PSYCHOLOGY AND WORK: an introduction

Macmillan Business Management and Administration Series
edited by Alan Hale

David Brown and Michael J. Harrison: *A Sociology of Industrialisation:
an introduction*

Terry Green and John Webster: *Managing Mathematically*

Peter Haine and Ernest Haidon: *Computers in Business*

Arthur Hindmarch, Miles Atchison and Richard Marke: *Accounting:
an introduction*

Peter Ribeaux and Stephen E. Poppleton: *Psychology and Work: an introduction*

Psychology and Work:

an introduction

Peter RIBEAUX
Senior Lecturer in Psychology,
Middlesex Polytechnic

Stephen E. POPPLETON
Principal Lecturer and Subject Leader in Psychology,
Wolverhampton Polytechnic

First edition 1978
Reprinted 1980, 1981 (twice), 1982, 1983

Published by
THE MACMILLAN PRESS LTD
*London and Basingstoke
Companies and representatives
throughout the world*

Typeset in Great Britain by
REDWOOD BURN LIMITED
Trowbridge & Esher
Printed in Hong Kong

British Library Cataloguing in Publication Data

Ribeaux, Peter
   Psychology and work. – (Macmillan business
   management and administration series).
   1. Psychology, Industrial 2. Work – Psychological
   aspects 3. Psychology
   I. Title II. Poppleton, Stephen E.
   158.7   HF5548.8

   ISBN 0–333–22066–8
   ISBN 0–333–22067–6 Pbk.

Editor's Introduction

This series is a direct outcome of the opportunities and challenges created by the rapid expansion of higher and further education in the past decade.

The expansion involved changes in the structure of advanced education, through the CNAA, the Polytechnics, the Regional Management Centres and the professional bodies which encouraged staff to develop new and experimental teaching. Substantial changes have taken place in the definition, scope and methodologies of the social, administrative and management sciences leading to modifications in the presentation of these subjects. Many new full-time students and staff have questioned traditional approaches and methods and have established more open discussion and debate on their courses. Demands for qualified manpower led to an expansion in part-time education and increased questioning by students in full-time jobs of the relevance of their studies.

Each of these developments has had a profound impact on the structure and content of courses and given fresh impetus to the discussion and modification of curricula and teaching methods in polytechnics, universities and colleges of further education. The editor and authors of the books in this series have made a deliberate attempt to respond to these changes.

The books set out to provide a comprehensive and up-to-date introduction to the ideas and methods of their subjects for specialist and non-specialist students in fields such as business and management studies, social science and administration. Their aim is to help students who have little or no previous knowledge of them to achieve a mastery of the scope and basic techniques of their subjects and to use them critically and with imagination for further study or for practical professional applications. They also seek to make some contribution to discussions of teaching and learning problems in their field.

Many introductory books present their subjects as a coherent body of knowledge of which the logic is self-evident and the concepts and methods clear to the careful reader. Students do not always find this so. Confronted as they are by a well-established discipline which has developed a particular method that may not bear any obvious relationship to the way in which they have been accustomed to think or to realities as they see them, students often have difficulty in comprehending the significance and detail of the forms of analysis it employs.

The editor and authors of the series felt that they should not take for granted the 'self-evident logic' of their subjects, but try to demonstrate to readers the ways in which their disciplines provide an effective framework for the analysis of problems in their field. When abstractions or concepts are introduced their functions and limitations are explained. Where methods or techniques are described the authors show why they take the form they do and the ways in which they may be used for particular tasks of analysis.

Students often criticise courses because their subjects or parts of them do not have any obvious, or immediate, practical applications. They may present what appear to be unnecessarily complicated ways of dealing with quite straightforward problems or, paradoxically, they may be regarded as over-simplifying or ignoring difficulties which are experienced in real situations. Systems of knowledge provide generalisations which are derived from a variety of abstractions and models. Some of these yield tools of description and analysis that have direct applications. Others suggest ways of looking at problems that, however fruitful, may have only limited or indirect applications.

The authors have tried to make clear the relevance of their subjects. Where concepts and methods have direct applications they show how, and under what circumstances, they can usefully be applied. Where they are of indirect use they show how a process of simplification may isolate and draw attention to the important characteristics of a complex problem, or how the study of complicated or abstract aspects of a problem may throw fresh light on it.

The authors have rejected a view, reflected in many basic textbooks, that students at an introductory level should concentrate on 'learning up' the information and techniques of their subjects and not be troubled with discussions of concepts and analytical method. This 'descriptive' approach, which divorces the study of techniques from that of conceptual and analytical structures, makes it more rather than less difficult for students to appreciate how a technique has developed, why it takes a particular form and how it functions. As a result students can spend a considerable time trying to understand, with limited success, a method of describing and presenting information or a method of analysis and fail to achieve any real facility in using it. The discussion of concepts and analytical method also acquaints a student with some of the difficulties and controversies surrounding the ideas and techniques he is studying. Without such knowledge he is unlikely to appreciate their limitations or establish any real ability to discriminate between alternative approaches and methods.

One of the more important aims of education is to develop a student's capacity to formulate and solve theoretical and practical problems. It is clear that few business and administrative problems are in practice separable into the neat categories represented by disciplines such as economics, accounting, law, sociology, psychology and computing. But most courses are based on combinations of studies in these and similar discrete disciplines which are rarely effectively integrated. It is recognised that the development of bodies of knowledge which provide rigorous rather than superficial integrative approaches will be a long and difficult task. The editor and authors of the books in this series are aware of this problem and within their limitations have attempted to indicate points at which contributions from other disciplines are necessary to the analysis of the problems with which they are dealing. It is thus hoped that in the long run the series will make some contribution to the development of interdisciplinary approaches.

The problems outlined above are common in the teaching and learning of many subjects which, although emerging historically as systems for analysing and solving practical problems, have developed advanced methodologies and a logical order of presentation that may not bear an obvious relation to the practical problems with which they are supposed to be concerned.

Many students are attracted to the study of psychology, perhaps because they already have considerable experience of human behaviour and that studies in the discipline will increase their knowledge of their own and others' motivations and actions. It is therefore surprising how frequently the subject presents students with unexpected difficulties. This may be due to the fact that psychology employs sophisticated forms of analyses and technical language to interpret phenomena and situations that are part of everyday human experience and which are normally understood and discussed in simple 'layman' terminology. The transition from the one to the other can prove extremely difficult and sometimes irrelevant. Psychology is also a field in which there is a multiplicity of differing and sometimes conflicting explanations for what may appear to be either obvious or objectively testable behaviour. The authors of this text have sought to show what is agreed and what is a matter of dispute in behavioural analysis and to what extent common-sense ideas are reinforced or questioned by experimental evidence. They have also set the discussion of the psychology of work within the framework of general psychological theory so that the student who successfully completes the text will have not only a thorough grasp of the practical applications of psychology to fields in which he is interested but also a firm understanding of their general theoretical background for further professional study.

The editor and authors of the books in this series are conscious of their limitations in attempting to implement their ideas in writing and teaching and do not suppose that their presentation will solve students' learning problems. They do not ignore the critical importance of motivation and sustained and disciplined study as factors in effective learning. But they felt that if subjects were presented in a way that made their form and justification explicit rather than implicit this would aid teaching and learning.

In seeking to achieve their aims the books in the series have been subjected to a great deal of critical scrutiny. Each is written by more than one author. This has enabled authors to combine a comparison of views with a considerable, and sometimes uncomfortable, degree of mutual criticism. The editor and authors have all, in recent years, had considerable experience of designing and teaching new CNAA honours degree, diploma or professional courses. Their manuscripts have been discussed with colleagues in education and the professions and have been tested in classes with students.

My thanks as editor are owed to the authors who responded to my request to write the books in the form that I have outlined. This has involved them in an extremely demanding process. The fact that we shared some basic assumptions about education and learning was of great help. The editors and staff of Macmillan with whom we have worked have showed great patience and could not have done more in difficult circumstances to encourage the series. My thanks are also due to George Brosan, Maurice Peston and Bruce May, who through many discussions have significantly influenced my educational ideas, and to my wife Diane, who has kept a discerning eye on my activities and the progress of the series.

February 1976   ALAN HALE

Contents

Preface

This is a book about psychology in which the authors have attempted, where-ever possible, to discuss its relevance to the world of work. There are many texts available which give a good introduction to either basic general psychology or occupational (industrial) psychology. Perhaps the most noticeable characteristic of these two types of text is the small amount of overlap in subject-matter. In particular, we feel that neither of these introductions is particularly appropriate for the student of business and administration who wishes to know the relevance of psychology to his subject-matter. If he is presented merely with general psychology, he is left with the very difficult task of deducing for himself its relevance to the work situation. As his knowledge of psychology at this stage can only be an introductory one, this task, we feel, is too demanding. On the other hand, if he is presented merely with occupational psychology, his lack of appreciation of basic psychological theory and methodology is likely to impair his ability to use the techniques and methods wisely. We feel that basic psychology has more relevance to work than the content of most texts on industrial psychology would suggest. Thus in the present text we shall consider both general psychology and industrial psychology, but treat them in such a way as to try to overcome the objections raised above. We would like the reader of this book to glean from it an insight into the way psychologists approach problems in the world of work. In order to achieve this objective, we have divided the book into a number of parts. Each part comprises chapters of both general and occupational psychology. We have chosen to do this rather than divide the book into two sections, one on general and the other on occupational psychology, in order to illustrate more clearly the relationship between them. This caused problems because it was very difficult to decide which areas of basic psychology to put with which areas of occupational psychology. Many concepts such as those of 'motivation' and 'perception' are clearly relevant to a number of different areas. Certainly groupings other than the one we have chosen could have been equally logical.

The book, *in toto*, therefore constitutes an introduction to psychology and work. However, by reading selectively, it is also possible to use it for two other purposes: either as an introduction to general psychology; or as an introduction to occupational psychology. None the less, we do feel that it is best read from the point of view from which it was originally conceived as an introduction to psychology and work.

We should like to thank Alan Hale for his helpful advice on the manuscript, and those of our colleagues, friends and students who have commented on various parts of the text. Not least we must thank our long-suffering wives and families, of whom we have seen rather less than we would have liked while writing this book. Finally, we would like to thank Mrs Janet Saunders and Mrs Betty Lansdell for their very rapid and efficient typing of the manuscript.

1978

P. RIBEAUX
S. POPPLETON

Acknowledgements

The author and publishers wish to thank the following who have kindly given permission for the use of copyright material:

Academic Press (London) Limited and Academic Press Inc., New York for figures from *The Evaluation of Personal Constructs* by D. Bannister and J. M. Mair, *Advances in Experimental Social Psychology*, Volume I, edited by L. Berkowitz and *Organizational Behavior and Human Performance*, Volume 2, by E. E. Lawler and L. W. Porter;
The American Association for the Advancement of Science for the extract from 'Genetics and Intelligence: A Review' by L. Erlenmeyer Kimling and L. F. Jarvik from *Science* Volume 142, December 1963;
Baillière Tindall for the figure from *The Measurement and Appraisal of Adult Intelligence* by D. Wechsler;
The British Psychology Society for the figure from the article 'The Pattern of Personal Response Arising during the Office Work Day' by Nelson and Bartley from *Occupational Psychology*, 42 (1968) published by Cambridge University Press;
Raymond B. Cattell for figures from *Motivation and Dynamic Structure* (Cattell and Child, 1975) and *Scientific Study of Personality and Motivation* (Cattell and Kline, 1977);
Mark Cook for a diagram from *Interpersonal Perception;*
The Institute of Personality and Ability Testing for a table from 'The Sixteen Personality Factor Questionnaire' by R. B. Cattell;
The McGraw-Hill Book Co., New York for figures from *Human Engineering Guide to Equipment Design* by C. T. Morgan *et al; A Theory of Leadership Effectiveness* by F. E. Fiedler, and *New Patterns of Management* by R. Likert;
Methuen and Co. Limited for extracts from *The Structure of Human Abilities* by P. E. Vernon; *The Structure of Human Personality* by H. J. Eysenck; and *Human Intelligence* by H. J. Butcher by permission of the author.
N.F.E.R. Publishing Company Limited for extracts from the National Institute of Industrial Psychology, Paper No. 2 'Studying Work';
Penguin Books Limited for a figure from an article by Roy Payne and Derek Pugh in *Psychology at Work* (Penguin Education, 1971) and a figure from 'A

Technology of Training' by K. Tilley in *Industrial Society* edited by Denis Pym;

Pergamon Press Limited for a diagram from *Perception and Communication* by D. E. Broadbent;

Prentice-Hall Inc., New Jersey, for the extracts from *Social Psychology* by J. M. Carlsmith, D. Sears and J. L. Freedman; *Perception* by J. Hochberg and *Industrial Psychology* by E. J. McCormick and J. Tiffin;

Rand McNally College Publishing Company for extracts from *Handbook of Industrial and Organizational Psychology* edited by Marion Dunnette; Professor Alec Roger for Table 12.1;

Scott, Foresman and Co. for a diagram from *Performance in Organizations* by L. L. Cummings and D. P. Schwab;

University of Chicago Press for an extract from *Attitude Towards War* by Droba (1930);

George Weidenfeld and Nicolson Limited and McGraw-Hill Book Company for the drawing from *The Intelligent Eye* by R. Gregory;

John Wiley and Sons Inc. for a table from *The Motivation to Work* by F. Herzberg, B. Mausner and B. Snyderman.

Every effort has been made to trace all the copyright holders but if any have been inadvertently overlooked the publishers will be pleased to make the necessary arrangement at the first opportunity.

Part I
INTRODUCTION

1
An Introduction to Psychology and Work

1.1 Introduction

The purpose of this chapter is to introduce the reader to psychology as a discipline, to indicate the main perspectives from which psychologists operate and to see how applied (particularly occupational or industrial) psychology is related to the basic discipline.

Section 1.2 is a discussion of the subject-matter of psychology. The chapter continues (Section 1.3) with an examination of the nature (scientific or otherwise) of psychological theories and explanations. Section 1.4 is an examination of the major perspectives in psychology, in particular the behaviourist, psychoanalytic and cognitive ones. The existence of these different perspectives has been, and is, responsible for many of the initial difficulties experienced by newcomers to psychology. For this reason early discussion is important. In Section 1.5 we discuss the relationship between general psychology and occupational psychology (the psychology of man in the world of work). This is followed by Section 1.6, which describes the applied branches of psychology, with particular emphasis on occupational psychology. Section 1.7 offers a brief history of occupational psychology. In Section 1.8 we consider methodology, in particular the research methods used by occupational psychologists. The final section of the chapter (Section 1.9) summarises the structure of the rest of the book.

1.2 What is psychology?

'Psychology' is one of those words which often produce emotional reactions in people. The man in the street may be inclined to think of a psychologist as someone who can see into the mind and find all sorts of strange tendencies hidden there. To the businessman the word may conjure up the idea of an academic in an ivory tower who indulges himself in theories of behaviour having little or nothing to do with real life.

Sigmund Freud (1940), the father of psychoanalysis, must bear some of the responsibility for this image. It is not the authors' wish to start this text with an anti-Freudian tirade. Indeed, both the authors have great respect for the

originality of his thought and work. Rather, it is to warn the reader against
accepting fashions of thought, be they pro- or anti-psychology, at face value.
Freud, more than anyone in the field of 'psychology', has a massive retinue
of popular followers and critics. The former have been responsible for attributing to his work a power which its practitioners probably do not have, and
the latter for overemphasising the inadequacies of some of the more exaggerated versions espoused by some of the converted. At this level of discussion,
the true merits of his work are barely touched upon. With this kind of atmosphere, the psychologist confessing his profession can regularly expect to meet
the equally common reactions of 'Oh! I must be careful what I say', or the
often suppressed attitude of 'What does he know about *real* life?' These reactions may communicate almost anything – envy, aggression, fear, interest or
admiration – but the main point is that psychology is an often misunderstood
profession. Our hope is to make its role a little clearer.

Later in this chapter we discuss various schools of psychology and their
perspectives (viewpoints), but we must also introduce the topic now, for the
perspective adopted determines one's definition of psychology.

For illustrative purposes we shall consider two viewpoints, perhaps more
important historically than currently, and examine the implications of each:
(i) the psychodynamic (psychoanalytic), stemming from the work of Freud,
Jung and Adler in the early years of this century; and (ii) the behaviourist,
deriving from the work of Watson and others in an overlapping but slightly
later era.

Essentially, the conflict between the two groups centres on three major
related areas of difference: (1) the methods of studying people; (2) the subject-
matter of psychology; and (3) the attitudes adopted towards the status of
psychology as a science.

(1) The psychodynamicists use methods which encourage the individual
(usually their patient) to talk about himself – his experiences, feelings and
dreams. The behaviourists, on the other hand, use experimental methods
under controlled conditions to determine how specific variables affect observed
behaviour in a given situation. This difference in method is allied to a
difference of opinion about subject-matter.

(2) The psychodynamicists claim to be studying 'the dynamics of the mind'
(both conscious and unconscious). This includes thoughts and feelings of all
kinds. The behaviourists (e.g. Watson, 1919; Skinner, 1938) reject the study
of experience as unscientific, and claim that only observable behaviour is
suitable for scientific study. This alone, therefore, should be the domain of
psychology.

(3) The third point of difference refers to the status of psychology as a
science. Behaviourists think that psychology should attempt to construct
theories based on a foundation of publicly observable and replicable data on
the model of the natural sciences. They reject the psychodynamic approach
as being non-scientific. The psychodynamicists, on the other hand, do not
believe that the study of behaviour alone can lead to a real understanding of
human beings. For them the human mind cannot be neglected.

The result of this basic and continuing split between the two schools has
been to yield at least two kinds of psychological theory and explanation. Only

in the last twenty years has this state of affairs begun to be remedied. Illustrations of the kinds of reconciliation that certain psychologists have attempted to achieve lie in the work of G. A. Kelly (1955) and G. A. Miller (1964). Kelly's personal-construct theory is concerned with identifying the kinds of construction each individual builds up about the world around him. His approach seems to have the merits of doing justice both to the individuality of each human mind and to assessing this in a manner which is both quantifiable and repeatable. The title of Miller's book, *Psychology: the Science of Mental Life*, also indicates the possibility of some kind of synthesis between the two approaches.

Where does this leave us in our quest for a definition of psychology? For the purposes of this book we shall go no further than the point of view suggested in the previous paragraph. We propose to adopt a rather broad approach, incorporating the views of both schools of thought mentioned so far. Something like this would do justice to our standpoint: 'Psychology is the study of behaviour and experience pursued by methods the status of which is continually under review.' The first part of the definition is concerned to include both psychodynamic and behaviourist contributions, and the second ensures that not too many illusions creep into the body of knowledge as a result of methodological inadequacies. We have come a long way since the days of Freud and Watson, and although their schisms are to some extent still with us, a tendency toward *rapprochement* heralds a more promising era. Whilst on the subject of definition it is worth pointing out that our definition includes the study of animal behaviour.

1.3   The status of psychological explanation

We shall now consider a question which has become something of an old chestnut for students of psychology and the philosophy of science: 'Is psychology a science?' The answer will enable us to know something more about the kind of status psychological investigations should aspire to.

First, we have to decide what a science is. Let us state it as follows: 'A science is a body of knowledge which has been achieved by means of scientific method. Scientific method involves the systematic testing of a theory using observation or experimentation in such a way that the experiments or observations in question are both publicly observable and repeatable. A science sets out to explain events within its sphere of relevance and to predict future events.' Popper (1968) suggests that a theory is satisfactory if it is in principle falsifiable. This is a criterion which has been regularly used in connection with the physical sciences. However, it is quite clear that its use would exclude as unscientific a lot of the material which would be included in our definition of psychology, in particular that of psychodynamic origin.

In the terms of this book this criterion would probably put the 'unscientific' label at least on parts of the chapters on motivation and personality, as well as on much of Part V. For this reason and for several others, wider meanings of the word 'explanation' than the purely scientific have been put forward. Possibly the most extreme of these has been to count as an explanation anything which serves to cast light on the occurrence of an event, be it even simply a new and interesting way of looking at that event. There are obviously a number of intermediate points between this position and that of Popper. The behaviourists chose to adopt a Popperian type of view and excluded the kind of account which the Freudian tradition and social psychology tended to generate. It is not our wish to do this, but, rather, to be aware of the status of our knowledge when we use material which is not 'scientific' in a Popperian sense.

Two characteristics of human beings have helped to bring about this problem concerning the scientific nature of psychological explanation: (i) they are purposive, i.e. they do things in order to achieve some end – inanimate objects do not have purposes in what they do. Rather they are acted upon; (ii) human beings have minds, i.e. they think thoughts, have emotions and sensations. Neither of these two characteristics is obviously observable or measurable, but is expressed indirectly through speech and behaviour.

The problem then becomes a question of whether in any indirect way, these characteristics can be made publicly observable. If this can be achieved satisfactorily, then psychological science and explanation will be of a similar status to the physical sciences. If not, and it is our contention that attempts so far have all been more or less unsatisfactory, then psychological explanation includes 'explanations' which would not be classed as scientific using Popper's definition.

1.4 Perspectives in psychology

In a short introductory chapter of this kind, it is impossible to adumbrate even the bare bones of all the viewpoints which have graced the discipline of psychology. We shall focus particularly on the two with which we started. Historically they have certainly been the most influential. However, the fact that other currently very important approaches are included together in a composite subsection should not be seen as reflecting on their value. As indicated, the behaviourist and the psychodynamic approaches have both generated extreme proponents and a series of less rigid positions.

THE BEHAVIOURIST APPROACH

The work of J. B. Watson (1919) was the immediate antecedent of a series of theories propounded by psychologists known collectively as 'stimulus–response', or 'associationist', or 'connectionist'. Their basic contention is that a number of psychological phenomena (centred around learning and memory, but expanding into the wider field of personality) are explicable in terms of some stimulus (S), to which a response (R) is attached as a result of some kind of experience. The first flush of enthusiasm for the new scientific psychology soon moved into a phase of no less enthusiastic controversy about what behaviour was. After all, it was one thing to point out that the contents of the mind could not give rise to scientific data, but what about things like speech and its content? At one stage, speech was taboo as a subject of study for a behaviourist, but later it was decided that only the inferences made from verbal evidence about any underlying mental states were suspect. However, topics such as thinking could be studied and people began to draw inferences about thinking processes (e.g. while tackling problems) from the behaviour of the organism rather in the manner in which the existence of the atom was inferred before it was actually discovered. This departure from the simple *S–R* paradigm heralded the birth of the *S–O–R* (stimulus–organism–response) approach whose novel feature was the postulation of some kind of mediating activity (internal to the organism) between the stimulus and the response in the linkage system. Further departures from the original extreme position, such as the recognition that what might be one sort of stimulus to one person might be a different stimulus to another person, helped to breach the original Watsonian position. The 'neo-behaviourists', or cognitive psychologists, as the new generation are called, drew down upon themselves the wrath of the purists because of their enlarged field of study. However, there are two positive features to this development. First, they brought an improved methodology to bear on topics which had only previously been studied by introspection (the conscious process of examining one's own thoughts, feelings and experiences – a highly subjective method particularly prone to error). Second, the road was open for the human mind to be studied in a more precise and scientific manner. True, the philosophical problem that explanations at the level of mind are different in kind from explanations in terms of behaviour had not been solved. However, neo-behaviourists' models of thinking and memory, for example, are highly suggestive as to the actual mechanisms likely to be involved in the physical counterparts of mental activity. What is more important, they are capable of empirical testing.

THE PSYCHODYNAMIC APPROACH

From the psychodynamic viewpoint, such issues posed no problems. After all, psychoanalysts had been speculating about the mind for years. However, they, too, had their problems. Starting with an initial split between Freud and Jung over the nature of man and the role of sexuality, which degenerated into a personal squabble between them about each other's psychopathology, the initial tight band of analysts began to split up. The main bone of contention was the degree of emphasis to be placed on the respective roles of biological make-up and the social environment in the shaping of the individual's development. Freud himself had emphasised the idea of a biologically pre-ordained unfolding of the personality, and Jung had suggested a blueprint of a somewhat more flexible kind. In the 1930s a group later to be called the Neo-Freudians came to place a greater emphasis on the importance of the child's social context. Modern psychoanalytic thought has achieved something of a synthesis between these two positions. It has also become much more amenable to rigorous scientific research into many of its propositions.

OTHER PERSPECTIVES

We should emphasise that psychologists use a number of perspectives and that so far we have mentioned only two. Each of these perspectives tends to have a particular focus of interest. For example, the behaviourist has been primarily concerned with the area of learning (see Chapter 3) and the psychoanalyst with personality (see Chapter 3). Other more recent perspectives are the biological, cognitive, humanistic and social psychological ones.

The biological approach attempts to relate behaviour and experience to physiological events. We cite some of this work in Parts II and III of the book, though relatively little since its importance for the world of work is limited largely to the design of equipment and working conditions (see Chapter 5).

Of ever increasing importance is the cognitive approach. Here the focus is on the mental processes of perception, attention, imagery, problem solving, remembering and thinking. Central to the cognitive approach is the model of man as a processor of information. This model is an underlying theme of much of the material in Part II. The cognitive approach has also played an increasingly important role in work on motivation.

The main feature of the humanistic approach is a respect for the whole human being with an emphasis on his need for self-fulfilment. It also calls into question the determinism which underpins the other perspectives we have mentioned. Man is the possessor of a free will. Humanistic psychologists (e.g. Rogers, 1951; Maslow, 1954) have primarily focussed their attention on motivation (Part III) and personality (Part IV). Their approach has had considerable practical influence in the fields of motivation and counselling.

The social psychological perspective, whilst it derives a great deal from the others outlined above, is distinctive in that it uses concepts which apply at the level of the group rather than that of the individual. Some of its concepts stem from a sociological tradition and at certain points in the text we shall enter the rather nebulous hinterland between psychology and sociology. We feel that there is no clear criterion for what to include in a psychology text and what in a sociology text. A degree of overlap is inevitable and this is particularly evident in the final part of this book.

1.5 General psychology and applied psychology

The different perspectives outlined above, and the fact that general psychology is something of a hotch-potch of perspectives, pinpoints a great difficulty for the applied psychologist, namely the considerable shortage of clear, comprehensive, rigorous and precise models and theories.

Rodger (1950), writing on industrial psychology, has pointed out that these applied psychologists (see Section 1.6 for fuller clarification of this term) are both scientists and technologists. The problems of most technologists (e.g. engineers) lie in finding methods of using the body of knowledge of the science they are applying to solve practical problems. For the psychological technologist the basic body of knowledge is less secure. This is certainly the case, for example, when he starts to apply psychodynamic principles. But it is also the case with theory in social psychology (Part V) and motivational theory (Part III). The continuing controversy between competing theories and the lack of clarity in the connection between theory and application has been responsible for suggestions that occupational psychology is simply a series of fashions tenuously based on more or less well-substantiated theories. We are afraid that this accusation has a certain substance. Nevertheless, we cannot go all the way with it; with Broadbent (1971) we feel that the applied perspective has generated, and is likely to continue to generate, its own theoretical advances.

We have mentioned the discontinuity both within general psychology and between general and applied psychology, but what do we mean by 'applied psychology', and what kinds of psychologists are there?

1.6 The branches of applied psychology

In this section, we will consider what psychologists do, both in their capacity as pure research investigators in 'pure' psychology and in the applied field.

'Pure' psychologists often work in laboratories (in which case they are often called 'experimental psychologists') but not necessarily so. They study various aspects of human and animal behaviour. In man, work may concern his intelligence and personality, motivation, memory, perception and attention, as well as the way he learns, thinks and solves problems. Academic psychologists also study how he behaves in a social context (social psychology) and what happens when his behaviour is inappropriate or strange (abnormal psychology). As indicated earlier, they do this from a variety of different standpoints – the behaviourist, the psychoanalytic, the physiological, and others which may or may not overlap.

We defined psychology as the study (scientific wherever possible) of experience and behaviour. Much of the work of experimental psychologists has concerned itself with animal species other than man. Particularly popular has been the white rat. Much theorising about behaviour, particularly theories of learning, has arisen from animal experimentation. Many psychologists believe that such theories may illustrate fundamental laws governing behaviour in all higher species, including man. Others (e.g. Beach, 1960) argue against this assumption, and suggest that theories of laws governing behaviour should be 'species specific'. We are largely sympathetic to the views of Beach. Animal experimentation, along with theories based on it, is not presented here unless we believe it to be of relevance to human behaviour. Where animal studies are cited, this will usually be because no comparable studies on man have been carried out. Their results should be generalised to apply to man only with the greatest caution.

Applied psychologists may be divided according to their areas of application:

(1) The clinical psychologist is concerned with the diagnosis and treatment of psychiatric disorders. In this connection two other kinds of profession should be mentioned: psychiatry and psychotherapy. Psychiatrists are medically qualified doctors who have a qualification in psychological medicine and are hence able to prescribe treatments, such as drugs, which psychologists cannot use. Psychotherapists may be trained in a variety of techniques from

psychoanalysis to one of the less intensive forms of counselling. The central component of psychoanalysis is a one-to-one personal relationship between the therapist and the patient, together with a particular kind of listening and interpretative role on the part of the therapist. Forms of psychotherapy include non-directive therapy, where the therapist plays a more passive role, and a Skinnerian approach, where the therapist intervenes at a much earlier stage and indicates his approval when the patient comes to make an increasingly appropriate adaptation.

(2) The educational psychologist is concerned with the diagnosis of educational potential, problems of individual maladjustment and, increasingly, with the social aspects of educational life and school organisation. He is also concerned with educational technology (teaching methods – e.g. programmed instruction).

(3) The occupational psychologist is concerned with the world of work. His main areas of expertise lie in vocational guidance, personnel selection and occupational training (Rodger (1950) has called these 'fitting the man to the job', or 'F.M.J.'), and equipment design, methods of work, and working conditions and rewards ('fitting the job to the man', or 'F.J.M.'). These various fields are seen to be complementary and interdependent. Thus, depending on the labour market, it may turn out that a difficult problem of recruiting suitable people for a particular job becomes not a question to be solved by personnel selection, but rather by selecting someone less well-qualified and then training him, or else by redesigning the job. An example of a combination of these approaches was in the nursing profession in 1964 when the qualification of State Enrolled Nurse was instituted. These people, who require only two years' training (as opposed to three) in order to be able to carry out practical nursing duties, have helped to free the better-qualified State Registered Nurses for more advanced work.

Contrary to the oversimplified picture painted earlier, occupational psychologists have been making advances in both the applied and theoretical fields. As mentioned earlier, Broadbent (1971) suggests that the major theoretical advances in the future are likely to come from an applied perspective. They have begun to answer general questions such as: Why do people work? What makes them satisfied in their work? What organisational structures are most likely to encourage (i) satisfactoriness, and (ii) satisfaction on the part of workers? In addition, the occupational psychologist continues to develop his work as a technologist in promoting his two main concerns, the increase of satisfaction and efficiency at work.

1.7   A history of occupational psychology

First, a word about terminology. We shall use the word 'occupational' to describe the kind of psychologist whose concern is the world of work. However, the words 'industrial' and 'organisational' are also used. The word 'industrial' was the first on the scene, reflecting a predominant concern with industrial, as opposed to commercial or service, occupations. To an extent it has been replaced by 'occupational', a word less limited in its connotations.

The term 'organisational' has emerged even more recently with the growing interest of psychologists in the effects of organisational characteristics on the satisfactoriness and satisfaction of workers.

In both the United States and Europe the first real period of growth was generated by the First World War. Previously Munsterberg (1913) and Scott (1911) had been working in the United States, and they and others earned the first real recognition for their profession during the war with their work on personnel selection and assessment and the construction of the first group intelligence test to be widely used, the Army Alpha. In the United Kingdom the war precipitated investigations into the effects of physical conditions of work on performance, accidents and absenteeism. This work culminated in the setting up of the Health of Munition Workers Committee by the government in 1915. From this time industrial psychology continued to develop on both these fronts and on both sides of the Atlantic. In the United Kingdom, in 1922, the National Institute of Industrial Psychology was established, and carried out much pioneering work in the design and use of tests of intelligence and abilities for the purposes of personnel selection and occupational guidance. The next important milestone, the Hawthorne Investigations, began in the mid-1920s and ended during the Great Depression, some six years later. What had begun as a study of the effects of such aspects of working conditions as illumination and rest pauses on worker performance started to accumulate surprising evidence of the influence of unexpected social factors. This was to influence strongly the development of occupational psychology for some three decades at least. Indeed, research into topics such as the effects of supervision and the role of work groups continues today. The Second World War intensified the developments of the First World War, but on a larger scale. Psychologists played a major part in the allocation of conscripts to all types and levels of work in the armed forces. They also trained military personnel for this role, as well as participating in the design of other kinds of training. (For a fuller review, see Vernon and Parry, 1949.)

The post-war years heralded an era of investigation into work groups and later into organisations. One of the central focuses has been the relationship between variables of supervision, performance and satisfaction. One of the unproven but fashionable beliefs referred to earlier (Section 1.5) had involved the idea that work performance could be improved by increasing the satisfaction of workers. Brayfield and Crockett (1955), in an influential review, exploded the myth with their conclusion that there was little or no consistent relationship between satisfaction and performance. The late 1950s and early 1960s were a period of moral and professional crisis in occupational psychology. Attacks were being made from various parts: (i) 'pure' psychologists were concerned with the lack of rigour in the work of occupational psychologists, and in the prostitution of their trade as a tool of management; (ii) they were no longer getting the results suggested by the promise of the war-time work. The consequent heart-searching served to do two things. First, occupational psychologists began to take into account more variables (previously left uncontrolled) in their increasingly sophisticated models of the work situation. Second, an increased awareness of methodological problems led to an increased ingenuity in attempting to solve them. This is not to say that all is now well with occupational psychology. Indeed, the era of fashionable transient techniques is not yet over; nor will it ever be as long as the applications are ahead of the theory. What is hoped is that this book will equip the reader to ask, as occupational psychologists are doing, some of the right kinds of questions concerning those things they see (or perhaps do not see) going on around them in the world of work.

1.8   Methodology in occupational psychology

We noted in the last paragraph that the occupational psychologist has become increasingly aware of methodological problems within his field of study. We believe that the methodology brought to bear by the psychologist to the study of man at work is at least as important a contribution as are his theories. We shall therefore outline some of his major methods of investigation. Specific examples will be brought out later at relevant points in the text.

With respect to research methodology, one basic purpose of scientific research is to determine the relationship between variables. There are two main types of research paradigm which may be used in an attempt to achieve this result, namely the experimental method and the correlational method. The former involves manipulating one variable, named the independent variable, in order to observe the effect on another variable, the so-called dependent variable. The experimenter tries to hold constant all other variables which might have an effect on the dependent variable. In so far as the experimenter succeeds in this, then it may be said that a change in the independent variable causes a change in the dependent variable. The correlational method, on the other hand, does not generally lead to causal inference. It consists of determining the relationship between two variables as they exist in real life. It is possible to control for other variables using this method, but this usually requires considerably larger samples than would be the case without control. Underlying both of these approaches are a number of scientific characteristics: (i) research is purposeful rather than random – the problem is chosen on the basis of a theoretical or practical reason; (ii) research is cumulative and self-correcting – this necessitates a review of the relevant research literature before tackling a particular problem; (iii) procedures are stated explicitly and clearly so that research is repeatable; (iv) the same concepts are used by experts in a particular area of research so that results can be easily communicated.

So far we have rather oversimplified the alternative scientific approaches available. For example, the multiple correlation approach allows for the investigation of the relationships between more than two variables. Similarly, we can distinguish between a number of types of experimental methods: laboratory, field and simulation. In laboratory experiments all conditions are rigidly controlled except for the independent variable, which is allowed to vary in certain specified ways. This usually involves the use of at least two groups of people, known as the experimental group (for whom the independent variable is varied) and control group (for whom it is not) so that any changes in the behaviour of the experimental group can be attributed to the effect of the independent variable. The field experiment is similar, but it attempts to apply the experimental method to on-going, real-life situations, so that there is less control over other variables. The simulation experiment attempts to duplicate the relevant parts of the real-life environment on a small scale, so that changes can be brought under more control than in the case of the field experiment. The objective of this latter method is to enable greater generalisation of the results than would be the case with the laboratory method.

Over the past decade or so it has become increasingly acknowledged, however, that the experimental methods described above may be subject to systematic distortions, such that results tend to be influenced in the direction hypothesised by the experimenter. A number of explanations for this finding have been suggested. For example, Orne (1962) attributes it to the experimental subjects' wish to do what the experimenter wants as they place themselves under his control, and to act like 'good subjects'.

Argyris (1968) believes that the experimental situation may lead to biased results because of the subject's subjugated status. He suggests that it may lead to passive, withdrawn, hostile and generally non-cooperative behaviour. To overcome this danger, he recommends four possible alternatives: (i) to give the subjects a more active role in the planning and design of the project; (ii) to make the relevant measurements less obtrusive; (iii) to set subjects to 'role-play' the purpose of the experiment; and (iv) to use post-experimental enquiries to determine how much the subject was responding to the 'real' purposes of the research. For example, one of the authors studied direction of 'eye-gaze' of the subjects. After the experiment he asked them whether or not they had been aware that eye-gaze was being studied (Poppleton, 1971). Had they been aware of it, then their eye-gaze behaviour would probably have been different because of this awareness.

When the psychologist has used one of the methods which we have outlined, experimental or correlational, he then has the problem of analysing the data. He attempts to do this by using appropriate statistical inference techniques to assess the degree of relationship between variables, and to assess the significance of that relationship (i.e. the confidence he can have that the relationship is a real one, rather than being due to chance factors alone). A detailed description of when and how to use statistical tests is to be found in any introductory text on the subject.

1.9 The structure of this book

Most of what needs to be said about the lay-out of this text has been said in the Preface. However, we shall spell out here what is included in each of the four remaining parts.

Each part, as we have said, is made up partly of a chapter or chapters of 'pure' psychology relevant to a particular area of application and a further chapter or chapters specifically on that applied field. The 'pure' chapters cover their topics in rather more depth than is absolutely necessary for an understanding of the applied chapters, which in some cases would be quite intelligible on their own, reflecting only a tenuous connection with the 'pure' field.

One of the major problems we faced in writing this book concerned the structure of our subject matter. Due in part to the contrasting perspectives already mentioned there exists a discontinuity within the subject matter of 'pure' psychology. There is also a discontinuity between pure and applied psychology. What we have tried to do is to emphasise what continuity there is by putting together in the different sections those areas of pure and applied psychology which are most closely related. At the same time it is quite clear that in some cases the degree of relatedness is quite small, reflecting the current state of knowledge.

Part II focusses on basic psychological processes. We are concerned with the way in which man selects and receives information impinging on his sense organs, how he processes this information and how he learns to respond appropriately. These basic processes are particularly relevant to two applied areas of occupational psychology, training and ergonomics. These topics, therefore, constitute the final two chapters of this part of the book.

The emphasis in Part III is on motivation. Motivation has received considerable attention in the context of work performance. Because of this we are devoting a separate part of the book to it. Further, the concept of motivation has played an important role in theories of personality. Thus Part III acts as a kind of bridge between Part II (basic psychological processes) and Part IV (personality, intelligence and assessment). We have included a chapter on attitudes in this part rather than Part V because although often considered in the social context the concept of attitude is closely related to that of motivation. Further, one attitude in particular, that of job satisfaction has been much studied in the work situation and theories of job satisfaction are intimately linked with those of motivation.

In Part V we examine an important area of social psychology, focussing initially on the behaviour of individuals in social groups and then upon the nature of work organisations. A fuller itemisation of what is contained in each chapter will be found in the table of contents and at the beginning of each chapter.

Finally, it is hoped that this book will be relatively easy to use as a reference book by making use of the author and subject indexes at the end of the book.

Part II

BASIC PSYCHOLOGICAL PROCESSES AND HUMAN PERFORMANCE

Basic psychological processes include perception, attention, memory and learning, and it is these that we consider in this part. In considering these processes we shall often make reference to the human-information-processing model. According to this model, man is conceived as a processer of information. He initially perceives information impinging on his sense organs, which he processes, then responds to it and/or stores it. Such stored information may be called upon when required for some further activity. The nature of attention, perception and memory is the subject of Chapter 2. These processes are largely dealt with in terms of a cognitive information processing model. In this part we do not discuss the more complex aspects of information processing such as thinking, problem-solving and decision making. Individual differences in these processes are the main focus of Chapter 10.

Human learning also has been approached from an information processing point of view, at least for the learning of relatively complex skills. Other approaches to learning have focussed upon simpler tasks often using animals as experimental subjects. This work has given rise to a number of 'learning theories' which we shall consider, along with skill acquisition, in Chapter 3.

Chapter 3 illustrates the increasing 'cognitisation' of psychology by contrasting earlier behaviorist approaches to learning with the more recent emphasis on mental processes, as illustrated by the information processing approach. This part, like Part III with the development of process models of motivation, reflects a general trend in psychology. In this part too, we are concerned not only with basic psychological processes, but also in their relationships with human performance in the work situation.

Thus in Chapter 4, we turn our attention to training and development, which, it might be thought, should rest heavily on learning theories. However, we should bear in mind that other areas of psychology have relevance for training, notably the individual's capacity for change in attitudes (see Chapter 8) and his abilities (see Chapter 10). None the less we have chosen to place our discussion of industrial training in this section. General principles of learning and skill acquisition are both relevant and important even though it is also fair to say that much of the psychologist's contribution to training does not rest neatly on basic principles of learning. Rather, such principles are often too general to be applicable to many tasks for which training is required. This is a problem which arises in much of applied psychology, including ergonomics, which constitutes the final chapter in this part (Chapter 5). Ergonomics is concerned with equipment design and the installation of 'man-machine systems'. As such, it is very much concerned with man's capacity to process information, the subject matter of Chapter 2. Again, we find that much of this information is too general to be of much value to many specific ergonomic problems.

Such differences between 'pure' and 'applied' areas of psychology tend to result in some degree of discontinuity between pure and applied chapters reflecting the actual discontinuity between 'pure' and 'applied'. However, such discontinuities need to be made explicit, as do the points of continuity, and it is this belief which has given rise to the particular organisation of this part of the book.

In this section, we also raise a number of methodological issues which are of general importance in psychology, particularly in its applications. They are relevant both to training and ergonomics, and also to other topics covered in this book, notably selection and performance appraisal. They include the evaluation of a programme's effectiveness, the choice of criteria (often measures of effectiveness) and the question of generalisation from laboratory to real life situations.

2
Attention, Perception and Memory

2.1 Introduction

This chapter sets out to consider the ways in which we process information, from our perceptions of incoming sensory stimulation to complex memory processes. We shall focus initially on attention (Section 2.2). We shall then discuss the processes of perception (Section 2.3) and memory (Section 2.4), examining both theoretical and empirical work. Although attention, perception and memory are intricately related, we shall treat them separately for purposes of presentation. Attention is the process by which we narrow down the mass of stimuli which impinge on us into a manageable amount of information. Perception is the process of sensing in a meaningful way the stimuli we attend to. Memory is the process of storing this perceived information for the purpose of future recall. In this chapter we are concerned with a broad overview of the processes involved, leaving a discussion of their relevance to work to the later chapters.

2.2 Attention

Because the brain is bombarded with more information than it can process, it is frequently necessary first to reject some information in order to focus upon what is important. Indeed, the greater part of the over-all perceptual input is regularly rejected. As you read this, consider all the things going on around you to which you are not attending. Efficiency in a task will to some extent depend on the efficiency of this selection. One way of studying this problem is by considering the process of 'selective attention'. Selective attention is defined as 'The ability of a listener, whether human or animal, to process only part of the information which he receives and to ignore the rest' (Moray, 1969).

Most of the early evidence is based on two kinds of experiment: (i) 'split-span' experiments, in which listeners receive two or more messages simultaneously (e.g. one to each ear) and are asked to respond by repeating what they have heard or answering questions about one or more of them; and (ii) 'shadowing' experiments, in which the listener is asked to repeat back verbatim relatively long messages as they hear them. These are sometimes referred to as 'verbal tracking experiments'. Most of the relevant experiments require subjects to shadow information presented in one ear and to reject that presented to the other.

We shall look at Broadbent's early (1958) attempt to account for the data generated from such work. In his 'split-span' experiments two series of three digits were played simultaneously, one to each ear. Subjects reported what they had heard ear by ear rather than in temporal sequence. Thus if the left ear heard 1, 3, 5 and the right 2, 4, 6, the subject would respond 1, 3, 5, 2, 4, 6, and not 1, 2, 3, 4, 5, 6. Broadbent tried to develop a system which would explain this tendency to respond to the stimulus according to its source rather than the order of presentation (see Figure 2.1). He proposed a short-term memory store, where messages from one ear might be held for a matter of seconds while the messages from the other ear were being processed in a limited capacity channel. Then messages are filtered from the store to a limited capacity channel which leads to further memory storage and processing mechanisms.

Limited channel capacity means that a person can only process so much information at any one time. If the amount of information held in the short-term memory store exceeds this limit, then only part of it can be filtered through, leaving the rest to decay. Consequently only a certain amount of it can be processed into the long-term memory store or can generate directly a behavioural output. However, it is possible to pass unprocessed signals back into the short-term memory store (rehearsal) in the way that one repeats a telephone number to oneself in order not to forget it between looking it up and dialling it.

The chief characteristic of the filter which Broadbent proposed is an on–off switch for each input channel such that only one channel is attended to at a time. Originally Broadbent thought that the filter defined channels on the

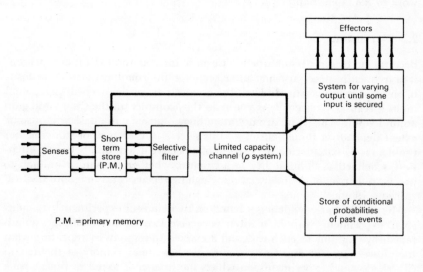

Figure 2.1 Broadbent's (1958) information-processing model

basis of their crude physical characteristics (location in space, volume, voice of speaker, etc.). However, an experiment by two Oxford undergraduates, Gray and Wedderburn (1960), and, later variations on the same theme, caused him to modify his ideas. Gray and Wedderburn presented the different syllables of words alternately to different ears of the subjects in the manner of the original split-span experiments. They found that the subjects did not report a jumble of syllables which Broadbent's model would predict if one physical channel (in this case an ear) were being attended to at a time. In fact they reported the original words. This suggests that the selection of material for attention occurs not on the basis of its crude physical characteristics but on a much more complex basis involving if necessary the analysis of words.

Treisman (1964) suggests a more complex, tree-like filter mechanism which carries out a series of tests on incoming messages. The first tests distinguish between the incoming information on the basis of its physical or sensory aspects (like Broadbent's original filter). The later tests distinguish syllable patterns, sounds and the meaning of words and sentences. Thus if two messages have very different physical characteristics they are separated very early, but if they differ only slightly in content and are spoken by the same voice only a very late test will distinguish between them and they will tend to interfere a great deal with each other in shadowing experiments. This kind of 'filter' is also compatible with findings concerning those aspects of the non-attended or non-shadowed channel which cause a spontaneous switch of attention to it. These include not only physical factors such as changes in a speaker's voice, changes from speech to music and changes in volume or language but also emotionally significant pieces of content such as the listener's name, a familiar bit of literature, or a call of 'fire!'. Such events switch attention to them because a filter such as Treisman's would be sensitive to them. The main advantage of the Treisman model is that it does justice to the Gray and Wedderburn and other similar experiments. However, it does require a rather complex kind of filter, and Deutsch and Deutsch (1963) propose that it is in fact simpler to move the selective mechanism back a little in the process. They suggest that the incoming material is analysed physically (à la Broadbent) but that what is finally selected for attention is also determined by a matching process in the long-term memory storage system on the basis of what is most pertinent to the individual at the time.

The debate as to whether early or late selection is the case has not been resolved one way or the other. Moray (1969) carried out a complex experiment in which he found both Treisman's and the Deutschs' model to be wanting and a current view has been expressed by Norman (1976) when he concludes that both models may be correct but incomplete. He suggests that it is probably misleading to see information processing as a kind of funnel in which incoming messages are subjected to a filtering out by some kind of mechanical process until only a small proportion of the incoming material remains. Rather, he says, we should ask 'what resources are required by a task and see if the demand exceeds the supply'. Thus depending on the task and our situation we may process either on the basis of crude physical characteristics or on the basis of its pertinence to our personal situation at the time. Our (limited) capacity (and hence the amount of our resources) may vary too. When we are alert and involved our capacity is greater than when we are bored or tired. Clearly the manner in which we attend to a message depends both on filtering it on the basis of relatively simple characteristics of the message and on a matching of it with our stored experience. It also depends on the effort we are prepared to invest, our state of arousal (fatigue or alertness) and the other resources we may possess. The search for a single bottleneck like Broadbent's filter which determines our ability only to do one thing at a time has been unsuccessful; but what has been achieved is a multi-causal view of the nature of selective attention.

This has been a very rapid look at a very complicated field. Our purpose here is to emphasise the idea that what we perceive has already gone through a complex process of selection by the time we perceive it and that this selection is made necessary by the limited capacity of the human organism to process information. We hope to have given the reader some idea of how this comes about but must refer him to a recent review (Norman, 1976) if he wishes to enlarge his knowledge of this area.

In the next section we shall consider the process of perception proper, confining ourselves largely to object perception and leaving person perception to Chapter 11.

2.3   Perception

The physiological perspective referred to in Chapter 1 has been of considerable importance in the study of perception. We know a good deal about the sense organs used in vision and hearing and to a lesser extent those used in smell and taste. Physiologists have also investigated skin sensations and those concerned with movement and balance. For a stimulus (e.g. an object or event) to be perceived it must activate a sense organ. A minimum amount of physical energy of a specific kind is required to activate a sense organ. For each relevant measure of physical energy there is a psychological correlate. For example, the correlate of sound frequency is pitch and that of intensity is loudness. Much research has been concerned with relating physiological processes and biological structures to perceptual processes. We shall illustrate this by considering vision.

VISION

The retina at the back of the eye contains two kinds of cells: rods, which are cylindrical in shape; and cones, which are more bulbous. These cells are sensitive to the light reflected from the objects we see around us. The cones are active in daylight conditions and the rods only under dim illumination. When we walk from a well-lit into a dark room we are unable initially to see anything. After a while we become able to see shapes and objects. This is because the rods take time to be activated, and the cones are no longer activated under the dim illumination. When the cells of the retina are stimulated they send electrical impulses back along the optic nerve to the optic cortex of the brain where the pattern of stimulation at the eye is reproduced on a more or less point-for-point basis. What is perceived was at one stage thought to be a function of the interaction of the optic cortex with other brain areas responsible for visual learning, motivation, emotion and other factors. This may still turn out to be broadly true, but the complexity of the process may be indicated by a consideration of the rest of this section. In particular we shall be considering those phenomena of perception which are not easily accounted for on the basis of a simple physiological model like the one outlined above.

For reasons of space and because most is known about it we shall confine ourselves to visual perception, and we shall be concerned mainly to show that there are aspects of the subject which at present can best be accounted for in terms of psychological rather than any other sort of explanation.

The perception of objects

We shall first attempt to discover how far we can get with a simple explanation of perception like the very basic physiological one just presented. We shall then put forward two examples of the type of account which seems to be needed in order to handle those perceptual phenomena with which the simple structuralist account seems unable to deal.

Structuralist theories (those which attempt an explanation in terms of the structures involved: e.g. the retina, optic cortex and other parts of the brain) attempt to account for perception on the basis of combining structural elements together. Thus a psychological structuralist theory would consider two main kinds of elements: (i) sensations which are received as each individual receptor is stimulated; and (ii) memory images, which are memories of sensations. These two are combined in order to form our perceptions. A simple physiological structuralist theory would combine the physiological equivalents of (i) nerve impulses from the retina, and (ii) nerve impulses from a memory store. Thus what we perceive is the sum of all our retinal stimulation at a given time plus the memory image associated with similar patterns of stimulation in the past. We recognise objects by somehow combining and matching the sensations with the memory image. How this combining and matching takes place is what the structuralist sets out to discover.

What is wrong with this simple structuralist view of visual perception?

Three kinds of phenomena will serve to cast doubt on the simple structuralist account and with it also the idea that perception is for physicists and physiologists alone: (i) the perceptual constancies; (ii) the illusions; and (iii) the effects of organisation.

The perceptual constancies. In general, our perceptual world is a pretty stable one. Objects do not change in shape or size as we move in relation to them. Yet their retinal image does change. Take, for example, a boy three feet tall, ten feet away and a man six feet tall, twenty feet away. Their retinal images will be the same size. But, of course, they do not appear to be the same size. This effect is known as 'size constancy' – the tendency to perceive the object as we know it, not as it appears on our retina. The structuralist explains constancy by saying that the retinal images interact with the memory images which make the man look larger and the boy smaller. However, the same result is achieved with entirely unfamiliar objects (see Figure 2.2).

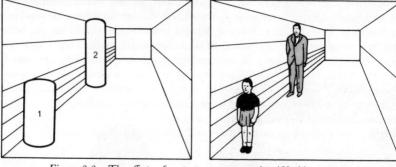

Figure 2.2   The effects of context on apparent size (Hochberg, 1964)

Thus the structuralist is forced to argue that the size of the object is computed from the size of the retinal image and its apparent distance. He has to explain the man's and the boy's constancy of size in terms other than simple sensations and memory images. He must have recourse to some higher-order computation involving the different parts of the retinal image.

The illusions. These have in common the characteristic that they give rise to perceptions very different to what one would expect on the basis of the retinal stimulation they produce (see Figure 2.3). In the case of the Müller–Lyer

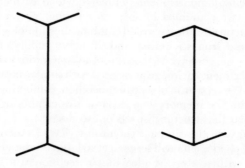

Figure 2.3   The Müller–Lyer illusion

illusion, the perceived length of the same stimulus object (the arrow shaft) changes depending on whether the arrow-heads at each end of the shaft are ingoing or outgoing.

Why? There have been many attempts at explanation but at this stage it is sufficient to indicate that the structuralist is in some difficulties if he is trying to explain these phenomena in terms of sensations and memory images. He would need to have recourse to some rather sophisticated processing of his retinal images before he can account for the illusion. We shall return to this topic later.

The effect of organisation. That this can influence perception is indicated by the manner in which various creatures, e.g. chameleons, are able to escape detection by becoming inconspicuous against their background. Ambiguous pictures, such as the young and the old lady or the vase and faces, are other instances of how identical retinal stimulation can produce two different perceptions (see Figure 2.4). How we will perceive a whole object cannot in

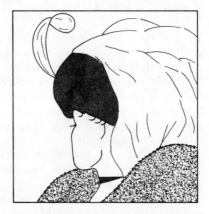

Figure 2.4   Look steadily at these – they may not be what you think they are

this case be predicted simply by adding up our sensations of the parts. Indeed, the parts may become unobservable when combined with other parts.

It seems clear that the simple structuralist position has been considerably undermined. What have we to offer instead?

First, let us be clear about what it is we have rejected. We are not saying that perception has nothing to do with the structure of our retinal sensations, our memory images and some sort of combination of the two. But we are saying that the picture is a great deal more complicated than that, for size constancy can occur without any memory image and the same retinal image can give rise to two totally different perceptions. Two alternative approaches, those of Hochberg (1964) and Gregory (1966), will now be outlined. Both promise to aid our understanding of perception.

Hochberg's approach (1964)

Hochberg favours an explanation in terms of higher-order variables in perception, i.e. he believes that there are laws by which we order our sensory data into perception. He takes into account, for example, work by Hubel and Wiesel (1962), who have recorded from single neurones in the cat's optic cortex. What they found was that there appear to be certain neurones that are tuned specifically to particular patterns (e.g. a line or the edge of a slope) if these stimulate a whole field of retinal receptors. This discovery immediately gives us a more sophisticated analysis of our retinal sensation; no longer are we confined to a simple addition of the points of stimulation on our retina. Hochberg suggests that the discovery of such cells makes the postulation of higher-order analyses of retinal stimulation in the brain a realistic proposition. He goes on to look for other possible higher-order analyses of retinal images, not physiologically, but by attempting to indicate the sort of task they would carry out. In particular he considers two higher-order variables: (i) the gradient of texture density; and (ii) simplicity of interpretation as a determinant of what is perceived.

The gradient of texture density. Gibson (1950), emphasising the importance of considering real out-of-doors situations, argues that if a pattern of retinal stimulation is analysed adequately it should be sufficient to explain perception. An example of this sort of higher-order analysis is the gradient of texture density. If one looks straight ahead at a homogeneously textured surface, say a squared sheet of paper, the density of the texture does not change from one part of the sheet to the next. The texture density gradient approximates to zero. As the top of the sheet is slanted away, the further squares come to change in shape and become smaller in relation to the nearer ones. This, says Gibson, is a powerful depth cue. Each surface has a texture the gradient of which provides an indication of slope and distance. Such a cue enables us to locate the distance of objects standing on or adjacent to the surface in question. In theory this cue should make our perception of the location of objects in space absolutely accurate.

The gradient of texture density is still of uncertain status as an analysing principle in perception. It is certainly inadequate in the following respects: (i) we have no quantitative information on how gradients determine slope, nor on how two gradients combine to give an angle between two surfaces; (ii) we need more information on what causes this cue not to be used to the fullest extent possible, for it provides enough information for the constancies to be complete and for space perception to be perfect – neither of these happens (Smith and Smith, 1962); and (iii) we have no evidence for specific physiological bases in the nervous system for this sort of analysis.

Simplicity of interpretation as a determinant of what is perceived. This analytic principle derives from the *Gestalt* laws of organisation. The *Gestaltists* (from the German word for 'figure' or 'form') argued that we perceive whole figures rather than their component parts and therefore put forward a number of laws to explain the manner in which we derive these whole figures from the stimulation applied to the thousands of retinal receptors. Hochberg (1964) argues that several *Gestalt* laws are specific instances of a general principle of simplicity of interpretation. In effect they cut down the information load on the perceiver by enabling him to code a whole configuration in the optic array as a figure. In the case of an ambiguous figure two alternative interpretations are equally simple. In the case of the illusions the simplest interpretation turns out to be misleading. An illustration of the way in which simplicity might be calculated in order to determine whether we see a line figure as two- or three-dimensional is shown in Figure 2.5.

The more complex a two-dimensional drawing becomes, the more likely it is to be seen in three dimensions if it is possible to perceive it as being in three dimensions. Complexity is measured by the number of angles, *a*, the number

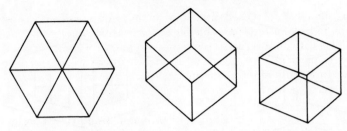

Figure 2.5   Measuring simplicity: information and organisation (Hochberg, 1964)

of continuous lines, b, and the number of different angles, c, using the formula $a + b + 2c$. Applied to the three figures above, it is clear that their degrees of perceived three-dimensionality are predicted by the formula.

Similar points may be raised with respect to simplicity as a higher-order unit of analysis as we raised with texture density gradients: (i) Do we in fact use them? (ii) Do we have any evidence for physiological structures which perform such an analysis on our retinal sensations? Unfortunately, the answers are (i) that we do not as yet know, and (ii) that we have not.

None the less, Hochberg's approach is challenging as an attempt to solve the problems of perception in terms of higher-order analysis of our retinal stimulation. Certainly we cannot yet condemn it while it is still in the hypothetical stage.

Gregory's approach (1966, 1970)

Gregory's approach is rather different. His view is that our perception of objects involves the testing of hypotheses about what they are (object hypotheses). The idea is that we try to make sense of ambiguous retinal stimulation by seeing how well it fits our hypotheses. We shall illustrate Gregory's approach by reference to his treatment of visual illusions. Similar principles apply to other illusions, but we will confine ourselves to the Müller–Lyer illusion (see Figure 2.3 above).

Almost everyone is subject to this illusion. How does Gregory account for it? He does so by suggesting that we bring into play our size-constancy apparatus, the system which compensates for changes in the size of our retinal image with viewing distance. Optically the image of an object doubles in size as its distance is halved. Yet over a considerable range of distances objects do not appear to change much in size. Thouless (1931) found that constancy was almost perfect for fairly near objects but that it tended to break down for more distant objects and when depth cues were absent. Whatever the actual mechanisms mediating size constancy, Thouless has shown us the manner in which it works to counteract the effects of a changing retinal image. Gregory suggests that it is because the illusions trigger perspective depth cues that they bring into play our constancy apparatus.

The Müller–Lyer arrows are seen as indicating perspective in the way suggested by Figure 2.6. The ingoing arrow-heads suggest typically an outside corner of a building, bringing the shaft nearer, whereas the outgoing arrow-

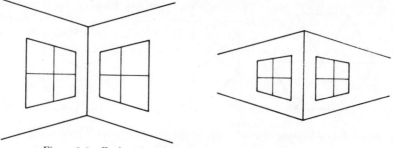

Figure 2.6   Explanation of the Müller–Lyer illusion (Gregory, 1970)

heads suggest typically an inside corner, moving the shaft further away. Thus if the shafts give similar retinal images, our constancy-scaling apparatus will make the further-appearing one look longer than the other. This is in fact what happens. How does Gregory test this idea? There are two main questions to be answered: (i) Why do the figures look flat if the arrow-heads are supposed to indicate perspective? (ii) How can constancy be set even though the figures look flat?

Gregory suggests that the figures look flat because the perspective cues are counteracted by the texture cues from the surface on which they are printed. He reports that two-dimensional wire arrows painted with luminous paint and suspended in the dark are seen monocularly (to remove all but perspective depth cues) as three-dimensional. This would indicate that the surface texture cues probably do counteract the perspective depth cues. Further, when the apparent depth of luminous Müller–Lyer arrows viewed monocularly is measured by a special apparatus (see Gregory, 1966) and the amount of distortion of the shaft is also measured, the distortions are highly correlated with apparent depth for the full range of arrowhead angles. Thus we can conclude that distortion occurs when depth is indicated by perspective but counteracted by background texture (Gregory, 1971). Although others (Fisher, 1968; Day, 1972) have suggested that this mechanism is too specific to cover more than a few particular cases, its general principles seem likely to be more or less correct.

A phenomenon which has fascinated psychologists over the years has been the Necker (1832) cube (see Figure 2.7). It gives rise to alternative perceptions

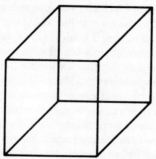

Figure 2.7   The Necker cube

of depth while the retinal image remains constant. Further, we get no constancy scaling of the kind that we would expect from a real cube's retinal
image. The face appearing furthest away does not look larger. It is not
expanded in the way a retinal image of a real cube would have to be in order
to make it look like a cube.

Gregory suggests that depth reversal of Necker cubes is due to our selecting
alternating hypotheses of what the image may be representing. But the hypotheses represent three-dimensional objects which have typical sizes and shapes.
So we arrive at the idea that size and shape can be scaled directly from the
object hypotheses. Selection of an inappropriate hypothesis (such as the
reversed cube) selects inappropriate size for front and back, and so it appears
distorted even though there is no misleading retinal information.

Interestingly, Gregory goes on to suggest that our collections of object
hypotheses are the raw materials of our thought processes and the concepts
to which the names in our language are attached. He is thus attempting the
beginnings of a unified theory of perception, language and thought.

Hochberg and Gregory represent two different approaches to the problems
of perception. They have chosen to develop different aspects of the simple
structuralist position. Hochberg emphasises the potential value of discovering
what higher-order analysis the perceptual system performs on our retinal
stimulation. Gregory stresses the importance of the non-sensory aspects of
perception in the form of object hypotheses which influence what we make
of our retinal stimulation.

The discussion so far has confined itself to our perception of objects and
space under relatively simple conditions. The question we now wish to
address is what happens when we take into account such things as the motivational and emotional state of the perceiver, his personality and his choice of
what to perceive.

OTHER FACTORS RELATED TO PERCEPTION

Motivation and emotion
Most research in this field has been done using material which is vague,
ambiguous and out of focus. The thinking behind this work is as follows. If the
subject is under a particularly strong motivation, then this will colour his
perceptions. In one study subjects were shown blurred pictures of articles
related to food at varying periods after their last meal. There was an increase
in the number of food-related objects perceived up to about six hours after
the last meal, but thereafter a decrease. There was also an increase in the
tendency to give no response at all (Levine, Chein and Murphy, 1942).

More persisting motives also seem to influence perception. Aggressive subjects chosen on the basis of the T.A.T. (see Chapter 9) were quicker to perceive pictures of aggressive acts than they were less aggressive ones (Eriksen,
1951). Likewise, subjects high in need for achievement perceived words
related to achievement at a lower intensity of illumination than those with
less need of achievement (McClelland and Liberman, 1949). The T.A.T.
itself makes use of the phenomenon being discussed by presenting a non-
committal picture and asking subjects to describe what is happening in it.

Further evidence that motivational/emotional factors affect perception comes from studies of perceptual defence.

Perceptual defence

An experiment by Bruner and Postman (1947) was the first to demonstrate the phenomena of perceptual defence and perceptual sensitisation. They measured the time taken for free association (saying the first word to come into the subject's head) to each of ninety-nine words. A fortnight later the subjects were presented tachistoscopically (i.e. via an apparatus capable of presenting visual material for short precise exposures) with the six words to which their free association time had been longest, the six to which it had been shortest and the six to which it had been intermediate. It was found that for some subjects the words which had the longest free-association times were the most quickly perceived, while for others they were most slowly seen. This curious finding led to the hypotheses of perceptual sensitisation and perceptual defence. These hypotheses involve one very strange aspect. They imply that, at least in the case of perceptual defence, the subjects had a sort of pre-perception of the words which caused them to put up their defences and led to a slowing up of their perceptions. A slow free-association time is supposed to indicate a word with strong emotional significance.

An objection to this interpretation is that subjects may just have been reluctant (in the case of 'perceptual defence') to speak words which were embarrassing or taboo to them. This may be so, though Beier and Cowan's (1953) subjects reported that they did not consciously stop themselves from speaking the words. The possibility of an unconscious blocking of perception comes from the research of Dixon (1958), who found that when sexual words were presented tachistoscopically at an intensity just below threshold (the level at which they were able to perceive them), the subjects showed a rise in psychogalvanic skin response (P.G.S.R.) in spite of the fact that they were not conscious of the nature of the words. (P.G.S.R. is a measure of emotional arousal.) McGinnies (1949) found that P.G.S.R. was greater to sexual words than to neutral words, that they were more slowly perceived and that P.G.S.R. appeared before the words were correctly perceived. However, Aronfreed, Messick and Diggory (1953) report that in their experiments the P.G.S.R. occurred only after the words had been perceived.

Vernon (1962) concludes that probably some awareness, though of a rudimentary nature, occurs which has the effect of retarding or accelerating fully conscious perception. Which of these occurs will depend on the inhibitions or freedom from inhibitions of the subject. It is interesting to speculate on the relationship of the phenomenon to the mechanisms of attention (discussed in Section 5.2).

Effects of attitudes and interests

It is difficult to assess the work on interests and the way they influence perception. Postman, Bruner and McGinnies (1948) administered the Allport–Vernon–Lindzey study of values test to subjects and then showed them tachistoscopically a series of words related to the values in the test. Subjects perceived most readily the words corresponding to the particular values which the test had shown them to possess. This, together with the experiment of Postman and Schneider (1951), in which the same result was obtained by using words which were equally infrequent in the valued and non-valued categories, suggests that people certainly do perceive more readily words associated with their own special interests. However, this may be due to a special vocabulary which has been acquired rather than the interest itself.

Prejudice

This can also influence perception. Secord, Bevan and Katz (1956) found that subjects prejudiced against blacks tended to exaggerate the extent to which characteristics like the width of nose and fullness of lips (characteristics related to the black stereotype) appeared in actual photographs of blacks, in comparison with less-prejudiced subjects.

Perception and personality

Individual differences in the ability to perceive items or components of a picture as discrete from their surroundings appear to be related to an important personality dimension known as 'field independence' (Witkin *et al.*, 1954).

This dimension also shows itself in the ability to impose organisation and structure in coping with perceptual material of an unstructured kind. Field independence is measured by either the rod-and-frame test or the embedded-figures test. The rod-and-frame test consists of a movable rod which is presented visually in a frame that may be tilted either to the left or to the right. The subject, seated in a chair which may also be tilted to the left or right, must adjust the rod to the true vertical position with no background cues or guidance apart from the misleading frame and his own sense of orientation. The embedded-figures test requires the subject to find a simple figure embedded in complex ones. Research has shown that field independence increases with age from 8 to 21 but that there is a strong correlation between early and late scores for individuals. Thus although field independence increases with age over this period each individual's degree of field independence in relation to his peers is likely to remain more or less constant (Witkin, Goodenough and Karp, 1967). Witkin (1959), referring to a study of 10-year-old boys, reports that the degree of field independence is related to the kind of upbringing the boy has received. Thus a mother who restricts her son's activities, whether because of her own fears or anxieties or because of particularly strong ties to him, who stresses conformity and who does not encourage him to take responsibility for himself, is more likely to have a field-dependent child. In addition, field-independent children are likely to have a higher intelligence test score (Witkin *et al.*, 1966) and Witkin (1967) has related field independence to cultural background. Other studies (Witkin, 1965; Witkin, Lewis and Weil, 1968) show it to be related to mental health. Field-dependent and field-independent personalities seem to show their psychological disturbances in different ways. Disturbances in field-dependent personalities seem to be those that stem from a relatively primitive and chaotic personality structure. These include identity problems, passivity, alcoholism, ulcers, obesity, character disorders and hallucinatory states. On the other hand, disturbances in field-independent personalities seem to spring from a personality structure characterised by over-control, over-intellectualisation and isolation from reality, as, for example, in obsessional and compulsive reactions and delusional thinking. These findings seem to suggest that field independence is associated with the coherence and cohesiveness of a person's ego defensive system (see Chapter 10) but that it is certainly no guarantee of emotional stability.

More generally, the evidence is that field independence is related to a person's ability to cope effectively with ambiguous and misleading stimuli encountered in everyday life. For example, scores on Crutchfield's embedded-figures test have been found to be related to other people's judgements of their insight, reliability, and ability to cope with complexity (Crutchfield, Woodworth and Albrecht, 1958). Even more interesting is the report (Witkin, Goodenough and Karp, 1967) that older people who were still actively involved at work were more field-independent than those who had retired.

Individual differences in the susceptibility to visual illusions have also been investigated and there is some evidence that field-independent people are less susceptible to them (Gardner, 1961; McGurk, 1965). Susceptibility to some illusions (e.g. the Müller–Lyer illusion) decreases with age, while for others (e.g. the Ponzo illusion) it increases (Leibowitz and Judisch, 1967). Susceptibility also depends on cultural background, with people living in a more 'carpentered' environment being more susceptible to the Müller–Lyer illusion and people from more primitive regions being more susceptible to vertical–horizontal effects.

2.4 Memory

When discussing attention we presented an information-processing model and discussed modifications to it on the basis of more recent work. That discussion and the following one on perception show how much each process is functionally dependent on access to the individual's memory of past experiences. Thus, while it is convenient for present purposes to conceptualise memory as a late component in the information-processing sequence, as did Broadbent (1958), this does not represent accurately its true role in relation to the other two processes. In this section we shall be concerned chiefly with two main aspects of memory: (i) the storage system and how material is stored in it; and (ii) how material is retrieved from memory. In the final part of the section we shall mention some of the simpler and more obvious ways of using our knowledge of how memory works in order to improve our ability to remember.

THE INFORMATION STORAGE SYSTEM

Evidence from a number of sources, largely concerned with the manner in which we forget, seems to suggest that there are three different kinds of information storage in memory. While agreement with this statement is not total (see Craik and Lockhart, 1972), it does seem to be held by the vast majority of researchers in the field. The first of these stores is a sensory memory which retains most or all of what impinges on our senses but only for a very short time. Estimates suggest a maximum of between a quarter of a second and two seconds. The second kind of storage is usually called primary memory (P.M.). This is equivalent to Broadbent's (1958) short-term store but estimates of the maximum storage time without rehearsal range from about five to thirty seconds. The third kind of storage is a long-term secondary memory (S.M.). Here a memory trace may remain for years. As far as is known this store is of virtually unlimited capacity.

The sensory memory can deal with much more information than secondary memory, but the information is lost within two seconds at best, the time depending to some extent on the duration and intensity of the particular stimulus and on subsequent stimulation. Sperling (1960) pioneered research into visual sensory memory or iconic memory (see Neisser, 1967). He presented cards containing twelve letters (three rows of four letters) for fifty milliseconds and found that on average people could recall four or five of them. However, when they were required to report only the letters in one row (indicated by a high, medium or low tone presented immediately after the card), their success rate ranged from three to four. When there was a gap of half a second between exposure of the slide and the tone, then the number of items in the row recalled dropped to one or two, the same as if no tone were presented. This experiment shows that material seen briefly ceases to be available to us after a very short time unless we direct our attention specifically to it. There is also evidence for sensory stores for hearing and touch.

The short-term primary memory (P.M.) storage is seen as a store in which the information called from the sensory memory is quickly lost (though not nearly as quickly as in the sensory system) unless it can be transferred to a relatively permanent store, the long-term secondary memory (S.M.). For example, if we are introduced to a large number of strangers, we forget many of their names within thirty seconds. The names of those whom we regard as more important are more likely to be 'rehearsed' for a limited period of time until we have to attend to some new information. It is as though information in the P.M. is only intended to be held there long enough for it to be coded and transferred to the S.M.; P.M. is seen as having a limited capacity, and when it is full, new information entering it must replace something already there.

On the other hand, S.M. is seen as having a virtually unlimited capacity. The amount of information going into permanent storage is colossal. In fact it is so large that we often have difficulty in retrieving information when we want it, even though we may find it at a later date.

Experimental studies of 'forgetting' have given rise to a number of theories which try to explain why we are unable to retrieve certain material. Three main ideas have been proposed: (1) decay through disuse; (2) forgetting through interference; and (3) motivated forgetting.

(1) There is no direct evidence to support the decay theory (the idea that

the memory trace decays over time unless it is worked on, as in rehearsal). Studies of hypnosis and brain stimulation suggest that many apparently inaccessible memories are stored. Further, it is impossible to test this idea conclusively since the human organism is never inactive. Consequently there is never an occasion when the memory trace is definitely not subject to interference. The theory can at best provide only a partial explanation of forgetting and seems likely to apply to sensory memory and P.M. only.

(2) The interference theory, based on free-recall studies (see below), holds that (i) new learning may interfere with material learned previously (this is known as retroactive inhibition), and (ii) previous learning may interfere with learning and recall of new material (proactive inhibition). These effects have been demonstrated frequently (e.g. Underwood, 1957). Interference effects are considerably less with meaningful rather than meaningless material and they, too, seem to apply to P.M. more than to S.M.

(3) The third theory was proposed by Freud (see Chapter 10) using his concept of 'repression'. This refers to the tendency for people to 'forget' experiences or feelings which they do not wish to acknowledge. This forgetting occurs unconsciously, and is not under the control of the person concerned. This theory is difficult to test experimentally. However, psychoanalysts hold that it is revealed regularly in their psychoanalytic treatment of patients, the treatment being based on the uncovering of experiences which, though forgotten, are responsible for the patients' later problems.

Evidence supporting the distinction between P.M. and S.M. comes from two main sources: (1) patients with certain kinds of brain damage; and (2) recall experiments.

(1) When lesions occur in a region of the brain called the hippocampus, the person cannot store new information permanently. There appears to be no functioning transfer mechanism from P.M. to S.M. For example, a person with whom a patient has just been conversing may leave the room and return a few minutes later and not be recognised (Milner, 1966). Knowledge and skills learned before the damage are unaffected. Information can also be held in P.M. by rehearsal, but it disappears when new information replaces it without transfer to S.M.

(2) In the typical free-recall experiment the subject is presented with a list of items. At the end of the presentation he is asked to recall the items in any order. If probability of recall is plotted against the order of presentation of the item, then a U-shaped curve results. Items coming at the beginning and end of the list are more likely to be recalled than those in the middle. This would be expected, given the P.M.–S.M. model. Initial items are more likely to have reached S.M., and final items are more likely still to be in P.M. at the time of recall. Furthermore, if this task lasts for a minimum of thirty seconds, this recency effect (the greater ease with which final items are recalled) is eliminated if the subject is given another task to perform (and so fills the P.M. with new material) immediately after presentation of the list (Craik, 1970). This finding is to be expected since the final items would then no longer be held in the P.M. Conversely, when factors hypothesised to affect only S.M. are varied, then it is found that the recall of early items is affected, but not that of the final ones. For example, Murdock (1962) found that shortening

the interval between items on a twenty-item list from two to one seconds resulted in poorer recall of the early items. It seems likely that the shorter presentation interval prevents rehearsal and other work being done on the early items. This would lessen their likelihood of reaching S.M. since such rehearsal, integration and coding seem to be necessary for the transfer from P.M. to S.M.

It was thought originally that rehearsal was the chief manner in which information was transferred from P.M. to S.M. However, more recent work has suggested that it is also processed into a convenient form for retention in S.M. This seems to be more important than simple rehearsal of material for long-term remembering. It is as though S.M. has a complex filing system such that incoming information has to be coded and integrated into the system. Coding of two kinds have been suggested for this purpose: reduction coding and elaboration coding. Reduction coding converts material into a more compact form, as in the use of mnemonics. Thus the colours of the spectrum (red, orange, yellow, green, blue, indigo and violet) become 'ROYGBIV' if reduction-coded. An example of elaboration coding by adding semantic meaning to the letters is the well-known classroom expansion into 'Richard Of York Gained Battles In Vain'.

There is fairly general agreement that the nature of the filing codes for S.M. is largely semantic, i.e. material is sorted in S.M. according to its meaning. Material coded according to meaning appears to be better remembered than material coded according to sound (Sachs, 1967). However, there are situations in which coding according to sound is more effective, for example where the material is relatively meaningless (Gruneberg *et al.*, 1970), or when there is insufficient time to make a meaningful whole out of a series of unconnected words (Baddeley and Levy, 1971).

There is evidence that many memories are stored which are not normally accessible to a person. We see this when we are unable to recall something and yet can recognise it. Sometimes we cannot recall something we have learnt, but we are able to relearn it more quickly than completely new learning of similar material. Ebbinghaus (1885) referred to this phenomenon as 'savings'. More dramatic illustrations occur sometimes under hypnosis, when memories from many years ago are vividly recalled. Vivid memories of a similar type, in which the scenes and sounds of an early memory are clearly evoked, come from electrical stimulation of certain parts of the brain (Penfield, 1969). If that specific part of the brain evoking the memory is destroyed, however, it does not eliminate the memory. This suggests a highly complicated, as opposed to a simple, anatomical representation of memory in the brain. It has been proposed that the biochemical basis of memory involves the complex molecule, ribonucleic acid (Hyden, 1969). There is some tentative evidence to support this idea, but as yet we are far from understanding the nature of these underlying biochemical processes.

INFORMATION RETRIEVAL

The distinction between information storage and retrieval is in practice a difficult one to make, for many ideas about storage stem from studies of information retrieval. It is possible that some memories are stored in a different way from others, and that there are two corresponding retrieval processes: (i) recall of something which has been learnt; and (ii) redintegrative memory. The latter refers to memories of life experiences, which may be quite vivid. Such memories can go back to childhood, though very early experiences during the first two to three years are rarely recollected. Memories of this kind are subject, of course, to error. Perception and memory appear to involve in part a process of construction, whereby people often remember what they expect to see or hear, even though they may have been mistaken. This is why witnesses sometimes give conflicting evidence in good faith. The use of elaboration coding to store material is compatible with this (Bransford and Franks, 1971).

Recall and redintegrative memory require retrieval from S.M. An interesting case of total retrieval of information is that of eidetic imagery. This is a kind of visual memory which enables the person to recall with almost photographic clarity a picture which has just previously been briefly presented. The person reports seeing an image of the picture somewhere in space which can be kept in attention for up to several minutes. Only about 5 per cent of children report clear detailed images which last for thirty seconds. After adolescence, such eidetic imagery is much less frequent. Eidetic imagery may not be related to S.M. but appears to be visual rather like the visual sensory system investigated by Sperling (1960).

In contrast to eidetic imagery the more usual information retrieval from memory may be only partial, or only partially correct. When we are trying to remember a specific word but are unable to do so, other words may come into awareness, most of which are similar in sound and a few similar in meaning to the required word. This state of search is known as the tip-of-the-tongue phenomenon. Brown and McNeill (1966) found that people in this state could give accurately the number of syllables and the initial letter of the required word, and frequently could give the final syllable, that receiving particular stress. This implies something about the organisation of memory, in particular about semantic memory (memory necessary for the use of language). They proposed that words might be stored according to a kind of two-dimensional filing system, according to their sound and meaning. Thus someone with a word on the tip of his tongue finds a number of words of similar sound coming to him but none has the right meaning and vice versa.

The retrieval of information from S.M. seems to require not simply regurgitation of its contents as with P.M., where the material is stored more or less as a whole without having been filed away according to its sound or meaning, but S.M. material has to be looked for in the right place, as it were. The right questions need to be asked either by a questioner or the individual himself. Thus you might not remember what you did on the Friday two weeks ago if the question was put to you in that way, but if you were asked whether you went to work or stayed at home you might find it easier to remember that you spent the day working at home, that you had been incessantly interrupted by telephone calls, had finally stopped answering the phone and consequently missed an offer of free theatre tickets from a friend who had failed to get hold of you. The events of the day were stored under a number of different headings in terms of their significance to you. But one of those headings needed to be cued in before you could remember what you had done. This kind of process is typical of S.M., and forgetting in S.M. has been called cue-dependent (Tulving and Madigan, 1970) because the lack of access to the stored material is due to the failure to provide a cue enabling its release. Cue-dependent forgetting is contrasted with trace-dependent forgetting, i.e. forgetting due to the decay or loss of the memory trace. Research into trace-dependent forgetting is subject to the same problems as trace decay theory in that the lack of accessibility of a memory does not mean it has decayed. It may have been subject to interference or the appropriate cue for its release may not have been used. On balance it seems likely that trace-dependent forgetting plays less part than one might expect from one's own experience of forgetting. Certainly methods such as hypnosis and electrical stimulation of the brain can elicit material which has long since been forgotten.

We have so far presented a summary of facts and theories concerning memory processes. Let us now turn to a discussion of their implications for ways in which memory can be improved.

THE IMPROVEMENT OF MEMORY

We suggested earlier that there might be two different ways in which memories can be stored or encoded: one involves knowledge stored in verbal form and illustrated by the free-recall experiment; the other involves material stored in a sensory form, perhaps primarily visual but also auditory, as illustrated by redintegrative memory. Paivio (1971) referred to these two different processes as the verbal symbolic and non-verbal imagery processes. He suggested that the non-verbal imagery process is most suited to encoding concrete spatial events and objects, and the verbal symbolic one for abstract verbal material. This distinction is an important one, for the use of non-verbal imagery can increase greatly the recall of objects in a particular serial order. Luria (1968) describes how this can be done using the method of loci. In this method a person visualises each of the objects to be remembered in a particular sequence. Each object is located at a point along a well-known route (e.g. along a well-known journey to work) such that objects are located in the desired order along the route. Similarly, it has been found that linking two objects together by a visual image can greatly enhance recall (Bower, 1972). For example, if we wish to remember that Mr X is very keen on stamp-collecting, we might conjure up a mental picture of a postage stamp which has on it the head of Mr X.

Retrieval is often difficult, and sometimes impossible, if there is insufficient time to consolidate information into S.M. When it is particularly important that we encode and retrieve adequately a certain piece of information or a particular skill, then over-learning (i.e. learning beyond the point of successful recall through repetition) is the most effective technique. This is critical especially in the training of a skill which could have drastic consequences if not recalled adequately (e.g. in pilot training).

The effectiveness of practice in aiding recall is increased by self-recitation during practice. In fact self-recitation is itself practice in recall. Self-recitation also aids memory in that it focusses the learner's attention on to the relevant material.

Finally, we noted earlier that memories are organised in some way. Material which is meaningless presents difficulties in organisation for storage (in relating it to other material), and we noted that meaningless material is particularly subject to interference effects, and hence to forgetting. We might infer from this that successful retrieval will be related to the degree of organisation present in the material to be learned. There is evidence for this. For example, Mandler (1974) found that when lists of words are learned, recall increases with the degree of organisation that can be imposed on the material. An illustration of this might be that it would be easier to remember all the names of a team of footballers who can be organised with respect to the position in which they play than it would without the positional knowledge and corresponding means of classification.

In this chapter we have considered some of the features of human information processing. We have seen that there are some things that can be done well and with ease and others which are difficult. One particular factor which determines this is the limited capacity of human beings to process information. Even though S.M. has an extremely large capacity, there are limits on the rate at which coding for storage and decoding for retrieval can take place since these activities require the use of the information-processing channel, thus excluding other material from access. The nature of the limits to human capacity in the work situation has been the subject of a great deal of investigation. It will be referred to again in Chapters 3 and 5 in connection with skill acquisition and ergonomics.

3
Learning and Skill Acquisition

3.1 Introduction

In this chapter we are concerned with the acquisition of behaviour. While we shall slant it towards the possible applications of work in this field, this introduction to the field must cover much that is basic and academic. Only in this way will the true flavour of psychological research into learning be clear. In Section 3.2 we shall discuss the concept of 'learning' and distinguish it from other, related concepts. We shall then move on in the next three sections to consider the theory of learning. First (Section 3.3), we shall define the main technical terms used and orientate the reader towards Sections 3.4 and 3.5, in which the two main general theories (stimulus–response theory and cognitive theory) are discussed. Section 3.6 reviews the considerable *rapprochement* and integration which has occurred between the two. Other recent developments are discussed in Section 3.7, including research into social learning. Section 3.8 draws some conclusions about the relevance of learning-theory principles for training and instruction. The chapter concludes with a discussion of the learning of complex skills (Section 3.9) and research into skill acquisition (Section 3.10).

3.2 The concept of 'learning'

Learning is probably not a unitary phenomenon. Psychologists who study such different activities as tooth-brushing or acquiring an attitude have tended to take up different standpoints when examining different learning activities.

This is most striking in the different approaches to the study of (i) simple forms of learning which often use animals as experimental subjects and stem mainly from the behaviourist tradition, and (ii) more complex human learning, particularly the acquisition of motor (physical) skills which generally operate within an information-processing framework (see Section 3.10 on skill learning).

The first problem with learning is that we cannot know whether something has been learned until we can infer it from the behaviour of the person concerned. This means that unless a person is sufficiently motivated to behave in such a way as to show his learning, we do not know whether or not he has learnt something In fact what may appear at first to be a learning problem may on inspection turn out to be one of motivation and vice versa. A manager is not infrequently confronted with the problem of deciding whether the poor performance of an employee is due to the fact that he has not learnt adequately what he is supposed to do, or whether it is due to a lack of interest or application. The correct diagnosis of the cause is clearly very important for effective remedial action.

Not all changes in behaviour are due to learning. Maturation (i.e. a genetically based development common to all normal members of a species) or fatigue can also cause changes in performance. Hence the definition of learning which we shall use is 'a process within the organism which results in the capacity for changed performance which can be related to experience rather than maturation'.

However, it is often difficult to distinguish between maturational and experiential causes of a change in performance. The two causes sometimes interact with each other, as can be seen, for example, in the acquisition of language in the child, typically between the ages of 1 and 3. At particular stages of maturation the child has the greatest ability to benefit from particular kinds of experience. Particularly striking is the young child's ability to learn to speak a foreign language perfectly, without much apparent difficulty – something which becomes extremely difficult at a later stage.

We shall now turn to a consideration of the kinds of activity which come under the heading of 'learning'. The list will not be exhaustive, but will serve to indicate to the reader the magnitude of the task facing anyone who attempts to evolve a comprehensive theory of learning.

Consider a new-born baby – it comes into the world needing to adapt to an environment totally different from that to which it has hitherto been accustomed. In the womb it has had no problems of nourishment or deprivation. It comes into a world in which, during the ensuing years, it will be expected to walk, talk and feed itself as well as discovering the nature of reality and understanding a large amount of 'dos' and 'don'ts' in the realm of what is or is not allowed. Initially the kinds of things it learns are simple things – such as screaming when it wants something – but later it starts to need motor skills like climbing or riding a bicycle. Children also have to acquire information in school lessons as well as understanding new words and concepts. In addition to this a great deal of emotional learning takes place – the child discovers which kinds of things are pleasant and which are frightening or unpleasant.

This illustrates the massive changes which must occur if the individual is to adapt to his environment. These changes will be partly due to learning and partly to other factors, such as the following: (i) the biological readiness to learn a given activity at a given age; (ii) personality (see Chapter 9); (iii) abilities and the capacity to learn a given task (see Chapter 10); (iv) past experiences, involving previous learning, including emotional experiences; (v) motivation (see Chapters 2 and 3); and (vi) situational variables, e.g. distraction, family problems and working conditions. These factors may all interact in a given person.

3.3   Theories of learning

We indicated in Chapter 1 that many of the controversies in psychological theory stemmed from differences in basic viewpoint concerning the proper concerns of psychological science. Such is the case for theories of learning. The key concepts used in these theories are 'stimulus', 'response' and 'organism'.

A stimulus is (i) 'some specific physical energy impinging on a receptor sensitive to that kind of energy', or (ii) 'any objectively describable situation or event (whether inside or outside the organism) that is the occasion for an organism's response' (Hilgard, Atkinson and Atkinson, 1975). The difficulty arising from these definitions often lies in discovering which aspects of the 'objectively describable situation' are responsible for the 'specific physical energy impinging on a receptor sensitive to that kind of energy' – in other words, how one can tell whether a person will respond to what someone says, to how he says it, or to his general appearance. Spence (1956), Gibson (1960) and Underwood (1963) have all distinguished between these two aspects. Spence refers to situational *versus* effective stimuli. Gibson refers to potential *versus* effective stimuli, and Underwood to nominal *versus* functional stimuli. Clearly, it is the functional or effective stimulus which is of interest to the psychologist. Unfortunately, there seems to be no general way in which the effective stimulus can be specified in advance for a given individual. Thus Underwood has shown that, depending on the task, different parts of the stimulus are effective. The nature of this phenomenon seems to be so specific that no rules are available for determining which part of the stimulus is effective in which case. The term 'stimulus' is therefore intrinsically circular, and the various ways of trying to escape from the circle have been less than successful. It is not possible to define what an effective stimulus is without reference to the response it is supposed to elicit. The response, however, as we shall see, is defined in terms of the stimulus.

A response is defined as (i) 'the behavioural result of stimulation in the form of a movement or glandular secretion', (ii) 'sometimes, any activity of the organism, including central responses (such as an image or fantasy), whether or not the stimulus is identified and whether or not identifiable movements occur', or (iii) 'products of the organism's activity – such as words typed per minute' (Hilgard, Atkinson and Atkinson, 1975). For the purposes of this chapter, which is concerned with learning, the relevant parts are (i) and (ii). Since the terms 'stimulus' and 'response' in learning theory are generally used in connection with theories which state that learning involves some kind of connection between the two, it follows that (ii) above must be taken to mean an activity with an identified stimulus.

The organism is a term 'used to refer to the living individual animal, whether human or sub-human' (Hilgard, Atkinson and Atkinson, 1975). There is a tendency for learning theorists to refer to the internal mental workings of the person as well as physical processes when they talk of the organism.

The theories of learning which we shall discuss have all evolved in the experimental psychology laboratory. The vast majority of experiments have been carried out using animals, usually the white rat, as experimental subjects. Theorists have, on this basis, attempted to find general laws governing the learning process which, it was hoped, would be valid for other species, including man. In their search learning theorists have not usually been interested in individual differences between animals and in how any such differences might affect the learning process. Such theories, however, have not been very successful in explaining animal behaviour and so it is not surprising that they have had relatively little influence in apparently relevant areas of human behaviour, e.g. in the training situation. One theory which has considerable applicability to human behaviour is Skinner's reinforcement theory, which Skinner himself does not consider to be a theory since it concerns only the description of behaviour.

Before examining learning theories we shall briefly describe their antecedents. Ebbinghaus (1885) and Thorndike (1898) were the first workers to attempt rigorous empirical investigation of learning. Their early work served to justify laws of association describing learning in terms of an association being found between two elements in the human psyche. Later, however, learning theories became split into two main strands: S–R (stimulus–response) and cognitive theories. The former, which include those of Thorndike (1932), Hull (1943, 1952), Guthrie (1952) and Skinner (1938), have in common that they assume learning to involve the building of a bond between S and R (the old associationist view, but restricted to links between S and R). They differ in their views of the nature of these bonds and how they are formed. Cognitive theories include a number of somewhat different approaches, all of which have in common a rejection of S–R theory. The theory of Tolman (1932) is the best developed of these. Essentially, the emphasis of cognitive theorists is that it is not links between Ss and Rs which are dominant in learning but links between Ss, such that one stimulus leads the subject to expect the next (Tolman, 1932) and between the parts of a whole configuration (the *Gestaltists*, e.g. Köhler, 1925). In general, we can say that the conflict between these two groups of learning theorists centred around those aspects of learning for which the others' theories failed to account and for which theirs was successful in accounting, e.g. Tolman's studies of latent learning (see below). There has been a degree of convergence between the two kinds of theory, but recently the trend has been away from the idea of a general theory to less comprehensive models such as the work on social learning, imitation and identification by Bandura and Walters (1963), which will be discussed later in the chapter.

Inasmuch as the newer models have been generated as a reaction to the older, general theories of learning, we may conclude that while the latter have yielded a number of general principles which are neither exhaustive nor sufficiently precise, the former leave us with a number of increasingly precise formulations which lack the comprehensiveness of the earlier models.

3.4 *S–R* theories

S–R theorists see learning as the process by which a particular stimulus comes to evoke a particular response. Generally they have distinguished between two types of *S–R* learning process. These are usually called 'classical' conditioning (Pavlov, 1927) and 'instrumental' or 'operant' conditioning (Skinner, 1938).

The starting-point for classical conditioning is a stimulus which leads automatically to a response. This stimulus (e.g. food) is known as the unconditioned stimulus (U.C.S.) as it evokes an automatic, unconditioned response (U.C.R.) (e.g. salivation). When another stimulus (e.g. a bell) is presented just before the unconditioned stimulus for a number of trials, this stimulus (the conditioned stimulus) presented alone comes to elicit a response very like the U.C.R. (i.e. salivation). In this example, the bell is the conditioned stimulus (C.S.) and the salivation to the sound of the bell is the conditioned response (C.R.). This paradigm is illustrated in Figure 3.1.

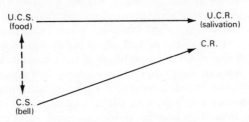

Figure 3.1   Classical conditioning

There followed a number of further discoveries in connection with the classical conditioning process.

(i) If the C.S. is administered many times unaccompanied by the U.C.S., the C.R. begins to weaken. This is known as 'extinction'.

(ii) A number of stimuli similar in nature to the C.S. will also evoke the C.R. but in decreasing strength as they depart further in similarity from the original C.S. This is known as 'conditioned stimulus generalisation'.

(iii) If certain stimuli cease to be paired with the U.C.S., whereas others continue to be so paired, only the latter will continue to evoke the C.R. This process is called 'discrimination'.

(iv) Certain features of the timing of the C.R.–U.C.R. pairings were also noted. In particular, a half-second delay between the onset of the C.S. and the U.C.S. leads to the fastest learning (Wolfe, 1934; Spooner and Kellogg, 1947).

(v) Noxious stimuli can be used as the U.C.S. (Bechterev, 1932).

(vi) If an interval of time is allowed to pass after the extinction of a C.R. and the C.S. is then administered without the U.C.S., it will again tend to elicit the C.R. This phenomenon is known as 'spontaneous recovery'.

(vii) In discrimination, if two potential C.S.s are sufficiently similar for the animal to be unable to distinguish between them, 'experimental neurosis' may occur (i.e. the animal breaks down), presumably as a result of a conflict over whether or not to respond.

As a model classical conditioning does not account for all types of learning. However, there are a number of everyday situations for which it has, more or less successfully, been shown to have some explanatory value, the learning of emotions, conflict and the learning of word meanings.

On the learning of emotions, Watson and Rayner (1920) succeeded in conditioning a fear response to a stimulus which did not elicit it previously in a small boy called Albert. Albert came to fear a variety of objects (generalisation) which bore increasing degrees of similarity to a tame white rat, in whose presence the experimenter had sounded a loud gong behind Albert's back. The reader will be happy to know that it proved possible to extinguish this fear response by means of a technique which came to be known as 'reciprocal inhibition'. Albert was given some delicious meals to eat, and during the meals various balls of wool, furry toys, rabbits and white rats were brought closer and closer to him in such a way that he came to fear them no longer. As far as is known, the episode caused Albert no permanent harm. This work has implications for the treatment of nervous disorders such as phobias.

On conflict, Pavlov identified one kind when he demonstrated experimental neurosis. Another kind of conflict occurs in connection with complex stimuli, of which one of the most common is man himself. Different aspects of the same person can evoke different responses, thus generating a conflict of emotions in relation to that person on the part of the subject. One example is the child's attitude to his parents when it involves a mixture of positive emotions arising from their association with many pleasant experiences in life and negative emotions resulting from experiences of parental anger and frustration.

A phenomenon known as higher-order conditioning has been suggested as an explanation of the way in which we learn to understand the meaning of words. The basic phenomenon is as follows. The C.S. from one experiment is used as the U.C.S. in the next. Thus a striped flying object may become a U.C.S. for a painful sting or a panic reaction on the part of parents. Later on, the word 'wasp' becomes the C.S. for the striped flying object.

Thorndike (1898) first suggested that the most common kind of learning was of a trial-and-error type. Later (1913) he proposed the law of effect which states that when a stimulus is followed by a response and then immediately by a satisfying state of affairs, that response is stamped in. If it is followed by a dissatisfying state of affairs, the response decreases in strength. Later still (1932) he modified the law of effect to take account of the discovery that dissatisfying states of affairs did not weaken responses as much as satisfying states strengthened them.

Skinner (1938), like Thorndike, emphasised the importance of reward, which he called 'reinforcement'. Specifically, a reinforcement is something which follows a response and so increases the probability of that response being repeated in a particular stimulus environment. The process of increasing the probability of a response in this way is known as 'operant' conditioning.

Like classical conditioning, it involves the acquisition of a new response to a stimulus. However, the means of acquisition are different. The essential components of operant conditioning are: (i) a response R which serves to bring about a particular outcome; and (ii) the reinforcement. This is illustrated in Figure 3.2.

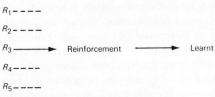

Figure 3.2 Operant conditioning

Skinner distinguishes between two kinds of behaviour. 'Respondent' behaviour involves the kind of behaviour elicited through the triggering of a reflex, e.g. salivation, as in classical conditioning. 'Operant' behaviour has as its chief characteristic that it operates on the environment; no particular stimulus can be relied upon to elicit it. Most behaviour is of this kind, e.g. walking and talking. Operant behaviour can be brought under the control of a stimulus, and most learning involves just this, according to Skinner. When a piece of operant behaviour occurs in the vicinity of a stimulus and is reinforced, it will tend to recur in similar situations.

Reinforcement may be positive or negative. The occurrence of a positive reinforcer, for example food or praise, is rewarding, as is the termination of a negative reinforcer, for example punishment. Thus a person will learn to use a piece of operant behaviour in order to terminate a painful situation. However, Skinner suggests that negative reinforcers are not as effective as positive ones.

Their effectiveness is in question for the following reasons:

(i) Punishment (the administration of a negative reinforcer) generates an emotional response, such as fear, which may be incompatible with the response it is desired to remove; hence the response is suppressed. However, the effects may not be long term and the response will re-occur when the emotional response disappears.

(ii) Punishment can be conditioned to the situation which elicits the unwanted response. Thus a rat comes to fear the cage in which it receives an electric shock to its feet. It can be difficult to get rid of such a connection.

(iii) When the individual avoids the punishment stimuli, he obtains reinforcement for so doing. This process has a number of undesirable aspects, the worst of which is likely to be that the punisher himself may become the stimulus for an avoidance response (avoidance conditioning). Others include a tendency for such emotional responses to the punishment to be unacceptable and the likelihood that the effect may only be temporary.

Skinner is concerned with description and not with generating constructs to explain learning. Hence he is more of a behaviourist than other theorists who propose intervening variables between stimulus and response, such as S–R bonds or habit strength (e.g. Hull, 1952), as these are simply constructs which cannot be observed.

One of Skinner's greatest contributions lies in his work on the scheduling of reinforcements. His work was mainly carried out on animals, though some human experiments have been carried out, mainly with children.

Reinforcements may be given on various schedules which can be of two main kinds: (i) *interval*, where reinforcements are dependent on the passage of a given interval of time; and (ii) *ratio*, where reinforcement depends on the number of responses emitted. These in turn may be divided into fixed and variable intervals or ratios. In fixed schedules the reinforcement occurs every, say, two minutes or every two responses. In variable schedules the reinforcement occurs on average every, say, two minutes or two responses. Thus it may be that a subject on a 2/1 variable interval or ratio schedule can at times obtain reinforcement for each response or receive none for several responses, much in the same way that a tossed coin could come down heads several times running.

The effects of these different kinds of partial reinforcement may be summarised under three headings: (i) ratio schedules usually elicit a higher rate of response – the animal is in a hurry to obtain the next reinforcement; (ii) with both types of fixed schedule, the rate of response is slower immediately after the previous reinforcement; and (iii) intermittent reinforcement (e.g. the man on a one-armed bandit) is more resistant to extinction than is continuous reinforcement.

Among Skinner's other contributions is his work on shaping, a method whereby behaviour is moulded into what is desired by reinforcing closer and closer approximations to the required behaviour until it is finally perfected. This is his most valuable contribution to the field of training, from the habit training of mental patients to the refinement of sophisticated social skills such as selling. Skinner and workers in his tradition have used this method to produce some quite dramatic results, such as teaching pigeons to play a modified version of table tennis or causing a lecturer to increase the use of certain mannerisms by nodding and smiling when they occur (e.g. the use of 'er' or 'um' or causing him to address particular parts of his audience by planting an attractive female there to do the reinforcing). Modification of psychotic behaviour by operant conditioning is another application (e.g. Ayllon and Haughton, 1964).

Skinner's work, though of considerable significance and value in the work context, suffers from a number of limitations. First, it is atheoretical in that it does not lead to an explanation of why a particular event does or does not act as a reinforcer. Such an explanation must take account of what happens within the organism. It is only possible to discover whether or not an event will act as a reinforcement in retrospect. Second, due to the relatively small number of studies of human behaviour, particularly in real-life situations, any general statements about the effects of reinforcement, such as those given above for the effects of scheduling, must be accepted with great caution. Third, Skinner is concerned with behavioural change and modification, not with learning processes. Doubtless reinforcement is very important for behavioural change. Whether or not it is so important for learning itself to occur is much more dubious, as will become clear when we consider cognitive theories in the next section.

Having introduced the reader to *S–R* learning 'theory', we shall end this section by quoting from Hilgard and Bower (1967) a number of general principles derived from such theories which are of importance when we come to the question of training and instruction. These principles are relatively uncontroversial within *S–R* theory. It will be interesting to note how they differ from a similar list derived from cognitive theory.

1. The learner should be active, rather than a passive listener or viewer. The *S–R* theory emphasizes the significance of the learner's responses, and 'learning by doing' is still an acceptable slogan.
2. Frequency of repetition is still important in acquiring skill, and in bringing enough overlearning to guarantee retention. One does not learn to type, or to play the piano, or to speak a foreign language, without some repetitive practice.
3. Reinforcement is important; that is, repetition should be under arrangements in which desirable or correct responses are rewarded. While there are some lingering questions over details, it is generally found that positive reinforcements (rewards, successes) are to be preferred to negative reinforcements (punishments, failures).
4. Generalization and discrimination suggest the importance of practice in varied contexts, so that learning will become (or remain) appropriate to a wider (or more restricted) range of stimuli.
5. Novelty in behavior can be enhanced through imitation of models, through cueing, through 'shaping', and is not inconsistent with a liberalized *S–R* approach to learning.
6. Drive conditions are important in learning, but all personal–social motives do not conform to the drive-reduction principles based on food-deprivation experiments. Issues concerning drives exist within *S–R* theory; at a practical level it may be taken for granted that motivational conditions are important. (See Chapter 6.)
7. Conflicts and frustrations arise inevitably in the process of learning difficult discriminations and in social situations in which irrelevant motives may be aroused. Hence these have to be recognized and their resolution or accommodation provided for (Hilgard and Bower, 1967).

3.5 Cognitive learning theory

Cognitive learning theory is sometimes called *S–S* (stimulus–stimulus) theory. It has been most fully developed by Tolman (1932) and is different from other behaviourist learning theories: (i) his units of analysis are somewhat larger; (ii) he sees behaviour as purposive; (iii) he proposes that what is learnt is not a connection between *S* and *R*, but an expectation based on a meaningful connection between two stimuli, i.e. between *S* and *S*; and (iv) he replaces reinforcement by confirmation, and behaviour is generated by expectancy and need.

He does not regard the organism as a simple thing in which direct *S–R* connections can take place, but rather postulates intervening variables which establish connections between (i) the need system, (ii) the 'belief–value matrix', and (iii) the behaviour space. We shall explain these below.

Tolman's explanation of learning is that, on repeated trials, the learner develops expectations of what follows what. For example, a journey may be divided up into choice points where certain signs at particular cross roads in a town are linked with expectations that the goal (part of the need system) is, say, to the right. If this expectation is confirmed, then next time the man wishes to reach his destination he will be more likely to take that path. This adds a further component to his belief–value system, a belief that turning right is related to achieving his valued goal. Ultimately, the man develops a cognitive map of the signs and their meanings and uses this to guide his actions in his behaviour space.

Tolman's theoretical framework has received support from animal experiments on learning through insight, sign (or place) learning and latent learning.

The original insight-learning experiment is that of Köhler (1925), carried out while he was interned on an island off the coast of Africa during the First World War. He turned the situation to good use by studying the behaviour of chimpanzees. One experiment involved placing the chimpanzee in a cage with fruit outside but out of reach of the short stick available to him. After trying various methods, such as pulling at the wire of the cage, to no avail and generally surveying the scene, he eventually picked up the small stick and used it to pull a larger stick lying outside the cage towards him. He was then able to use the larger stick to pull the fruit towards him. The main characteristic of this learning is that it does not apparently require any previous linking of the desired response to a stimulus (S–R learning). It seems that by surveying the scene the chimpanzee was able to link different stimuli (S–S) together, the long stick, the short stick and the fruit. Then, because he was hungry, he would act on this stimulus learning.

Tolman and Honzik (1930) performed an experiment which further showed the possibility that animals can learn by means other than the reinforcement of responses. Three groups of rats (A, B and C) were put in a maze one by one. One group (A) was rewarded with food on each successful attempt, while the other two groups (B and C) were simply allowed to wander through the maze without reward. After eleven days the reward group (A) were regularly performing better at solving the maze than the unrewarded group. At this point half the unrewarded group (B) were rewarded with food each time they reached the end of the maze. Their performance improved immediately to equal that of those rats that had been rewarded all the time. The remaining unrewarded rats (group C) continued to perform at the same level as before. This experiment has posed problems for S–R theorists in that group B clearly learnt something during the first eleven days even though, apparently, it was not the connection between stimulus and response through reinforcement. Another experiment in which rats have been towed through a maze on a trolley without reward prior to being rewarded for running the maze also shows the same sudden improvement in performance with the introduction of reward. This method of measuring learning is called the 'method of savings'. The phenomenon itself is called 'latent learning'.

Tolman's explanation was that the rat learned about the special arrangement of the maze (a cognitive map of what is connected to what). However, only when food was offered as a reward were the rats motivated to perform. Thus rewards do not serve to reinforce or 'stamp in' responses in learning, but to determine whether knowledge acquired will be used in performance. The distinction between reward as a reinforcer in learning (*S–R* theory) and reward as an incentive to performance (Tolman) is an important one which most clearly characterises the split between *S–R* and *S–S* theories.

As with the section on *S–R* theory we shall end with a direct quotation from Hilgard and Bower (1967) on the principles emphasised within cognitive theory. It is interesting that though the theoretical base is different, some of the principles for application are very similar.

1. The perceptual features according to which the problem is displayed [see Chapter 2] to the learner are important conditions of learning (figure-ground relations, directional signs, 'what-leads-to-what', organic inter-relatedness). Hence a learning problem should be so structured and presented that the essential features are open to the inspection of the learner.
2. The organization of knowledge should be an essential concern of the teacher or educational planner [see Chapter 4]. Thus the direction from simple to complex is not from arbitrary, meaningless parts to meaningful wholes, but instead from simplified wholes to more complex wholes. The part–whole problem is therefore an organizational problem, and cannot be dealt with apart from a theory of how complexity is patterned. [See section 3.10.]
3. Learning with understanding is more permanent and more transferable than rote learning or learning by formula. Expressed in this form the statement belongs in cognitive theory, but *S–R* theories make a related emphasis upon the importance of meaningfulness in learning and retention.
4. Cognitive feedback confirms correct knowledge and corrects faulty learning. The notion is that the learner tries something provisionally and then accepts or rejects what he does on the basis of its consequences. This is of course the cognitive equivalent of reinforcement in *S–R* theory but cognitive theory tends to place more emphasis upon a kind of hypothesis testing through feedback.
5. Goal-setting by the learner is important as motivation for learning and his successes and failures are determiners of how he sets future goals.
6. Divergent thinking [see Chapter 10], which leads to inventive solutions of problems or to the creation of novel and valued products, is to be nurtured along with convergent thinking, which leads to logically correct answers. Such divergent thinking requires the subject to perceive himself as potentially creative through appropriate support (feedback) for his tentative efforts at originality.

3.6 The meeting of *S–R* and *S–S*

We have so far examined learning theories derived from two main traditions, the connectionist (*S–R*) and the cognitive (*S–S*). At an earlier stage in the chapter we indicated that there had been a trend away from the original behaviourist approach towards a more flexible one. The original approach saw the human organism as a kind of black box with a stimulus input and a response output.

Animal experiments on latent learning and sign learning (Tolman, 1932) are illustrative of the kind of work which in the end sounded the death knell of the old black-box idea. No more was there to be a simple black box with an input and an output – but there had to be something inside it. Both Hull (1952) and Spence (1956) had their contributions to make in this move towards a more cognitive interpretation when they postulated intervening variables (e.g. Hull's concept of an internalised goal response).

Another cognitive development in *S–R* theory is that of Mowrer (1960). It starts with Miller's (1948) demonstration of fear as an acquired drive, in which a rat is placed in a box with two compartments, one painted black and the other white. The white one has a grid floor through which electric shocks can be administered. Initially the rat is allowed to explore both compartments and shows no preference for either. It is then placed in the white compartment and given a strong shock through the floor. The majority of rats soon learn to escape the shock by running into the black compartment. After this process has been completed for a number of times, the rat is placed in the white compartment without shock. The rat runs immediately to the black compartment. What has been learnt is fear of the white compartment. This fear can then serve as the motive for future learning, as shown by the next part of the experiment in which the opening between the two compartments is blocked off and the rat is only able to escape from the white to the black compartment if he learns to turn a wheel on a wall near the door. Miller's analysis is that fear of the pain produced by the electric shock was conditioned to the white compartment. Miller used a drive-reduction explanation of the acquisition of fear. He said that fear responses in the white box were reinforced by the termination of the pain. Mowrer could not accept this, for on this principle we should learn to beat our heads against walls and all manner of other unpleasant things simply because they would be followed by a reduction in pain when we stopped. Mowrer proceeded to do a number of experiments which contradicted Miller's explanation.

Thus Mowrer proposed a two-factor explanation of fear acquisition, in which fear was acquired by a process akin to classical conditioning and escape was learned through a kind of instrumental conditioning brought about by reinforcement through drive reduction. He called these two types of learning 'sign' and 'solution' learning. However, later developments caused Mowrer to revert to a one-factor theory, but one of a different kind, in which the fear occasioned by the pain response in the white compartment is conditioned to the stimuli of the white compartment, and similarly the (pleasant) outcome occasioned by his escape behaviour is conditioned to the stimuli from that behaviour. The walls become a sign for fear and the proprioceptive stimuli from a response become a sign for hope. Both kinds of learning are sign learning.

A further illustration of the way in which cognitive and *S–R* theories have grown closer together lies in Harlow's work (1959) on learning sets. In the basic experiment a monkey is confronted with two blocks, each with a different pattern or colour on it. Under one of these is a small reward such as a raisin. Once the monkey has discovered under which one it is, he has solved the problem and will continue to find the raisin under the same block. With each new task (using a different pair of blocks) the monkey has to begin again the task of discovering under which one the raisin lies. Now it is clear that by adopting a strategy of always going to the other block after failing to find the raisin under the first one, the monkey can guarantee that he is always correct on all the following trials. If he is correct on the first trial he goes on with the same block on ensuing trials. What Harlow discovered was that most monkeys had learnt the strategy well enough after 200 trials to be correct 90 per cent of the time on their second attempt at each new task. The implications of this for a connectionist–cognitive *rapprochement* are that if an *S–R* generalisation of the form 'If not block *A* then block *B*' can be made in behaviour, why should not proprioceptive stimuli (from within the organism) from the responses, without the responses themselves, be available as an explanation of cognitive phenomena. Such a learning process would not be too far from being a connectionist account of the phenomenon of understanding.

We shall now turn away from attempts to formulate all-embracing learning theories (like the *S–R* and *S–S* debate) to more recent developments.

3.7 Recent developments in learning theory

In this section we shall consider work on social learning, the substrate of learning (the biological base on which learning takes place) and, more briefly, other developments. We have selected the two areas mentioned because they are of the most general interest and relevance. In social-learning theory the key figures are Miller and Dollard (1941) and Bandura (1965) and the key issue is what mechanism is responsible for the particular form of behaviour acquisition in question, namely imitation through the observation of others. Simple *S–R* theories find this difficult to explain. Indeed, the learning theorists of the 1930s and 1940s avoided the issue. Miller and Dollard, making use of their four-part analysis (drive, cue (stimulus), response, reward) as the basic requirements for learning, put forward the idea that a response deriving from imitation had exactly the same status as any other unreinforced response until it was brought into the individual's habitual repertoire by appropriate reinforcement (i.e. it is not learnt until rewarded). They say that the tendency to imitate is itself learned. In one piece of research, 5-year-old children were able to obtain sweets from a machine, sometimes by turning a handle and sometimes by pressing it down. Prior to the child operating the machine, he would watch either another child or an adult doing it. In different forms of the experiment, the child was rewarded either for imitating the adult or for imitating the child. The children were able to learn to imitate either the child or the adult. They also learnt to generalise from the original child to other children and from the original adult to other adults. Miller and Dollard suggest that the reward is responsible for imitation.

Bandura and his co-workers, however, have done a number of experiments which go against reward or reinforcement as the mechanism for learning imitated behaviour. Rather, they say that learning is the product of observation, and imitative behaviour is the product of reinforcement. They have shown that this is the case by demonstrating that children may not show that they have learnt the behaviour until they are, sometimes considerably later,

offered a reward for doing so. They have also identified some of the characteristics of people and behaviour which are particularly liable to be imitated.
Bandura, Ross and Ross (1961) demonstrated the generalisability of imitated
responses. They later (1963a) showed that children who had recently seen
aggression in a film reacted more aggressively in response to frustration than
others who had not been exposed to such aggression. They further found
(1963b) that children seeing aggressive behaviour on film followed by gene-
rous reward, or by no consequences at all, imitated the aggressive actor more
than those who had seen his actions severely punished. It seems that what
happens to an aggressive model does play a part in whether or not he is
imitated. However, Bandura and Walters (1963) have shown that if children
are offered incentives for reproducing the behaviour in question, they can
reproduce it immediately, to the extent of removing completely the difference
previously attributed to their earlier treatment.

Bandura, Ross and Ross (1963c) set out to test two of the existing hypotheses about the choice of models for imitation: (i) Whiting's status-envy
theory (1960) – that the child envies the status of certain people whom it
copies in order to attain a kind of share in that status – and (ii) the social-
power theory put forward by various people (e.g. Mussen and Distler, 1959)
which states that the child will imitate the person who wields the greatest
power in a given situation or the person who controls the most valued resources. In this experiment there were two adults, one of whom controlled
a collection of very fine toys. For one group of children the controller gave
the other adult the toys. Then both adults carried out a series of idiotic
actions (a kind of comic turn), each adult, however, acting differently
from the other. If the children imitated the controller this would support
the social-power theory and if they imitated the recipient it would support
the status-envy theory. For a second group of children the controller simply
gave the toys directly to the children, with the second adult standing by. The
result was that the children tended to imitate the controller in both conditions. It seems that the findings support the social-power theory and that
children do not seem to be influenced by the status of the recipient, though
they may be by that of the controller. Bandura and his co-workers have
investigated a number of further characteristics of the model and his behaviour for the way these affect imitation. They have also varied the instructions given to the child subjects. Their results may be summarised as follows:
(i) high-status models and models similar to the subject tend to be imitated
most; (ii) aggressive behaviour and the moral values of adult models tend to
be most imitated; (iii) instructions to the child indicating that he will be paid
in proportion to how much of the observed behaviour he is later able to
reproduce increases his tendency to imitate, as does telling the child to verbalise what he is observing (Bandura, Grusec and Menlove, cited in Bandura,
1965).

Bandura's research tells us a great deal about what is imitated, but provides very little on the explanation of imitation. Bandura suggests a process
by which it could occur – a kind of direct sensory–sensory conditioning (for a
review, see Seidel, 1959) in which contiguous stimuli become linked. That
this kind of process takes place is more or less sure (Morrell, 1961) but it still

does not tell us why such learning forms the basis for an imitation, or why children choose certain behaviours to learn in this way.

It is clear that there are still outstanding controversies in the behaviourist account of learning. However, it is possible to identify a continuing trend away from the initial rigid formulations of Watson towards a greater preparedness to recognise that learning phenomena embrace topics not easily included by formulations incorporating just observable data. We have seen on the one hand that Skinner attempts an atheoretical approach in that he regards his task as the systematic gathering of data. In all probability, his work represents the climax of this tradition. On the other hand, the work of Tolman and the *Gestaltists* (see Chapter 2) has required the postulation of unknown organismic factors within the behaviourist scheme. The original S–R model has become an S–O–R model (in which O stands for organism), one which, in addition to enabling a *rapprochement* between S–R and S–S theorists, has also opened the way to dialogue between behaviourists and others, such as personality theorists. Thus there is a large amount of evidence available as to the nature of the organism which is doing the learning. The work of Penfield (1958), for example, has yielded certain findings about the nature of memory mechanisms which suggest that we carry within us permanent detailed representations, possibly analogous to tape recordings, of past events. What is interesting is that electrical stimulation of certain areas of the brain causes the subject to relive the memory as though it was actually happening, complete with associated emotions. This suggests that emotions are attached permanently to the original experience and this must be taken into account when considering the nature of learning. It also raises the likelihood of one trial learning to the level of probability rather than possibility. Eysenck's work (1955) indicates that there are probably individual differences in the susceptibility of different individuals to conditioning. Eysenck proposes that introverts are more easily conditioned than extroverts. Other theorists have emphasised the influence of anxiety on the learning process, suggesting that learning is improved under conditions of average anxiety, but deteriorates under conditions of high or low anxiety, the points of deterioration ranging with the complexity of the task. Investigation of the organism and its nature will also, it is hoped, lead to a *rapprochement* with the psychodynamic school (see Chapter 9), an early indication of which occurred as early as 1941 with the arrival of Miller and Dollard's work on social learning. This draws heavily on psychoanalytic concepts, but is mainly concerned with the manner in which each of us activates his own particular pattern of learned habits, which forms the personality.

Numerous researchers have found that certain kinds of response are learnt more quickly than others, even though they are not apparently dissimilar. Initially it was thought that transfer and stimulus intensity were responsible for these differences but, later, evidence began to accumulate indicating something else. Thus Bolles (1970) suggested that successful avoidance conditioning must be built on the particular set of species-specific avoidance responses possessed by the particular species (the substrate of learning). Thus it may be extremely difficult to condition a pigeon to avoid an electric shock by pecking a key, but very easy if the desired response is that it fly away. The suggestion is that certain response patterns are linked instinctively to certain kinds of stimuli, but in a somewhat tenuous way, rather in the manner of a broken line which needs filling (as illustrated in Figure 3.3).

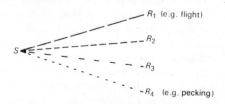

Figure 3.3   The substrate of learning

In Figure 3.3 R_4 will be difficult to condition to S but R_1 will be much easier. Estes (1972) suggests that it is simply a question of directness, i.e. the number of associative links that need to be made between S and R. In view of the innate biological organisation of the animal's behaviour, activation of a drive mechanism by a painful stimulus delivers facilitatory input to a family of defence and flight reactions (R_1), but not to the family of responses involving pecking and swallowing (R_4). If a pecking response is required, more linkages need to be set up. Garcia and Koelling (1966) found that, whereas it was relatively easy to condition radiation sickness to the drinking of sacharine-flavoured water, this was virtually impossible in the case of visual or auditory stimuli. The crucial element was the gastric nature of the stimuli. On the other hand, an avoidance response to electric shock to the feet could easily be established to visual and auditory stimuli but not to the sacharine-flavoured water. This seems to indicate that the most rapid learning is that which makes use of species-specific organisations of behaviour. On the other hand, the human organism is extremely flexible in what it can learn, as illustrated by the discovery of our ability to control many subconscious processes like blood pressure, heart rate, and so on (Di Cara and Miller, 1968; Miller, 1969). The reader who wishes to pursue other recent approaches is referred to a review by Estes (1972).

3.8   Some conclusions on learning and instruction

While we have made it clear that we think that the era of the general, all-embracing learning theory is over, at least for the time being, we do not wish to suggest that such theories are worthless. They are certainly compatible with a large amount of data. However, the problem is that they do not cover all the data and that the requirements necessary to make this possible render these theories increasingly unwieldy with *ad hoc* additions. When the reader has digested the principles from cognitive and *S–R* theory listed above, having first of all stripped them of their jargon, he may conclude that it is all good common sense and not much more. Now, it is true to say that there are good instructors who would automatically put into practice a large number of these principles. On the other hand, there are probably an even larger number who would not. The pertinence of this to Hilgard and Bower's points is that the points taken singly may be pretty obvious, but when taken in combination they actually generate something which is far from obvious unless a good deal of thought (and effective thought at that) has been directed to the matter.

That said, it becomes clear that we do have some principles deriving from learning theories which could be of use to the amateur instructor starting out from scratch. For the professional the message is less exciting. He has probably done a lot of thinking about the matter and has settled down to a particular manner of proceeding, though the chances are that he has left one or two aspects of the matter out of his considerations and may be helped by making an acquaintance with them.

As far as the applicability of cognitive and *S–R* theories to different kinds of task is concerned, Hilgard, Atkinson and Atkinson (1975) suggest that automatic physical activities are best understood in terms of habit formation, and higher mental skills are best understood in terms of insight and understanding. The suggestion is that *S–R* theories are most appropriate in the case of the former and cognitive theories in the case of the latter. In between these two types of activity there lies a large range of activities to which the two kinds of theory are both applicable. Fitts (1962), in his review of complex skill training, emphasises what he calls the 'cognitive phase'. In particular, he quotes the researches of Williams and his associates into the phase of pilot training prior to the first solo flight (Williams and Flexman, 1949; Flexman, Matheny and Brown, 1950). Striking improvements in the time up to the first solo flight were noted. Without use of a ground trainer the accepted time to solo was about eight hours. Using a ground trainer and a number of special procedures deriving from learning theory forty-eight students averaged 5.28 hours. With more intensive use of these special procedures forty-two students achieved an average time of 3.82 hours. What strikes Fitts as particularly significant is the use of techniques designed to promote an understanding of flight problems and procedures. In particular, he selects the use of knowledge of results, establishing appropriate sets or expectancies, 'talking through' manoeuvres and 'intellectualisation' of the task in hand. The point we are making here is that 'cognitive' principles can also be of particular value in the case of physical skills as well as in the acquisition of knowledge or understanding. We shall not go beyond these rather general comments on the relevance of learning theory, for this will be the task of the next chapter. As we have pointed out, general learning theories have been developed largely from animal laboratory experimentation. More recent learning models or theories have been more specific in their aims and some of these have developed from the context of human learning, particularly from the area of skill learning. It is to this area that we now turn.

3.9 Skill learning

For the psychologist the word 'skill' has come to refer to the performance of any task which, for its successful and rapid completion, requires an improved organisation of responses making use of only those aspects of the stimulus which are essential to satisfactory performance. Many tasks in the work situation fit this description, from the work of the typist to that of the skilled craftsman. Many workers who do not have any skilled trade to their name may also exhibit varying degrees of skill in their work. For example, the filing clerk may be distinguished from her less efficient colleague by the speed with which she can locate where the particular item has to go, and the rapidity with which she actually places items in, or removes them from, a file.

Research into skill acquisition has followed a pattern similar to that for learning in general. Initially, *S–R* theory dominated the field, to be challenged by the advent of Tolman's work (1932). Later, Lashley (1951) argued against the ability of any simplistic *S–R* approach to explain the problem of serial order (what follows what) in behaviour, such as is exhibited in skills like riding a bicycle.

He showed that, for many skilled movements, the operator is moving so fast that this cannot be accounted for by an explanation involving any kind of control by sensory feedback. The reason for this is that kinaesthetic (from the muscles) or even visual reaction times (which are faster) are far too slow to keep pace with the movements. The motor mechanisms must be pre-primed in some way to fire independently of sensory control. Thus, in skilled performance, both stimuli and responses are grouped together in batches for processing. Lashley's big contribution was to detach the notion of skill from that of habit.

What has been said above should not lead the reader to minimise the role of feedback (i.e. information which can be 'fed back' into a machine or organism in order to guide its next piece of activity) in the acquisition of skilled performance. Indeed, we are saying only that feedback has to operate at a level of organisation higher than the immediate stimulus–response level. The concept of 'feedback' fits in quite well with the idea of the skilled operator as someone who sets out with a particular goal and constantly modifies his behaviour in order to keep it in line with the attainment of that goal.

Three main approaches to skill acquisition have been used: (i) the learning-theory approach in the behaviourist (*S–R*) tradition; (ii) the information-processing approach; and (iii) the study of individual differences, inasmuch as they can affect the speed and effectiveness of skill learning.

The first two approaches will now be familiar to the reader. Although the material to be presented will be different, the traditions from which it comes will be recognisable. The third approach introduces an area which will be expanded upon in Chapters 9 and 10.

THE *S–R* APPROACH

It has been shown in many instances that *S–R* principles can be used to explain at least some of the phenomena of skill acquisition. For example, Noble (1969) gave subjects the task of learning which of a number of keys to press in response to each of a series of stimulus lights. He found that the number of reinforced or corrected trials played a large part in determining success rate for each response.

A further example will show the relevance to skill acquisition of more sophisticated learning-theory concepts. Digman (1959) used a 'tracking task' to demonstrate a now well-known effect, namely that performance is a function of the length of the learning trial and the gap between trials. (Typically psychologists use two laboratory tasks to simulate skills: (i) choice reaction time (C.R.T.) tasks in which subjects are asked to react as quickly as possible to a particular stimulus or stimulus configuration in an array of stimuli; and (ii) tracking tasks (in which the subject is required to follow with a stylus a moving target which might be either moving around different parts of a rotating disc or along a track). The former task simulates skills where most effort lies in perceptual organisation and the latter where the essence lies in perceptual-motor co-ordination.) Digman found that longer rest pauses between trials were associated with more time on target during the trials. Further, subjects who have been on a regime of short breaks between trials showed an immediate improvement in performance following an overnight break. Irion (1969) has used the concept of 'reactive inhibition' ($_sI_R$) to explain this.

'Reactive inhibition' is the term Hull (1943) used to describe the observed decrement in the performance of the learnt response following repeated performance of that response. It is due supposedly to some kind of fatigue in the part of the nervous system affecting the new performance. This reactive inhibition comes increasingly to act as a resistance to that performance. Therefore, an explanation of Digman's results is that the subjects on massed learning trials (short intervals between them), as well as building up the strength of the learnt response (habit strength [$_sH_R$]), also increasingly develop $_sI_R$, which counteracts the S–R linkage. For subjects on spaced trials (long intervals between them) the $_sI_R$ has time to subside between trials, as it does for the massed trials subjects overnight. The likelihood of a successful response is computed by the simple formula: $_sH_R - _sI_R$.

Thus, while it is clear that the S–R model by itself is not adequate as an explanation of skilled performance in view of its lack of flexibility and its inability to handle the speed with which feedback is clearly made use of, it is none the less useful in other respects. The most important of these is that it can explain those features which skill acquisition has in common with habit formation. It is not of any great value in respect of those aspects unique to the concept of 'skill', namely its flexibility and over-all purposiveness.

THE INFORMATION-PROCESSING APPROACH

The main assumption of this approach is that the human operator functions as a limited capacity information-processing channel. This limit refers to the total combined information processed at the three stages shown in Figure 3.4, perception, translation and response. The acquisition of skill is seen as the progressively more efficient use of this channel through (i) the coding of the stimulus at the perception stage by making use of the redundancy of the different parts of the stimulus, (ii) the more rapid selection of responses at the translation stage, and (iii) the more efficient performance of responses. The unskilled operator is subject to overloading caused by a tendency to attend to irrelevant aspects of the stimulus, to the relatively slow and hesitant nature of his translation methods and to the fumbling nature of his responses. The two latter characteristics in turn generate further stimulus inputs which cause a 'log jam' in the system. Applications of this approach would suggest methods of training designed to cut down the information content of the situation by such techniques as guidance on which aspects of the stimulus to attend to, and the use of part methods of learning which prevent new inputs from entering the channel until the old ones have been processed satisfactorily.

Fitts (1964) emphasises the use of feedback whereby information indicating the results of the response is fed into the system. This enables corrective action to be taken. Miller, Galanter and Pribram (1960) suggest that the operator proceeds by means of a series of 'TOTE' units, which are in essence a different way of presenting much the same idea.

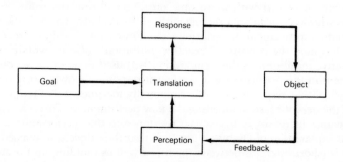

Figure 3.4   Flow diagram for perceptual-motor skills

'TOTE' stands for test–operate–test–exit. The process is as follows: The operator first tests the situation (*test*); then he makes a response (*operate*); then he checks on the effectiveness of the response (*test*); these first three steps are repeated until the task is completed (*exit*). Complex skills are regarded as hierarchies of TOTE units, united by a master plan involving the topmost TOTE. Learning consists of adding appropriate sub-routines to the repertoire and organising these into an effective programme.

INDIVIDUAL DIFFERENCES

The previous two sections have considered 'the human operator' as a fixed entity without consideration of differences in individual make-up. This is to some extent inevitable when one is concerned to explore to the full the ramifications of a particular approach. However, a balanced perspective requires recognition of as many as possible of the relevant variables. Some of the most important of these concern how the individual operator differs from other individuals, and the extent to which these differences interact with the learning processes of the operator to influence the way in which he acquires skills.

Relevant evidence is cited by Perl (1934), who reports a lack of correspondence between those learners who do best on the first trials and those who do best later on. Using correlation as a measure of correspondence, he found that inter-trial correlations tended to reduce to zero within a few trials. This seems to show that different abilities are probably involved early and late in training. This has been confirmed in a study by Fleishman (1962), who found that some specific abilities, in particular for understanding spatial relations (see Chapter 10), play more part earlier than later.

In contrast, Seashore (1951) found it impossible to discover any pattern of abilities which made skill acquisition easier on simple motor tasks. He suggested a 'work methods' hypothesis (see Chapter 4), arguing that simple skills are acquired by trial and error until the first successful trial, whereupon the learner continues to elaborate this until he becomes relatively accomplished. This means that different methods will be struck upon by different individuals, and this in turn almost certainly means that some will be more efficient than others. Jones's work (1969, 1970) makes use of this likelihood. He has found different patterns between simple and complex skills. In simple skills individual differences vanish relatively quickly as everyone acquires a more or less satisfactory work method, whereas in complex skills the combination of various parts of the skill means that inefficient work methods will have increasing difficulty in combining with other inefficient work methods, with the end result that increasing and stable individual differences occur in performance.

It is clear that a lot remains to be done in this area not only in respect of the influence of differences in ability but also in investigating any personality differences that might be important. Having briefly described three approaches to the study of skill acquisition, we shall review the ways in which they have, in combined form, been helpful in analysing the research findings.

3.10 Research into skill acquisition

This section will follow Annett's (1971) review in dividing the main findings into four areas: (i) stages of skill acquisition; (ii) perceptual organisation; (iii) receptor–effector organisation; and (iv) effector organisation and feedback control. Like Annett we shall end the section with a discussion of some of the 'old chestnuts' of skill research, part *versus* whole learning, feedback and guidance.

Stages of skill acquisition
Fitts (1964) describes three stages: (i) the cognitive stage in which the operator comes to understand what is required and how to achieve it; (ii) the associative stage in which S–R links are established; and (iii) the autonomous stage in which the motor patterns are refined until voluntary control is no longer necessary. Clearly there is some overlap between the stages, but the suggestion is that at different stages of learning different processes are involved. Clearly the first stage is equivalent to the concept of 'plans', in the sense of aims (Miller *et al.*, 1960). The role of explanation and demonstration in this area is clearly important. Unfortunately, this is one of the least researched areas in the field, but we can note here that Hilgard and Bower (1967) report that the one significant factor enhancing instruction in general, as found in the literature on instructional techniques, after the obvious general principles derived from learning theory have been applied, is that learning is

enhanced if the learner is made to verbalise what he is doing or attempting to do.

Perceptual organisation

Bryan and Harter (1897), in their study of Morse key operators, were probably the first investigators to report that their subjects first learned to recognise letters individually. Then, after a period of relative lack of improvement (commonly called a 'plateau'), they more or less suddenly came to recognise groups of letters as words.

At a later stage still they were able to respond to larger units such as phrases or sentences. The identification of redundancies in the stimulus and consequent earlier recognition of the items, then, can lead to a quicker response (Annett and Kay, 1956). Fuchs (1962) used an analogue computer to match subjects' performance on a tracking task and found that their corrective movements could be analysed into three components: position, velocity and acceleration. He found that in early practice position errors played the greatest part, while at later stages velocity and acceleration errors became more significant. The process could then be 'regressed' by adding a further 'stressing task'. Pew (1966) reports that in a compensatory tracking task subjects initially used one key at a time for control purposes, but then some subjects developed the further strategy of using the keys in combination. All of these investigations point to the conclusion that in acquiring a skill subjects reorganise their perceptions into more complex and relevant units.

Receptor–effector organisation

The S–R model is difficult to apply to receptor–effector organisation since (i) there are problems in fitting it to such tasks as continuous tracking, and (ii) there is more than one way to perform a skilled task successfully. Indeed, flexibility is often a crucial characteristic. However, it is difficult to escape from the conclusion that one feature of improvement in the performance of a skilled task is improvement in S–R reaction time (Fitts and Deininger, 1954; Fitts and Switzer, 1962). Likewise, the effects found by Bryan and Harter (1897) and Pew (1966) may be due to receptor–effector organisation as well as to perceptual organisation.

Effector organisation and feedback control

At least some of the improvement in performance during skill acquisition is due to improved organisation and control of response due to the more efficient use of feedback. Woodworth (1938) suggested that one effect of practice was to switch from visual to proprioceptive feedback and eventually to a minimal reliance on the latter. Fleishman and Rich (1963) tend to confirm this with the finding that subjects who scored high on a test of kinaesthetic sensitivity tended to do better on a two-handed co-ordination task than those who scored low. Rubin and Smith (1952) found that if they divided movement time into travel time and manipulation time, it was the latter which gained most improvement through practice. This again may be due to improved use of feedback, or to improved organisation of response, or to both.

As with simple and complex learning, a number of important general principles may be derived for the learning of skills. Before discussing these it is important to note that the greater complexity of skilled over unskilled tasks makes the general principles, too, more complex. Indeed, we shall present them not as principles but as issues to be considered. These issues concern such matters as feedback, guidance and part *versus* whole learning. We shall discuss each of these in turn.

Feedback

There are two basic kinds of feedback, intrinsic and augmented. Intrinsic feedback includes the usual visual and kinaesthetic cues occurring in connection with a response. Augmented feedback is any other kind of information from sources external to the operator. Augmented feedback may be concurrent (occurring with the performance) or terminal (after it). The terms 'knowledge of performance' and 'knowledge of results' are sometimes used synonymously with these. This distinction is important because the two kinds of augmented feedback seem to have different effects, an important fact often forgotten by those trainers who make too much use of concurrent feedback. We shall now discuss these differences.

Although terminal feedback has much in common with reinforcement, it differs in certain respects. Here we shall mention three of these differences: they concern (i) frequency, (ii) detail, and (iii) timing of the feedback. (For fuller reviews, see Bilodeau (1969) and Annett (1969).)

(i) *Frequency*. Bilodeau and Bilodeau (1958) report that the speed of learning depends on the frequency of trials in which feedback is provided. This is in contrast to the more complex picture with reinforcement (see Section 3.3). There is no evidence that learning can occur without practice or feedback. Certainly feedback appears to be crucial in the learning of perceptual-motor skills.

(ii) *Detail*. Feedback can vary considerably in the amount of detail provided. Beyond a certain point it seems that extra information does not result in faster learning. Thus Bilodeau (1953, 1955) found that in positional tasks (e.g. dart-playing) information over and above the direction of an error did not improve learning.

(iii) *Timing*. Unlike simple animal learning, the provision of reinforcement (feedback) is not dependent on its proximity to the response for its effectiveness. Indeed, quite large intervals may elapse between response and feedback with humans before the rate of learning is impaired, provided that no new trials take place between the response and the feedback.

Concurrent feedback is different in kind to terminal feedback. While it can be useful in moderation, the great danger seems to be that if it is available continuously in very precise form, though performance is often of a very high standard during training, it drops considerably as soon as the feedback is removed. One possibility is that the subject uses concurrent feedback as a kind of crutch which causes him to neglect the use of the intrinsic feedback on which he will later have to rely (Miller, 1953). An alternative and non-conflicting explanation is provided by Smode (1958), who suggests that the

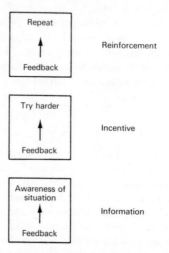

Figure 3.5　Examples of transformation rules for the use of feedback

on-going feedback also serves to motivate the subject. Annett (1970) and Smith (1962) provide evidence which suggests that concurrent feedback can actually distort the intrinsic cues and hamper learning, perhaps by overloading the system.

In the terms of our earlier discussions of learning and motivation, augmented feedback may be considered to have three different functions. These are informing, reinforcing and providing incentives. Which one or more of these actually occurs depends not only on the nature of the feedback itself but also on the kinds of transformation rule available to the subject (see Figure 3.5). Thus the informative function serves to provide further understanding, enabling the subject to alter an on-going response. The reinforcement function serves to strengthen the preceding *S–R* connection and the incentive function operates by reference to the goal of the individual. The incentive function ensures that partial success or progress encourages him and may help to clarify the goal so he feels that it is worth trying some more. These functions are brought into play depending on which transformation rules are available to the operator.

Guidance

Relatively little work has been done in this area, as indicated earlier in the chapter. However, guidance has been found to be useful in the form of concurrent information which helps the subject to make the correct response in perceptual discrimination (Annett, 1966) and positioning tasks (Fox and

Levy, 1969). In the latter case the effect is greatest when the guidance is given early in practice. In tracking, mechanical guidance can be effective (Bilodeau and Bilodeau, 1958; Holding and Macrae, 1964), but guidance by concurrent augmented feedback is subject to the disadvantages described in the previous section. This seems to be the case particularly where the guidance is more informative than the intrinsic feedback.

Part versus *whole learning*

The question at issue is whether it is better to learn new skills as a whole or in parts. Naylor (1962) suggests that it should be possible to classify tasks in terms of their complexity and organisation and on this basis to select the best learning method. Complexity means the difficulty of the component sub-tasks, and organisation means the extent of their interrelatedness. Naylor suggests that for tasks high in organisation an increase in complexity should

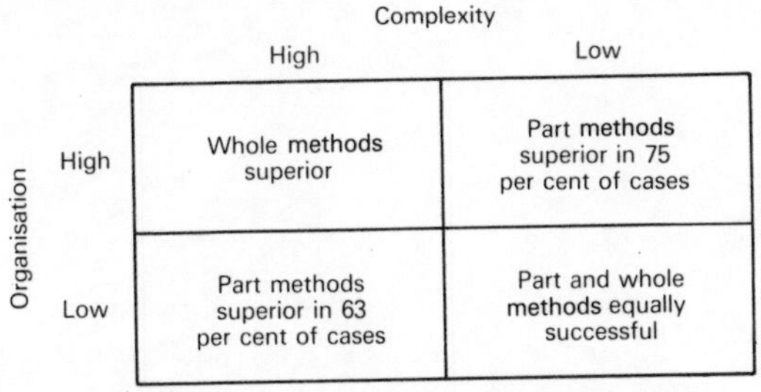

Figure 3.6   Diagrammatic summary of Naylor's (1962) survey of research into whole and part methods of skill training

favour the whole method, and for tasks low in organisation an increase in complexity should favour the part method. Thus the method preferred in the cases where the sub-tasks are high in complexity depends on the extent to which these sub-tasks are interrelated. The hypothesis derives some support from an analysis of previous studies (see Figure 3.6) and further research (Naylor and Briggs, 1963; Briggs and Naylor, 1962) which uses a three-dimensional tracking task and a serial prediction task. However, the problem remains as to how exactly to define the terms 'part', 'whole', 'complexity' and 'organisation' across tasks.

More recently, Annett and Duncan (1970) and Annett, Duncan, Stammers and Gray (1971) have developed the ideas of Miller *et al.* (1960) to try to tackle this problem of task analysis into parts and wholes. They have emphasised the hierarchical nature of skilled tasks in such a way that the whole at each level can be defined in terms of the goal of the operator and the part in terms of sub-goals. Annett *et al.* go on to define four different types of part–whole relations: type (i) is simply a chain of sub-objectives temporarily linked and of about the same difficulty; type (ii) is where the objective can be met by carrying out sub-objectives when necessary, as in sorting letters; type (iii) is where the over-all objective is met by selecting the sub-operations according to a strategy, as in fault-finding on electronic equipment; and type (iv) is where achieving the goal involves carrying out two sub-operations simultaneously, as in driving a car or riding a bicycle, giving hand signals at the same time. Here a considerable level of skill may be needed before the two can be put together.

Part- and whole-learning strategies are likely to be successful in different proportions for each type. So far there are no clear conclusions as to these precise proportions. However, such an approach shows promise in doing justice to the complexity of the problem.

4

Training and Development

4.1 Introduction

In the last chapter we considered the process of learning in connection with both simple and complex activities. Here our purpose is to examine the way in which the learner may best be enabled to acquire such skills and knowledge. This process by which the organisation imparts these skills and knowledge which are required in a particular job is called 'training'. This is usually but not always distinguished from 'education', which is more general in character, and 'development', which while still orientated towards the work situation tends to refer to the more distant career development of the individual. Training and development are closely related to personnel selection and other personnel functions in that the activities complement each other in the interest of achieving an effective and satisfied work-force. (For a fuller discussion of this point, see Chapter 12 on personnel selection.)

In this chapter we shall start with a discussion of the relevance of the psychology of human learning to personnel training (Section 4.2). We shall follow this with a discussion of the steps involved in the development of a training programme (Section 4.3). Section 4.4 is a discussion of some of the most commonly used methods and techniques of training. Section 4.5 discusses some of the characteristics of trainers and trainees likely to be associated with successful training. Finally, in Section 4.6, we shall examine the wider concept of organisation development; this involves seeing training in the context of the future of the organisation as a whole.

4.2 Training and the psychology of learning

We have seen in the previous chapter that the psychology of learning has yielded a number of general principles which apply to most learning situations. Such principles include the use of practice, reinforcement, feedback, motivation, and so on. The reader will find a more comprehensive list in Chapter 3. As suggested there, general principles of this kind have had a rather unexciting impact on the average training officer in industry. A usual reaction is that they are too obvious. However, the situation is perhaps more complex than that. Many training schemes neglect a number of these 'obvious' factors, not least the 'elementary' needs to motivate the learner and to provide him with feedback. Surveys of organisations testify regularly to the paucity of systematic training based on sound principles. It seems probable that, as suggested in the previous chapter, the general principles are often too general to be applicable to many tasks for which training is required. Often there are requirements specific to the particular task which require techniques of a special kind. The development of the required technology of training is a job which is too often avoided. None the less, the possibilities are there and a great deal of work has been done. In the next section we shall examine an approach to the development and design of training schemes, making reference to some aspects of the technology of training.

4.3   The development of a training programme

We have argued that most tasks in the work situation for which training is probably required are likely to be too complex for any simple application of the general principles mentioned in the last chapter. It follows from this that what is needed is a 'one-off' approach to training, i.e. the design of a training scheme which is appropriate to the particular job or task in question while still bearing in mind those general principles of learning which derive from our knowledge of the learning capacities of human beings.

Tilley (1968) describes what he calls a 'technology of training', i.e. a basic series of steps aimed at applying what is known about training to any given situation, with the final aim of creating a satisfactory training procedure. Figure 4.1 is a flow diagram which illustrates the basic steps involved. We shall describe each of the steps.

(1) *Analysis of the over-all system.* The job for which it is thought that training will be required is examined in the context of its position in the organisation. Training is only one of several possible ways of solving a 'training' problem. Alternative methods could involve the use of personnel selection (see Chapter 12) to select trained workers or ergonomics (see Chapter 5) to re-design the job, to mention but two. This conception is very much in line with the view of an organisation as a complex system (see Chapter 15), which has as a consequence the conclusion that there is seldom one simple, best, solution. Rather, each possible solution is likely to have advantages and disadvantages. Thus selecting ready-qualified men for a particular job might save the cost of a training programme, but there might be a scarcity of such men on the labour market; similarly, breaking a job down into a number of simpler jobs may enable the use of less well qualified operatives but generate boredom and dissatisfaction; and so on. The management task is to determine whether training is the appropriate solution to a particular problem.

(2) *Job description.* If it is decided to go ahead with the design of a training course, the first step is to obtain a job description. In common with many other activities (e.g. personnel selection, equipment design and the setting of pay rates) a description of what work has to be carried out is an essential prerequisite for training. This goes some way towards specifying the objec-

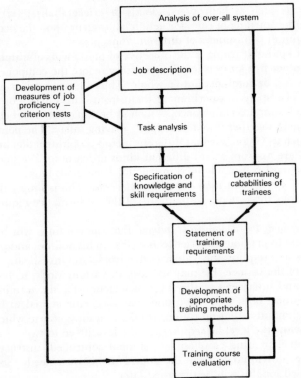

Figure 4.1   Steps in developing a technology of training (Tilley, 1968)

tives of a training course in terms of the overt performance required and of establishing criteria for the successful employee. In addition, a good job description identifies which parts of the job are carried out most frequently and which provide most difficulty. A good training scheme will emphasise these.

(3) *Task analysis.* While a job description tells us what is done in a job, task analysis goes into this in more detail and specifies how it is done in terms of the kind of learning (and, consequently, training) required. Although a number of similar taxonomies of learning (and, consequently, tasks) are available (e.g. Gilbert, 1969), Tilley makes use of Gagné's (1965) classification into six increasingly complex categories: (i) response differentiation (being able to reproduce a stimulus recognisably when required, for example writing clearly the different letters of the alphabet); (ii) associations (stimulus–response learning); (iii) multiple discriminations (being able to discriminate a number of responses and associate them with their appropriate stimuli, for example in learning the vocabulary of a foreign language); (iv) behaviour chains (a series of associations and multiple discriminations linked together, as in wiring up a simple electrical circuit); (v) concepts (classifying objects or events which may be reacted to in a similar way, for example the bird-watcher who gets out his binoculars to watch birds but not other kinds of

flying objects such as helicopters, clouds or cricket balls); (vi) principles (involving the learning of rules for action contingent upon the occurrence of different stimuli or instances of different concepts).

This last kind of learning is the objective of most forms of training. Learning of the other five kinds is usually necessary before the component parts of a principle can be combined into a whole. Thus a learner driver has to learn a number of responses, discriminate them from others, carry out chains of actions, understand certain concepts such as braking distances before he can assemble them together into a principle – driving safely. The point of classifications such as Gagné's is that different methods of instruction and instructional aids are appropriate to different kinds of learning. We shall consider some of the most commonly used instructional methods later.

(4) *Specification of knowledge and skill requirements.* This is simply the product of the previous three steps, an itemising of the performance requirements of the job.

(5) *Determining the capabilities of trainees.* Each new trainee will be different from the next in previous experience as well as in his abilities and personality. Simply this step requires the trainer to determine and investigate the current capability of the trainee. He may use tests of various kinds, including questionnaires and interviews at the stage of selection for the training scheme. This will ensure both that the trainee has a scheme geared to his current capabilities and also that no trainee is taken on for a course which is either above or below the level he requires. In the last fifteen to twenty years there has been an increasing emphasis on 'student-controlled' instruction which enables the individual to gear the course to his own needs. Some of the methods used for this will be discussed later.

(6) *Statement of training requirements.* This derives from the previous two steps and simply involves the identification of the 'gap' between the current capabilities of the trainee and the performance requirements of the job. The bridging of this gap is the purpose of this course.

(7) *Development of appropriate training methods.* This step, which is of crucial importance, concerns the choice of the best method of imparting the knowledge and skills required. A discussion of the details of some of these methods is left to the next section. Clearly the general principles of learning and skill acquisition are also relevant here, together with the devising of methods specific to the task in question and the use of instructional aids, such as simulators. Another matter involved in this step is the question of where the training shall be done, on the job, in the organisation's training school, or delegated to an external body.

(8) *Training-course evaluation.* In evaluating training we are concerned with trying to establish its reliability (consistency) and validity (effectiveness in achieving its goals). This involves establishing a relationship between the training method and some criterion or measure of performance. For practical purposes this criterion or measure should approximate as closely as possible to the ultimate criterion, i.e. some measure of the total effectiveness of training in terms of cost, turnover, productivity, etc. over a long time period. However, for research purposes, more specific intermediate and immediate criteria give clearer information concerning cause–effect relationships. Typi-

cally intermediate measures would be assessments of job performance, while immediate criteria would be post-training tests of knowledge, skills and attitudes acquired during training. These should as far as possible measure behaviour which is the result of training, not extraneous factors such as age, experience, etc.

In order to draw valid conclusions about training effectiveness, we need to design true experiments, either in the laboratory or in the field, which involve random assignment of subjects to treatment groups (which include control groups). Thus a particular training method represents the independent variable and the criterion or measure the dependent variable. While laboratory experiments are easier to control they may be somewhat artificial and their results may not be generalisable outside the laboratory. Field experiments, on the other hand, while overcoming the problem of artificiality are less easy to control for unwanted influences (Orne, 1962; Chapanis, 1967). Consequently, true field experiments should possess the following characteristics: they must (i) be sensitive and powerful enough to demonstrate cause and effect, (ii) rule out all other variables which might provide alternative explanations of the cause–effect relationship, (iii) eliminate alternative hypotheses about constructs involved in the relationship, and (iv) lead to generalisability of findings across time, settings and persons. Such experiments have been implemented successfully and maintained in field settings, though only infrequently (for a review, see Cook and Campbell, 1976).

Tilley makes the distinction between education (which is broader and more general) and training (which is specific to a particular kind of job). Because of its specificity it is easier to state the desired outcomes of training and consequently to determine the extent to which a training course has achieved these outcomes. Tilley also suggests that Gagné's first four categories of learning, response differentiations, associations, multiple discriminations and behaviour chains are amenable to straight-forward testing as to what has or has not been learnt. However, his other two categories involve the use of concepts and hence the transfer of the learning to different situations. These latter kinds of learning come closer to education and it is less easy to specify accurately what is a successful outcome to training. This problem is particularly evident in the field of management and supervisory training (e.g. Harris and Fleishman, 1955; Warr *et al.*, 1970). In both of the studies referred to it was found that the environment to which the trainee returned played a large part in determining whether he displayed evidence of what he had learnt. This is not to say that one should give up attempts to evaluate training where more complex learning is involved. Rather, we would argue that the necessity for evaluation is even greater in view of the scarcity of good validation studies. The literature is abundant in reports of successful validation of training in perceptual-motor skills (e.g. Seymour, 1966; Singleton, 1959). The conclusion in relation to management and supervisory training remains much less definite. We are not saying that management and supervisory training are not effective, only that it is very difficult to demonstrate their effectiveness.

Having seen something of what is involved in the development of a systematic training programme, we can now move on to consider in greater detail some of the methods which may be used.

4.4   Methods used in training

There are many different training methods which are used regularly. Some of these have been developed for specific kinds of performance, others for more general use. They can be classified under the following headings.

THE LECTURE

In terms of the principles of learning presented at the end of our discussion of learning theories (Chapter 3), we should expect the lecture to be a relatively ineffective training technique. It does not (i) allow for active participation by trainees, (ii) provide feedback to them, (iii) allow them to learn at their own pace, (iv) ensure that material is meaningful, (v) ensure that prior learning has taken place before introducing new learning. On the other hand, it is an economical technique in terms of trainer time. Proctor and Thornton (1961) have suggested that it can be a useful technique when (i) presenting completely new material, (ii) working with a large group, (iii) introducing another instruction method, (iv) training time is limited, (v) summarising material developed by another instruction method.

There has been relatively little research into its efficacy as a training technique. An unpublished study by one of the authors found that undergraduate students asked to recall the main points at the end of a lecture recalled only 14 per cent of what the lecturer considered to be the main points. This study underlines the lecture's negative aspects listed above, a conclusion further endorsed by McGehee and Thayer (1961), who suggest that it is of minimal value in promoting behaviour or attitude change.

AUDIO-VISUAL AIDS

There are a wide variety of instruments falling into this category, including films, film strips, slides, overhead projectors, opaque projectors, tape recorders, closed-circuit television and teaching machines. There is less evidence than one might expect to suggest that training utilising these instruments is more effective than other training methods for most kinds of material. However, in some circumstances they have advantages, e.g. in the presentation of close-ups to large audiences. Thus Fryer (1951) found that the training of American Air Force personnel in code learning was more effective with film presentation than with a lecture or the use of a manual. However, Schramm (1962), in a survey of 114 studies, concluded that eighty-eight of them found no significant differences in effectiveness between television and classroom instruction.

Closed-circuit television is much used in the training of such skills as interviewing. Probably this is because it allows for participation and provides for both auditory and visual feedback of a precise kind. However, it is difficult to determine which aspects of the use of closed-circuit television (the participation or the feedback) contribute to its effectiveness.

THE GROUP-DISCUSSION METHOD

In this method a group of trainees are brought together under the direction of a trainer to discuss and through discussion to learn relevant material and/ or change attitudes. The technique involves participation which can facilitate both learning and attitude change. Much depends on the trainer, whose task it is to encourage participation and at the same time direct discussion so that training objectives can be achieved. This requires a considerable degree of social skill on his part. (A fuller discussion of group processes will be found in Chapter 13.) However, in the present context it is worth reporting the study of Levine and Butler (1952), who found that group discussion helped to improve errors in the way in which supervisors rated their subordinates whereas a group given a lecture only or no instruction did not change.

The technique is probably of most use for the development of problem-solving and decision-making capacities, the presentation of new and complex material, for the changing of attitudes and where the presentation of material is likely to need classification or amplification. A special case of this method is T-group or sensitivity training, to which we now turn.

T-GROUP TRAINING

This technique is sometimes referred to as sensitivity training, laboratory training or human-relations laboratory training. Usually it is used for supervisory or managerial training and development. Typically it is run on a residential basis and may last for anything between a few days and a few weeks. Although a trainer is present in the group, discussion proceeds in a most unstructured way. The role of the trainer is a minimal one, it being solely to facilitate interaction and to prevent undue pressures being brought to bear on any particular individual. The unstructured nature of the situation leads almost invariably to anxiety in trainees, and it is hoped that anxiety reduction will be brought about as a result of the interaction achieving the objectives set for it. These objectives are to increase trainees' self-awareness, sensitivity and understanding of others and to improve social skills and hence the ability to form satisfactory interpersonal relationships.

A number of aspects of the T-group situation should facilitate learning: (i) feedback is provided as a result of exposure of one's behaviour to the comments of others; (ii) a task of the trainer is to generate a supportive atmosphere so that defensiveness is reduced and learning and attitude change maximised; (iii) each trainee has the opportunity to experiment with new behaviour and practise social skills; (iv) the situation is one which not only encourages the learning of social skills but also facilitates learning about the basic learning processes. On the other hand, if the trainee is not able to reduce sufficiently his anxiety and defensiveness, this can act as a barrier to learning. Furthermore, the anxiety generated by the situation can be so great for some individuals that it becomes intolerable and may even result in emotional breakdown. This, though not very frequent, suggests that trainees should be preselected carefully for this type of training.

Campbell and Dunnette (1968) reviewed thirty-seven studies which attempted to evaluate T-group training. Their main conclusions were as follows: (i) there is no clear evidence that T-group training has any different effects on people's self-ratings (how they see themselves) than do other group experiences, but that increased sensitivity and flexibility do result; (ii) there is reasonably convincing evidence that T-group training results in changes in job behaviour. However, these changes vary with the individual and it is not clear how or whether such changes are related to effective job performance. Further, it is difficult to tell in advance what the results will be for each individual. One study in an oil refinery, for example, found that six months after training trainee ratings of its relevance indicated that they perceived the greatest change in their work behaviour and relationships, less in their ability to change the organisation's methods of dealing with people, and least in helping the organisation. This suggests that T-group training might be more helpful to the individual than to the organisation, though such self-ratings may be subject to various sources of error (see Chapter 11). These conclusions are in line with those of Furlong (1969), who suggests that the effectiveness of T-group training is crucially dependent on the organisational atmosphere to which the trainee returns. The T-group atmosphere is very democratic and the organisational atmosphere needs to be similar for the most effective results and for the prevention of frustration and conflict on the trainee's return.

CASE-STUDY METHODS

Typically case-study methods are used for the training and development of supervisors and managers. It is a variant of the group-discussion technique in which a real or hypothetical problem often involving interpersonal relationship difficulties, is presented to the trainees for discussion, analysis and solution, usually in the form of a report. Usually cases are presented in written form, but they may also be introduced via role play (see next section) or film. The main objectives of the technique are to help trainees to analyse problems and to discover underlying principles by illustrating the multiple causes and effects involved in the problem. A frequent objective is also to make trainees aware of the inter-group interactions involved in discussion and so develop their knowledge of group processes and skills in interaction.

The case-study approach is probably most appropriate for those trainees who (i) need training in the identification and analysis of complex problems which they have to face in the real-life situation, (ii) need to become acquainted with a variety of approaches, interrelations and personalities in order to broaden their awareness of the ways in which problems can be solved, (iii) are sophisticated enough to arrive at general principles and to formulate problem solutions themselves, and (iv) like to tackle difficult problems themselves, particularly when they appear to be relevant to real-life situations. It is unlikely to be appropriate for people with little knowledge or experience of the problem area, for those lacking in maturity or greatly lacking in self-confidence. All group-discussion methods are only likely to be effective if the group composition and atmosphere is such as to enable and encourage people to speak freely and openly.

Perhaps the greatest benefit of the case study is its face (apparent) validity. This means that trainees will tend to see its potential relevance fairly readily, and consequently are likely to approach a case-study session with considerable commitment. Of course, the real test of any training method is its true validity (i.e. the degree to which it achieves the objectives set for it), and face validity can sometimes contribute towards true validity by ensuring commitment to the training programme. Unfortunately, the present authors are unaware of any satisfactory validation studies.

ROLE-PLAY METHODS

Role-play training methods resemble the case-study method in that they involve the presentation of a difficult problem to which trainees are required to try and find solutions. However, unlike the traditional case study, participants are required to play the parts of the characters portrayed in the problem situations. Any kind of interaction can be simulated in this way, provided that at least two people are involved. Most commonly role-playing is used to simulate two-person interactions, which usually take the form of an interview, e.g. sales interview, selection interview, performance appraisal and counselling interviews, grievance interviews, etc. In such role plays, one of the trainees takes the role of the interviewer, and his job is to try to conduct the interview to the best of his ability. Another trainee adopts the role of the interviewee, which involves typically some play-acting ability on his part in order to illustrate the characteristics of the interviewee as described in the brief or case study. Commonly this technique is used both to improve the trainees' handling of specific kinds of interviews and to increase their interpersonal skills more generally. One very frequent result of this approach is the development of a very real-life situation in which the participants become genuinely involved. This helps to give the technique face validity and provides a very interesting and life-like demonstration of a way of coping with the problem for other trainees who may only be observers for a particular case. Thus trainees learn by observation, participation and perhaps most importantly from the discussion which follows each role play. One variant is to get several groups of trainees to perform the same role-play situation independently and then to have them compare the different ways in which the problem was tackled.

Role-playing can be particularly effective in changing attitudes. There are possibly three reasons for this. (1) Typically role-playing requires a person to cope with a situation and a set of problems which he has not had to face before. Consequently he thinks about the problem, searches for information and tries to justify ideas which previously he had not thought about or needed to justify. The discussion may therefore act as a learning process for him, with new information acquired or new ways of seeing already acquired information leading to attitude change. (2) There is evidence that attitudes are changed most readily when people are involved emotionally, a state engendered by role-playing. (3) Role-playing sometimes puts the trainee in a position of having to put forward arguments contrary to those he would normally express. Dissonance theory (see Chapter 8) would predict that to the extent such behaviour is not perceived as being 'coerced' by the situation, dissonance will be aroused due to the inconsistency of behaviour and previously held attitudes. The dissonance may then be reduced by a concommitant change in attitude. On the other hand, there are a number of drawbacks to the use of role-playing. For example, trainees may regard it as childish or artificial and they may overact, exaggerating their roles. Further, it seems to be not the role-playing itself that leads to change but adequate discussion of it afterwards and whether it is part of the general analysis of case material (Lawshe, Bolda and Brune, 1959).

MANAGEMENT GAMES

Like case-study and role-playing techniques, management games simulate aspects of the real-life situation. As such they not only possess a high degree of face validity but any learning occurring might be expected to transfer to the job situation. They simulate real-life situations in requiring the same kinds of operating and policy decisions.

Trainees, usually managers, are placed in teams, each of which represents a company. Each team is presented with a problem about which the game centres. Problems may concern both general and specific aspects of management, from running an organisation to making its marketing decisions. The teams are provided with all the information they need and are required to organise themselves. Usually this involves some allocation of roles to individuals in order to arrive at policy and operating decisions. The effects of such decisions are computed and fed back to the team. Games may last from several hours to several months but will always represent far lengthier time spans. At the end of the game winners are declared and each team's actions are analysed.

Objectives of management games can be any or all of the following: (i) to indicate which are the key factors to observe; (ii) to focus attention on established policies and strategies and so focus on long- rather than short-term planning; (iii) to enable trainees to make better use of various tools in decision-making, e.g. financial statements; (iv) to encourage trainees to use analytical techniques such as mathematical models.

There is little evidence on how well these objectives are attained, though reports of participants indicate that they often feel that games have been useful to them. However, in evaluating the use of a business game in a 'Management by Objectives' course at Harvard, it was felt that it needed to be more closely integrated with the rest of the course (McKenney, 1962).

SIMULATORS AND TRAINING AIDS

The last three techniques have all involved simulations of job situations. Here we are concerned solely with the simulation of equipment used on the job. Such simulations may take the form of mock-ups, models or prototypes, and range from simple to very complex designs. Usually they are employed when the use of job equipment is either too dangerous or too expensive. As we mentioned earlier, the psychological rather than physical similarity of the equipment is necessary for positive transfer of training to the job itself. Provided that this is accomplished, there is considerable experimental evidence which indicates that such simulators can add to the effectiveness of training (Valverde and Youngs, 1969).

PROGRAMMED INSTRUCTION (P.I.)

In programmed instruction material is presented in a series of steps which usually become progressively more complex in that each step is based on the one or ones preceding it. Each step involves the presentation of a question or task to which the trainee must make a response. The response is followed almost immediately by knowledge of results, i.e. whether or not the response was correct. Incorrect responses require either back-tracking or following an additional sub-routine until the correct response is given.

Programmed learning rests on a number of learning principles: (i) by requiring the learner to make only small steps at a time, it minimises the probability of incorrect responses – there is evidence to show that errors, once made, can be difficult to eradicate, particularly in older people (Kay, 1951); (ii) a response is required from the trainee – the learner is active, and this facilitates learning; (iii) knowledge of results is supplied after each response, helping both to motivate and guide the trainee towards the correct response; (iv) the fact that people go at their own pace through the programme allows for individual differences.

Methods of presentation include (i) teaching machines of varying degrees of sophistication (these may be linked to computers and present material either visually or aurally), (ii) programmed books, (iii) simple illustrations, diagrams and other printed material. Typically the programmes themselves consist of a series of frames, each dealing with a small amount of information and requiring a response from the trainee. Responses may be either constructed (i.e. unrestricted) or multiple-choice, no consistent superiority having been demonstrated for either method. Programmes may be either linear (i.e. the learner goes through every frame in sequence) or branching (i.e. special loops allow for adaptation to the learner's level of achievement). Construction of any kind of programme is time-consuming and demanding of expertise.

However, their value has largely been demonstrated, at least inasmuch as they enable more efficient use of training manpower once the programme has been constructed. For example, Nash, Muczyk and Vettori (1971) reviewed over a hundred studies carried out in the work situation and concluded that programmed instruction almost always reduced training time as compared with conventional methods of instruction, on average by about one-third. It is unclear to which aspect of P.I. this was attributable. No differences were found in immediate learning or retention and some studies have shown P.I. to be inferior to classroom instruction for long-term retention (Goldberg *et al.*, 1964). Programmed instruction is particularly useful for the learning of factual material, not least because it ensures that the trainer pays a great deal of attention to the nature and sequencing of information to be learnt.

A development of P.I. is computer-assisted instruction (C.A.I.), in which a complex learning programme is stored in a computer and the trainee inter-acts with the computer. This has been little used in the work situation, prob-ably because of its high cost. However, if computer facilities are available at *per capita* cost, then C.A.I. can be used to aid the trainee in practising re-sponses, in problem-solving and through simulation business games. Above all it can cater with great flexibility for individual differences in trainees. Such research as has been carried out in industry comparing C.A.I. with P.I. suggests that the former may result in savings in time but that there are no clear differences in achievement or performance (Schwartz and Haskell, 1966; Schwartz and Long, 1967). Successful educational uses of C.A.I. have included the teaching of reading to children (Atkinson, 1974) and the teach-ing of first-year Russian at university (Suppes and Morningstar, 1969).

INTERPERSONAL SKILL TRAINING

A number of methods have evolved over the past ten years with similar goals to those of sensitivity training. The evidence concerning the effectiveness of sensitivity training is less than adequate. There is a real dearth of evidence when different techniques and such variables as the trainer's directiveness, active participation, his structuring of sessions, authoritativeness and the extent of his focus upon individual's specific needs are considered.

One of the more recent techniques to appear in this area is transactional analysis, stemming from the writings of Eric Berne (1963). People are seen as playing various familial roles in the work situation, ranging from that of the mature adult to the immature dependent child. Such techniques often seem to behave like fashions in clothes: they are extremely popular for some years but are replaced by newer models. Like fashions, people tend to use them because they look good (i.e. have face validity) in spite of the fact that very little or nothing is known of their true validity in the work situation. It is notable that sensitivity training, rational training and transactional analysis all stem from the clinical tradition, and such techniques have received very little rigorous research in the clinical and work situations. This may reflect less on the adequacy of the method rather than on the problems of evaluation (see the section on T-groups).

NEED FOR ACHIEVEMENT TRAINING

Attitude and motivational change is infrequently made the major objective of training, and then not very explicitly. An exception to this is McClelland's (1965) work. He has developed a set of propositions which draw eclectically from theories of learning. These propositions, twelve in all, are to be used in designing training programmes aimed at increasing achievement motivation. The propositions are general in nature and presumably would apply to attempts to change any motive, though McClelland and his co-workers have focussed exclusively on the need for achievement. The propositions emphasise (i) social reality as defining the appropriateness of the motive, (ii) the impor-tance of meaningfulness of the motive, (iii) self-determination as an influence on behaviour, (iv) the role of feedback, and (v) the role of the chance to improve both oneself and others.

What little evidence there is (Kolb, 1965; McClelland, 1965) suggests that training programmes based on these propositions usually do increase significantly the level of need for achievement of trainees. For example, Mc-Clelland reported two studies involving small samples of Indian businessmen whose entrepreneurial activity increased significantly after training compared with their before-training scores and compared with a control group. The difficulty in interpreting such findings is that it is not clear which aspects of the course are effective in producing change. It may be, for example, that the commitment of the trainers to the programme led to high motivation among the participants. Also the study does not provide evidence as to the long-term results of such training. Little subsequent research evidence is available on the technique, though clearly this could be an important factor in increasing productivity.

4.5 Trainer and trainee characteristics

There has been little systematic research concerned with delineating the importance of individual characteristics of trainers and trainees for particular training techniques. We must therefore draw upon indirect evidence to suggest how such variables might be of importance. With respect to trainer variables we would expect that supervisory effectiveness would be in part a function of the supervisor's ability to change subordinates' attitudes and to help them develop their knowledge and skills. If this is the case, then those variables associated with supervisory effectiveness should also be associated with training effectiveness. Recent leadership theories emphasise the contingent nature of effectiveness on both individual and situational variables. For example, Fiedler (1967) predicts that permissive, democratic leaders will be most effective under moderately favourable situational conditions (the task and the group being led), whereas more controlling, active and less democratic leaders are more likely to be effective at the extremes of favourableness (see Chapter 14). If this is the case with training, desirable trainer characteristics will vary with the nature of the task and with the characteristics of the group. Similarly, from our discussion of attitude change, we would expect that the success of attitude-change attempts would be greatest with communicators (trainers) of high prestige who are similar to group members in such aspects as background, values and interests (see Chapter 8).

Many studies indicate that trainees with certain characteristics are more likely to be successful in training and educational programmes. Probably the variable of significance most commonly found is general intelligence (see Chapter 10), which has been found to be related fairly consistently to success on academic, supervisory and management development programmes (e.g. Gruenfeld, 1966; Neel and Dunn, 1960) as well as frequently being a factor in training success. Intelligence, however, is usually a better predictor of training success than of job performance.

Another factor likely to be of considerable importance for trainee success is the trainees' level of self-esteem. Indirect evidence for this comes from work by Shaw (1968) and Boocock (1966); they found that a person's degree of favourableness of self-concept was correlated positively with his ability to cope successfully with tasks requiring new learning.

A number of studies have indicated that age is an important factor in trainee performance. In general, training programmes take longer for older workers (in research studies workers over 35 have in general been classified as older workers) to achieve a given performance level. Belbin and Belbin (1968) suggest that the most appropriate training methods for older workers for perceptual-motor tasks involve minimising errors (i.e. by guiding the correct response) and slowing the pace, as Kay (1951) found that older workers found it particularly difficult to 'unlearn' errors. There is evidence that it is not age *per se* which is responsible for much of the decline in learning capacity with age, for older people who have engaged in learning activities throughout their lives show much smaller decrements in learning capacity.

Other trainee characteristics likely to be of importance are levels of knowledge and skills acquired prior to training, motivation, interest levels and temperament. It seems that attention to these variables in selecting people for appropriate training courses, as well as in designing appropriate courses, can be of considerable importance. For example, people with too high levels of skill and knowledge for a course are likely to become bored and those with too low levels to become discouraged. People who really want to receive a particular kind of training are much more likely to benefit from a training programme than another person reluctantly pressed to do it. Temperament may also play its part, as illustrated by those people who are insufficiently stable emotionally to benefit from T-group training and who may even break down during such training.

4.6 Organisational development

Recently a number of psychologists have emphasised the importance of an organisation's ability to change in the modern technologically complex industrial society. This has led them, along with other behavioural scientists, to focus upon the social processes and environments of organisations rather than upon individuals, their selection and training. They have developed a number of techniques for dealing with organisations as total systems, called 'organisational development' (O.D.) techniques. Like training, they focus upon change, but on changing group rather than individual behaviour. They were given impetus by such studies as those of Fleishman, Harris and Burtt (1955) and Sykes (1962), who found that training programmes were ineffective if they were in conflict with the organisational climate, such that transfer of training did not carry over to the job situation.

The methods used in O.D. rest on a few basic principles: (i) data feedback and action research (Lewin, 1947); (ii) the use of groups for individual and group change; (iii) the use of groups as agents for change; and (iv) participation as a means of achieving involvement in the change. (See Chapter 13 for a discussion of the theoretical basis of these principles.) Historically many of these techniques have been based on the T-group and its variants. Typically such techniques, along with others, are used for team-building and the development of work groups. The other set of techniques used in O.D. are diagnostic interventions which depend upon data collection and feedback. There are many methods of collecting data (e.g. interview, questionnaire) and of feeding them back. One example of the latter is the confrontation meeting, in which two work groups describe each other separately and then get together with a behavioural scientist to confront each other with these descriptions.

An important feature of O.D. is the role of a behavioural-scientist consultant who plays the part of an active change agent. His role is to apply behavioural-science knowledge, theories and techniques in order to bring about organisational change. Thus he may well make suggestions which involve changing job design, pay systems or organisational structure. An important aspect of his role is that of counsellor to participants in the change programme.

O.D. techniques are as yet in their early formative stages, and very little research has been done to evaluate them. Perhaps all that we can therefore say at the moment is that there is no established theory for changing organisations as total systems in a field dominated by change attempts which tend to focus exclusively on the individual approach. O.D. techniques do, however, represent the area of greatest increase in activity concerning change attempts. (For a further discussion of organisations, see Chapter 15, and for a full review of work in this field see Beer (1976).)

5
Ergonomics

5.1 Introduction

This chapter sets out to examine the role of human beings in relation to the equipment they work with. In particular, we shall be concerned with the design of equipment to suit human needs and capacities, to improve performance and to minimise errors. In Section 5.2 we will consider basic concepts. This will be followed with a discussion (Sections 5.3, 5.4 and 5.5) of the main principles involved in taking the human operator into account when designing equipment. This discussion will be in three parts based on the view of a human being as someone who (i) perceives, (ii) processes and (iii) acts on information presented to him. Consequently Section 5.3 concerns information displays in the equipment (for example, the lay-out and design of dials from which readings must be taken). Section 5.4 considers the relationship between the information load placed on the operator by the equipment and his capacity for processing it. Section 5.5 concerns the design of controls (such as the steering-wheel, gear lever or pedals of a car) for optimum human performance. The subsequent sections are concerned with the design of work methods, rules and procedures (Section 5.6) and with the over-all working environment (Section 5.7).

5.2 Basic concepts

Ergonomics may be defined as an interdisciplinary approach to the problem of fitting the task to the man (Davies and Shackleton, 1975). Rodger (1950) distinguished between two main areas of occupational psychology, fitting the man to the job (F.M.J.), comprising the selection, training and occupational guidance, and fitting the job to the man (F.J.M.). He saw the latter as including equipment design, work methods, working conditions and rewards. Each of these three areas of study is included in a broad definition of ergonomics, such as that of Davies and Shackleton. However, equipment design is generally considered to be the essence of ergonomics, with method study and working conditions being overlapping areas.

The term 'ergonomics' is most widely used outside the North American continent. In North America a similar area of work is called 'human engineering' or 'human factors engineering'. For example, McCormick and Tiffin (1974) define the field of human factors engineering as designing for human use. They see it as overlapping with the design of work methods, but as being more concerned with the design of equipment and other physical facilities as they relate to human performance. In fact, Chapanis (1976) states that human (factors) engineering and ergonomics can be considered to be synonymous for all practical purposes.

The field of ergonomics first emerged during the Second World War. The purpose was to consider human factors in the initial stages of the design of complex systems. The Davies and Shackleton definition points out the interdisciplinary nature of ergonomics. Apart from the basic engineering required to build the system, problems of system design are handled in the main by methods and techniques from a variety of disciplines, most particularly experimental and engineering psychology, anatomy and physiology. Ergonomics also uses methods and techniques from environmental medicine, toxicology, anthropometry, time and motion study, operations research and sociology. The introduction of increasingly complex systems for both military and industrial purposes has led to increased effort in trying to reduce human error and improve the performance of such 'man–machine' systems (see below for clarification of this term).

That human error can be an important determinant of system unreliability or failure has been demonstrated in several studies. For example, Willis (1962) analysed shipboard collisions and found that human error was responsible for over 60 per cent of them. It was responsible for over 70 per cent of aircraft accidents in the United States Air Force in 1961. It is certainly not outside the experience of most of us that accidents involving man–machine systems (e.g. motor-cars) are very often attributable to human error. Hence the role of the engineering psychologist (or ergonomist) is potentially one of considerable importance if he can help to design such systems to minimise human error.

Let us look at this role more specifically, and see what kinds of tasks engineering psychologists address themselves to. Kraft (1970) asked a group of human factors specialists to specify their activities. He categorised their replies into seventy-three different types of activity, the most common of which were man–machine system analysis, analysing control-display requirements, designing work lay-outs, developing operating procedures, analysing task–equipment relationships, evaluating engineering designs, developing simulators (see Chapter 4), analysis of human errors and analysis of the safety of systems.

Typically ergonomists have viewed the human operator from an engineer's perspective, i.e. as part of a man–machine system. The concept of 'system' is taken from engineering, and essentially it implies number of components, men and machines working together towards some common purpose. This means that a change in any one part of the system will have an effect on other parts of the system and on the over-all result. A system can often be viewed in terms of a number of sub-systems. Typically ergonomists are concerned with what is known as the 'personnel sub-system' (that part of the over-all system which particularly involves the human operator). It includes the selection and training of operators, as well as the immediate work environment, equipment design, rules and operating procedures. A change in any one of these five components can have consequences for any of the others. This means that whenever we contemplate a change in, say, equipment design, we must bear in mind its implications for selection, training, rules and operating procedures and the work environment. Any evaluation of such a change needs to be made in terms of its costs and benefits for the system as a whole.

Of the five aspects of the personnel sub-system listed above, two (selection and training) are the subjects of separate chapters in this book. Later sections of this chapter are devoted to the others.

In addition to the concept of 'system', ergonomists frequently use another concept from the engineering field, one which we have met in earlier chapters, namely that of man as a processor of information. This is closely allied to the idea of man as a component in a man–machine system. The human operator receives information via his sense organs, in particular that coming from some kind of display in the equipment. This information is then monitored and processed by the operator. These mediating processes include the use of memory and problem-solving, which require the operator to draw on past experience. They also include the use of strategies which help to co-ordinate and bring together various perceptions. Finally, such mediating processes result in some kind of decision which is then translated into an output. This output in the present context is usually a motor (physical) action via a control device (such as the brakes of a car or the dial of a telephone), though one important action output might be for the operator to do nothing until further information is received.

Before examining the field of ergonomics more closely, we need to consider three important methodological issues, those of (1) generalisation, (2) criterion selection, and (3) evaluation. These issues are common to other applied areas such as selection and training. Here we shall briefly consider each of them in turn.

(1) Applied psychologists must be cautious in generalising from results obtained from laboratory experimentation to real-life situations. There are many instances where relationships found in the laboratory situation have not been found in real life. Hence laboratory experimentation is not a substitute for field studies; rather, its use is in generating hypotheses. Further, we should also be cautious in generalising from field studies, for results may be biased in some systematic way. For example, Chapanis (1974) notes that almost all ergonomic studies have been conducted with large-boned, English-speaking people of Western customs, habits and ways of life.

(2) A related problem involves the selection of appropriate criteria for evaluation of a system. Typically laboratory experimentation makes use of such criteria as accuracy of response, physiological measures such as cardio-vascular responses (to moderate stress), psychophysical thresholds, ratings of annoyance, comfort, reaction time or the number of learning trials necessary to achieve a given standard of performance. On the other hand, ergonomic field studies often employ such systems criteria as the anticipated life of the system, appearance, ease of operation, cost, safety, training or manpower

requirements. These latter criteria are the ones which are most important to the user of the system and their relationships with the former kind of criteria are usually both complex and unclear.

(3) The third methodological issue we shall raise in connection with ergonomics and other applied areas of psychology is that of attempting to evaluate the effectiveness of changes in the system, whether that system be one of selection, training or man–machine interaction. Evaluation goes beyond the establishment of relationships between various independent and dependent variables. For example, we might find a very significant negative relationship between noise level in the work-place and performance. One way of increasing performance might be to reduce noise, but the cost of this may far outweigh the benefits of improved performance. Evaluation, therefore, usually takes the form of a cost–benefit analysis, where an attempt is made to place a value on each cost and benefit following from any particular method of operation. This must be done in terms of a common unit, usually money. Of course, benefits and costs, particularly those of a long-term nature, are often extremely difficult to estimate. Nevertheless, it should always be attempted.

Earlier in this section we mentioned that an idea central to ergonomics is that of the man–machine system. Typically such systems involve display devices which are monitored by the human operator, who then adjusts control mechanisms as he considers necessary. We shall now consider in turn three basic aspects of man–machine systems: displays, the operator's mediation processes and controls in more detail.

5.3 Displays

Ergonomists attempt to design displays (indirect presentations of information from the environment) to make accurate perception as easy as possible. This requires detailed, accurate knowledge of the operator's capacity to perceive and process information received from displays. The nature of this capacity was a main theme of previous chapters. However, much of that information is too general to be of direct benefit to the ergonomist. Evidence on the efficiency of different types of displays stems rather from a large number of highly specific studies.

Displays can vary in many ways. One of the most important is in the use of different sense modalities, the selection of which should depend upon the purpose of the display, existing demands on the senses and the complexity of the message to be transmitted. Vision and hearing are the modalities predominantly used, though sometimes touch is employed (e.g. to sense vibration).

It has been found in general that visual displays are most appropriate when the information to be transmitted is complex, lengthy, not urgent, concerned with spacial orientation, required for comparison with a standard, unsuitable for hearing (e.g. through overloading of the auditory channel), or aimed at an operator in a fixed position. On the other hand, auditory displays are usually better when the information to be transmitted is simple, short, urgent, not needed later for referral, aimed at a moving operator, or to be located in time (Chapanis, 1976).

There are many kinds of visual display, including mechanical indicators (e.g. clocks, thermometers) and various designs of letters and numbers. Mechanical indicators may be further subdivided into moving-pointer indicators (suitable for checking, setting and tracking tasks), moving-scale indicators, where the pointer remains still while the scale moves (generally less suitable) and counters (suitable for quantitative reading and setting tasks). Moving-scale indicators are rarely the most efficient because they must always violate one of the following design principles: (i) the scale should move in the same direction as the indicator; (ii) clockwise rotation should result in increased scale settings; and (iii) numbers on the scale should increase in a clockwise direction (Chapanis, 1976).

Research on the most effective styles of letter and number presentation shows that no one style is consistently superior for all conditions. There is a considerable amount of research in this area (see McCormick, 1970), and we can only present an illustrative finding here. For example, it has been found that characters illuminated from the side should be narrower than those illuminated from the front. This is due to the tendency of white light to spread out over a black surround.

Auditory displays may be subdivided into tonal signalling systems and speech. The former are generally superior for transmitting simple, urgent or secret information, information aimed at a person who is trained to decode the signals or information transmitted in conditions unfavourable for speech. They are used in such systems as Morse code, aircraft navigation and burglar alarms. Speech, on the other hand, is most suitable when the information must be transmitted and when flexibility is required: where the source of information must be identified, where an operator untrained in code learning must process the information, where the message requires some kind of preparation and when there is stress (as codes may then be forgotten).

Typically speech communication systems modify speech in some way. One way is to use language in specific prescribed ways. Sometimes alterations are made to language to facilitate its transmission. This is shown in the construction of specialised languages for particular purposes, of which one of the best-known examples is the international word–spelling alphabet used for radio messages in civil aviation; readers are probably familiar with the use of Alpha, Bravo, Charlie, Delta, etc. to transmit the letters A, B, C, D, etc. under noisy conditions. Another approach is to modify components of speech systems by the use of such devices as noise-cancelling microphones or microphone noise shields. A third approach involving the human engineering of speech communication systems is to design such systems as a whole. To do this, individual components and language are selected in order to match each other and work together in effective combinations (Chapanis, 1976).

We have discussed a number of advantages and disadvantages of presenting displays in different ways, in particular to the different senses. More generally, whenever we need to design displays, it is necessary to take account of each of the following aspects: the normal and maximum distances required for viewing them; the speed with which information needs to be transmitted to the operator; the required accuracy of the information; the amount of information needed; and the range of equipment error.

Displays may be categorised in a number of ways, as noted earlier. For example, they may be either static (e.g. signs and labels), or dynamic (e.g. clocks and radios). They differ in terms of the kinds of information which they present according to whether it is quantitative or qualitative in form, whether it simply checks information by illustrating whether or not a continuous changeable variable is within a normal or acceptable range, or whether it presents alpha-numeric (letters and numbers) or symbolic information. The particular way in which information is presented should of course depend upon the design requirements. For example, qualitative displays are most suitable when an operator must discriminate between only a small number of states (e.g. open or shut, on or off). The general requirement for a qualitative display is that different environmental states are distinctively represented so that they can be distinguished easily. This may be done by auditory (e.g. bells or buzzers) or visual (e.g. warning lights) means. On the other hand, quantitative displays are necessary when numerical information is required. This may be indicated either by analogue or digital indicators. Analogue devices (e.g. meters, gauges) provide a visual analogue of a numerical value and are required for rapid transmission of information. They also give fairly accurate readings and hence provide considerable flexibility. Digital indicators present numerical information directly and frequently take the form of counters. They are most suitable when a high level of accuracy and specificity is required. Of these two kinds of indicator, more research has been carried out on analogue displays. For example, Singleton (1969) found that if scales were divided into four or five subdivisions, and numbers were marked against only the major scale divisions, then the most satisfactory speed–accuracy trade-off resulted. The important point is that scale subdivisions need to be sufficiently large to be clearly discriminated by an operator at an appropriate distance from the display. Other factors to be taken into account in achieving this objective are the contrast of the scale numbers, marks and pointers with the scale background, and the illumination level of the work environment.

Much research has been concerned with design features of scales (see Morgan, Cook, Chapanis and Lund, 1963). For example, it has been found that (i) circular dials give better results than linear scales, (ii) horizontal scales are inferior to vertical ones, and (iii) a pointer moving against a fixed scale is superior to a fixed pointer and moving scale. In general, the most effective scales have been found to be those which are compatible with the operator's expectations and established perceptual habits. For example, circular scales are better if they increase in a clockwise direction, horizontal scales are better if they increase from left to right, and vertical scales for upward increases.

Finally, in this section we should note that displays are tending to become increasingly complex, particularly in the large remote control systems of modern automated processes. The requirement here is for quick and accurate information concerning faults or problems in the process. This has lead to representational displays which represent the processes involved in a simple and logical way. Hence the position of displays is decided on such criteria as similarity of function, importance and sequence in the process. Typically the operator is presented with a visual display and is required to check the readings, noting any deviations from the normal state. It has been found that deviations are most easily perceived if points of the null or normal position are arranged in some systematic manner, so that any deviation leads to a break in the pattern. This is illustrated by an extended pointer design (Oatman, 1964) which enabled more rapid detection of deviant points than with short pointers and the more accurate location of those detected (see Figure 5.1). This type of display is made particularly effective by breaking up the visual field, so that deviant instruments are easily detectable.

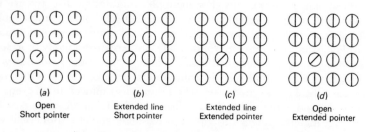

(a)	(b)	(c)	(d)
Open Short pointer	Extended line Short pointer	Extended line Extended pointer	Open Extended pointer

Figure 5.1   Extended pointer designs (c *and* d) *are more easily detected and located than short pointers* (a *and* b) (*Oatman, 1964*)

Having discussed the design of displays, we now turn to the mediation processes required of the human operator. These include such mental processes as making judgements or evaluations, reasoning and computing in order to arrive at an appropriate decision or course of action. These processes regularly have as their starting-point information received from displays of the kind we have just described.

5.4   Mediation processes

Those mediation processes of particular interest to ergonomists involve much of what was discussed in the chapter on attention, perception and memory. We should note, however, that just as there are no clear distinctions between these processes themselves, it is also impossible clearly to distinguish them from other processes such as computation and problem-solving.

It is clear from the discussion in the last section that the form of display is of great importance for accurate perception. We would therefore expect that decision quality depends upon the effectiveness of displays, and there is considerable evidence to support this contention (e.g. Silver, Jones and Landis, 1966). Other evidence comes from laboratory and field studies of monitoring and inspection work. These tasks require an operator to detect whether or not a relatively uncommon event has occurred, and, typically, it is found that man is poor at such tasks (Davies and Tune, 1970). Laboratory studies have usually involved an observer watching a display for faint and infrequent signals arriving erratically over a considerable time period. Not only is performance poor, but large performance decrements occur after short periods of time. These decrements can be either reduced or sometimes prevented by the provision of immediate feedback (i.e. 'correct' or 'not correct') after each response. When this is not feasible, as is the case in many work situations, then either the provision of artificial signals or short rest pauses can prevent decline in performance (Davies, 1970). More recently the usefulness of computer assistance has been investigated in this context (Poulton, 1974). However, the use of batteries of tests to select people for monitoring tasks have been largely unsuccessful as a means of improving monitoring performance (McGrath, 1968).

Effective decision-making is not only a function of the display but it also depends on the number of alternative responses available. For example, Hilgendorf (1966) measured reaction times in a key-pressing task and found that response time varied directly with the logarithm of the number of alternatives for up to 1000 of them. Reaction time is determined by both recognition time (i.e. a memory mediational process) and movement time.

An aspect of mediational processes which is particularly important in ergonomics is compatibility. This refers to the extent to which the spatial, movement or conceptual qualities of stimuli (displays) and responses (control movements) either individually or in combination are consistent with human habits and expectations. The concept is related to that of transfer of training in that such habits and expectations transfer from one situation to another. Many studies have found that the use of compatible relationships facilitates performance as measured by such criteria as speed of reaction and accuracy.

There are a number of different kinds of compatibility. Spatial compatibility refers to the physical features or arrangement of items in man–machine systems. It often refers to display–control relationships, the relationship of a control to its corresponding display. For example, an automatic vending machine on which the choice buttons are adjacent to the items to be bought is easier to operate than one where they are distant. Spatial compatibility has been shown to be a very important determinant of performance in man–machine systems (e.g. Chapanis and Mankin, 1967). Movement compatibility is concerned with the relationship between the direction of some physical movement (e.g. of a control mechanism) and the direction of response of a system. For example, turning the steering-wheel of a car to the right causes it to turn right. Finally, conceptual compatibility deals with culturally learned expectations such as the use of red for danger or the use of a curved line to represent a bend in the road.

In addition to perceptions and expectations, short-term memory is also an important mediational process in the human operator. Its particular characteristics may affect the design features of both displays and controls. This may be illustrated by a data-entry keyboard task much as it is performed by computer operators. Conrad (1966) found that errors increased with the length of time required to retain the necessary information in short-term memory, a factor which appropriate keyboard design was able to reduce.

Much of what we have said concerning human mediation processes applies also to control devices and displays. We shall now consider in more detail the factors affecting the design of controls.

5.5   Controls

Perhaps the most obvious general principle in the design of controls is that their lay-out should take into account the anatomy of the human body and the functions which the limbs are capable of performing. Further, no limb should be overburdened. Although obvious, this principle is not always adhered to. For example, one author heard of a tank designed during the First World War which had a bad effect on morale because it was extremely difficult to get out of in a hurry. The size of the exit had not been designed with anatomical considerations in mind.

As we mentioned in the previous section, compatibility is an important design consideration. For example, Loveless (1962) demonstrated the importance of control movements conforming with previously existing expectations or direction of motion stereotypes. Warrick (1947) found that the best results were obtained when the control and display moved in the same direction. It has also been found that the symbolic association of shape with use improves learning of the appropriate response, thus a triangular knob pointing in the direction of movement of a lever can help to reduce errors. A similar principle is that controls should mimic the movements they produce in the system, as with car steering-wheels.

An important finding has been that different kinds of control are best suited for different tasks. For example, Ziegler and Chernikoff (1968) found that for a tracking task a static pressure control was superior to a displacement control, which was in turn superior to an on–off control. Morgan *et al.* (1963) recommend the use of different controls for different types of tasks, as indicated in Figure 5.2.

Control design should take account of a number of other factors, including the working environment (e.g. temperature, oscillation, acceleration), the operator's clothing and working position, direction of movement relationships, methods of coding controls and the prevention of accidental activation. When all of these factors are taken into account, it is often best to combine a number of related controls if possible. A simple example is a dimmer switch, which combines an on–off switch with a light-dimmer control.

We have mentioned previously the importance of people's expectations for equipment design. When there are universally held expectations about control movements, these are referred to as 'population stereotypes'. These affect direction of movement relationships in that when they are in accord with population stereotypes the results are shorter reaction or decision times, a greater probability that the correct control movement is attained initially, faster control use, more precise adjustments and faster learning (Chapanis, 1976).

Recently, powered control systems have become increasingly important. The essence of these systems is the transformation of a control output (e.g. the actions involved in driving a car) to a system output (e.g. an accelerating vehicle) via some kind of machine. This may occur in a number of ways: (i) zero-order control, where control movements directly affect system output, (ii) first-order control, where operation of the control determines directly the rate of change of machine output, and (iii) second-order control, where con-

Control movement	System (or equipment component) response				
	Directional				Non-directional Increase*
	Up	Right	Forward	Clockwise	
Up	Recommended	Not recommended	Conditionally recommended	Not recommended	Recommended
Right	Not recommended	Recommended	Not recommended	Conditionally recommended	Recommended
Forward	Recommendation depends on other variables	Not recommended	Recommended	Not recommended	Recommended
Clockwise	Recommendation depends on other variables	Recommendation depends on other variables	Recommendation depends on other variables	Recommended	Recommended

*Increase refers to increase in power output, brightness, rpm, etc., and to 'on' or 'start' as opposed to 'off' or 'stop'

Figure 5.2   Recommended relationships between control movement and system or component response (Morgan et al., 1963)

trol operation affects acceleration of machine output. As the order of control increases, so increasingly complex skilled movements are required to produce the desired change in system output. Further, control movement has a decreasing correspondence with system movement, making such control movements increasingly difficult. To cope with this difficulty a number of techniques (involving augmented feedback) have been devised which reduce training requirements and make possible control which would not otherwise be possible (Kelley, 1968). These techniques serve largely to provide the operator with additional helpful information on his system which would not otherwise be available. Examples of this are the provision of information about his past movements and computer predictions on the basis of these about the future behaviour of the system if current trends are continued.

Before ending this section we should again note that equipment display and control lay-out should be designed for (i) optimal performance of the specific task required, and (ii) a range of individual differences by catering for the range of operators who are likely to operate the system.

We now turn away from equipment and towards two other aspects of job design of interest to the ergonomist: work methods and working conditions.

5.6   Work methods, rules and procedures

Barnes (1968) observes that principles of motion economy or work methods are related to the use of the human body, the arrangement of the work-place and the design of tools and equipment. A number of examples of the application of these principles follows:

1. The two hands should begin as well as complete their motions at the same time.

2. The two hands should not be idle at the same instant except during rest pauses.

3. Motions of the arms should be made in opposite and symmetrical directions and should be made simultaneously.

4. Hand and body motions should be confined to the lowest classification with which it is possible to perform the work satisfactorily. The five general classes of hand motions include, first, the fingers by themselves, with the others involving, progressively, other body members in this order: wrist, forearm, upper arm, and shoulder. Generally speaking, lower classifications require less time and physical effort than the higher classifications. There are, however, exceptions to this generalization.

5. Momentum should be employed to assist the worker whenever possible, and it should be reduced to a minimum if it must be overcome by muscular effort.

6. Smooth continuous curved motions of the hands are preferable to straight-line motions involving sudden and sharp changes in direction.

7. Ballistic movements are faster, easier, and more accurate than restricted (fixation) or 'controlled' movements.

8. Work should be arranged to permit an easy and natural rhythm wherever possible.

9. Eye fixations should be as few and as close together as possible (Barnes, 1968).

Most of these applications have received some support from laboratory and field studies, though there are exceptions to this. For example, Lauru (1954) found that the principle of bimanual symmetry (application 3) did not hold for an experimental study using the 'Lauru platform', a mechanism measuring the forces resulting from the activity of a person when standing on a small work platform. In general, there has been very little rigorous testing of such principles and their range of application.

Once work methods have been established they are often formalised into operating rules and procedures.

The basic set of rules and procedures for particular jobs are described in technical manuals of which instruction booklets and maintenance guides are a simplified version with which the general public is familiar. Their importance in safe and efficient practice is coming to be increasingly appreciated as research indicates their importance. For example, Chapanis (1965) found that the design and wording of written materials accompanying equipment can be at least as important as the design of the equipment itself.

5.7   The working environment

In this section we shall consider four aspects of the work environment which have received a considerable amount of attention from researchers: (i) illumination; (ii) temperature; (iii) noise; and (iv) hours of work.

ILLUMINATION

The ability to make visual discriminations is not only a function of the surrounding level of illumination but also of certain intrinsic characteristics of a task. The characteristics include the brightness contrast between the 'figure' and its background, the size of the 'figure' and the time available for seeing it. A change in one of these aspects can be compensated for by an appropriate change in one of the others. For example, Blackwell (1959) found that for a given level of illumination, a decrease in viewing time had to be accompanied by a concomitant increase in brightness contrast to maintain the same level of visual discrimination.

Research has found that different levels of illumination are appropriate for different tasks. We tabulate illumination levels recommended for a number of tasks (see Table 5.1). These recommendations, taken from the *IES Lighting*

Table 5.1

Task	Recommended illumination, (footcandles)
Operating table (surgical)	2500
Very difficult inspection	500
Proof-reading	150
General office work	70–150
Food preparation	70
Wrapping and labelling	50
Loading (materials handling)	20
Hotel lobby	10

Source: *IES Lighting Handbook* (1972).

Handbook (1972), were obtained using rather complex methods developed by Blackwell (1959). Not only is the over-all level of illumination important, but so is its distribution throughout the work area. This is related to the location of lights, which should also be installed so as to minimise glare. Glare may interfere with vision as well as being a source of discomfort.

TEMPERATURE

This has received more research attention than other aspects of the atmosphere such as air pressure, the presence of varying amounts of gases or other toxic conditions. Closely related to temperature is humidity. In conditions of high temperature and humidity, particularly when the temperature of surrounding buildings and objects is high, heat stress can arise. This occurs because, in addition to the reduced heat loss through convection and radiation, humidity reduces the effectiveness of perspiration in losing body heat.

The effects of heat are greatest when people are expending physical energy, as this energy expenditure itself increases body temperature. For example, Mackworth (1950) found that when subjects were given a heavy task which required a substantial effort to work a weighted lever, the error rate increased with the increases in the effective temperature. A similar effect,

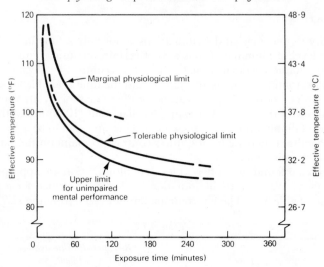

Figure 5.3   Tentative upper limit of effective temperature for unimpaired mental performance as related to exposure time; data are based on an analysis of fifteen studies (comparative curves of tolerable and marginal physiological limits are also given: Wing, 1965)

though less pronounced, was obtained for a telegraphical task which required relatively little energy expenditure. This relationship between temperature and performance is also illustrated by Wing's (1965) review of fifteen studies. Figure 5.3 illustrates the increase in exposure time before performance starts to be impaired as the effective temperature is reduced between 120 and 80 degrees Fahrenheit. The recommended tolerance limits illustrated by the middle curve are based on other studies, but show a similar pattern. It should be noted that such tolerance limits vary from person to person, depending upon physical fitness and general health.

At the other end of the air-temperature spectrum there is evidence that low temperatures can result in performance decrements, at least for manual tasks. Such decrements occur below skin temperatures of about 55 degrees Fahrenheit. Fox (1967) has suggested this effect is due to a lowering of hand-skin temperature. Five-finger movements are more susceptible to low temperatures than grosser movements (Dusek, 1957). There is insufficient information concerning performance in mental tasks at low temperatures to draw any conclusions with respect to performance. The temperature at which people feel most comfortable varies a little depending on the time of year. In the United States it is about 71°F in the summer and 68°F in the winter (*American Society of Heating, Refrigeration and Air-Conditioning Engineers Handbook*, 1967).

NOISE

This is an area of research which has received considerable attention over the past twenty years or so. However, conclusions regarding its effects on work performance remain much the same as Broadbent's (1957) conclusion based on a review of research that no significant performance decrements were apparent at noise levels up to 90 decibels. From this level upwards, significant decrements did occur. He also concluded that there was no apparent variable common only to tasks which were affected adversely by noise. However, Cohen (1968) has suggested that there is some evidence to indicate that although simple, repetitive tasks are relatively unaffected by noise, such may not be the case for complex mental tasks, those requiring skill and speed and those placing heavy demands on perceptual capacities. There is clear evidence showing that vigilance tasks (requiring monitoring of displays) are susceptible to decrements in performance because of noise.

There is more conclusive evidence concerning the effects of noise on hearing. An impairment in hearing due to prolonged exposure to high noise levels has often been demonstrated. For example, La Benz, Cohen and Pearson (1967) studied earth-moving operatives exposed to noise levels of 90 to 120 decibels. People with different periods of exposure of up to thirty years were compared with each other, and it was found that, after a correction had been made for deterioration of hearing due to age, those with longest exposures showed the greatest impairments, particularly at the higher sound frequencies. Hearing loss is also a function of a number of other factors, namely the noise characteristics of intensity, sound frequency range, duration and continuity, as well as certain individual characteristics.

Even when noise does not affect performance or hearing it can have other negative consequences. It can cause annoyance or discomfort, and has been found to be related to absenteeism (Cohen, 1972). It may, therefore, be a cause of dissatisfaction at work (see Chapter 8). Cohen (1972), in a five-year follow up of workers exposed to noise levels over 95 decibels, found that, as compared with a control group, the noise-exposed workers complained more frequently of illness and had more disorders diagnosed. All this evidence points to the likelihood that noise can act as a significant source of psychological stress.

Having said this, a striking phenomenon of life today is many (particularly young) people's liking for music played fairly loudly. Certainly, it is important to distinguish between background noise and the more harmonious musical 'noise'. According to Uhrbrock's (1961) conclusions, music can have either positive or negative effects on work performance depending upon both individual and task variables. His conclusions are presented below:

1. Unqualified claims that increased production results from the introduction of music into the work situation are not proven.
2. The social implications of music in industry as an incentive system ultimately should be faced. A question may be asked, 'Is this a legitimate device that gives pleasure to workers and profit to employers?'
3. Feelings of euphoria during periods of music stimulation have a physiological basis which is evidenced by changes in blood pressure that occur in some subjects while listening to music.
4. Factory employees prefer working where music is played rather than where it is not played.

5. Not all workers like music while they work. From 1 to 10 percent are annoyed by it.

6. Quality of work can be adversely affected by the use of music in the work situation.

7. Instrumental, rather than vocal, music is preferred during working hours by the majority of workers.

8. There is a negative correlation between age and preference for work music.

9. At least three investigators have reported that young, inexperienced employees, engaged in doing *simple*, repetitive, monotonous tasks, increased their output when stimulated by music.

10. Evidence has been presented which demonstrates that experienced factory operators, whose work patterns were stabilized and who were performing *complex* tasks, did not increase their production when music was played while they worked.

11. At times music has had an adverse effect on the output of individual employees, even though they reported that music was 'quite pleasant' (Uhrbrock, 1961).

It is possible that, at least for relatively easy tasks, music may have little effect on performance. It is, however, widely appreciated by workers, though preferences are variable depending on the population studied. For example, Newman, Hunt and Rhodes (1966) varied the kind of music, including having none at all, over a five-week period. They found that it had no effect on either the number of units produced or on the proportion rejected. However, the subjects preferred to have music while they were working.

HOURS OF WORK

Research concerning hours of work has focussed on three different areas: working long hours, rest periods, and the effects of shift work.

Much of the early work in this field concerned the length of the working day. For example, studies by the British Industrial Fatigue Research Board on munitions workers during the First World War showed that when the working week was increased above a certain level, over-all productivity hardly increased and even decreased for a very long working week. There were also increases in the accident and absenteeism rates as the number of hours worked increased. Similar findings are cited by Kossoris *et al.* (1947) in an American study of workers during the Second World War. They found that an eight-hour day and a forty-hour week was best when over-all efficiency and absenteeism were considered. As hours were increased a relatively low increase in production occurred. For example, if work exceeded an eight-hour day and a forty-eight-hour week, then extra hours worked resulted in a gain in output equivalent to two normal hours. For heavy work the output was reduced to less than half that for normal working hours. Similarly, increases in accident rate were found with increases in the hours worked.

Research work on the effects of introducing rest periods into work also goes back well over fifty years. For example, Farmer and Bevington (1922) found that rest periods did not diminish over-all production for a group of British production workers. More strikingly, Miles and Skilbeck (1944) found that performance increased by over 14 per cent when two fifteen-minute breaks were introduced. McGehee and Owen (1940) found that the introduction of similar rest periods had two beneficial effects in that they reduced the number of 'unofficial' breaks as well as increasing the speed of work. More recently in the United Kingdom Bhatia and Murrell (1969) found that for female operatives productivity remained about the same when an eight-hour work day was reduced to seven hours by interposing rest periods. Six ten-minute breaks were slightly more effective and were clearly preferred to four periods of fifteen minutes.

We have already mentioned that performance on vigilance tasks declines after a period as short as twenty to thirty minutes, and frequent breaks and relatively short over-all sessions are necessary to keep performance at a high level. It is likely that many tasks show some deterioration in performance over any reasonable length of time. Such appears to be the case for driving, though the evidence is indirect (Herbert and Jaynes, 1964). They found that performance (on a driving test taken immediately after driving by groups of people who had been driving for one, three, seven and nine hours) declined the longer people had been driving prior to taking the test.

The effect of rest periods in many of these examples would appear to be a function of people's psychological state rather than of physical tiredness. This contention is supported by a study of female office workers (Nelson and Bartley, 1968). Figure 5.4 shows the importance of cognitive factors in feelings of tiredness, boredom and effort. Similar findings were obtained by Griffith, Kerr, Mayo and Topal (1950) for manual, office and supervisory workers.

There are two main kinds of shift system, permanent and non-permanent.

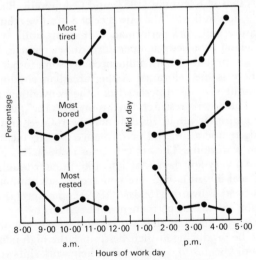

Figure 5.4   Percentage of female office workers reporting hours during each half day when they felt most tired, bored, and rested – data points are plotted at mid-points of the hours (Nelson and Bartley, 1968)

Permanent systems require individuals to work the same (usually eight-hour) shift each day. Non-permanent systems involve rotation between shifts, e.g. morning shift for the first week, afternoon shift for the second week and night shift for the third week. There are a wide number of variations on these systems, but we shall confine ourselves to these two. Three main kinds of variable affect the satisfactoriness of the different kinds of shift system. These are sleep loss, the circadian rhythm of rest and activity, and social factors.

Research into sleep loss is relevant here because it appears to be the case that sleep at an unaccustomed time is not as long or as deep. The nature of the rotating, non-permanent shift system described above is such that workers have to do just that for at least one week in three. In addition, social activity, which is usually based on the conventional working day, is also likely to eat into sleeping time at one end or the other. However, sleep loss is perhaps the least important factor of the three mentioned above, since the evidence indicates that it needs to be considerable before significant decrements in performance occur. Thus Williams, Lubin and Goodnow (1959) report few errors on the first seven minutes of a vigilance task with a thirty-minute to one-hour sleep loss, but a rapidly increasing error rate after two minutes with a fifty-four hour loss of sleep. This suggests that the effect of sleep deprivation is likely to be greater for longer tasks than for short ones.

The twenty-four hour circadian rhythm of rest and activity has been studied since the 1850s. The circadian rhythm is a kind of internal biological clock whereby bodily processes fluctuate at different times of the cycle. The cycle may be illustrated by means of the body temperature of an individual on a conventional day and night schedule. Body temperature is at its lowest at about 4 a.m. rising gradually to a peak which can vary any time from noon to late evening, depending on the individual and his social habits. Research such as that of Kleitman (1963) and Colquhoun, Blake and Edwards (1968*abc*, 1969) has indicated the existence of a positive relationship between body temperature and work performance. It seems unlikely (see Wilkinson, 1971, for a review) that body temperature causes changes in performance; rather, they are probably both influenced by some other factor(s). What concerns us here is the relevance of the circadian rhythm for shift work, in particular shift systems different from the conventional 9 a.m.–5 p.m. working day. The crucial research for this involves the question of the extent to which the entire circadian rhythm may be rotated around the clock so that peak body temperature and performance times coincide with the times when a person is working. The answer seems to be that complete reversal is possible within a very few days (Aschoff, 1969) under totally isolated conditions. Where real-life situations are concerned, adaptation is slower. Colquhoun, Blake and Edwards (1968*abc*, 1969) report progressive but incomplete adaptation to various permanent shift systems over a period of twelve days. Such research suggests that workers on weekly rotating shift systems are unlikely to be producing at their best, since the high point of their circadian rhythm only begins to coincide with their work shift at the point when they are due to change shifts again. This is in accordance with the reported findings of Bjerner, Holm and Swensson (1955) concerning errors on different shifts in a gas-works. Workers on afternoon and night shifts were most prone to error. Unfortunately, as far as is known, no studies have compared non-shift workers with shift workers in this connection.

We have already hinted at the social factors which are relevant to our discussion of shift work and these will not occupy us long here. The problems they pose centre mainly round the disruption to social life caused by working unconventional hours. These may vary from missing a drink with one's friends at the pub to intolerable domestic strain. Clearly, such factors, while they may not affect production directly, seem likely to influence the extent of a worker's satisfaction with his work.

What, then, are the conclusions to be drawn with regard to shift systems? Clearly work on circadian rhythms suggests that non-permanent rotating systems are bad for output. Other evidence suggests that the results of shift work are not as bad as one might predict. Certainly there are compensating factors such as more pay and more time off. Further, some people may actually prefer shift work. A study by de la Mare and Walker (1968), in which workers were allowed to choose the shift they worked, showed that some men actually preferred permanent night shifts. If such people were available in sufficient numbers, the problems of the three-shift system might be overcome by adopting what has been called the permanent night, double day system'. This involves a permanent night shift with alternating day shifts. Such a system would enable the night-shift workers to adapt totally, provided they could safeguard their sleep by being insulated from daytime noises. The adjustments required by the alternating day shifts would be far less than for a three-shift system. (For a fuller review of this area, see Wilkinson, 1971.)

We have examined in some detail four environmental factors which can significantly affect human behaviour at work. We might have added more unusual factors such as radioactivity, weightless environments or acceleration and gravitational forces. For all these factors and others, ergonomists have compiled tables of acceptable tolerance levels (Morgan *et al.*, 1963). However, ergonomists have not as yet addressed themselves very much to the effects of a number of these variables in combination. The data to which we have referred have been concerned with the effects of only one environmental variable. We should also note that much of the data have been collected from young, healthy male subjects and we should therefore be extremely cautious in generalising to different work populations.

Part III

MOTIVATION AND ATTITUDES

Motivation has been called the power house for all human activity. Ultimately we only do things because we are motivated to do so whether by choice or by coercion. Hence, it may be seen as fuelling the basic processes discussed in Part II. We start with a discussion of the main current views of motivation (Chapter 6). This includes an examination of the various constructs which have been proposed to explain motivational phenomena. It also includes discussion of the relationship between motivation and emotion, and an evaluation of the importance of cognition in motivation. Two main types of motivational theory are introduced, process theories, which usually take an incentive view of motivation and content theories which attempt to specify different kinds of motive or need. This forms a relatively detailed basis for a consideration of how these views have been extended and applied to the world of work (Chapter 7). In particular, we devote considerable attention to one kind of process theory (Valence-Instrumentality-Expectancy theory) because it has been primarily developed in the context of work situations. We also discuss other theories which have particular relevance to the work situations such as Adams' equity theory (derived from dissonance theory) and more briefly, content theories.

The latter type of theory is taken up more extensively in Chapter 8 which presents a further extension of the theme of motivation. In the sense that attitudes are persisting dispositions to think, feel and act in particular ways towards aspects of our environment (human or otherwise), they derive, at least in part, from our view of whether such objects or persons are conducive to the satisfaction of our motives. An attitude upon which particular emphasis is placed is that towards work, commonly known as 'job satisfaction'. It is work on job satisfaction, specifically that initiated by Herzberg and his associates, which is closely bound up with content theories of motivation.

We have included the chapter on attitudes here, rather than in Part V (social aspects of work). This is to draw attention to their inextricable relationship with motivational phenomena. In particular, we see one of the major functions of attitudes as that of enabling basic needs to be satisfied while at the same time serving to help an individual adjust to his 'social world'. Because of this, the reader will be able to discern a number of underlying perspectives and theories which are common to each of the chapters in this part of the book.

6
Motivation

6.1 Introduction

In this chapter we shall be considering what might be called the power-house of man – his motivation. The kind of questions we shall be trying to answer will concern matters such as 'What makes a person feel hungry or thirsty?', and 'What makes him turn his head as an attractive member of the opposite sex walks past?' Essentially we shall be considering what fuels these activities, how the process takes place and how it is aimed in a particular direction.

Consider the two following situations: 'You are walking with your grand-mother down the street on the way to an appointment. It is twelve noon. The smell of food in preparation drifts out of a nearby restaurant. You suddenly feel hungry'; and 'A young man is walking down the street on the way to visit his grandmother. It is the first pleasantly hot day of the year. Suddenly his thoughts are filled with the attractiveness of the women in their summer dresses. He no longer feels like going to see his grandmother.' In both situations a previously neutral motivational state has been switched into one of motivational arousal. In the first case, the arousal involves hunger; in the second, sex. In both cases there had been apparently no great feelings present prior to the appearance of the smell or the young ladies in summer dresses, except possibly for the desire to meet granny. How has this change in moti-vational state occurred?

We can use these illustrations to describe the two main answers which have resulted from the theorising and empirical research of psychologists. One possible kind of answer to the question posed at the end of the last paragraph might be as follows: 'It was just coming up to lunchtime and he was getting hungry anyway', or 'He had been craving for a romantic involvement for some time and it had just come to the fore again.' Such answers suggest that it is factors *internal* to the individual, e.g. his personal needs, which generate this kind of motivational arousal. This kind of concept will reappear in Section 6.2. An alternative kind of answer might be that a particular stimulus in the environment (the smell of food or the young women) generates the motivation. In other words, factors *external* to the individual are responsible. This kind of concept will be further amplified in Section 6.2 under the head-ings of 'incentive' and 'reinforcement'.

Section 6.3 is devoted to a concept closely related to motivation, namely emotion. Emotions, we need hardly say, involve feelings like love, hate, jealousy and joy, and they, like motivation, are associated with psychological and physiological arousal. In this section we focus particularly on the cognitive aspects of emotion, i.e. how the manner in which we perceive and understand our environment affects what we feel. This is followed in Section 6.4 by a discussion of how cognitive factors enter into motivation. Particular emphasis is laid on how they have contributed to the development of incentive theories. These are considered at length in relation to work in Chapter 7 (see the V.I.E. model). Section 6.5 attempts to place all the concepts and ideas discussed so far into perspective by describing two very similar models of motivation which include both internal and external factors in what attempt to be comprehensive models.

In Sections 6.6 and 6.7 we come to the vexed question of the 'content' of human motivation. How many motives are there (Section 6.6)? How are they organised and which are the most powerful (Section 6.7)? In our theoretical discussion so far we will only have touched on this difficult topic since we shall have been mainly concerned with the motivational process rather than the content of the motives themselves. In Section 6.7 we attempt to do justice to what many empirically orientated psychologists consider to be a conceptually untidy area.

6.2   Motivational concepts

A number of different motivational concepts have been suggested to explain motivated behaviour. In this section we shall divide them into those whose main aspect is internal to the individual (instinct and drive) and those whose main aspect is external (incentive and reinforcement)

INTERNAL FACTORS

Instinct
An instinct may be defined as an innate, biologically based predisposition to behave in a particular way. Instinct explanations of human behaviour became popular amongst psychologists early in this century, mainly due to McDougall and Freud. McDougall (1908) proposed that there are ten instincts (e.g. acquisition, construction, curiosity, flight) and later added others. Freud, on the other hand, distinguished between two types of instincts, the life instincts underlying sexual behaviour (in a very wide sense) and the death instincts underlying aggression (see Chapter 9).

There were a number of problems with such explanations of behaviour: (i) lists of instincts were arbitrary and there were no grounds for choosing one list rather than another; (ii) such 'explanations' were sterile in the sense that they did not lead to any testable propositions; (iii) many of these so-called instincts were not found in all cultures, suggesting the importance of learning in their acquisition.

Because of these problems the concept of instinct disappeared from psychology for a time, until it re-emerged in modified form due to the work of ethologists (students of animal behaviour in their natural habitat).

In studying birds and fishes they have observed species-specific patterns of behaviour which appear to be present innately in all normal members of a species. Releasing stimuli were discovered which triggered these fixed action patterns. For example, Tinbergen (1942) discovered that a red patch, typical of the chest colour of other males, triggered aggressive behaviour in the male stickleback. There is no evidence, however, that human behaviour is so clearly biologically based. Instinctual tendencies in men appear to be much more susceptible to modification by environmental influences.

The unsatisfactory nature of instinct as an explanation of human behaviour led to the proposal of the concept of 'drive', to which we now turn.

Drive and homeostasis

A drive may be defined as a state of arousal caused by a biological need, such as lack of food or water. Although drive and need are sometimes used interchangeably, psychologists have generally considered drive to be the psychological counterpart of a physiological need. Much early research (e.g. Cannon, 1918) was concerned with the question of how drive operated, whether locally (e.g. through stomach contractions in hunger, or dryness of the mouth in thirst), or centrally (in the brain). The evidence indicated that drive could operate without local stimulation (e.g. people with most of their stomach removed still experienced hunger), presumably due to some homeostatic mechanism. A homeostatic mechanism is a self-regulating mechanism designed to maintain a constant bodily state, rather in the manner of a room thermostat by which the heating is switched off when the room temperature reaches a certain level and on again when it falls below that level. For example, lack of food leads to a bodily imbalance which results in the experience of hunger, which leads to behaviour aimed at eating, which in turn restores the deficit, and so on.

The concept of drive itself arose as a behaviourist reaction to untestable instinct explanations. Drive could be both specified and controlled by varying deprivation of food, water, etc. and observing its effect on behaviour. Much animal experimentation of this kind was carried out, and a number of findings appeared to be compatible with a drive explanation of motivated behaviour, for example (i) activity increased with deprivation, (ii) animals showed periodicity in behaviour such as eating and sleeping related to the extent of their deprivation, and (iii) consummatory behaviour increased in vigour as deprivation increased.

Central to drive explanations of motivated behaviour is the idea that an organism seeks to reduce 'drive'. Drive is conceived to be a state of deprivation which is unpleasant and which the organism seeks to reduce or eliminate.

The concept of drive, however, has become less popular as an explanation of motivation for a number of reasons. It was realised that many behaviours thought to result from drive are affected very much by learning and other types of previous experience. For example, Harlow (1959) found that effective sexual behaviour in rhesus monkeys did not occur if, as babies, these monkeys had been separated from their mothers. Furthermore, it became apparent that drive reduction was not a sufficient explanation of the cessation of motivation. In experiments rats would perform responses to obtain saccharin, a sweet-tasting but non-nutritive substance (Sheffield and Roby, 1950) which could not have reduced any physiological need. Sexual arousal without consummation also appeared to be rewarding (Sheffield, Wulff and Backer, 1951) and observations of spontaneous curiosity and exploratory behaviour in animals appeared to be incompatible with drive reduction.

Because of such difficulties a number of refinements to drive theory have been suggested. For example, Dollard and Miller (1950) proposed that behaviour not traceable to some specific physiological deprivation was due to secondary drive (i.e. learnt by association with a basic drive). They proposed that a secondary drive was learned in a way analogous to the acquisition of fear (Watson and Rayner, 1920; Miller, 1948) where a previously unfeared object comes to be feared through association with a frightening experience (see Chapter 3).

A number of non-homeostatic drives have been proposed, e.g. a curiosity exploration or general boredom-avoidance drive, in order to explain activity not traceable to drive reduction. Such explanations have not generated research beyond a certain point, however, and this has led to the use of such concepts as incentive and reinforcement, to which we now turn.

EXTERNAL FACTORS

Incentive
The notion of incentive refers to stimuli or outcomes which both instigate approach or avoidance behaviour and evoke a state of arousal which motivates such approach or withdrawal. Incentives may be objects such as money or beer, environmental conditions such as a beautiful view or humid weather, or states such as fatigue or contentment. They may also be memories or fantasies, both of which can have arousal properties and which can lead to behaviour aimed at making such thoughts more or less vivid. They may be either pleasant or unpleasant in that they instigate either approach or avoidance behaviour.

The incentive value of an outcome is not the same as its actual reward value. The incentive value refers to the anticipated or expected reward which the outcome should bring. For example, a promotion may have a very high positive incentive value and lead to great effort in our work performance. We may find, however, that on achieving promotion we do not get the anticipated satisfaction. As a result of this experience the incentive value of further promotion might decrease or even become negative.

The notion of incentives is one widely prevalent in everyday life. The 'carrot and stick' approach to management involves using positive and negative incentives respectively. In this approach an employee is led to anticipate that if he attains a particular outcome (e.g. high productivity), then a certain reward (e.g. money) will follow. In the example above the carrot (i.e. the money) will only act as an incentive in this situation if the employee believes that high productivity will in fact be followed by the incentive of money and if he believes that the outcome of high productivity is contingent upon his performance. If high productivity is paired with higher wages, then high productivity itself may develop incentive value, and become an end in itself. High productivity in this example might be described as a goal, goal object or objective. When managers set objectives they are using an incentive framework of motivation, hoping that an objective will act as a positive incentive. 'Management by objectives' schemes (Humble, 1966) attempt to fix goals which will act as incentives and motivate people to achieve those objectives.

In our example above we suggested that an outcome may not have incentive value if a person does not believe that he is likely to achieve that outcome; that is, the force on a person to perform an act is determined not only by the anticipated attractiveness of an outcome, but also by his expectation of his act achieving the desired outcome. Vroom (1964) has expressed this relationship as follows:

$$\text{force of motivation} = \begin{array}{c}\text{expectancy of desired} \\ \text{outcome}\end{array} \times \begin{array}{c}\text{'valence' of desired} \\ \text{outcome.}\end{array}$$

Vroom defines 'valence' as anticipated satisfaction. Other psychologists have defined valence in terms of 'attractive–unattractive' and/or 'desirable–undesirable' (Dachler and Mobley, 1973; Lawler and Suttle, 1973). We can see from Vroom's formulation that the motivational properties of outcomes are dependent not only upon their attractiveness (valence) but also upon the perceived likelihood of their being attained. Vroom's theory, and various modifications of it, are known as expectancy theories. They may also be described as incentive theories, in that they are concerned with the motivational consequences of anticipated outcomes.

An incentive theory has been proposed by McClelland *et al.* (1953). He proposes that motivated behaviour takes the form of an approach or withdrawal from a situation, depending on whether pleasant or unpleasant consequences are anticipated. According to McClelland all motivated behaviour depends upon the anticipation of affective (emotionally pleasant or unpleasant) outcomes, and hence involves learning. Thus anticipations are evoked by the situation as a result of the latter's prior association with pleasant or unpleasant feelings. Further, he proposes that for the arousal of such feelings there must be a discrepancy between what a person expects and what he perceives. More specifically, he proposes that small discrepancies are pleasant and large ones unpleasant.

The concept of incentive has much in common with that of reinforcement, to which we shall now turn.

Reinforcement
The notion of reinforcement may be defined as any event following a response which increases the strength of that response and its likelihood of recurrence in the future. Premack (1959) has suggested that a reinforcer is simply an event which has a higher preference value for the person being reinforced

than the behaviour being reinforced. Similarly Bolles (1967) has proposed that to judge whether or not an event is likely to have reinforcement properties it is first necessary to determine its preference value and then to contrive situations where an opportunity to do the preferred thing is made contingent upon doing something else.

Reinforcement, then, involves finding something relatively high in a person's preference hierarchy of outcomes, and giving that reward when the desired behaviour of a lower preference value occurs. The more this is done, then the stronger the desired behaviour should become. For example, if praise is a highly valued reward for a particular person, then by praising him each time he produces a good piece of work, he should be more likely to produce good work in the future. Reinforcement could also be negative, criticism for example, in which case, other things being equal, the strength of the criticised behaviour should be decreased. If negative reinforcement (punishment) is too strong, then neurotic, maladjusted behaviour may result.

The reinforcement approach assumes that behaviour is determined by our past history of reward. That behaviour which has been most reinforced will be most likely to occur when the situation is similar to that in which it has been rewarded in the past.

It is clear that the concepts of incentive and reinforcement have much in common. They both refer to the power of external events that affect behaviour, either through anticipation of reward (incentive) or through the strengthening of some behaviour because it is followed by reward (reinforcement).

Furthermore, any situation explicable in reinforcement terms is also explicable in incentive terms, for the occurrence of a reward on a particular response might not only strengthen that response, but may lead to an expectation that a repetition of the response would be similarly rewarded. Hence the 'reinforcement' comes to have incentive value. In fact this acquired incentive value may be the mechanism which strengthens the so-called 'reinforced response'.

Perhaps the greatest problems of both incentive and reinforcement explanations are concerned with determining what constitutes a reinforcement, incentive or preference for a particular individual and explaining how an outcome acquires a particular strength or value.

Both incentive and reinforcement explanations of behaviour attach great importance to a search for pleasant or rewarding outcomes. Outcomes which are pleasant or unpleasant often arouse characteristic feelings which we call 'emotions', and it is to these that we now turn.

6.3 Emotion

We recognise emotions in ourselves by the pleasant or unpleasant feelings associated with them and often by awareness of certain physiological changes, such as a rapid heart-beat. We can often recognise emotions in others by their appearance (e.g. facial expression, posture, gesture) and by them telling us how they feel. Emotions seem to be closely related to motives and McDougall (1908) proposed that each motive had a corresponding emotion. Emotions may be aroused by an outcome or merely by the imagination or anticipation of some outcome. An unpleasant emotion is often experienced when a negative outcome occurs or when an expected positive outcome does not materialise. Thus emotions frequently accompany motivated behaviour. They also themselves affect motivation in that we strive after outcomes which have resulted in pleasant emotions and try to avoid those which have resulted in unpleasant ones. Previously we have said that an incentive refers to something which can evoke a state of arousal which motivates approach or withdrawal. This state of arousal may itself be experienced as an emotion, and thus an incentive might be seen as something with emotionally arousing properties. Similarly, a reward or reinforcement can often give rise to an emotional state. We may perhaps say that emotion refers simply to the pleasant or unpleasant feelings and the concomitant physiological changes which seem to underlie incentive and reinforcement explanations of behaviour.

Duffy (1962) has suggested that emotional phenomena can be explained in terms of level of arousal or activation, where arousal refers to some kind of physiological arousal. This poses problems, for different measures of arousal do not intercorrelate very highly. Another difficulty for this position derives from the work of Schachter and Singer (1962), who attempted to manipulate emotion by injecting subjects with epinephrine, a substance which has arousal properties. One group of these subjects was placed in the company of a stooge (in reality a confederate of the experimenter) who was acting as though he were angry, and another in the company of an apparently euphoric stooge. Subjects not aware of the properties of the drug, or misinformed about it, acted more like the stooges than a control group (injected with a placebo, a non-effective substance) and another injected group correctly informed about its effects. This experiment suggests that the kind of emotion experienced is determined not only by physiological arousal, but also by some kind of cognition (i.e. some kind of evaluation of the situation).

A later study by Valins (1966) suggested that behaviour may be affected if subjects *think* they are aroused, without *really* being aroused. This was done by giving false feedback about the rate of heart-beat. Male subjects were shown slides of nude women and recordings of rapid heart-beat were paired with certain slides and normal heart-beat with the rest. The subjects later tended to report the former slides as more attractive.

These experiments suggest that the kind of emotion experienced may be influenced by cognitive factors. The importance of cognitive factors in motivation has become increasingly apparent, and it is to a consideration of some of these factors that we now turn.

6.4 Cognitive aspects of motivation

Incentive theories of motivation allow considerable scope for the influence of cognitive factors. An important variable is the expectation that a given outcome will follow a particular action. The incentive value of an outcome seems to be dependent on a number of cognitive factors. One of these is the actual reward experienced as a result of attainment of a particular outcome. The pleasantness of the outcome will affect its future incentive value. In general terms, our past experience of an outcome, its difficulty of attainment and its effect will help to determine its incentive value.

Vroom (1964) has suggested that the valence (and hence its incentive value) of an outcome not otherwise desired is a function of its instrumentality (the degree to which the person sees the outcome in question as leading to the attainment of other desired outcomes).

Attribution theory (see Chapter 11) also has interesting implications about the effect of cognitions on motivation. It is in essence a theory about the way in which we attribute characteristics, particularly causal and dispositional ones, to people and events, including ourselves. Weiner *et al.* (1971) have put forward a classificatory scheme for allocating causality in situations relevant to achievement. Success or failure are attributed mainly to one of four causes: ability, effort, luck and task difficulty.

In Figure 6.1 locus of control (which can be either internal or external to

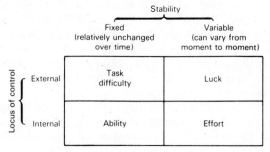

Figure 6.1   Scheme for allocating causality in situations relevant to achievement (Weiner et al., 1971)

the individual) refers to whether the individual perceives the outcome as being under his (internal) control or due to factors beyond his control, e.g. the organisation, fate, etc. (external). Stability refers to whether the individual perceives such factors as being constantly present (fixed) or variable over time.

Weiner *et al.* suggest that locus-of-control variables determine the extent to which a person desires a particular outcome, and thus the strength of his motivation (the locus of control/valence of outcome hypothesis). They also suggest that the stability variables determine the subject's perceived probability of success (the stability/expectancy hypothesis). Incentive theorists consider this to be an important determinant of effort. Clearly Weiner's investigations serve to put some meat on to the basic Vroom formula.

There is some support for the above ideas in the form of a number of experiments. For example, Weiner, Heckhausen, Meyer and Cook (1972) tested the locus of control/valence of outcome hypothesis by allowing children to reward themselves for their achievements. They were supposed to take as many plastic poker chips as they thought fit after a success and return as many as they thought fit after a failure. The results showed that attribution of success to effort increased the amount of reward they gave themselves. Attribution of failure to lack of effort generated the greatest amount of self-punishment. In connection with the stability/expectancy hypothesis, they found that reductions in expectancy of success were found following failure attributed to task difficulty and low ability and the reverse if failure was attributed to lack of effort or bad luck. Thus if one thinks one's failure is due to either of the variable stability factors, bad luck or lack of effort, then one expects that next time things will be different. Conversely, if failure is seen as due to low ability or task difficulty (the fixed stability factors), the expectation is that the future pattern will be similar to the past.

The implications of this theory for a manager would seem to be that to obtain the maximum effort from his subordinates he should be concerned that the subordinate sees his success in obtaining an outcome as being dependent on his own ability and effort rather than external factors. This should lead to high satisfaction and the outcome should have high incentive or reinforcement value. He should also be concerned that failure should be perceived as being due to lack of effort or bad luck rather than low ability or task difficulty, so increasing expectancy of success and hence effort.

6.5   Towards a comprehensive theory of motivation

It is clear from our discussion so far that simple homeostatic physiological models of motivation cannot explain motivated behaviour on their own. The evidence reported indicates the extent of the influence of situational (incentive and reinforcement) factors on both the direction and intensity of motivated behaviour. A number of theories, which we shall now review, attempt to explain this apparently double-ended or push–pull nature of motivation.

BINDRA'S THEORY

Bindra (1969) proposed a theory, based in large part on studies of animals, suggesting that motivation is generated by a combination of physiological and incentive stimuli. He uses the term 'central motive state' to define that motivational condition created by the interaction of the physiological arousal and the directionality brought about by the influence of a significant external stimulus. Thus both external stimulation and internal need can bring the central motive state into play. For example, a person will become hungry (defined in terms of the behaviour he is prepared to undertake to get food) either if his blood sugar level becomes low enough (internal stimulation) or if he sees food (external stimulation).

Incentive processes (stimulated externally) may therefore account for the wide variety of motivated behaviour which does not have a clearly physiological or instinctive component, and even those motives which have traditionally been regarded as physiological contain both physiological and incentive components. According to Bindra, then, the directionality of the central motive state may be determined partly innately and partly through learning. Events which are satisfying to the organism can create a motivational state by setting up a capacity for anticipation of that particular outcome. This capacity becomes attached to the central motive state. Young (1959) attributes to this capacity for anticipation a dynamic characteristic which is brought into play when the event in question becomes potentially available. Thus it seems that incentives operate as a result of the activation of some kind of system in the organism which is specifically primed to be activated by that particular kind of stimulus. Further, the stimulus (incentive) in question must have had some part in setting up the system. The theory of McClelland *et al.* (1953) discussed earlier proposes a similar mechanism, as does that of Cofer and Appley, to which we now turn.

COFER AND APPLEY'S THEORY

Cofer and Appley (1964), like Bindra, postulate two mechanisms, the sensitisation–invigoration mechanism (SIM) for internal stimulation and the anticipation–invigoration mechanism (AIM) for external stimulation. They propose that the SIM comes into action in response to particular stimuli in an innately determined manner. There is evidence from some animal studies that some stimuli seem to elicit arousal behaviour in the organism without prior learning. Whether such arousal occurs in human behaviour is more questionable. Indeed, McClelland argues that the most biologically determined motives, such as hunger, can be accounted for solely in terms of incentives (the AIM mechanism). As a result of previous experience internal hunger cues come to be associated with the anticipated pleasant emotional state of having eaten food. The internal cues deriving from deprivation of food and the food itself thus acquire incentive value.

Cofer and Appley proposed the idea of an anticipation–invigoration mechanism on the evidence that objects external to the individual can take on motivating and arousing characteristics which are not innate. For example, particular times of the day elicit hunger when there is no physiological deprivation. Similarly, the smell of food can arouse hunger. In essence AIM is brought into play by stimuli in the environment. These stimuli have been regularly associated with events such as feeding time which involve some kind of gratification. In time they come by themselves to evoke the expectation that gratification will follow, and they encourage the person to become active. Even frustration of these expectations seems to further energise the person. Thus the essential feature of AIM is that arousal is brought into play by situational determinants (factors in the environment), and the exact nature of these situational determinants decides which of a variety of available responses will occur. This connection is made by one of the kind of associative learning mechanisms reviewed in Chapter 3. Cofer and Appley suggest that the two mechanisms (SIM and AIM) can work together in many situations. Both biologically and situationally determined arousal can combine in order to generate activity. The cessation of motivational activity is determined by the degree of arousal capacity the stimulus possesses. Thus in a stimulus generating fear, escape will reduce the capacity of the stimulus to elicit fear.

Some motives such as the need for achievement seem to operate in such a way that obtaining the gratification actually encourages the person to become even more motivated. Other kinds of factor, such as a stronger kind of motivation or possibly demoralisation and failure, seem to be required in order to reduce an achievement need.

To conclude, we can see that the theories of Bindra and Cofer and Appley place great emphasis on the 'pull' or incentive aspect in motivation, particularly in human motivation. Incentive-type models of the motivational process, like that of Vroom, are currently most used in explaining human behaviour in the work situation. We shall deal with some elaborations of this model applied to the work situation in the next chapter.

Until now we have dealt with motivation in general terms, in a search for some general mechanisms of the process of motivation. Now we turn to some specific motives of importance in human behaviour, the content of motivation.

6.6 Content in human motivation

So far we have mentioned a number of human motives, but these have by no means been an exhaustive list since almost anything can acquire incentive value. An exhaustive list is therefore impossible but psychologists have nevertheless been concerned to classify motives into different types. Classification schemes for motives are many and various and rather than try to review them we shall opt for one which is probably no better than the others simply in order to indicate the range of phenomena we are dealing with. Murray (1964) differentiates the following five kinds: (i) the more biologically based motives, such as hunger, thirst and thermo-regulation; (ii) sexual motivation; (iii) emotional motives, such as fear, anger, delight and affection; (iv) intrinsically motivated behaviour, such as curiosity, exploration and manipulation; and (v) social motivation, such as dependency, affiliation, dominance, self-esteem, aggression and approval. Murray also includes the need for achievement in the last category, but we shall treat it separately as it is not so clearly a social motive as are the others. We shall also discuss a further type of motivation which we shall call the need for self-development, and which covers two aspects, namely the need for a consistent self-image and the need to develop and 'improve' the self-image. In particular, we shall consider the evidence for a need for such consistency.

We shall now briefly describe each of these in turn, spending more time on the later motives in our list which are probably of more importance in the everyday work situation.

HUNGER AND THIRST

These motives might be described as needs in that they require satisfaction, otherwise the individual dies. Two areas of the hypothalamus (part of the brain) have been found, injury to which produces in one case overeating and in the other case no eating at all. These two areas seem likely to correspond to the 'on' and 'off' switches of a homeostatic mechanism. A homeostatic model, therefore, comes nearest in applying to these motives, but even here it suffers from the problems which we have already discussed. These problems are further exemplified by the fact that, at least in Western society, eating and drinking are often occasions for social interaction rather than for satisfaction of hunger and thirst.

SEX

Sex differs from the more homeostatic motives mentioned above in that the relationship between drive strength and deprivation is markedly different from what would be predicted from a homeostatic model. Sexual motivation appears to be highly dependent on learning and cultural factors, and particularly on early experience with other people. Freud suggested that sexual motivation was the predominant human motive and that the constraints imposed on its gratification, both internal and external, often result in substitute behaviour. Although many psychologists would not agree that sex is as important a motive as Freud suggests, there is no doubt that, at least in Western society, it is very important. Argyle (1969) suggests that the constraints on sexual behaviour affect social behaviour such that the end-product of sexual motivation may be conversation, proximity, eye contact, and sometimes bodily contact rather than sexual intercourse. He suggests that the net effect is to convert sex into generalised social-approach drive. If this is the case then sexual motivation at work is no doubt of considerable importance. This is clearly the case in certain areas of advertising and publicity, and in government and C.B.I. warnings to businessmen going abroad! It is also probably important in such areas as personnel selection and appraisal and in day-to-day interaction. One of the authors was once on a selection panel which discussed the candidates at great length. Finally, the panel (all male) were swayed by the chairman's final statement of 'Well I like the lady with the big . . .'!

EMOTIONAL MOTIVES

These are many and various, but psychologists have concentrated their studies on fear and anger. A number of similar physiological changes have been identified for each motive: (i) overt bodily patterns such as facial expression and muscular tension; (ii) internal physiological changes of a kind which prepare the person for emergency action; and (iii) brain mechanisms which mediate these processes. The internal changes which occur involve the sympathetic nervous system, which brings about an increase in heart beat and a constriction of blood vessels to transmit the blood faster to the brain and to the muscles. Breathing is faster and the liver secretes extra sugar to give more energy. At the same time certain other activities, such as digestion, are slowed down. In addition to these main activities of the sympathetic nervous system, the endocrine system secretes hormones which also have effects on the circulation, sugar production and a number of other functions. Funkenstein *et al.* (1957) found that students working on a frustrating task tend to show one of three reactions: fear, anger or depression. The angry students secreted more of the hormone noradrenalin and the fearful and depressed students more adrenalin.

Two brain areas are primarily involved in emotional motivation, the limbic system and the reticular formation. Areas of the limbic system of the brain seem to be concerned particularly with motivation. Nearby areas stimulated electrically elicit fear, rage and other emotional reactions. This fear can be conditioned to be elicited by other stimuli. Thus Delgado, Roberts and Miller (1954) paired electrical stimulation of the limbic system with a tone for a group of experimental cats and the animals later showed fear reactions in response to the tone. The reticular activating system of the brain stem is a general arousal mechanism, having an energising effect and this also appears to be involved in emotion.

What possibly happens in emotion is that a stimulus occurs in the environment which is felt by the sense organs, and identified and assessed by the cortex and limbic system of the brain, with the effect of generating an anticipatory state of either a pleasant or an unpleasant kind. The reaction generated is likely to be partly learnt, partly innate and derives from the limbic system which determines whether the behaviour will be of an approach or avoidance kind and the experience pleasant or unpleasant. The reticular system determines the intensity of the reaction. The limbic system probably also initiates the bodily changes and these bodily changes probably summate with the initial perceptions to determine the total emotional experience.

At a more psychological level, perhaps most work has been done on fear and anxiety motivation, or, more accurately, the need to escape fear. Taylor (1956) defined 'anxiety' as a drive which causes people to behave in such a way as to try to reduce the anxiety. A number of different concepts and measures have been used in this area, and their interrelationships are not always clear. Atkinson (1953) proposed a motive which he calls 'fear of failure'. People who possess this tend to avoid situations which might result in failure at some task. Certainly there is evidence that fear of failure might be very important in certain work situations. For example, Poppleton (1975) has noted the strength of this kind of motive in a number of life-assurance salesmen, this fear being known as 'fear of rejection' within that industry. (Particularly relevant also to this whole topic is the work on cognitive aspects of emotion of Schachter and Singer (1962), which we have mentioned above.)

INTRINSIC MOTIVATION

The evidence for intrinsically motivated behaviour (behaviour which is satisfying in itself) derives from such areas as research into sensory deprivation and curiosity in play. The main finding concerning sensory deprivation is that people find it most unpleasant. In such studies subjects experience only the minimum of sensation, wearing translucent goggles which admit diffuse light only, ear muffs, long cuffs from the elbow covering the hands to prevent touch, and air conditioning set so as to minimise temperature sensations. Most subjects lasted only two or three days despite good pay (see, for example, Bexton, Heron and Scott, 1954). They experienced increasing difficulty in keeping their thoughts coherent, became irritable and finally suffered hallucinations. It seems that there is a minimum level of sensory input without which human beings cannot function. From this we can conclude that there is a motive to seek stimulation when this is lacking in the environment.

Curiosity can be shown to be a motive inasmuch as it will serve as a means of bringing about learning (e.g. Butler, 1953). Maddi (1972) reported that children tended to choose collections of toys of intermediate novelty with which to play, avoiding both the familiar and the very different. McClelland's incentive theory postulates that intermediate deviations from what is expected are pleasant whereas extreme deviations are unpleasant and no deviation leads to indifference. Certainly there is evidence that a number of activities such as manipulating new objects, and exploring and seeing new things can be rewarding in themselves.

We now turn to some very important motives in the work situation, the social motives. We shall begin with what is probably one of the most fundamental of social motives, the need for affiliation.

SOCIAL MOTIVATION

Affiliation (the motivation to be with others)

Affiliative tendencies are often manifested in the forms of play and conversation that people adopt. The origins of affiliative motivation are uncertain, but studies of maternal deprivation suggest that the early relationship with the mother is important (Bowlby, 1952; Goldfarb, 1955). Sampson (1965) found that first-born children were lower in affiliative motivation than the later born. What is probably needed for the satisfactory development of affiliative motivation is initial appropriate mothering followed at a later stage by satisfactory contact with peers.

Schachter (1959) found that fear brought about by subjects being told they were to receive a painful electric shock increased the subjects' desire to affiliate, probably because affiliation serves to reduce fear. Indirect evidence for this comes from the finding that first-born children have a stronger tendency to affiliate when frightened than later-born ones. Thus first-borns who are likely to have had more benefits from affiliating when frightened in their early years are more likely to affiliate when frightened, even though they may show a lower resting level of affiliative motivation. There is evidence from a study by Sarnoff and Zimbardo (1961) that anxiety may reduce affiliation, when anxiety was aroused by telling subjects that they were to perform an embarrassing task such as sucking artificial nipples. It seems there is a kind of anxiety (which might be called neurotic anxiety) which is not reduced by the presence of others since the prospect of confessing to the anxiety actually makes it worse.

A number of studies seem to support Festinger's (1954) theory of social comparison, which states that where a person is experiencing strong emotion or is uncertain about himself he may wish to compare himself with others in order to evaluate either himself or his experiences. In this way he may clarify both the type and the strength of his emotions. For example, Schachter (1959) found that subjects preferred to wait with others about to undergo the same experience.

Approval

Work on this motive has stemmed principally from Crowne and Marlowe's (1964) scale of social desirability. People with high scores on this scale tend to be more conforming, cautious and easily persuaded than others. Their behaviour tends to be more anchored in the norms of society or in those of their social groups. In the laboratory they tend to (i) react more favourably to a dull task, (ii) condition more easily in verbal conditioning experiments (see Chapter 3), (iii) conform more in social situations, and (iv) show cautious goal-setting in risk-taking situations and be more susceptible to persuasion. There is evidence that people with a high social-desirability score are more likely to avoid threats to their self-esteem (this probably has much in common with what we have called 'fear of failure') and seek affiliation with others than are people with a low score. They also tend to depend more on the favourable evaluations of others and avoid self-criticism. Summarising this evidence, Cofer (1972) has defined the approval motive as the 'desire for social support, self-protection and avoidance of failure'; its goals 'include social recognition, status, protection, dependency, love and affection'. We can see from this definition that there is considerable overlap between some of the social motives which we are describing, including the need for approval, and the next we shall consider – dependence.

Dependence

Dependent behaviour lasts longer in humans than in other species. During childhood it takes the form of touching or holding a parent, being near, seeking attention, reassurance, affection or need satisfaction. Often these do not go together in the same child (Sears, 1963). During later childhood dependence may be discouraged or punished by parents. During adolescence children try to break out of this dependent relationship and boys try to do this earlier since it is not an approved behaviour pattern for them (Kagan and Moss, 1962). Walters and Parke (1964) report that children and adults who are strong in dependency are more subject to social influence. Gewirtz (1961) found that isolation for twenty minutes increased dependency in children, but it is not clear whether it was the isolation itself or the anxiety produced by it which was responsible for the dependent behaviour.

Walters and Parke (1965) suggest that early dependent behaviour grows out of earlier innate orientating and following responses. Thus Carr (1965) found that infants aged three months were more aroused by stimuli consisting of circles and spots when placed in a manner representative of human eyes than when these were in a different configuration.

Schaeffer and Emerson (1964) suggest that for the first six months of life attachment is to certain stimuli but that during the period from six to nine months attachment to particular individuals develops. Children reared in institutions of the poorest kind may become apathetic to adults and not show a dependent response (Yarrow, 1964). Freud believed that feeding by the mother reinforced dependence, but work by Schaeffer and Emerson (1964) indicated that dependent attachments may be formed with adults who have no part in feeding, and Sears, Maccoby and Levin (1957) found no correlation between dependence and maternal feeding habits. Factors influencing the amount of dependence shown in later childhood seem to be the responsiveness of the mother to the infant's crying and the amount of interaction between them (Schaeffer and Emerson, 1964) and the style of discipline used. Love withdrawal as a disciplinary technique has been found to produce a stronger conscience but also greater dependence than physical punishment (Bronfenbrenner, 1961).

Self-esteem

This is the need to be evaluated highly by others and to compare favourably in performance with others. Secord and Backman (1964) note that parents usually evaluate their children favourably – which results in children forming favourable self-images which they continue to seek confirmation of in their dealings with others. At the moment it is not clear whether they are simply seeking congruent responses from others or whether there is a specific need for self-esteem, as proposed by Rogers (1951). We shall discuss the need for consistency later in this section, as well as the need for achievement, which appears to resemble to some extent the need for self-esteem in that it results in a concern to increase one's competence.

Dominance

Little is known about the conditions under which dominance (as a motive) is aroused, nor about its origins in socialisation. However, it is part of a male role which is acquired through identification with the father or other available male models (Kagan, 1964). Thus the kind of father likely to produce a dominant son could be the one who is both dominant himself and rewarding to the son. A similar analysis could also apply to dominant women. Authoritarian personalities tend to be dominant when in a position of domination, and submissive when in a subordinate one (Adorno *et al.*, 1950). Poppleton (1971, 1975) reports that dominance as measured by 'factor E' in Cattell's '16 Personality Factor Questionnaire' correlates both with eye-gaze behaviour in students and with effectiveness as a life-assurance salesman.

Aggression

Aggression may be aroused in various ways. It may occur in response to attack or unnecessary frustration, and it may be instrumental for other needs, or there may be a spontaneous aggressive drive which operates purely on its own account. There is little evidence for the latter hypothesis except from animal studies by, for example, Lorenz (1966). Socialisation studies have shown that aggression is strongest when children have been frustrated by rejection or in other ways, frequently punished especially by physical punishment, or exposed to aggressive models. It is lowest in those who have had warm relations with parents and where parents have discouraged the use of aggression and used love-orientated methods of discipline. At the present time it remains an unresolved question whether aggression is an innate drive (Freud, 1920), a learned drive (Dollard *et al.*, 1939), or a piece of socially learnt behaviour (Bandurce, 1965). It seems likely that all three ideas may be correct.

Aggression is frequently aroused but less often expressed; this is due to social restraints. As a result, displacement is often used to channel the aggression in a different direction. For this reason verbal aggression is more common than physical violence.

We turn next to the need for achievement, which we have said is perhaps less of a social need, certainly in its expression, than are the other social needs we have discussed.

ACHIEVEMENT MOTIVATION

Achievement motivation has been defined by McClelland (1961) as the concern over competitition with a standard of excellence. On the basis of a number of laboratory studies, McClelland proposed the following hypotheses: (1) Individuals differ in the degree to which they find achievement a satisfying experience. (2) Individuals with high achievement motivation tend to prefer the following situations: (*a*) situations of moderate risk as opposed to those of high or low risk, (*b*) situations where knowledge of results is provided, and (*c*) situations which permit individual responsibility. (3) Since the business entrepreneurial role has the characteristics outlined in (2), individuals of high achievement motivation will be attracted throughout their lives to the entrepreneurial role.

On the basis of research evidence McClelland suggests that people high in such motivation are more likely to have grown up in environments which expected competence of them, gave them independence at an early age and evaluated them highly.

In support of McClelland a number of studies (e.g. Cummin, 1967) has found that general administration management success was positively correlated with achievement motivation. However, a review by Klinger (1966) is less supportive of some of McClelland's work, and it is likely that some revisions to our ideas about the achievement motive will have to be made. It has certainly been probable from very early on in this research that the need for achievement is not a unidimensional motive. Thus Atkinson (1953) suggested that what may appear to be low need for achievement may in fact be high fear of failure. Atkinson (1964) further suggests, on the basis of experimental evidence, that the need for achievement operates only when a person with a high need for achievement perceives the situation as an evaluative one. The need for achievement appears to have something in common with a need suggested by Maslow (1954) for self-actualisation, which refers to the individual's desire to express and develop himself and to use his capacities to the full.

SELF-CONSISTENCY MOTIVATION

A number of consistency theories (see Chapter 8) suggest that a state of imbalance or inconsistency between our attitudes gives rise to a need to reduce such a state. Dissonance theory (Festinger, 1954) states that inconsistency between attitudes and behaviour will also lead to such a motive. Dissonance theory states that when two cognitions are held which are the opposite of one another, then a state of dissonance, which is unpleasant, will exist. A person in such a state will then try to reduce the dissonance. Dissonance and the other consistency theories will be discussed in Chapter 8, so we need only note here that many studies, several relating directly to the work situation, lend support to the consistency motive: (i) Adams and Rosenbaum (1962) found that when a person was paid by piecework he tended to adjust his productivity according to whether the payment was higher or lower than he felt he deserved. (ii) Aronson, Carlsmith and Darley (1963) found that people who expected, on the basis of previous experience, that they would have to do something unpleasant chose to perform the unpleasant task even when they could have chosen a more pleasant one.

Korman (1971) has suggested another kind of consistency theory, namely that people perform in a manner consistent with their self-image. Evidence supporting this comes from Korman (1968). He found that people told that they were not competent to achieve a specific goal performed worse than people told they were competent. He further found that people of low self-esteem were less likely to achieve difficult goals which they had set for themselves than high self-esteem people.

Korman (1967) found that people of high self-esteem were more likely to choose occupations consistent with their self-perceived needs and their self-perceived abilities.

Having looked at the range of human motives, we shall now turn to their organisation and how they relate to one another.

6.7 The organisation of motives within individuals

There are two aspects of the organisation of motives which we wish to treat here. The first concerns the problem of several motives competing for expression at the same time. The second concerns the relationship between different categories of motivation, e.g. drive and incentive. We shall start with the first.

Maslow (1943) has suggested that motives (he calls them 'needs') are organised hierarchically, and that the more basic (lower-level) needs in the hierarchy are prepotent (the most powerful), i.e. if a lower-level need is not satisfied, its satisfaction is sought before any of the higher-level needs. Thus a hungry man should put food before safety – a well-fed man should put safety before friendship, and so on (see Figure 6.2).

A stripped-down version of Maslow's hierarchy of needs has been put forward by Alderfer (1969, 1972), combining Maslow's lower two levels into one (existence needs), retaining his middle level (relatedness needs) and

Figure 6.2   Maslow's hierarchy of needs

combining his top two levels (growth needs). The three-level model (known as the 'ERG model') operates in a similar though slightly different manner to Maslow's. One major difference is the proposition that the less a higher-level need is satisfied, the more an individual will seek satisfaction of the next need below, even though it has previously been satisfied. Thus frustration leads to a kind of regression in the level of need at which the individual operates. This proposition helps to account for the negative research findings on the Maslow model of prepotency to be reported later (Alderfer, 1969; Hall and Nougaim, 1968). What is the status of such hierarchical models? We shall mention a number of the most relevant studies and then attempt to draw a conclusion. Porter's (1964) study of 2000 members of the American Management Association (A.M.A.) is perhaps the best known. He administered a thirteen-item questionnaire based on a modified version of Maslow's hierarchy aimed at ascertaining the importance of each need, how much it was met and how much it should be met. The study showed that higher-level managers placed more importance than lower-level managers on self-actualisation and autonomy needs. This one might expect if one assumed that in proceeding up the hierarchy of the organisation they had proceeded up their hierarchy of needs. If that were the case the study could be regarded as supportive of Maslow. Unfortunately, the Porter studies (1961; 1964; Porter and Mitchell, 1967) show no other differences in the extent to which different levels of management emphasise the other levels of need in the model.

Directly negative evidence for Maslow's notion of prepotency comes from the studies of Alderfer (1969) and Hall and Nougaim (1968). Alderfer correlated the extent of satisfaction with lower-level needs with the purported importance of the next higher-level need for a sample of managers. He found that the relations were in the opposite direction to that predicted by Maslow. Thus satisfaction of a need level seemed to be associated with its own importance rather than the importance of the next higher-level need. Hall and

Nougaim's study confirms these findings. Clearly, as everyone, including Maslow, knew, the prepotency notion needs modification. For further discussion of Maslow, and particularly self-actualistion, see Chapter 15.

A mention should be made, while we are reviewing Maslow-type models, of some work which has been done on the question of classification of motives. Questionnaires have been constructed on the basis of Maslow's classification in order to discover whether the various component motives of each level (e.g. hunger, thirst, thermo-regulation, etc. for the bottom level) do in fact cluster together in terms of their importance or level of satisfaction. Factor analysis (a technique designed to identify such clusters – see Chapter 10) has yielded no evidence in favour of Maslow's classification. However, Alderfer (1972) has used the same technique and has found support for his ERG classification.

Whatever the current state of content theories in general, Maslow's theory has been very influential in industrial and organisational psychology, probably more than it should have been, for it rests on very little evidence. One problem with it is that it suggests that at any one point in time one motive should be all important. Vroom's incentive theory, on the other hand, through the concept of instrumentality, allows for the simultaneous action and fulfilment of different motives through a summation procedure. In addition, as Maslow himself suggests, it seems probable that different people and different cultures have different orders of priority, in which case the Maslow hierarchy becomes over-flexible in the sense that it ceases to generate testable predictions. None the less its influence has been undoubted and as a common-sense approach to motivation it remains appealing.

The second aspect of the organisation of motives concerns the relationship between different types of categories of motive and specific objects which have motivational properties – we might almost say between drive and incentive.

Cattell (1965) gives an answer to this problem through his dynamic lattice (see Figure 6.3). He proposes that each attitude (i.e. interest of a certain intensity in some course of action with respect to some object), 'subsidiates' to another attitude, which in turn 'subsidiates' to another, etc. That is to say, we do *A* in order to do *B* in order to gain the satisfaction of *C*, etc. The various attitudes in the dynamic lattice 'subsidiate' in the last resort to basic 'instinctive' goals, which Cattell calls 'ergs'. Cattell suggests that by factor analytic techniques (see Chapter 10) it is possible to delineate meaningful clusters of attitudes which make up sentiments. He defines these as major acquired dynamic trait structures which cause their possessors to pay attention to certain objects or classes of object, and to feel and react in a certain way with regard to them. They tend to be organised around important cultural objects such as social institutions or people, and toward which elaborate constellations of attitudes accrue during a person's life experience. Cattell cites evidence, mostly based on young adult and predominantly male populations, for the following sentiments: career or profession, sports and games, mechanical interests, religion, parents, spouse or sweetheart, and the self.

A similar paradigm is compatible with an incentive view of motivation, as illustrated in Figure 6.4. It seems likely that particular classes of outcomes

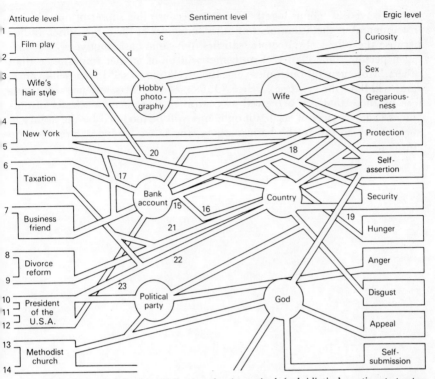

Figure 6.3 Fragment of a dynamic lattice, showing attitude 'subsidiation', sentiment structure and ergic goals (Cattell and Child, 1975)

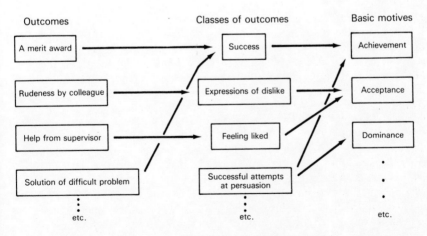

Figure 6.4 Relationship between incentives (outcomes) and basic motives

are perceived as 'going together', either because this subset of outcomes is instrumental in the attainment of other outcomes of the same subset and/or because the subset of outcomes 'satisfies' the same basic motive(s). For any given person, some classes of outcomes will be of greater importance than others. More general outcomes (e.g. those relating to self-image/self-evaluation) will have the greatest valence. Outcomes of greatest valence will therefore be those that are perceived as central to these general classes of outcomes. The valences of classes of outcomes will be modified by the ability of such classes to satisfy the basic motives, the latter having a large genetic component.

7

Motivation and Work

7.1 Introduction

In the last chapter we discussed a number of theories of motivation. These may be divided (following Campbell et al., 1970), broadly speaking into content theories (relating to *what* the motivation is about: food, sex, money, etc.) and process theories (relating to *how* the motivation is aroused, maintained, satisfied, etc.). In view of the multiplicity of content theories, the inconclusiveness of research aimed at establishing a satisfactory classification system (or taxonomy) and the consequent complexity of the task of relating particular motives to work criteria, industrial psychologists have, at least since 1960, preferred to make use of process theories in their thinking and research. Consequently in this chapter we shall place more emphasis on these (Sections 7.2 and 7.3). Since some of the work on content theories has been discussed in the previous chapter (Sections 6.6 and 6.7), we shall not dwell on them at length here except to consider (in Section 7.4) the potential usefulness of this kind of theory for the work situation in view of some of the limitations of process theories.

This is followed by a discussion (Section 7.5) of the influence of certain specific factors in the work situation which have been found to exert motivational influence. Clearly manipulation of these is one way in which managers can influence the motivation of workers. Certain variables which form the subject-matter of other chapters (e.g. work groups (Chapter 13), leadership and supervision (Chapter 14), and organisational structure and climate (Chapter 15)) are omitted here. The final section of the chapter (Section 7.6) is devoted to a discussion of some of the techniques which have been used to measure motivation at work.

As in the previous chapter, the words 'theory' and 'model' will be used more or less interchangeably. Furthermore, they are both used in a manner which the students of philosophy of science would be likely to characterise as slipshod. However, such is the nature of this field.

7.2 Process theories

The theories we shall be discussing here all fall into the category which Campbell and Pritchard (1976) refer to as V.I.E. (valence, instrumentality, expectancy). The prototype of these is Vroom's model (1964). As we saw in Chapter 6, its basic components are valence and expectancy expressed in the equation:

$$\text{force of motivation } (F) = \text{expectancy of desired } \times \text{ valence of desired}$$
$$\text{outcome } (E) \qquad\qquad \text{outcome } (V).$$

Valence, the reader will recall, refers to the extent to which an outcome (e.g. pay, food, praise, etc.) is attractive and likely to produce satisfaction. The instrumentality of an outcome refers to the extent to which the outcome above can be instrumental in obtaining another desired outcome (e.g. a three-piece suite, a full stomach, an increase in self-esteem). In general, later V.I.E. models are elaborations on Vroom's basic theme, incorporating other relevant variables in order to increase the sophistication of the model. Such models have been produced by Porter and Lawler (1968), Graen (1969), Campbell *et al.* (1970) and Cummings and Schwab (1973). The common elements are summarised in Figure 7.1 in a composite scheme presented by Campbell and Pritchard (1976).

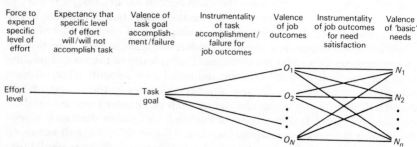

For purposes of simplicity this schema portrays only one level of effort and one level of success on one task goal. A similar set of relationships exists for alternative levels of effort and alternative tasks or alternative levels of success.

Figure 7.1   Composite expectancy–valence model (Campbell and Pritchard, 1976)

The dependent variable to be explained is the individual's effort towards the required work performance. The remaining variables interact to produce the level of effort. The nature of this interaction has been the subject of a great deal of research, some of which we shall be reviewing later. For the time being it is important to note that the model as it stands in Figure 7.1 is by no means complete, that a large number of additions have been made to it by the authors mentioned above, and that a large number of further additions will turn out to be necessary. We shall elaborate on some of these additions, but it is perhaps ironic that one of the reasons for adopting the V.I.E. model originally was that content approaches to human motivation had become too cumbersome and complex. We shall be discussing this point later.

Clearly there are a number of factors which are missing from the model as illustrated. One of these is the fact that effort is not the only determinant of performance. Lawler and Porter (1967) have included in their model two modifications which help to overcome this difficulty. On the left of Figure

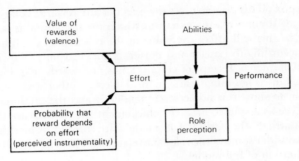

Figure 7.2   Lawler and Porter's (1967) model

7.2. is the basic V.I.E. model (with the difference that perceived instrumentality rather than expectancy is included); on the right, moderating the influence of effort in determining performance, the notions of ability and role perception.

Ability is defined as the individual's currently developed power to perform, and refers to such characteristics as intelligence, manual skills and personality traits. Role perception refers to the kinds of activities and behaviour the individual feels he should engage in to perform his job successfully, and determines the direction in which effort is applied. Role perceptions, like effort, are a particular type of attitude, and both are crucial antecedent attitudes for effective performance, or else the effort might be misdirected involving perhaps energetic but organisationally ineffective performance. Graen (1969) uses a similar concept to role perception when he speaks of the role expectations of persons in power and the multiplicity of roles involved at work. However, he concentrates on the roles of the standard performer and the effective performer.

Another dimension which has been specified by some writers (Campbell *et al.*, 1970; Graen, 1969; Cummings and Schwab, 1973) is that distinguishing between the internal (personal) goals of performance and the external (organisational) goals. Roughly speaking, this is equivalent to a distinction between pleasing others and pleasing oneself in task performance. Clearly the two can coincide; but to the extent that they do not they can be expected to produce different kinds of performance.

Possible modifications to the basic model are practically infinite and to describe them all is beyond the scope of this book. However, we shall mention one basic kind of modification which seems to add a dynamic and on-going aspect to the model which has not so far been apparent. This is the introduction of feedback loops which modify the basic components as a result of the individual's experience over time. Porter and Lawler (1968) show a feedback loop from the 'Performance' box to the 'Probability that reward depends on effort' box in Figure 7.2. They suggest that this perceived probability will alter as a consequence of the individual's experience of the rewards of performance. If these are satisfactory, the probability is maintained at a high level; if not, the probability will be reduced with a consequent deterioration in performance. Another feedback loop goes from the 'performance box' to the 'value of rewards box'. This also involves the effect of any rewards consequent upon performance. It concerns the extent to which the individual is satisfied with the rewards. This will affect the value of the rewards in the future. How it does this, according to Lawler and Porter, is not clear, for, following our discussion in Chapter 6, receipt of certain kinds of rewards (e.g. food) reduces their value. One is not hungry after a meal. Certain others (e.g. achievement) do not seem to show this homeostatic tendency and the attainment of these seems to serve as a spur to greater achievement (i.e. to increase their value).

Having outlined the basic V.I.E. model with some of its modifications, we shall now consider some of the relevant research findings. This will be followed by an evaluation of the model.

7.3   Research into process theory

In general, research into the V.I.E. model has involved investigation both of the relationship between pairs of individual components and of the whole model. The purpose of this section is to describe some representative evidence so that the reader will understand the basis of our conclusions as to the current status of the V.I.E. model. For the sake of easy classification we shall divide our review into four parts: research into valence, research into instrumentality, research into expectancy, and research into the composite V.I.E. model.

Valence

Unfortunately research into the effects of valence on effort and performance has been bedevilled by the fact that measurement of valence is extremely difficult. The reason for this has to do with the difficulty (some would say impossibility) of devising a measure for comparing the attractiveness of, say, a pound in one's pocket with a reduction in working hours, or a complimentary word from a supervisor with the personal satisfaction of a job well done. Even if they can be compared one with another in terms of preference the problem of finding a single scale for measuring all possible incentives in terms of attractiveness (valence) has thus far not been solved.

This said, the perceptive reader will be anticipating no very definite conclusion from the research we are about to review. He will be right. However, there are some positive studies. Pritchard and Sanders (1973) found a correlation (see Chapter 10) of 0.54 between the ratings of the valence of job outcome of 148 employees in an American government agency and their ratings of the effort they put into their work. However, the correlation between valence of outcomes and supervisors' ratings of effort was only 0.21. On the negative side is the finding of a correlation of only 0.16 between valence of outcomes and performance found by Hackman and Porter (1968) in a study of telephone operators. Another negative finding is the median correlation of only 0.05 between rated importance of pay and job performance in a simulated work situation (Jorgenson, Dunnette and Pritchard, 1973). Apart from the difficulties of measurement mentioned above, it is clear that the investigators did not include measures of all the possible intrinsic and extrinsic outcomes that might have been involved. Consequently, the correlations found are as likely to have been an underestimate as an overestimate of the kind of general relationships between valence and behaviour. It seems highly likely *a priori* that valence and behaviour are related, but at this stage methodological difficulties preclude any conclusion as to 'whether' and 'how'.

Instrumentality

In general, the research into the relationship between instrumentality (the likelihood that performance is followed by a desired outcome) and performance is more conclusive. Georgopoulos, Mahoney and Jones (1957), in a study of 621 production employees in a household-appliance factory, found that subjects who experienced high instrumentalities via the incentive system tended to produce more than those reporting low instrumentality. Lawler and Porter (1967), in a study of 154 managers, found low positive relationships between their perceptions of the instrumentality of their performance and ratings of their effort and performance by supervisors, peers and themselves. In general, the self-ratings and the ratings for effort showed the highest correlations with perceived instrumentality. These correlations were increased if the perceived instrumentality ratings were combined multiplicatively with a measure of the relative importance of the reward (valence). A number of other field studies (e.g. Porter and Lawler, 1968; Gavin, 1970; Wofford, 1971) and experimental studies (Jorgenson, Dunnette and Pritchard, 1973; Pritchard and DeLeo, 1973; Graen, 1969) have tended to support the general findings of a relationship between instrumentality and performance. However, we must also report Dachler and Mobley's (1973) finding of very low correlations indeed.

Expectancy

Two experimental studies by Arvey (1972) and Motowidlo, Loehr and Dunnette (1972) generally support the prediction that the greater the perceived relationship between effort and performance (the expectancy that effort will lead to successful performance), the better performance on a laboratory task was likely to be. In these studies subjects told that they performed well tended then to perform better on the next trial than those told that they had performed poorly. Field studies testing the hypothesis are somewhat scarce, the chief one being the virtually non-existent relationship found by Pritchard and Sanders (1973) in the study referred to earlier.

On the other hand, measures of perceived instrumentality (Lawler and Porter, 1967 (see Figure 7.2); Porter and Lawler, 1968; Hackman and Porter, 1968), which is a combined measure of effort–performance expectancy and performance–outcome instrumentality, do correlate with measures of performance. However, in view of the nature of this measure it is impossible to assess the contribution of effort–performance expectancy.

While it is fair to say that the results of field studies of expectancy and performance are disappointing, the results of experimental studies and the possibility of improvements in methodology keep this part of the V.I.E. model very much alive.

The Composite V.I.E. Model

We have seen that correlations between the individual basic components of the model and work performance, though they have ranged from zero to about 0.5, have in general been unspectacular. What happens if they are combined as the model as a whole would require? We have already seen (Lawler and Porter, 1967; Hackman and Porter, 1968) how combining pairs of components increased the size of correlations with work performance. We shall now examine two studies in which all these basic components of the model were combined and related to effort and performance.

Dachler and Mobley (1973) tested the model on semi-skilled workers on two manufacturing sites, one of which paid its employees by the hour, the other using an incentive scheme. They attempted to overcome the difficulty of specifying precisely what an outcome is by identifying by means of interviews and questionnaires forty-five relevant outcomes. The reader is referred to Dachler and Mobley for a precise description of how valence, instrumentality and expectancy were measured, but, in essence, workers were asked to specify the amount of effort required for given levels of performance (expectancy), the level of performance required for different levels of outcome (instrumentality) and the desirability of the outcomes (valence). Dachler and Mobley found that if they multiplied the three V.I.E. components together they obtained a composite measure which correlated 0.3 with work performance, but only on the site using the incentive scheme. Presumably this can be accounted for by the direct correlation between pay outcomes and performance level. The most important of the three variables was expectancy, and this accounted for a large part of the predictive power of the model. Lawler and Suttle (1973), in a study of sixty-nine retail managers, also obtained measures for the V.I.E. model. Combining these, they obtained correlations of 0.39 with self-ratings of effort, 0.27 with superiors' ratings of effort, and 0.15 with peer ratings of effort. This is very much in line with the Dachler and Mobley study, as are a number of other less sophisticated studies (e.g. Mitchell and Albright, 1972; Mitchell and Nebeker, 1973; Pritchard and Sanders, 1973).

THE STATUS OF PROCESS THEORY

The reader will be able to conclude from the above review that the V.I.E. model is only partially successful in relating the various aspects of motivation to performance. This applies both to the full model and to its components. We have pointed to difficulties in methodology which make it difficult to measure its component variables and consequently to test the model properly. It is therefore possible that the solution of the methodological problems could lead to a more definite confirmation of the model. As yet, however, the verdict must remain 'not proven'. Certainly the framework has been, and seems likely to remain, the most powerful generator of research in the field for some time to come. However, it is paradoxical to note that Vroom's simple model $(F = E \times V)$, which was preferred to content theories such as those of Maslow on the grounds (amongst others) that it by-passed the problem of classifying the mass of possible motives at work, has sprouted offspring which have generated a very similar complexity. Witness Dachler and Mobley's (1973) identification of forty-five outcomes of performance and the consequent forty-five valences and the abundance of possible variations on the model itself. There seems no way of avoiding the complexity of human motivation. As in the field of learning the days of the great comprehensive theory seem at an end. The future seems to point towards deeper study of smaller areas of motivation.

7.4 Content theory

We are including a section on content theories of motivation here because logically there ought to be one. However, we have already discussed these in Chapter 6 in the context of motivation in general. Also, as stated earlier this kind of theory has not turned out to be particularly fruitful in generating empirical research in the world of work. The chief reason for this has been the lack of empirical testability that has characterised a lot of the theorising. This applies as much to Maslow's hierarchy of five needs (reviewed in the previous chapter) as to Murray's earlier (1938) motivational theory incorporating as many as twenty needs. Both theories are based on the clinical experience of the author and can only be described as subjective in the sense that another author might have chosen as different a set of needs as they did from each other. None the less such descriptions of human motivation have an appeal which derives from the dynamic which they are discussing. In the way that process theories are just that, namely a description of a process devoid of any reference to the content, so content theories are about the dynamic of motivational forces. They are, as it were, about the fuel which energises people into action. Ideas such as sex, aggression, affiliation, achievement and power carry more spontaneous interest than valence, instrumentality, expectancy and outcome. Hence the charm and endurance of content theories. In the last chapter we looked at the work of McClelland and Maslow. In the next we shall review that of Herzberg. The research evidence is presented in three chapters. Consequently this section will confine itself to a few comments on the current situation.

In the 1960s the development of V.I.E. theory and the realisation that Herzberg's work was far from being the hoped-for end of the road seemed to have sounded the death-knell of content theory. However, encouragement has in fact come from an unlikely source – the field of empirical research. Essentially this encouragement is of two kinds. First, there was the identification of the necessity in testing V.I.E. theories of specifying the nature of outcomes (see previous section). If it is reasonable to postulate a large number of possible desired outcomes, it must also be reasonable to postulate a large number of desires (or motives) to match these outcomes. Indeed, if there is one conclusion to be drawn from the V.I.E. research it must be that the attempt to escape from the problem of the complexity of human motivation has only led us back to the same difficulty in another form. The present authors feel that this issue has to be confronted by accepting that human motivation has both content and process and that research into the former is inevitable. What researchers will have to bear in mind is that the evidence for a theory of motivational content bears a necessarily different relationship to the theory than that for process theory. The problems are discussed at greater length in the section on Freud in Chapter 9 on personality. Suffice it to say that in the context of work and motivation it is certainly arguable that empirical verification of V.I.E. models has turned out to be as difficult a matter as that of Freudian theory. Certainly the general level of statistical support is not a lot better.

Whereas the academic is entitled to sit on the fence until the case is proven, the manager or management consultant must opt for one kind of view rather than another. In our opinion, provided he has thought the matter through (and it is hoped that this book will help a little in this direction), it is still legitimate to opt for any one or more of the motivational theories put forward here and elsewhere in this book. However, this statement should be taken to exclude some of the more simplistic assumptions (e.g. 'rational economic' man) mentioned in Chapter 15.

Having examined theories of motivation and work, we turn now to an examination of those factors at work which appear to be of particular motivational significance: job design, payment, promotional opportunities and working conditions.

7.5　Motivational factors in the work situation

We shall omit here obviously relevant topics such as leadership and supervision, work groups and organisational structure since these are material for chapters on their own in the final part of the book.

In this section a major difficulty will be to distinguish between motivational influences and other determinants of performance. Most of the evidence we shall consider concerns the relationship between the above-mentioned variables and job performance, but, however, we do not know what other variables are involved. A second difficulty in interpreting the evidence is that many studies show apparently contradictory results, because other variables mediate their effects on motivation. For example, the nature of the work done affects styles of supervision, which in turn have motivational consequences.

JOB DESIGN

In terms of expectancy theory, Lawler (1969) suggests that changes in job design are likely to affect motivation because they have the power to influence the perceived probability that rewards will result from good performance, i.e. they affect the instrumentality of good performance (Vroom, 1964). In particular, Lawler argues that changing job content by making the job more challenging, by job rotation, or job enlargement (giving the worker more tasks), or job enrichment (giving him more challenging tasks), will increase the perceived probability of intrinsic rewards (e.g. feelings of accomplishment, achievement, developing skills) following from good performance. These outcomes are perceived as leading to the satisfaction of the higher-order needs in Maslow's hierarchy (i.e. self-esteem and self-actualisation).

He further suggests that jobs must possess three characteristics to satisfy the higher-order needs: (i) a person must receive meaningful feedback about his performance; (ii) the job must be perceived as requiring valued abilities; and (iii) the person must have a high degree of self-control over goal-setting and the paths to these goals.

Clearly, making a job more challenging will only be more motivating to the extent that people possess higher-order needs. Doubtless individual differences in motivation explain some of the variation in effectiveness of job-change programmes.

Job-change programmes may also vary in effectiveness for other reasons. (i) a simple job may allow scope for social interaction which may have higher reward value than the increased intrinsic motivation of a more complex job not allowing these contacts; (ii) people may not perceive themselves as being capable of coping with a new job (fear of failure) and hence may resist it; and (iii) people may see a more complex job as demanding more of them, and equity theory would predict that in this case they would expect higher outcomes – if increased intrinsic motivation was not great enough to satisfy this effect, then they may well seek more pay or holidays or a shorter working week.

We should finally note once again that we have only referred to the motivational consequences of job changes. However, job changes often also result in greater job clarity, more efficient work methods and fewer training needs – which also contribute to the over-all effect of such programmes.

PAYMENT

It is a commonly held belief that money is one of the most positively valent work outcomes for most people. Graham and Sluckin (1954) found pay the most important job factor in a survey of skilled and semi-skilled workers in England, and Wilkins (1949, 1950) found that 18- and 19-year-old men at a British Army Reception Centre ranked pay second to 'friendly work-mates'. Generally these measures have been of a self-report kind, and, as Opsahl and Dunnette (1966) state, 'it is easy to find people in industry who behave as though they value money highly'. They suggest a number of reasons for its high value: (i) it acts as a conditioned generalised reinforcer; (ii) it acts as a conditioned incentive; and (iii) it is an instrument for gaining a large variety of derived outcomes, for example sexual rewards, status rewards, physical rewards such as good food, freedom to do as one wishes, etc.

Support for V.I.E. theory comes from studies which show that people told that their earnings are contingent on effectiveness have higher performance levels (e.g. Kaufman, 1962; Dachler and Mobley, 1973). On this basis, we should expect incentive schemes to lead to higher performance. However, this is not always the case.

(1) People and situations vary and sometimes monetary incentives do not serve to motivate more work. One has to ask what money means to the individual. Only if he places a reasonable value on it will it serve to motivate him further. Reasons for not valuing money may range from a low need for what it can provide (e.g. the hermit) to an excess of it (e.g. football pools winners or people with other sources of income).

(2) Not infrequently incentive schemes may lead to restriction of output. Often through mistrust they are perceived as giving rise to negative consequences such as redundancies, changes in payment rate or disruption of good relations with work-mates. Such fears may lead to group pressures to restrict output. Poor worker–management relations are not a good soil for incentive schemes to flourish.

(3) A further reason why incentive plans may be less than successful is that workers often do not perceive the relation between pay and productivity in group incentive schemes. In V.I.E. terms, the probability of good performance leading to the first-level outcome (pay) is too low to be highly motivating. A number of studies also suggest that incentive plans are less effective for repetitive, destructive, boring and disliked tasks.

A theory which has been developed with particular reference to pay in the work situation is *equity theory* (Adams, 1963). It can, however, be broadened to encompass a variety of job behaviours and outcomes. The basic model is presented in Figure 7.3. It proposes that a person compares himself with

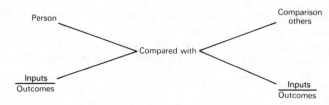

Figure 7.3   Adams's equity theory

other people ('comparison others') by comparing his ratio of job inputs (e.g. effort, ability, etc.) to job outcomes (e.g. pay, recognition, etc.) with the same ratio for the comparison person. If the two ratios are unequal, the person is motivated to reduce the discrepancy. Inputs include anything a person perceives as an investment in the job and worthy of some return. Outcomes are returns from the situation. The elements in the input–outcome ratios are weighted by their importance. In order to reduce any discrepancy 'tension' a person may change his perceptions of inputs or outcomes, leave the situation, attempt to change the inputs and outcomes of the comparison person, change his own input and outcomes or change the comparison person. The method chosen will depend on its worth to the individual (e.g. he will change a perception of a comparison person's ratio rather than his own).

The main implication of the theory is that a person who feels that his inputs are too high relative to outcomes should try to reduce his inputs (e.g. by reducing effort, time spent at work) and/or increase his outcomes (e.g. pay, promotion). Conversely, when a person perceives his inputs as being relatively low, he should try either to increase his inputs or decrease his outputs. There is some supportive evidence for these deductions, though the effect seems to be stronger when inputs are perceived as too low rather than too great, at least with respect to pay. Andrews (1967), Lawler (1968) and Pritchard, Dunnette and Jorgenson (1972) have all found that perceiving oneself as being underpaid had a greater behavioural effect than a perception of being overpaid! Possible reasons for this asymmetry are discussed by Campbell and Pritchard (1976), who conclude that people are less likely to feel inequity when an organisation is losing out (in the case of overpayment) rather than an individual (in the case of underpayment). One important problem with the theory is that the arousal of inequity can only be inferred from the situation and/or experimental manipulations. It cannot be measured directly. Therefore, we are faced with the problems of (i) knowing whether inequity has actually been aroused in a particular individual, and if it has, of (ii) knowing all the ways in which it can be reduced so that we can observe and monitor any changes in behaviour.

A further problem concerns a person's choice of 'comparison other'. We mentioned earlier that a change in comparison other is one of the possible results of inequity, as it involves 'less personal cost' than a change in one's own behaviour or attitudes. The theory as it stands, however, makes no predictions about choice of a comparison other. An illustration of this kind of problem was experienced a few years ago by the authors, who received a salary increase which put them ahead of their university colleagues. One of the authors experienced some feelings of dissonance or inequity for a short while until he stopped comparing his salary with them and thought about equally high incomes obtained by other groups which he felt resulted from lower inputs. Perhaps one implication of this aspect of equity theory is that if we wish to change people's attitudes to work, then we might do this more easily by giving them information about potential comparison others, rather than trying to change directly their attitudes concerning their own inputs and outputs. This, of course, would require some knowledge about their comparison other (i.e. groups or people with whom they identify or sympathise). (For a fuller discussion of this point, see Chapter 8.)

The previous suggestion would be compatible with the idea that consistency with respect to self-image is particularly important (i.e. that people react in a manner which is consistent with their cognitions about themselves). We suggested earlier that the method of low equity reduction chosen will be that which minimises the psychological 'cost'. By this we mean that cognitions which are more clearly related to the self-image, and which are particularly related to the most important aspects of the self-image (i.e. self-worth), will be the most difficult to change, and that changing them will involve the greatest cost to the individual in that he will experience great uneasiness or anxiety when his ideas about his identity or self-worth are threatened. This theory of course presupposes a motive to strive towards a consistent view of the world, and in particular of the self. Thus a person with a poor view of his worth or abilities (i.e. low in self-esteem) should put himself in situations likely to produce failure (i.e. by choosing impossible tasks) or not try very hard so that he fails and hence maintains a consistent view of himself. Conversely, a person with a high valuation of his worth and abilities will be most motivated to succeed in various tasks to enable this image to be preserved. In the previous chapter we looked at two studies which support these predictions (Korman 1967, 1968).

Adams' theory is probably the most rigorous and best-researched equity theory. Empirical evidence has generally supported it, with some reservations. Adams (1965) has tried to improve the theory by making several propositions about the choice of method of inequity reduction: (i) a person will maximise positively valent outcomes and the valence of outcomes; (ii) he will minimise increasing inputs which require effort and which are difficult to change; (iii) he will resist real and cognitive changes in inputs that are central to his self-concept and self-esteem (as we argued earlier); (iv) he will be more resistant to changing cognitions about his own outcomes and inputs than about another's outcomes and inputs; and (v) leaving the field (escaping from the situation) will be resorted to only when the magnitude of the inequity is high and other means of relieving it are unavailable.

Weick (1966) has pointed out that, like dissonance theory (see Chapter 8), it should allow for such possibilities as denial, differentiation, toleration of the discrepancy, alteration of the object of judgement, bolstering and task enhancement.

Finally, we should note that, as Vroom (1964) has pointed out, the theory implies that a person's satisfaction with pay (and possibly, therefore, his motivation to change jobs and other motivations) is a function of a number of factors. These include: (i) his belief concerning the degree to which he possesses various characteristics; (ii) his conclusions concerning the degree to which these characteristics should result in the attainment of rewarding outcomes from his job; (iii) his beliefs concerning the degree to which he receives these rewarding outcomes from his job; (iv) his beliefs concerning the degree to which others possess these characteristics; (v) his beliefs concerning the degree to which others receive rewarding outcomes from their jobs; and (vi) the extent to which he compares himself with these others.

Most of these factors have been shown to be related to satisfaction with pay. Perhaps of particular interest relating to (v) is that Lawler (1967) found that secret pay policies appeared to contribute to dissatisfaction with pay. Specifically he found that managers tended to overestimate the pay of subordinates and peers, and underestimate that of their superiors, and saw their own group as being paid too little by comparison with all three groups.

PROMOTION OPPORTUNITIES

Expectancy theory would predict that promotional opportunity would lead to high-performance motivation in so far as promotion is perceived as being contingent upon good performance. This is most likely to be the case when promotions are based on some kind of evaluation system, and that system is seen as being both fair and accurate. We might therefore expect that appraisal systems would increase high-performance motivation if promotion is perceived as being related to appraisal, this latter being perceived as fair and accurate, assuming that the person desires promotion. There is evidence that managers and executives have a particularly strong desire to move upwards in the organisation. Evidence supporting the above line of reasoning comes from a study by Georgopoulos, Mahoney and Jones (1957), who found a higher proportion of 'high producers' among workers who reported on a questionnaire that low productivity would hurt their chances of promotion than in those who did not. This was only the case for those workers who reported that promotion was important to them and who were free to set their own pace of work.

Although we know of no evidence, we should also expect opportunities of job transfer and training opportunities to function in a similar way to promotional opportunities. They should motivate people to higher performance in so far as they see transfer and training opportunities to be contingent on performance and transfer or training as bearing positive valence through their instrumentality to other outcomes, e.g. promotion and the satisfaction of higher-order needs.

WORKING CONDITIONS

We have already discussed social and financial working conditions. In this section we shall discuss the physical environment. One of the earliest sets of studies to investigate systematically the effects of the physical environment were the 'Hawthorne' studies (Roethlisberger and Dixon, 1939). Perhaps the most striking finding was how small were these effects on motivation compared with social factors.

Maslow's need hierarchy would suggest that physical conditions should be of great importance when physical danger is threatened and that people should be reluctant to do dangerous jobs, particularly when their basic needs can be satisfied without taking such a job.

Herzberg *et al.* (1957) have postulated the existence of the classes of work motivation: extrinsic and intrinsic. The extrinsic factors refer to working conditions in their widest sense: pay, supervision, company administration and policy, job security and physical surroundings. Herzberg *et al.* suggest that such extrinsic factors are only able to prevent the onset of job dissatisfaction or to remove it once it is there. They cannot affect job satisfaction which is determined solely by intrinsic factors (achievement, recognition, advancement, responsibility) and job-content factors. Herzberg (1966) further suggests that workers will be motivated to work harder only by intrinsic factors, and the extrinsic factors, including physical working conditions, will motivate people only to stay at or leave the job. A considerable body of experimental evidence does not support the satisfaction–dissatisfaction dichotomy, and the motivational implications are not borne out in a study by Schwab, DeVitt and Cummings (1971). They found that extrinsic factors were as instrumental in motivating high performance as were intrinsic factors. However, we might expect from earlier discussions that there will be considerable individual differences in terms of the relative importance of intrinsic and extrinsic factors. Those people with high needs for achievement, self-esteem and self-actualisation are likely to be relatively more affected by intrinsic factors.

Having looked at some specific aspects of the work situation of particular motivational significance, we now turn to a more general problem, that of the measurement of motivation.

7.6   The measurement of motivation

Much of our discussion of motivation has been from the viewpoint of expectancy theories. For these theories the variables of relevance to motivation are expectancy and valence. We shall therefore consider these first before going on to examine ways of measuring valences of clusters of outcomes in the form of needs, interests, attitudes and values, sentiments and ergs.

EXPECTANCY

The most usual way of measuring this is to obtain verbal reports of probabilities. Studies have often shown such reports to be meaningfully related to a number of variables. However, verbal-report methods of measuring expectancies, valences or other motivational characteristics are liable to errors: (i) people may be unaware of what their motives are or of their strength (unconscious motivation); (ii) people may find it difficult to compare the strength of their motives with those of others; and (iii) people may wish to conceal their motives.

An alternative way of assessing expectancies is to infer them from actual decisions or choices made by the person. The problem with this method is to disentangle the roles of expectancies and preferences in decisions. Of course, there is no reason why both methods of measurement should not be taken and some kind of estimate based on the two.

VALENCE

Since valence is a hypothetical construct it can only be measured indirectly. Consequently, a number of possible ways of estimating it are available. Each has its advantages and disadvantages:

(i) Verbal reports and questionnaires are often used. These have the advantage of being relatively quick and straightforward to obtain, but are open to possible deception, conscious or unconscious.

(ii) The attractiveness of outcomes may be inferred from the analysis of fantasy. This will be discussed in the next section under 'projective tests'.

(iii) If an outcome strengthens (reinforces) a response tendency, it can be assumed to be positively valent. If it weakens a response tendency, it is likely to be negatively valent. Valence is measured by the amount or rate of change in response probability. Such a measure would not be a very good indicator of the strength of valence. It is also difficult to set up situations to measure such behaviour satisfactorily.

(iv) Inferences may be made from the choices made between alternative courses of action. Again, it is likely that such inferences must be made informally, since systematic observation under controlled conditions is rarely possible.

(v) Observing consummatory behaviour is possible when this takes place, e.g. eating and drinking. Clearly, other kinds of outcome are less amenable to this kind of observation.

(vi) Decision time is a behavioural indication of differences in valence of outcomes. The length of time elapsing before a person chooses between alternatives could be assumed to reflect the extent to which the outcomes differ in valence.

It is apparent that the various methods of estimating valence are just that – estimates. The relatively disappointing research into V.I.E. models may be a reflection of this difficulty.

NEEDS OR MOTIVES

Motives or needs, i.e. the content of motivation, have generally been measured in three ways, by depth interview, by projective tests and by multiple-choice paper-and-pencil tests. We shall consider each of these in turn.

(1) The depth interview has been used primarily in the clinical situation and is based on psychoanalytic principles (Chapter 10). It tries to uncover the fundamental motivations (often assumed unconscious) of individuals. In the clinical situation a very large number of sessions may be required to elicit these motives, and methods such as free association and the interpretation of dreams may be used.

(2) Projective tests also stem from psychoanalytic origins. The subject is required to respond to an emotionally neutral stimulus such as a drawing or an ink blot. Since the stimulus is relatively neutral, any emotional or motivational content in the response is likely to derive from the subject. Thus a hungry person may see the characters '4OOD' as 'FOOD'. Similar interpretations can be responsible for content relevant to sex, aggression, power or achievement motivation in the response. The responses required may be interpretations of ink blots (as in the Rorschach Test), construction of stories (as in the Thematic Apperception Test (T.A.T.) used to measure the need for achievement), completion of sentences or stories, arranging or choosing among pictures or verbal alternatives and expression through drawing or play. These tests have often been found to be very much affected by methods of administration, the tester's personality and the subject's moods and attitudes. Their reliability (i.e. consistency of measurement) and validity (extent to which a test measures what it is supposed to be measuring) have often been very low. Exceptions have been the T.A.T. measure of achievement motivation and certain uses of the Rorschach Test where a complex scoring system requiring trained scorers has often had good reliability and moderate validity. These tests have some use as exploratory instruments in a clinical setting, but with the possible exception of the T.A.T., have not justified their use in the work setting.

(3) There have been very few paper-and-pencil tests (questionnaires) designed to measure basic needs or motives. One, which is still in the experimental stage but which is based on some research evidence, is Cattell's motivational analysis test. This purports to measure a number of basic needs (ergs) and sentiments, as mentioned in the last chapter. It is too early to say whether this will be of any value in the work setting, but the evidence so far has indicated that the measurement of such needs has little direct relationship with job performance.

INTERESTS

Interest inventories have been the measure of motivation most widely used in the work situation for assessment purposes. Usually they require a person to indicate the relative strength of his preferences for various activities and hobbies. This is done by presenting groups of activities and asking the person which he likes most or least, or by asking him to indicate for each of a number of statements the extent to which he likes or dislikes the activity in question. Interest inventories such as the Strong Vocational Interest Blank and the Kuder Preference Record have often showed good reliability and useful predictive validity (i.e. they can to some extent predict later job performance if given at the time of selection for the job). The Kuder Preference Record measures relative strengths of interests in ten areas, such as outdoor, practical-mechanical, scientific, artistic, literary and persuasive.

ATTITUDES, VALUES AND IDEOLOGIES

The next chapter concerns itself with attitudes, but here we will briefly discuss their measurement. We need only note here that clusters of attitudes may be measured in the work situation for various reasons. The questionnaire is the method most used. Perhaps the most widely used measure for research purposes is the Cornell Job Satisfaction Questionnaire. For selection purposes or occupational guidance, the Allport–Vernon–Lindzey Scale of Values has been used to measure six value dimensions, such as economic, religious and political. We have mentioned already Cattell's clusters of attitudes, called 'sentiments', and have suggested that one of these, the self-sentiment, may be of particular importance. Finally, we should note that Eysenck (1954) has designed a questionnaire based on factor analysis, measuring two bi-polar attitude dimensions which he calls ideologies, namely radicalism–conservatism and tough-mindedness–tender-mindedness. The present authors do not know of any studies using this in the work situation.

8
Attitudes and Job Satisfaction

8.1 Introduction

This chapter follows after two chapters concerned with motivation. We have considered the question of whether human motivation is generated primarily by internal needs or drives, or by external incentives and reinforcers. Broadly speaking we concluded that for purposes of studying work motivation it was most convenient at present to adopt some kind of incentive theory, though we anticipated a future resurgence of interest in content theories.

Our purpose in this chapter, however, is not to study the motivation to work but to see how our motives (our needs and drives) influence the generalised way in which we think feel and act in the wider world around us, i.e. how they influence our attitudes to significant aspects of our world.

In Section 8.2 we introduce some of the difficulties of defining the word 'attitude', while at the same time coming down, for the sake of simplicity, in favour of a rough, though more or less acceptable, definition. In Section 8.3 we attempt to draw together some of the main threads in the field of attitude change by presenting two 'consistency' theories and briefly mentioning the contribution of attribution theory (which is more fully presented in Chapter 11). Section 8.4 uses a framework described originally by Hovland and Janis (1959) to dissect the process of interpersonal persuasion (to change an attitude), making reference to a number of empirical studies. In a very elementary way it could be regarded as a kind of psychologist's cook-book for advertisers! Section 8.5 is concerned with the measurement of attitudes. Finally, Section 8.6 introduces one kind of attitude which is particularly relevant to this book, the attitude to work. Job satisfaction has been much studied and we shall present a review of the field together with some of the theories which have been put forward to account for the empirical findings.

8.2 The concept of 'attitude'

Everybody knows what an 'attitude' is. Or do they? Ask a sample of one's friends and they are likely to provide a rich variety of suggestions. We shall not dwell at length on this problem, only long enough to derive something acceptable. Fishbein (1967) notes that a person's attitude towards any object can be seen as a function of his belief about it. Fishbein also emphasised the extent to which a person feels for or against a particular kind of object. Doob (1947) saw an attitude as being a learned predisposition to respond in a particular way to a class of objects.

Combining three aspects, the belief about the object (the cognitive aspect), the feelings experienced (the affective aspect) and the predisposition to do something to or about the object (the conative aspect), the present authors, largely for the sake of simplicity, offer the following definition: 'An attitude is a learned predisposition to think, feel and act in a particular way towards a given object or class of objects.' This has much in common with Asch (1952) and Secord and Backman (1964). The predisposition arises because of its learned ability to satisfy basic motives. The use of the world 'predisposition' is important. The cognitive, affective and conative aspects of an attitude do not all need to coincide – voting behaviour in elections is an example. One may think and feel positively about a political party but not vote for it. Thus La Piere (1934) in an early study found that although many restaurant owners responded negatively to a written enquiry as to whether they would serve Chinese guests, the same restaurant owners raised no problems when the investigator arrived accompanied by two Chinese guests. Presumably the profit motive was too strong. Wicker (1969) has confirmed this kind of finding over a wide range of population samples. The cognitive and affective aspects are only slightly related to overt behaviour. Probably most people suppress the behavioural component of their attitudes. Indeed, Insko and Schopler (1967) argue that conation (behaviour) is conceptually distinct from cognition (belief) and affect (feeling).

There is one area, however, in which attitudes and behaviour are found related. This is in the field of attitude to work. Labour turnover has been found to be negatively related to job satisfaction (Fournet *et al.*, 1966). However, other behaviour is not so consistent in its relation to job satisfaction. Absenteeism seems to be negatively related to it but less consistently so (Vroom, 1964) and job performance is not clearly related at all (Brayfield and Crockett, 1955).

This said, let us now move on to a discussion of some of the empirical and theoretical work in the field. We shall be covering this in the next two sections, one devoted to empirical work and the other to theoretical work. Regrettably these two are not well integrated. Such empirical work as is closely related to the main theoretical formulations has been included in the section on theory, but we have felt it necessary to include also a review of empirical studies which, if not wholly atheoretical, have been designed to test hypotheses other than those contained in the classical theories which we shall be reviewing. Often their purpose has been simply to solve a practical problem in the field of advertising or public relations (e.g. Janis and Feshbach, 1953; Dabbs and Leventhal, 1966).

8.3 Theories of attitude change

The idea of attitudes changing so as to bring about greater consistency, meaning and organisation to the individual's belief is central to two theories of attitude change, balance and dissonance theories, which we shall review here. The earlier of these, balance theory, was first proposed by Heider (1946, 1958) (see also Chapter 11). Its original form of analysis was limited to the attitudes of one person towards himself, one other person and one impersonal entity. Its predictions were not always verified (Zajonc, 1960), probably because it was not concerned with the over-all cognitive structure, though later variations have attempted to come to terms with this. Congruity theory (Osgood and Tannenbaum, 1955) is a special case of balance, and deals specifically with the problem of direction of attitude change and the quantification of the relationships between attitudes. Common to balance and dissonance theories is the idea that human beings find inconsistency difficult to tolerate beyond a certain amount. This inconsistency, depending on the theory, can be an inconsistency between beliefs or an inconsistency between beliefs and actions. The common element, then, is a postulated need for consistency within the individual. Any level of inconsistency above that tolerable to the invidual becomes a stimulus for some kind of adjustment in the individual's behaviour or attitudes. Let us now examine the theories in a little more detail.

BALANCE THEORY

Balance theory derives originally from the pioneering work of Fritz Heider (1958). He suggested that we sense intuitively when a situation in which we find ourselves is unbalanced or uncomfortable cognitively. Thus if I discover that my newly acquired friend who had seemed to react favourably to all my favourite causes and interests suddenly shows an extremely unfavourable attitude to something I hold dear, say, my allegiance to a political party, I am likely to feel uncomfortable, perhaps because of an expectation that an argument will occur when the matter is broached in conversation or when my attendance at a meeting interferes with other, shared activities. Clearly there are individual differences in the ability to tolerate this kind of discomfort. Some people in fact may find this situation pleasurable as Heider (1958) suggests, but there is still a tendency towards imbalance, which for many is uncomfortable and generates what Newcombe (1961) calls 'a strain towards symmetry'. The nature of this is illustrated in Figure 8.1. The diagrams illustrate, on the left, balanced situations, and, on the right, unbalanced situations. Balanced situations are stable whereas unbalanced ones are unstable and under a strain to turn themselves into balanced ones. The means by which this can be achieved is by altering one or more of the bonds which link the three elements in the triangle. Rosenberg (1960) reports that their subjects chose the simplest methods of restoring balance. Thus what they tended to do was to change the sign of the single unbalanced relation – the less alterations the better. This kind of formulation has been incorporated into the theory. Thus, whether the attitude is changed towards the other person or towards the third party is simply a function of the simplicity of the transformation required to return the system to balance.

In the unbalanced situation (see Figures 8.2 and 8.3) I may either change my attitude towards my friend or my attitude towards the political party or alter my perceptions of my friend's attitude towards the political party.

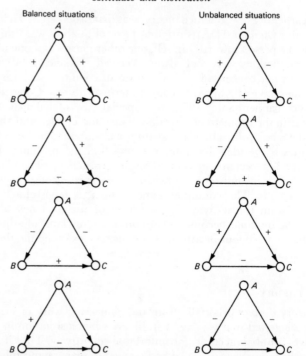

A represents the mind of the individual, *B* his perception of another person, and *C* his perception of a third person or object. Signs + or − represent positive or negative bonds between them.

Figure 8.1   Balanced and unbalanced situations

Other solutions are also possible, such as lying about my political affiliations, which would restore a kind of uneasy balance. However, we shall exclude these here in the interests of simplicity. So far we have three competing ways in which, by one alteration, we can restore the system to balance, but no criterion for choosing between them. Indeed at this stage it is not possible to formulate such a criterion in general terms. However, it is possible to apply Rosenberg's (1960) criterion of simplicity if we make a modification to the basic triadic situation that we started with. This modification involves introducing an extra element which is fixed, such as entry into an upper-class social club of which my friend disapproves. If I have a positive attitude towards entry into this upper-class social club, and membership of the party is positively related to such entry, this reduces the number of possible 'most economical adjustments' to the system to just one, a change in my attitude towards my friend. Adding the extra element makes prediction possible concerning which of the bonds will change.

This, however, is not the whole story. Later studies (Jordan, 1966, 1968; Price, Harburg and Newcombe 1966; Rodrigues, 1967) have shown that balance only seems to become a consideration when *A* likes *B* (Figure 8.2), i.e. when I like my friend. If I do not like my friend I am more likely to remove him from the system than tolerate the imbalance he generates in it. Newcombe (1961) has produced a reformulation of balance theory which only applies if *A* likes *B*, and Crockett (1974), Fuller (1974) and Crano and Cooper (1973) report results consistent with this formulation. Thus Fuller reports that subjects were able to distinguish in pleasantness (balance or imbalance) between situations in which *A* likes *B* and agrees or disagrees with *B* about *C*. But the situation in which *A* dislikes *B* seems to be such that subjects feel little or no difference in the 'pleasantness' depending on whether *A* and *B* agree or disagree. It seems as though *A* disliking *B* turns the system into a non-system. Other recent contributors to this field include Brickman and Horn (1973) and Touhey (1974) – who emphasise the interpersonal aspects of the model, as opposed to the purely cognitive, intra-personal aspects.

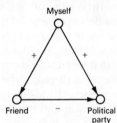

Figure 8.2   Unbalanced situation

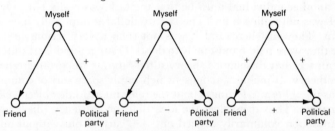

Figure 8.3   Possible resolutions of imbalance in Figure 8.2

We have said enough about balance theory to suggest that it is as yet very obviously incomplete in terms of predictive power. The basic problem is the one touched on above, namely the fact that there are a large number of possible ways of reducing imbalance: for example, leaving the situation, attempts to convince the other person, modification of one's perceptions, changing one's attitude to the other person, avoiding the issue, agreeing to disagree, as well as (the main method of interest in this chapter) changing one's attitude. In addition, as Heider (1958) himself points out, life is often made more interesting by disharmony or imbalance. People who are not totally consistent can be both more entertaining and interesting and get more excitement out of life than their more balanced and placid counterparts; there might even be a force towards imbalance! However, as an explanatory device and as a way of looking at the whole area of attitude change and social interaction, it remains a force which has generated a good deal of empirical research. This has led to the development of increasingly sophisticated versions of the model which begin to do justice to the complexity of the field. For a discussion of balance theory in relation to social interaction, see Chapter 13.

DISSONANCE THEORY

Another variation on the consistency theme is dissonance theory, put forward originally by Leon Festinger (1957). It is interesting in that some of its predictions which have in fact been empirically substantiated are surprising in that they differ from the usual guesses people make about the outcome of the experiments involved. Let us take an example: a group of subjects goes through the following procedure. First, they are asked to carry out two boring tasks, a request with which they comply. After this some of the subjects are offered one dollar to go into the waiting-room and inform the next subject that the task has been fun and interesting. Other subjects are offered twenty dollars to do the same thing. Afterwards all the subjects are asked what the real opinion of their task was. Perhaps the reader would like to say which of the two groups rated the task more interesting, the one-dollar group or the twenty-dollar group. Some people at least will be surprised to hear it was the one-dollar group. According to dissonance theory the reason is as follows. As a result of the procedure they went through, the one-dollar group could be imagined to have said to themselves 'I have just done two boring tasks and then told some one that they were fun and interesting, for which I have been paid only one dollar. It cannot be the money I told that lie for, since such a small amount was involved. The only explanation that there can be for deceiving another individual must be that the task was really not so boring at all. So I was not telling a lie.' The twenty-dollar group really have no such problems. They just lied (and it was not such a very serious lie anyway) because they were paid handsomely to do so (Festinger and Carlsmith, 1959).

We can see that dissonance theory differs in one important respect from balance theory. It includes actions (which imply some sort of commitment) as well as thoughts and feelings about the relevant attitude objects (elements) in its analysis. Thus it involves the idea that inconsistency (dissonance) between an action voluntarily carried out (i.e. carried out without any significant pressure) and an attitude held towards a particular object (element) brings into play a strain towards some kind of adjustment, which may be a change of attitude, in order to restore consistency (consonance).

A number of studies support this general formulation. Aronson and Mills (1959) found that female students who went through an embarrassing screening procedure before they were allowed to join a sex-discussion group had a more favourable attitude towards a boring tape-recording of that group than students who had had either a mild screening procedure or none at all. Aronson and Carlsmith (1963) report that children deterred from playing with a desired toy by a mild threat of punishment reduced their valuation of the toy, whereas those deterred by a severe threat did not. What the mild-threat children had to handle was the dissonance arising from having been deterred from playing with the toy by the threat of a very mild punishment. Surely the toy could not have been so attractive!

Four main criticisms may be made which concern the common elements of both balance theory and dissonance theory: (i) no account is taken of the variations in an individual's ability to tolerate dissonance; (ii) like a lot of other theories in social psychology, they seem to be much better at explaining things after the event than making predictions; (iii) very little is said about the much more common situations where the number of elements involved is greater than in the rather circumscribed situations involved in typical balance and dissonance experiments; and (iv) in both theories the exact nature of the basic components is not clearly defined.

There are also a number of points to be made which are specific to dissonance theory:

(1) Brehm and Cohen (1962) have pointed to a number of methodological problems with dissonance experiments. The most important of these is the problem of subject drop-out. For example, in the Festinger and Carlsmith (1959) study, out of seventy-one subjects eleven dropped out, seven from the one-dollar group, four from the twenty-dollar group and none from the control group. The point is that this differential drop-out rate might actually make it more likely that the results would conform to dissonance-theory predictions since presumably those subjects who had found the dull task most boring would be the ones most likely to drop out. This would raise the average interest score for the one-dollar group since less of such subjects dropped out from the other groups. On the other hand, if this was the case, and it is not proven, the dissonance theorist could rescue his position by arguing that a drop-out was in fact a way of preventing the dissonance that would have arisen had they remained in the experiment. Thus the debate continues.

(2) Since none of the basic components of the theory (elements, dissonance and commitment) is clearly defined (although obviously a cross between common sense and a sensitivity for psychology will provide an approximate version), it is clear that the theory can not have a very tight structure. Explanations other than dissonance ones are often equally acceptable for most dissonance experiments. In the Aronson and Mills (1959) study it is quite conceivable that the girls actually enjoyed the initiation process and registered their approval by being polite about the boring tape-recording. On the other hand, supposing they were indeed devastated by the initiation, they could have felt very relieved at the tameness of the discussion. Neither of these possibilities seems to have been excluded.

(3) Bem (1972) has been in the forefront of the assault against cognitive dissonance theory. Essentially, his argument has derived from simulations of typical dissonance experiments in which the subjects of the experiment are not put through the experimental procedure but are put in the role of an 'observer' of the experiment by being provided with information descriptive of the 'real subject's' situation. Bem's 'observers' were able to predict the results of the one- and twenty-dollar experiment, even though they themselves were not involved in a dissonant situation. Bem argues that the subjects in the dissonance experiment could simply have been seeing themselves as the observers might have seen them (see our discussion of attribution theory in Chapter 11). Thus they could have been making an inference about their own uncertain attitudes, for the sake of security labelling them on the basis of what they perceived to be expectations of an observer.

The authors do not intend to enter the dissonance *versus* attribution theory debate, which has at present reached a state of truce with no crucial experiment emerging to give victory to either camp. We would simply wish to make this point; it is quite possible that both theories are in a way correct and must coexist for the time being. Attribution is helpful particularly in considering the logic involved in the inference processes which influence our perceptions of the feelings of ourselves and others. However, it is very much a cognitive theory which does not devote itself much to the motivational dynamics which initiate such inference processes. A dynamic force of some kind is required for the initiation of all behaviour and mental activity. Balance and dissonance theories postulate a suggestion (albeit an imprecise one) of the nature of such a force for cognitive and affective change. As yet some kind of drive towards consistency cannot be discarded as a candidate for this position. Thus both dissonance and attribution theories see attitudes changing as a result of behaviour. On the other hand, incentive approaches (Vroom, 1964; Fishbein, 1967) (see Chapters 6 and 7) see behavioural disposition partly as a function of the valence of outcomes (or attitude towards the incentive object in question). There is evidence to support both types of theory. A study by Linder, Cooper and Jones (1967) suggests that incentive and dissonance effects may work against each other. When there is barely sufficient incentive for making a statement contrary to one's held attitude, then dissonance and subsequent attitude change may take place if the person makes the statement while feeling free not to comply. When the freedom not to comply is removed or markedly decreased, however, attitude change is greater, the greater the incentive for compliance. It would seem that in situations of unforced compliance, dissonance theory applies, whereas in situations of forced compliance, incentive theory applies.

8.4 Processes of attitude change

Controlled laboratory research into the determinants of attitude change are many and various. In discussing empirical studies of the factors influencing attitude change we shall adopt the scheme proposed by Hovland and Janis (1959) in their review (see Figure 8.4 which is a diagrammatic representation with slight modifications provided by Freedman, Carlsmith and Sears, 1974). This may make this section rather like an advertising man's cook-book, but it seems the simplest way of indicating something of the range of this work.

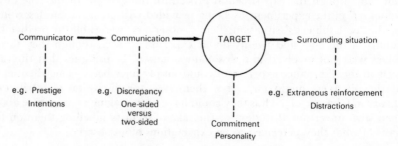

Figure 8.4   Model of the attitude-change situation, showing examples of important factors at each stage (the amount of attitude change that occurs is determined by variables at each point in the process) (Freedman, Carlsmith and Sears, 1974)

The basic components are: (i) the communicator, who is attempting to change the attitude; (ii) the communication (the means the communicator uses); (iii) the target, the person whose attitude the communicator is attempting to change; and (iv) the surrounding situation, which may in some way affect the giving or the receiving of the communication.

THE COMMUNICATOR

Prestige

In general the greater the prestige possessed by the communicator the more attitude change he is likely to produce. Experimental evidence to this effect is provided by Hovland and Weiss (1952), who found that communications about atomic submarines allegedly coming from J. Robert Oppenheimer, the famous physicist, generated more change in attitudes among the audience than if they were supposed to come from *Pravda*. The same was true of other topics. Aronson, Turner and Carlsmith (1963) found that an enthusiastic review of a piece of modern poetry had more effect in changing subject's attitudes if it was said to be by T. S. Eliot than by an unknown female student.

Intentions

If the intentions of the communicator are perceived as honest, he is more likely to produce attitude change. Thus Walster, Aronson and Abrahams (1966) found that a convicted criminal's message carried more weight if he was arguing in favour of greater powers for the police than if he was arguing for greater individual freedom. Walster and Festinger (1962) and Brock and Becker (1965) have found that a message is more effective if it is overheard rather than directed towards the listener. People seem to get suspicious if they think the communicator is trying to persuade them. The 'soft sell' was devised to avoid this effect; but a problem with this is that the sell may become too soft and fail to make any impact.

Liking and similarity

Both of these characteristics of the communicator contribute to the tendency of his message to be accepted by the subject. Balance theory accounts quite well for this phenomenon.

Reference groups

Groups influence people's beliefs in two main ways: (i) by changing their opinions to make them agree with the rest of the group, and (ii) by supporting a member's opinion so he can resist persuasion from outside the group. Kelley and Volkart (1952) found that the more boy scouts valued their troop the more resistant they were to a communicator who tried to change their opinions on subjects closely related to the troop's norms. Siegel and Siegel (1957) found evidence of attitude change in a natural social experiment concerned with the allocation of accommodation by ballot to third-year female students at an American university. The subjects were those who had expressed a preference for high-status accommodation at the end of the first year. At the end of the second year these were split into three groups: (*a*) those who had expressed a preference for high-status accommodation and had been successful in the ballot at the end of the first year (and hence were in such accommodation during their second year); (*b*) those who had been living in lower-status accommodation but still wished to move to the higher-status accommodation for the third year; and (*c*) those who were in the lower-status accommodation in their second year and did not wish to move. A political-values questionnaire (the E–F Scale), which should have been relevant to attitudes towards social status, was administered at the end of the first and second years and it was found that group (*c*) showed greatest change in a less authoritarian (perhaps status-conscious) direction with group (*b*) showing intermediate change, and group (*a*) very little change. This experiment seems to show that both reference groups and membership groups exert an influence on people's attitudes, with greatest influence occurring when the membership group becomes the reference group.

The sleeper effect

Noted by Kelman and Hovland (1953), this effect was discovered when a positive, competent, fair communicator initially had more influence on high-school students' attitudes towards the lenient treatment of delinquents than a negative, biased, uninformed one. However, over a period of three weeks the effect of the positive communicator decreased, while the effect of the negative one increased, until both effects came to be much the same. If the subjects were reminded of the communicator, the original effect was more or less restored.

THE COMMUNICATION

Discrepancy

This variable, the discrepancy between the attitude expressed by the communicator and that of the target, interacts with other variables in an interesting way and is an illustration of how a laboratory experiment can come up with a finding quite at variance with common sense, simply because it failed to take into account other critical variables. Thus Hovland and Pritzker (1957), using a communicator who was highly acceptable to the targets, found that over a variety of topics such as the likelihood of a cure for cancer within five years, the desirability of compulsory voting and the adequacy of five hours sleep per night, the greater the discrepancy, the greater the change of attitude. Similar results have been reported by Goldberg (1954) and French (1956).

This seemingly strange series of results is brought more in line with common sense by research done by Hovland, Harvey and Sherif (1957), who used an issue of far greater salience to the subjects, prohibition, in the states of Texas and Oklahoma. They concentrated on the following three aspects of the problem: (i) How favourably will the communicator be received when his view is at variance with that of the recipient? (ii) How will what the communicator says be perceived and interpreted by individuals at varying distances from his position? (iii) What will be the amount of opinion change produced when small and large deviations in the positions of communication and recipient are involved?

On the first point, favourableness of the reception was determined by the closeness of the communication to the views of the recipient. On the second point, the phenomena of distortion of the message and discrediting the communication were seen to be influential factors. The subjects whose views coincided with the message tended to perceive the message accurately. Those with slightly discrepant views tended to distort the message of their communicator and hence discount him, while those with highly discrepant views tended to discredit the source. On the third point, it was found that individuals whose position was only slightly discrepant from the communicator's were influenced to a greater extent than those whose positions deviated to a larger extent.

Thus we may conclude tentatively that where there is ambiguity about the credibility of the communicator and the subject is deeply involved about the issue, the greater the attempt at change, the higher the resistance. But with a respected communicator and a non-salient issue the greater the discrepancy, the greater the change.

One-sided versus two-sided communication

In general, the conclusion which may be tentatively drawn here is that the less informed and the less intelligent the target, the more likely that one-sided communication will be effective. However, in most situations two-sided communication seems more effective, probably because the communicator is likely to seem better informed, less biased and less as though he is trying to influence the target. This variable, being a relatively subtle one, probably only has its effect if there is some doubt as to the credibility of the message.

Stating a conclusion

This is another factor having a marginal effect. By stating a conclusion you make sure that the target knows what is being said. By not stating one the communicator is less likely to give the impression that he is trying to convince. Intelligent people seem to be more influenced by the latter method.

Order of presentation

Where both sides of the issue are to be presented, is there any advantage in being either first (primacy effect) or second (recency effect) to present one's case? It seems likely that the primacy effect often found in everyday life is due to the opposite side not being heard after presentation of the first message. Consequently it is difficult to control this factor. However, probably the best experiment is one by Miller and Campbell (1959). They had college students listen to a suit for damages. Half heard the defendant first and half the plaintiff. After both sides had been presented they were asked for their opinion.

The results showed that the first communication was most effective if followed immediately by the second, followed by a week's interval and then the test of effect. The second was most effective if the week's interval came between the two communications. It is clear that this is a highly complicated effect.

The novelty of the information

The main hard finding in this area is that if the target believes he is about to hear something new, the more likely he is to change his attitude after hearing the message (Sears and Freedman, 1965).

THE TARGET

Personality factors

Hovland and Janis (1959) have shown that subjects who are persuasible under one set of conditions tend to be persuasible under others. However, it is not clear which personality characteristic is responsible for this tendency.

One fairly consistent finding is that subjects low in self-esteem (i.e. who think poorly of themselves) are more persuasible. Typically such people have feelings of inadequacy, social inhibitions, social anxiety and test anxiety. The correlations between self-esteem and anxiety are generally low but consistent. Three different kinds of explanations have been offered for this finding. (i) people high in self-esteem have more effective defences than people with low self-esteem, who are more exposed and sensitive to persuasion; (ii) low-self-esteem people place a low value on themselves and their opinions which they are less reluctant to give up; (iii) a person low in self-esteem is more likely to be impressed by a given source than a person high in self-esteem. There is at present no evidence as to which explanation is correct.

Intelligence is a factor which is related to persuasibility under certain circumstances. However, the relationship is not a direct one, for example the finding that more intelligent people are more persuasible if a conclusion is not stated.

There is fairly consistent evidence that women are more persuasible than men and that they change their attitudes more (Janis and Field, 1959). This finding has been explained by the nature of the sex roles in our society. On this view submissiveness is associated with persuasibility and dominance with the opposite.

Defensive style

Another way in which people differ is in the style of defence they use when confronted by an argument or some other persuasive communication. Defences can broadly be divided into two types, those that are relatively cognitive and logical and those that are relatively non-cognitive and illogical. The former include such things as producing counter-arguments, discrediting the communicator and generally responding to the meaning and reliability of the message. The latter include what Freud called 'defence mechanisms', denial of the conflict between the persuasive message and the original position, misperceiving the message, suppression of the message and reaction formation (moving in the direction opposite from that advocated by the message). Katz, Sarnoff and McClintock (1956) investigated the effects of different types of message on two groups of people, one group who made extensive use of defence mechanisms (high defence) and one who relied less heavily on these (low defence). They were subjected to two kinds of message concerning prejudice against blacks. One contained a number of facts about blacks and whites, all of which were designed to show that prejudice was not based on sound reasoning (the information appeal). The second message showed the psychodynamic relationship between defence mechanism and prejudice (the insight appeal). The insight appeal was most effective with the low-defence group and the information appeal with the high-defence group. It seems likely that the high-defence group were strongly resisting the attack on their defence mechanisms by the insight appeal.

Commitment
This is another factor determining the likelihood that a person will change his attitude in the face of persuasion. If a person has committed himself to a course of action, any communication denying the rightness of that course is likely to be rejected. Likewise, a public statement commits a person to the attitude expressed. A variable affecting the degree of commitment is whether the subject had free choice in taking a given course of action. Freedman and Steinbruner (1964) found that subjects who had been made to feel they had made up their minds freely on a given subject were more resistant to changing their opinions than those made to feel they had had little choice in their decisions. This finding is very much in line with dissonance theory.

Innoculation and support
McGuire *et al.* (1961) have investigated two ways of making subjects resistant to attempts at attitude change. These two methods, which he named innoculation and support, are as follows. Innoculation involves subjecting a person's opinion to a mild attack and then helping to repulse the attack. This helps him to marshal his defences and make him more resistant to a stronger attack. Support involves supplying him with counter-arguments so as to prepare him for attack. McGuire and Papageorgis (1961) found innoculation to be more effective than support but that support was more effective than no preparation at all. It seems that support is most effective when the arguments used in the support are similar to those contained in the subsequent attack on the attitude.

Forewarning
Another method of strengthening resistance to attitude change is by forewarning the target. Thus Freedman and Sears (1965) found that teenagers told ten minutes in advance that they were about to hear a talk entitled 'Why teenagers should not be allowed to drive' were less influenced by the talk than others who had not been warned.

SITUATIONAL FACTORS

Reinforcement

It seems that if reinforcement, or something like it, is associated with a persuasive communication, it is more likely to persuade. Thus the country-side, mountain streams and elegant horses are linked with cigarettes. A good meal can help clinch a business deal. However, it is clear that there are probably other explanations apart from reinforcement which may account for these phenomena. The meal may simply put the target in a better mood. Whatever the mechanism we may note that Janis *et al.* (1965) have repro-duced these phenomena in the laboratory. They gave some subjects 'Pepsi Cola' to drink while they heard a communication on foreign aid. These subjects finished up more favourably disposed to the communication than other subjects who had no 'Pepsi Cola'.

Fear arousal

The original study in this field was by Janis and Feshbach (1953). They divided their subjects (high-school students) into three groups. All were shown films attempting to persuade them into regular tooth-brushing. They were shown a highly fear-arousing, a moderately fear-arousing and a non-fear arousing film, respectively. Immediately after the showing the first group reported being impressed by the message and agreeing with it more than the others. But a week later it was found that the subjects in the non-fear-aroused group had in fact changed their behaviour more than the others.

Unfortunately later researchers have in general failed to replicate this finding. For example, Dabbs and Leventhal (1966) subjected college students to varying degrees of fear-arousing communications and found that the most fear-arousing was the most effective in persuading students to have anti-tetanus injections. Janis (referred to in Freedman *et al.*, 1974) explains the difference between these findings and his and Feshbach's as being due to the amount of fear produced. A moderate amount of fear may enhance the per-suasive effect of a communication, but extreme fear may bring into play other factors such as the mechanism of denial or may disrupt the target so much that he is unable to act coherently.

The arousal of aggression

Analogous with the idea of arousing fear and then offering reduction of it through acceptance of the communication is the idea that if aggression is aroused people will be more willing to accept an aggressive idea (to release their aggression). Weiss and Fine (1956) subjected one group of students to a frustrating, annoying experience and another to a pleasant, satisfying experience. Then both groups were subjected to a persuasive communication that took either a lenient or a punitive attitude to juvenile delinquency. The hypothesis was that the frustrated subjects would be more aggressive and more likely to accept the punitive communication. This was confirmed by the results.

Distraction

Apart from the obvious possibility that distraction may serve to prevent the message ever reaching the target, distraction may also serve to facilitate the communication by distraction of the target's defences against persuasion. Festinger and Maccoby (1964) had half their subjects listen to a speech against fraternities at college while at the same time watching a film of the speaker. The other half watched a funny, non-relevant film during the same speech. Subjects who initially disagreed with the speech (who were in favour of fraternities) showed more change in the second (distraction) than the first (non-distraction) condition. Later studies have not given unequivocal support to this finding. The issue probably hinges on the amount of distraction involved; clearly this is difficult to control.

A BRIEF COMMENT

Attitudes are generally considered to be relatively enduring aspects of an individual's personality. When attitude change is being attempted it is worth considering the extent to which the subject is committed to it and the extent to which his resistance has been built up by some of the methods just considered. Lest the results of laboratory experiments give the wrong impression, let the efforts of politicians testify to the practical difficulties in engineering mass attitude change in the short term using methods which are acceptable in a democratic society.

8.5 Attitude measurement

Attitudes have been measured in various ways, via feelings, beliefs, behavioural intentions and behaviour itself, or any combination of these. Methods of measurement include self-reports in response to questionnaire items concerning beliefs, feelings and behaviour, projective techniques, situational tests with the purpose disguised, direct observation (e.g. through personal contact, interview or in some standard situation) and physiological reactions. In general, however, attitude measures have tended to concentrate on the affective and cognitive aspects of attitudes. This has been largely because the conative or behavioural aspect is more difficult to assess.

QUESTIONNAIRES

Questionnaires are most used, and these may take a number of forms. If they ask open-ended questions, requiring some form of content analysis, they are likely to be prone to error in that they do not necessarily sample the required attitude systematically enough, since the respondent may answer as he pleases. Consequently there has been a preference for requiring the respondent to place his response into one of a number of categories, e.g. by the use of multiple-choice answers. The culmination of this trend has been the use of attitude scales such as those of Thurstone, Likert and Guttman, which we shall discuss below. While these are likely to be more reliable as a measure

than open-ended questionnaires and interviews, they do suffer from one disadvantage in relation to the latter in that they sample only those aspects of
the attitude to which the respondent is forced to reply. Other important
aspects which might have emerged in a more open-ended approach where
the respondent can say what he likes are automatically excluded. Neither
approach) is clearly 'better' than the other. The important question is the
purpose to which the attitude measure is to be put. For statistically based
research of the survey kind the attitude scale is clearly more appropriate,
but for more exploratory work an open-ended interview or questionnaire
would be preferred. In view of what has been said so far, it is clear that the
present authors agree with Cook and Selltiz (1964) when they suggest that
probably the only really effective way of measuring attitudes is to use several
kinds of measuring devices as a check on each other. A full survey of such
methods is not included here for reasons of space. An excellent review will
be found in Cook and Selltiz (1964). However, because they have been widely
used we shall describe the construction of three different kinds of attitude
scale.

ATTITUDE SCALES

It is beyond the scope of this book to examine the technical and mathematical
details of attitude-scaling. The interested reader will find a useful short
summary in most comprehensive social-psychology textbooks (e.g. Secord
and Backman, 1964) and for a more detailed treatment he is referred to
Fishbein's (1967) collection of readings. We shall now describe three kinds
of scaling method.

(1) A Thurstone scale (Thurstone and Chave, 1929) is constructed by
arranging for a large number of independent judges to rate a large number
of attitude statements according to the extent to which they are either favourable to the attitude object in question on a continuum such as the one shown
in Figure 8.5.

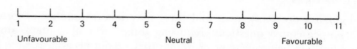

Figure 8.5

By combining the verdicts of the judges for each statement, an average value is obtained for that statement. The final version of the attitude scale is made up by selecting a number of statements which show a wide range of favourableness and on which there is a high degree of agreement between the judges. In Table 8.1 we have a scale of attitude towards war constructed in this way. The respondent's score is based on the average scale value of the statements he agrees with.

Table 8.1   Scale of attitude towards war

Scale value*			Put a check mark (√) if you agree with the statement. Put a cross (×) if you disagree with the statement.
7.5	( )	1	Under some conditions, war is necessary to maintain justice.
3.5	( )	2	The benefits of war rarely pay for its losses even for the victor.
9.7	( )	3	War brings out the best qualities in men.
0.2	( )	4	There is no conceivable justification for war.
6.9	( )	5	War has some benefits; but it's a big price to pay for them.
8.7	( )	6	War is often the only means of preserving national honour.
0.8	( )	7	War is a ghastly mess.
5.5	( )	8	I never think about war and it doesn't interest me.
1.4	( )	9	War is a futile struggle resulting in self-destruction.
8.3	( )	10	The desirable results of war have not received the attention they deserve.
4.7	( )	11	Pacifists have the right atittude, but some pacifists go too far.
2.1	( )	12	The evils of war are greater than any possible benefits.
6.8	( )	13	Although war is terrible it has some value.
3.7	( )	14	International disputes should be settled without war.
11.0	( )	15	War is glorious.
6.5	( )	16	Defensive war is justified but other wars are not.
2.4	( )	17	War breeds disrespect for human life.
10.1	( )	18	There can be no progress without war.
3.2	( )	19	It is good judgement to sacrifice certain rights in order to prevent war.
9.2	( )	20	War is the only way to right tremendous wrongs.

*Scale values are provided here for purposes of information and do not normally appear on the scale.
Source: Ruth C. Peterson. *Scale of Attitude Toward War* (University of Chicago Press, 1931).

(2) Likert (1932) has devised a somewhat different scaling method which in practice correlates highly with that of Thurstone. He has a large number of judges express their own attitudes to a large number of statements on a five-point scale (see Figure 8.6). The statements are then subjected to what is called an 'internal consistency analysis'. The purpose is to select for the final version of the scale only those statements which discriminate most effectively between the highest- and the lowest-scoring judges. Thus a statement with which the lowest-scoring judges (on all the statements) consistently

'strongly agree' and with which the highest-scoring judges consistently 'strongly disagree' is a suitable statement for inclusion in the final version of the scale. The respondent's score is the sum of his statement ratings. A Likert scale therefore consists of a number of items such as the one shown in Figure 8.7.

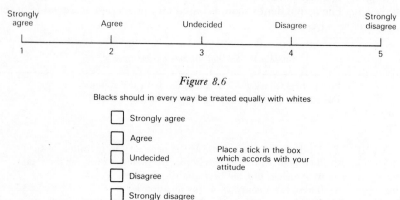

Figure 8.6

Figure 8.7

(3) The two previous kinds of scale may measure somewhat indiscriminately a number of aspects of an attitude. Thus, in Table 8.1, moral, economic and philosophical aspects are combined. Consequently, totally different patterns of responses may combine to make up the respondent's total scores. While sometimes a global score of this kind may be desirable, it is often necessary, particularly in research, to devise a measure which measures only one attitude dimension (e.g. the moral one). Guttman (1950) has devised a method for securing unidimensionality, called the 'scalogram method'. The chief characteristic of this method is that the respondent's score on the scale describes his pattern of responses. Thus only one pattern of responses can lead to each particular score, In Table 8.2. we know that if a person has a score

Table 8.2   Pattern of responses in a scalogram

Score	Says 'yes' to item			Says 'no' to item		
	3	*2*	*1*	*3*	*2*	*1*
3	×	×	×			
2		×	×	×		
1			×	×	×	
0				×	×	×

of three he has agreed with statements one, two and three. If he has a score of two he has disagreed with statement three and agreed with statements two and one and so on. In practice complete consistency of this kind is rarely achieved. Guttman (1950) has suggested that an appropriate criterion is that the response pattern should be 90 per cent reproducible in order that a scale be considered unidimensional.

8.6 Job satisfaction

We have defined an attitude as the degree of affect towards an object. Such feelings towards work are usually assessed via measures of job satisfaction. The best known of these is the Job Description Index (Smith, Kendall and Hulin, 1969). This scale measures attitudes towards work, supervision, pay, promotion and coworkers. Smith *et al.* cite intercorrelations between these five scales ranging from +0.28 to +0.42. This provides some evidence for a general factor of job satisfaction, though it suggests that each type of satisfaction being measured has a considerable degree of specificity.

THEORIES OF JOB SATISFACTION

Whether or not a general factor of job satisfaction exists has been debated since Herzberg's formulation of a theory of job satisfaction. His theory stems from an analysis of the experiences and feelings of 200 engineers and accountants in nine companies (Herzberg, Mausner and Snyderman, 1959). They were asked to describe job experiences in which they felt exceptionally good or exceptionally bad about their jobs and to rate how much their feelings had been influenced by each experience. These statements were then analysed, with the results shown in Figure 8.8.

Herzberg *et al.* found favourable job attitudes are usually associated with activities such as achievement, recognition, the work itself, responsibilities and advancement. Unfavourable job attitudes were usually linked to contextual factors such as company policy and administration, supervision and working conditions. The former activities are related to job content, being intrinsic to the job and, because of their relation to favourable attitudes, Herzberg called them 'motivators'. He called the environmental factors 'hygiene factors'. He further hypothesised that only motivators could lead to job satisfaction and only hygiene factors to dissatisfaction, i.e. there are two separate dimensions of job satisfaction and job dissatisfaction. Hygiene factors are considered to satisfy the need to avoid pain (i.e. Maslow's lower-order needs), whereas motivators are necessary for the satisfaction of self-relisation motives (i.e. Maslow's higher-level needs).

The theory has resulted in a number of investigations, some of which support it (e.g. Whitsett and Winslow, 1967), while others do not (e.g. House and Wigdor, 1967; Dunnette, Campbell and Hakel, 1967). The reasons for this lack of support are likely to involve a combination of the following: (i) supportive studies may be method-bound (i.e. the critical incident technique used by Herzberg may give biased results through a tendency in people to see good experiences as being caused by their own actions, and bad experiences as being due to situational (hygiene) factors) – in so far as people have a need to maintain a positive self-image, then one could expect this to happen; (ii) even Herzberg's study showed that motivators could be involved in dissatisfaction and hygiene factors in satisfaction (see Figure 8.8) – other studies have found this to a great extent (Dunnette *et al.*, 1967); (iii) there is some evidence (e.g. Goldthorpe *et al.*, 1968) that hygiene factors may be important sources of satisfaction as well as dissatisfaction for particular groups

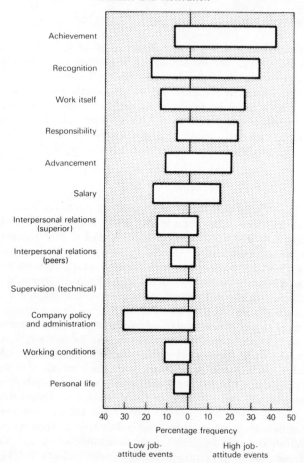

Figure 8.8 Percentage of 'high' and of 'low' job-a titude sequences in which each of the categories appeared (Herzberg et al. 1959)

of workers, notably 'blue-collar' workers; and (iv) a number of studies suggest that other factors play an important role in determining job satisfaction, in particular the attitude systems and beliefs of the workers concerned.

Wolf (1970) attempts to take greater account of these individual differences in proposing a need-gratification theory of satisfaction. He hypothesises that (i) people with ungratified lower-level needs (see Figure 6.2) derive both satisfaction and dissatisfaction from their degree of gratification; (ii) people with lower-level needs conditionally gratified receive both satisfaction and dissatisfaction from the degree of gratification of higher-level needs and dissatisfaction comes when continued gratification of lower-level needs is disrupted or threatened; (iii) people with lower-level needs unconditionally gratified obtain both satisfaction and dissatisfaction from the degree of gratification of higher-level needs; (iv) dissatisfaction results from the fustration of gratification of an active need and from interruption or threatened interuption of a previously gratified lower-level need; and (v) satisfaction results from the gratification of any need.

This theory sees attitudes as being dependent upon fundamental motives. However, this relationship is a complex one, being mediated by several intervening variables. Vroom (1964) identifies four classes of variables which appear to determine the attitude of a person towards his role in an organisation: (i) the amounts of particular classes of outcomes (e.g. pay, status) contingent upon role occupation; (ii) the strength of desire or aversion towards these outcomes; (iii) the amounts of these outcomes believed by the person to be received by comparable others; and (iv) the amounts of these outcomes which the person expected to receive or has received at earlier points in time (see Chapter 7).

While this view, which might be called the 'need-fulfilment' view of job satisfaction, is clearly a reasonable one to hold, unfortunately there is some evidence which appears to run counter to it. For example, Berger (1968) reports that for a heterogeneous group of workers job satisfaction was only related to the satisfaction of needs by the work situation in the case of individuals with high self-esteem. Other studies (Hulin, 1966; Katzell, Barrett and Parker, 1961; Form and Geschwender, 1962) offer evidence that the social group which acts as a reference point for the individual and to which he looks for guidance in his attitudes (the social reference group) has an influence in determining whether a need-fulfilment theory will apply. Thus only if his needs are in line with those approved by his reference group will satisfaction of those needs lead to job satisfaction. In addition, there is evidence that success at achieving task goals (presumably the fulfilment of a need, at least for some) is related to satisfaction for high self-esteem individuals but not for low self-esteem individuals (Korman, 1971). The same study seems to suggest that social reference group evaluations are of equal importance for both high and low self-esteem individuals. However, Blood and Hulin (1967) find that blue-collar workers (who, according to Ghiselli (undated) are lower in self-esteem and hence more susceptible to social-group influence (Cartwright and Zander, 1960)) do in fact show a closer relationship between social reference group processes and job satisfaction. Korman (1971) summarises the position we have reached so far as follows:

Individuals appear to find satisfying those jobs which are consistent with these cognitions, both about themselves and about others, both as viewed by themselves and as viewed by others. Thus to the extent that a situation 'matches' a person's conception of himself in terms of his ability to satisfy his needs and be competent and in terms of being in balance with these cognitions, he will be satisfied. Similarly, to the extent that a job situation also matches a reference group's conception for an individual of what is proper and appropriate for him and in balance with the group's conception of what he is, then to that extent he will also be satisfied. The former seems to be a greater determinant of variation in job satisfaction for the high self-esteem individual than for the low, since 'lows' will not generally go completely against themselves in the interests of balance due to social norms. Rather, they do tend to ignore their own desires in determining their levels of job satisfaction. However, whether or not they are any more dependent than HSE's on 'group-defined equity' is still a moot point (Korman, 1971).

The perceptive reader will recognise the theoretical connections between this statement and the author's comment towards the end of the theoretical section of this chapter to the effect that both attribution- and balance-type theories have something to offer, and must coexist for the time being. Korman's statement makes use of both the idea of balance and that of attribution (a person forming his attitudes on the basis of the way other people feel they ought to be (Bem, 1972)).

THE CONCOMITANTS OF JOB SATISFACTION

A large number of variables have been found to be associated with job satisfaction. We shall mention briefly a number which are more or less clearly established.

Situational determinants of job satisfaction
Job level. It is found consistently that the higher the occupational level, the greater the job satisfaction (England and Stein, 1961; Herzberg *et al.*, 1957; Vroom, 1964). This finding seems to provide further support for the position Korman is putting forward. People in higher-level jobs are more likely to find opportunities for need fulfilment and to have higher self-esteem.

Job content. There is evidence (Walker and Guest, 1952) that people with more varied jobs are more satisfied.

Supervisory behaviour. Vroom (1964) reports a considerable amount of evidence that considerate, democratic, employee orientated leadership produces greater satisfaction than a more autocratic, task-orientated style. (For further discussion of this, see Chapter 14.)

Personal factors and job satisfaction
Age. Research seems to show a curvilinear relationship between age and job satisfaction. Thus the relationship increases progressively until the immediate pre-retirement years when presumably the general tendency is for the individual's work load to taper off in its significance.

Educational level. Although there is a tendency for there to be a positive relationship with job satisfaction, this disappears and turns into a negative one when occupational level is held constant (Klein and Maher, 1966). Probably what is happening is that as educational level rises so do the expectations of the individual, and these are catered for by the increased opportunities for expectations to be met at higher occupational levels. However, with occupational level held constant, the higher educational level will generate expectations which are unlikely to be met.

Mental health. A relationship between job satisfaction and mental health is also suggested in a study by Kornhauser (1965). He combined the following component indices to provide a general measure of mental health: manifest anxiety and emotional tension, self-esteem (positive *versus* negative self-feelings), hostility *versus* trust in an acceptance of people, sociability and friendship *versus* withdrawal, over-all satisfaction with life and personal morale *versus* anomie, social alienation and despair. This measure was administered to a sample of skilled, semi-skilled and unskilled workers. Typically job-satisfaction surveys show significant differences between occupational groups in job satisfaction, with the more skilled jobs resulting in high satisfaction. For example, Hoppock's (1935) survey found job satisfaction to be highest in professional, managerial and executive groups, lower in a category of sub-professional, business and minor supervisory groups, again lower in skilled manual and white-collar groups, lower still in the semi-skilled, and lowest in unskilled manual groups.

Kornhauser found that jobs in which workers are better satisfied are related to better mental health. Within occupations, the better-satisfied individuals enjoyed better mental health than those less satisfied. The satisfied in lowest-level jobs had mental-health scores similar to those of workers in higher jobs, and the dissatisfied among skilled and semi-skilled workers tend to resemble the lower-skill groups.

Kornhauser also investigated the relationship between job satisfaction and over-all satisfaction with life. His results, like those of Iris and Barrett (1972) and McCormick and Tiffin (1974), suggest that one factor affects the other in the same direction. The latter study suggested that job satisfaction tended to spill over to life satisfaction. Hulin (1966) found the same tendency, though he used a joint measure of job and community satisfaction. Such satisfaction seemed to have significant effects on satisfaction with life in general.

Consequences of job satisfaction

Job satisfaction, labour turnover and absenteeism. The relationship between job satisfaction and turnover is generally a significant and consistently negative one (Fournet *et al.*, 1966). Vroom (1964) also concludes that the research evidence indicates a negative relationship between job satisfaction and absenteeism, though less consistently than with turnover.

Job satisfaction and performance. Job satisfaction is an important attitude not only in its own right but also because it is related to aspects of work, such as absenteeism and turnover. Brayfield and Crockett's (1955) review of studies concerning the relationship between employee attitudes and performance showed that there was no clear relationship between the two, probably because 'productivity may be only peripherally related to many of the goals towards which the industrial worker is striving'. Vroom's (1964) review is also in agreement on the low relationship. If productivity does not fulfil either a personal need or a social reference group need then, it would seem, there is unlikely to be a positive relationship between productivity and satisfaction.

Part IV

PERSONALITY, INTELLIGENCE AND ASSESSMENT

So far in this book we have been concerned with isolated psychological processes or functions such as motivation, learning or perception. Personality research and theory, however, tend to focus on the whole individual rather than on only one psychological process. The main themes running through this part are indicated by its title. The main substantive theme is that of personality, defined in its widest sense. Hence we focus not only upon alternative theories of personality (Chapter 9) but also on intelligence and abilities (Chapter 10). These latter characteristics which form part of the total personality are treated separately. One important aspect of personality which was covered in Part II was that of motivation. It will receive only brief mention here.

It is not only psychologists who have theories about personality. We all have our own theories about the meaning of the behaviour which others present to us, and we draw our own conclusions about their underlying personality. These, often implicit, theories are reflected in the ways in which we perceive others. Person perception (Chapter 11) is involved whenever we make a judgement about a person, and such judgements occur in almost any kind of interview situation. In fact, the purpose of certain interviews, such as those used in personnel selection and staff appraisal is to arrive at accurate judgements about others.

In arriving at accurate judgements of others, whether in personnel selection (Chapter 12) or appraisal (Chapter 11), we need to have valid and reliable measures of personality. In this part we shall examine such measures, including ability tests, various kinds of personality tests and interviews. These measures derive from the different theoretical perspectives which are the focus of our attention in Chapters 9 and 10.

The second major theme in this part is a methodological one. The key issues here are those of measurement, specifically those of reliability and validity. The methodological tools of the psychologist, involved in such activities as constructing and validating personality measures, are probably of at least as much value in personnel selection and appraisal as are his theories and empirical findings concerning personality. These methodological techniques are a major focus in this part.

Part IV

PERSONALITY, INTELLIGENCE AND ASSESSMENT

9
Personality

9.1 Introduction

The reader will by now be aware that most topics in psychology can be viewed from a variety of different perspectives. This is particularly true in the field of personality, which deals with the entire range of human activity. In order to clarify what we mean, we shall start with a definition: 'Personality consists of the individual characteristics, in particular the modes of thinking, feeling and behaving which in their organisation and patterning determine the individual's manner of interaction with his environment.' Thus we see personality as a kind of compendium of various processes, some of which we have covered in other chapters, e.g. motivation, perception and learning. This chapter, however, will not simply be a reiteration of other ones, for far more is involved in the definition than just that. Note particularly the words 'organisation' and 'patterning'. Personality is a network of interrelated tendencies, some of which act in concert and others of which oppose each other in such a way that each individual's pattern is different.

To survey this complex but most fascinating field we shall take a sample of it, choosing the most influential viewpoints and attempting to assess their main strengths and weaknesses. We shall start with a topic which was touched on in Chapter 1, the conflict between the psychoanalysts (Section 9.2) and the behaviourists (Section 9.3).

Another viewpoint we shall study will be the phenomenological one. The focus of attention here is upon the individual's perception of his total environment, including himself (Section 9.4). In section 9.5 we shall examine an attempt to bridge some of the contrasting viewpoints (Kelly's (1955) personal construct theory) and try to evaluate its success. After this, in Section 9.6 we shall mention certain specific areas of personality research, e.g. the authoritarian personality, in order to give the reader an indication of the breadth of psychological research in the field. We then discuss personality measurement in Section 9.7 and personality and its relation to performance in Section 9.8, ending with a conclusion in Section 9.9.

We start our discussion of personality with Freud's (1940) psychoanalytic theory, because in spite of its considerable limitations it is a comprehensive theory and can be used to illustrate many of the important aspects of personality.

9.2   Freud's psychoanalytic theory

There are two main parts to Freud's theory, the structural (the nature and interrelationship of parts of personality) and the developmental (how these parts develop during the course of life). Common to these two is the concept of 'instinctual energy' (*libido*), which provides the dynamic both for the development and for the interplay of the different parts of the personality.

Freud states that the personality structure consists of three parts, the *id*, the *ego* and the *super ego*. The id is the power-station, a reservoir of instinctual energy. This energy is sexual (libido), but this word is misleading in contemporary terms since it includes a whole range of pleasurable activities which only at certain stages involve a gratification shared with a partner of the opposite sex. Freud included in his later writings the concept of *thanatos* (aggressive or death instinct) as opposed to *eros* (the sex, life or love instinct). This was in response to his observation that many of his patients had a habit of resisting treatment in such a way that they seemed to want to bring about their own downfall. However, others (e.g. Reich, 1950) have concluded that the apparent evidence for the death instinct is better accounted for in terms of a frustration which dams and diverts the libido. Thus a person gets angry with himself and others as a result of frustration of libidinal outlets rather than as a result of a basic reservoir of aggressive or death energy. We shall elaborate upon the nature of libido when we discuss personality development.

The second important part of personality structure is the ego. At birth the infant is endowed with only a small amount of ego structure, which develops progressively throughout the early years and to some extent beyond. The ego is concerned with obtaining satisfaction for the demands of the id in the outside world. Initially the rudimentary ego achieves this impulsively in fantasy through what Freud called the 'primary process' (the pleasure principle), but as the ego develops 'the secondary process' (in which reality is taken into account, and id demands can be postponed or effective means undertaken to satisfy them) takes over. The ego subsumes all the faculties involved in mediating between the id and reality. Thus it is the agency which learns, thinks and perceives. It also has the task of defending the organism from overwhelming flows of energy, usually in the form of anxiety due to dangers from outside (e.g. physical and personal threats) and from inside (e.g. excesses of sexuality or aggression at inappropriate times or places). For this purpose a series of defence mechanisms are brought into play, e.g. repression (where the energy is simply blocked off, i.e. made unconscious) and displacement, where it is directed at another object rather than the original target (the man who is furious with his boss and takes it out on his wife when he gets home). There are a number of defence mechanisms; they are, in principle, neither good nor bad for the mental health of the individual, and they can serve an extremely useful purpose. However, constant use of a defence mechanism where it is not needed can lead to a distortion of a person's behaviour and perceptions. For example, a person who always displaces his aggression may find himself unable to stand up to his boss and always antagonising his wife. A positive use of the displacement mechanism, called 'sublimation', is where surplus sexual energy is displaced into creative work.

The third part of personality structure is the super ego. This represents, in internalised form, the demands of society, in particular the demands of parents and other influential figures during childhood. The super ego has two parts: the 'ego-ideal' affirms 'desirable' ways of acting, thinking and feeling; and 'conscience' passes negative judgements and attempts to punish the individual for 'undesirable' acts, thoughts and feelings, or to prevent them altogether, doing this by means of guilt feelings (a particular kind of anxiety) which either counteract the impulse or follow from the action.

The three parts are interrelated in the manner shown in Figure 9.1. As can be seen from Figure 9.1, the process involves a continuous selection from a large number of id impulses both by the ego in terms of what is feasible in reality and by the super ego in terms of what is acceptable to the internalised version of what society will allow.

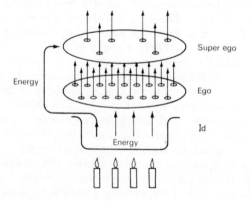

Figure 9.1   Schematic representation of Freud's theory

Freud also distinguished between the conscious and unconscious mind. Broadly speaking, the ego and super ego are conscious and the id is unconscious. Apart from ego and super ego material which is preconscious and available for recall, though not immediately available to consciousness, there is a large amount of material which, for example, has been repressed and which has therefore not been entirely lost but is consigned to the unconscious mind and hence is not accessible to consciousness. This unconscious, repressed energy can affect behaviour in devious ways and is the basis of mental symptoms and irrational behaviour.

For Freud personality development is a kind of biological unfolding. It proceeds in stages, depending on biologically determined outlets for the libido. For example, in the first year of life the chief area of the body through which the instinctual energy obtains its outlets is the mouth. Hence this is called the 'oral stage'. The outlets for the energy are in sucking and taking in through the mouth, blowing and spitting out, biting, the exploration of objects and the sensations of the mouth itself. The oral stage is itself divided into two parts, the early oral-receptive and the later oral-sadistic stages. The oral-receptive stage is based on the sucking reflex present at birth. The infant sucks automatically any object placed on its lips. Usually it is the breast or bottle which provides the pleasurable sensations but later the child takes pleasure in exploring objects by sucking. Initially the child cannot discriminate between himself and the objects which stimulate him; but eventually, as his own motor control grows, he finds out that 'me' involves those objects like his thumb over which he has instant control and 'not me' consists of those over which he does not have it, such as the breast or bottle. Later he attempts to control these latter objects by actions of his own, such as crying when hungry. He can also express his displeasure by biting, spitting or crying, and these functions come increasingly to the fore as the oral-sadistic stage is reached. These stages are not discrete but merge into each other and the influence of experiences throughout each stage continues to affect personality throughout life. For example, people with a history of oral over-indulgence tend to be optimistic (the desired feed always came), talkative, and enjoy food and wine. Those with a history of oral deprivation tend to become pessimistic (the desired feed tended not to come at the right time), abstemious and untalkative. There is a certain amount of evidence for some of Freud's propositions about the oral stage (e.g. Blum and Miller, 1952; Bernstein, 1955). (See Kline (1972) for a comprehensive review of this area.)

During the second year of life the anal stage begins to appear. The main focus for the libidinal energy is the anus. The child begins to be able to control his bowel movements and obtains satisfaction from this. He is able to delay defecation and this is pleasurable, as is the passing of the faeces. This is an activity over which he is able to have total control. In the oral stage others can force food into his mouth or deprive him of food, or take things from his mouth. No one, however, can either force him to defecate against his wishes or prevent him from making a mess if he does. There may be consequences, but this is something over which he can have complete control. The anal stage is accompanied by great strides in motor co-ordination and development and further this offers the possibility of increased independence and control, the main psychological developments of this stage. The anal stage is divided into two parts, the anal-retentive and the anal-sadistic. In physical terms the former, which occurs first, is concerned with retaining the faeces. In psychological terms it has to do with self-restraint both as a force for good, in that the child does not make a nuisance of itself, and also as a means of protest against a parent who is waiting for him to perform. The anal-sadistic phase is concerned with the expulsion of the faeces. In physical terms the sadism refers to the way in which it occurs, e.g. violent expulsion, making a great mess in the wrong place at the wrong time and vicious 'nipping-off' of the faeces. Psychologically Freud hypothesises that it concerns letting go of things or people, necessary skills in life, either in protest or aggressive non-compliance. The possibilities of character development stemming from this stage are very considerable, as with all stages. An 'anal character' has been suggested whose main characteristics are meanness, stubbornness and orderliness. Certainly these traits do seem to have a tendency to go together in later life (Beloff, 1957). However, no clear empirical connections with toilet-training practices in childhood have been identified.

The third stage is the phallic one; this may begin at any time from about $3\frac{1}{2}$ years. It is characterised by an increased interest in the genitals and feelings of attraction towards the parent of the opposite sex. This gives rise to conflict, in that the same-sexed parent becomes automatically a more powerful rival. Thus the child is torn between pre-existing love for the same-sexed parent and a newly developed hatred due to the rivalry. The conflict becomes intolerable and is repressed, the child gives up its attraction for the opposite-sex parent and its hatred for its rival, with whom it then identifies. This process forms the basis for super-ego development, in that the child is then able to introject (i.e. absorb) the values of the same-sexed parent and acquire the essential behaviour and attitudes involved in being a member of that sex.

If this is the case, then it is not universal. For example, Malinowski (1927) has found that the Trobriand Islanders have a different cultural pattern, with the parents playing totally different roles. Also, it does not appear to fit in with one-parent families, families in which the opposite-sexed parent is dominant, and hence likely to be the one who does the castrating, and cultures where the family as we understand it is not the chief or only factor in the development of the child.

Freud hypothesised that the next stage (the latency period) lasts from about 6 years of age to puberty. This is a period of consolidation, with minimal sexual activity, in which the child identifies far more with his peers and practices the behaviour appropriate to a member of his sex in his society. Again, the work of anthropologists (e.g. Malinowski, 1927) suggests that this is not universal. The Trobrianders enjoy increasing amounts of heterosexual activity from the age of 6 onwards during what ought to be the latency period. However, observation in our own society lends some support to the hypothesis.

The final stage, the genital one, starts at puberty, and is the period at which the adult heterosexual drive reaches maturity. It is expressed through non-ambivalent love of another. Whereas the object relationships of the pre-genital stages are narcissistic (i.e. self-centered, in that other people are involved only because they help to provide pleasure for the child), the genital stage heralds the channelling of the libido into genuine altruistic love relationships. Genital energy is sublimated into such activities as work, social activities and recreation. The developments of the earlier stages are consolidated into the genital stage in such a way that predominant modes of behaviour are carried through from earlier stages. The final adult organisation of personality contains contributions from all stages.

Such are the main strands of Freudian theory. We shall now attempt an evaluation.

A central criticism is that Freud's underlying procedures are unscientific. Freud obtained his basic data from individual patients and from his own self-analysis. There was therefore no systematic sampling to ensure the generalisability of his conclusions. He had no independent check on the data he was obtaining. The patients could have been deceiving him, or themselves, or both. His perceptions and interpretations were therefore of necessity subjective. Since the data were obtained in therapeutic sessions, the observations

cannot be repeated by an independent observer. Freud did not take verbatim records of his sessions, which means that a lot of relevant material
might have been lost and further that what has been published may be simply
that which fits in with his theory. These kinds of points, and there are many
more similar ones, must cause one to ask questions about Freudian theory.

The theory has been condemned for being too diffuse, and this is related
to the fact that many of its aspects do not seem to be easily testable empirically. Take, for example, the concept of 'repression'. If we wish to investigate
the hypothesis that little boys of five would like to kill their fathers and make
love to their mothers and we find no evidence for it in the statements of the
sample we are studying, then the convinced Freudian can answer 'Of course
not, the feelings have been repressed.' Concepts like the 'death instinct' raise
similar problems. It is easy to explain suicide or the breaking-off of therapy
by invoking a death wish, but such explanations are only possible after the
event and have no predictive force. Freudian theory is extremely weak in
predictive power.

Probably Freud's influence is attributable to two important considerations.
(1) Mental life, as opposed to behaviour, is an important field of study with
a live fascination of its own which makes it ask to be studied. Freud was a
pioneer in its study, using techniques which are still used, better methods not
yet having been discovered. The newer techniques tend to be more refined
variations on the old theme. The fact is that you cannot study mental life
without either examining your own or asking others to talk about theirs. It
is there to study and if the respectable scientific techniques are not applicable,
then other techniques have to be used with as many safeguards as possible.
It can be argued that there were insufficient safeguards, but such things are
not characteristic of pioneers. (2) Freud embraces a view of man on the
grand scale. As Hall and Lindzey (1970) say:

> Freud may not have been a rigorous scientist, nor a first rate theoretician,
> but he was a patient, meticulous, penetrating observer and a tenacious,
> disciplined, courageous and original thinker. Over and above all the other
> virtues of his theory stands this one – it tries to envisage a full bodied indi-
> vidual living partly in a world of reality and partly in a world of make-
> believe, beset by conflicts and inner contradictions, yet capable of rational
> thought and action, moved by forces of which he has little knowledge and
> by aspirations which are beyond his reach, in turn confused and clear
> headed, frustrated and satisfied, hopeful and despairing, selfish and
> altruistic; in short, a complex human being. For many people, this picture
> has an essential validity.

We turn now to a wholly different kind of approach to personality.

9.3 Trait and type theories – Cattell and Eysenck

One possible way of looking at personality is simply to describe a person at
a particular time. Two closely related ways of doing this are the trait and
type approaches. The trait approach involves the identification of a number

of relatively persisting characteristics of behaviour on which individuals differ from each other but which represent a tendency common to all. Take, for example, laziness. Everybody is lazy to some degree, ranging from 'not at all' to 'extremely'. The task of trait theorists is to identify the most significant human personality traits and to devise means for measuring accurately each individual in terms of them. The type approach is related to this. Essentially individuals are classified into types according to particular constellations of traits. Thus the type is a higher-order unit of description than the trait. The most well known and developed trait and type theories are those of Eysenck and Cattell. Eysenck operates chiefly at the type level and Cattell at the trait level. Their methods are in fact strikingly similar. Both operate by treating empirical data by means of factor analysis (see Chapter 10). In this they follow in the tradition stemming from behaviourism where a quantitative approach and objectivity in the best scientific tradition are of the utmost importance.

Initially it was hoped that the factors obtained would yield the key to the basic dimensions of personality; this was not to be, for just as the number 12 can be factorised in a number of different ways (6×2, 4×3, $2 \times 2 \times 3$), so also can a correlation matrix be factor analysed. Thus there is no one mathematically best way of obtaining the basic factors in personality. Indeed, one of the chief differences between Eysenck and Cattell is that they used different factor-analytic methods. None the less much fruitful work in other respects has emerged and it is this that we shall now describe.

CATTELL'S THEORY

For Cattell the main concept is that of 'trait'. He makes the important distinction between source traits and surface traits. Whereas the latter are simply groups of variables which seem to correlate together fairly consistently, the former are more important in that they represent the underlying variables which determine the events at the surface of personality. The source traits are identified by factor analysis of the interrelationships of the surface behaviour. Since surface traits are produced by the interaction of source traits with the enrivonment, they are less stable and consistent. Hence the source traits are likely to be more useful in explaining and predicting behaviour. Source traits may be divided into those which reflect predominantly the influence of the environment and those which reflect predominantly that of heredity. For example, intelligence has the greatest estimated hereditary contribution of the traits which Cattell has isolated. Of the temperamental traits (i.e. those concerned with the more or less persisting modes of reactions, e.g. speed, energy) isolated by him, that highest hereditary contribution occurs in factor *H*, a dimension of social boldness – shyness. On the other hand, he estimates that factor *F*, surgency (i.e. lively and talkative *versus* sober and taciturn) is almost completely determined environmentally, the early home background being critical. Another way in which Cattell divides his source traits is into ability (see Chapter 10), temperament and dynamic traits (concerned with motivation). More recently he has introduced the more transient concepts of 'states', 'roles' and 'sets'.

Thus anxiety may be a trait of a persisting nature but a person with this trait need not be anxious all the time. When he is, however, he is in a 'state' of anxiety. Likewise, people slip in and out of social roles on a temporary basis. Sets, again, are temporary. They are simply different predispositions to take in particular kinds of information.

Cattell obtains his data about personality from three main sources: *L* (or life-record) data, *Q* (or self-rating questionnaire) data, and *T* (objective-test) data. Thus Cattell's basic data come from three different sources of

Table 9.1   Descriptions of Cattell's sixteen personality factors

High-score description	Factor	Low-score description
Outgoing, warm-hearted, easy-going, participating (cyclothymia)	A	*Reserved*, detached, critical, cool (schizothymia)
More intelligent, abstract thinking, bright (higher scholastic mental capacity)	B	*Less intelligent*, concrete thinking (lower scholastic mental capacity)
Emotionally stable, faces reality, calm (higher ego strength)	C	*Affected by feelings*, emotionally less stable, easily upset (lower ego strength)
Assertive, independent, aggressive, stubborn (dominance)	E	*Humble*, mild, obedient, conforming (submissiveness)
Happy go lucky, heedless, gay, enthusiastic (surgency)	F	*Sober*, prudent, serious, taciturn (desurgency)
Conscientious, persevering, staid, rule-bound (stronger super-ego strength)	G	*Expedient*, a law to himself, by-passes obligations (weaker super-ego strength)
Venturesome, socially bold, uninhibited, spontaneous (parmia)	H	*Shy*, restrained diffident, timid (threctia)
Tender-minded, dependent, over-protected, sensitive (premsia)	I	*Tough-minded*, self-reliant, realistic, no-nonsense (harria)
Suspicious, self-opinionated, hard to fool (protension)	L	*Trusting*, adaptable, free of jealousy, easy to get on with (alaxia)
Imaginative, wrapped up in inner urgencies, careless of practical matters, bohemian (autia)	M	*Practical*, careful, conventional, regulated by external realities, proper (praxernia)
Shrewd, calculating, worldly, penetrating (shrewdness)	N	*Forthright*, natural, artless, sentimental (artlessness)
Apprehensive, worrying, depressive, troubled (guilt proneness)	O	*Placid*, self-assured, confident, serene (untroubled adequacy)
Experimenting, critical, liberal, analytical, free-thinking (radicalism)	Q_1	*Conservative*, respecting established ideas, tolerant of traditional difficulties (conservatism)
Self-sufficient, prefers own decisions, resourceful (self-sufficiency)	Q_2	*Group-dependent*, a 'joiner' and sound follower (group adherence)
Controlled, socially precise, self-disciplined, compulsive (high self-concept control)	Q_3	*Casual*, careless of protocol, untidy, follows own urges (low integration)
Tense, driven, overwrought, fretful (high ergic tension)	Q_4	*Relaxed*, tranquil, torpid, unfrustrated (low ergic tension)

Source: Cattell (1963).

observation: (i) the observation of others on the personality of an individual they know well (*L* data); (ii) an individual's own observations (*Q* data); and (iii) performance on specific situation tests (*T* data). Using data from all these three sources, Cattell has constructed correlation matrices describing the correlations of personality variables for each type of data. On some thirty or so occasions Cattell reports that the analytic picture shown in Table 9.1 has emerged from *L*- and *Q*-data studies. The last four factors, however, have only been obtained from *Q* data (Cattell, Eber and Tatsuoka, 1970). The *T* data seem to yield some factors corresponding to those emerging as a result of a further factor analysis of the *L*- and *Q*-data factors. Since the mathematical procedure Cattell uses yields factors which are intercorrelated slightly, it is possible to factor analyse the intercorrelations of these factors. The result is the identification of higher-order factors which include anxiety and 'exvia–invia' (so called because of its similarity to extraversion–introversion).

With the identification of the sixteen primary factors or source traits, it is possible to obtain a personality profile for each individual based on his score on each of the factors.

These source traits are mainly temperament traits, the only exceptions being *B*, an ability trait, and *E*, which has something of a dynamic nature. Cattell seems to see the dynamic traits operating mainly at the surface level. There are three kinds of these: ergs, sentiments and attitudes. Ergs are biologically based drives; sentiments are acquired attitude structures; and attitudes are the manifest expression of the erg/sentiment structure. A picture of Cattell's 'dynamic lattice' should clarify the interrelationships of these three dynamic features of the personality (see Figure 6.3).

Attitudes are subsidiary to sentiments, which in turn are subsidiary to ergs, in the sense that the first two are means to ends whereas the ergs are biologically given. One of the sentiments has a particular importance – the self-sentiment. Maintenance of a satisfactory self is an essential prerequisite to the functioning of all the other attitudes and sentiments. As Cattell (1965) states:

In the first place, the preservation of the self as a physically healthy and intact going concern is obviously a prerequisite for the satisfaction of any sentiment or erg which the individual possesses! So also is the preservation of the social and ethical self as something which the community respects.... Dynamically, the sentiment towards maintaining the self correct by certain standards of conduct, satisfactory to community and superego, is therefore a *necessary instrumentality* to the satisfaction of most other of our life interests. The conclusion to which this leads is that self-sentiment must appear in the dynamic lattice . . . far to the left and therefore among the latest of sentiments to reach a ripe development. It contributes to all sentiment and ergic satisfactions, and this accounts also for its dynamic strength in controlling, as the 'master sentiment', all other structures.

Whereas Cattell bases his work on sixteen to twenty-one factors, Eysenck prefers to work with three relatively broad, uncorrelated factors.

EYSENCK'S THEORY

In a similar way to Cattell, Eysenck administered a large number of measures to a large number of subjects. In addition to the kinds of measurements Cattell made, Eysenck also made clinical and physical ones. In his 1947 study, the sample consisted of 10 000 normal and neurotic soldiers. Two factors emerged from this study: extraversion–introversion and neuroticism–stability. In his 1952 study of normal subjects and mental-hospital patients he identified a third factor, psychoticism. These three factors constitute the highest level of Eysenck's model, which is diagrammatically reproduced here (see Figure 9.2).

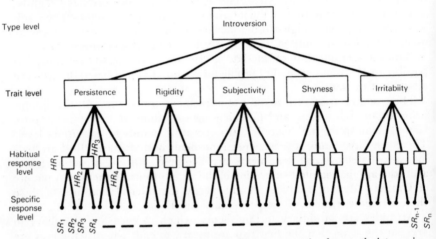

Figure 9.2   Eysenck's hierarchical model of personality structure as it relates to the introversion dimension (Eysenck, 1953)

The type level breaks down into traits, which in turn break down into habitual responses and these in turn into specific responses. The higher the hierarchical level, the more is the dimension characteristic of the individual.

Apart from this structural analysis of the personality, Eysenck has also attempted an analysis in terms of its biological determinants. He relates the introversion–extraversion factor to the relative degrees of excitatory and inhibitory potential in the cortex of the brain. Individuals who show a high degree of inhibitory activity in the cortex of the brain (which means that the cortex, which generally exerts a suppressing influence on expression, is not carrying out this suppressing function) tend towards extraversion, whereas those who show a high degree of excitatory cortical activity (and hence suppress expression) tend towards introversion. A further biological feature of Eysenck's analysis relates to neuroticism. Here he suggests that the basic reactivity of the entire nervous system determines the extent of neuroticism in the personality.

The immediate striking difference in the conclusions of these two workers is that whereas Cattell has identified some sixteen to twenty-one factors in his various studies, Eysenck has identified three only. Other workers in the field (notably Guilford and Zimmerman, 1949; Norman, 1963; Comrey and Jamison, 1966) have found different yet equally replicable sets of personality factors. A review by Howarth (1972) indicates that investigators have failed in the main to find a similar factor structure to that proposed by Cattell. In fact only a small number of factors have been found with any degree of consistency when all relevant studies are reviewed. As suggested earlier, there are a large number of possible factor solutions for any given batch of data and none of the workers mentioned above may lay claim to having discovered *the* structure of personality. Their main achievement has been that each of them in turn has identified a set of factors around which a large amount of empirical data have been collected. More than any other group of personality theorists, Eysenck, Cattell and Guilford (the third major contributor in the area) have first allowed their theoretical models to follow from empirical work of a replicable nature and then to test out their theoretical formulations in an empirical manner. This is in stark contrast to Freud, whose theory, as we have seen, has something of the character of a private dialogue between Freud and his patients. The empirical rigour of the current theorists is seen as their primary achievement.

An important point to note here is that the factors may only represent descriptive categories and not any actual psychological entities which can be observed in the manner of a particular bone in the skeleton. Rather, to carry the physical analogy a little further, a factor-analytic solution is somewhat like using a different set of categories to describe the body depending on the particular activity on which you are engaged. For example, the physical-education teacher and the doctor require different sets of categories to describe the same bag of bones. The differences between Eysenck and Cattell are due primarily to two causes. (1) They make use of different types of mathematical techniques to elicit their factors. The technique which Eysenck uses is one which yields orthogonal (uncorrelated) factors, whereas Cattell prefers to use a method which yeilds oblique (correlated) factors. Cattell's factors have some degree of overlap with each other and can in turn be factor analysed. Eysenck's, on the other hand, have zero intercorrelations. (2) What is interesting is that Cattell's second-order factors (exvia–invia and anxiety), obtained from factor analysis of his source traits, correspond very closely to Eysenck's factors of extraversion–introversion and neuroticism–stability (correlation $r=0.7$). It seems that Cattell's trait approach is at a different level of generality to the type of approach used by Eysenck. Figure 9.3 illustrates this.

The difference arises because Cattell's concern is with the relationship between personality and real-life variables such as occupation, marriage, leadership and musical preferences, whereas Eysenck's concern is with the theory of personality structure, in particular its physiological aspects. A more differentiated analysis at the trait level is more suited to the former task and more general analysis at the type level is more appropriate to the latter. Indeed, as we have suggested, analysis at the more differentiated level of attitude or interest (e.g. Strong, 1943; Kuder, 1965, 1970; Campbell, 1971) seems to provide even better prediction of occupational success than the trait level Cattell seeks to use.

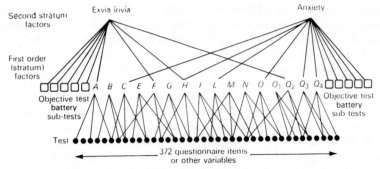

Figure 9.3   Second-order factor structures and the relation of questionnaire and objective test factors (Cattell and Kline, 1977)

However, these points of difference between the two should not be allowed to obscure the fact that it has been possible to find enough common ground to enable this detailed comparison. This common ground derives from their shared insistence on a sound empirical basis for their work and an eschewal of armchair theorising. It is epitomised in the convergence of their views at the level of type, in particular over the extraversion factor. They are both very different from the next theory we are going to consider, a phenomenological one.

9.4   Rogers' phenomenological theory

Like Freud, Rogers (1951) evolved his theory on the basis of his experience of treating patients in psychotherapy. Yet his experience took him in a somewhat different direction.

Structurally, for Rogers, personality comprises two parts, the 'organism' and the 'self'. The organism is the place where all psychological experience takes place. This includes everything that is happening within the organism and is available to awareness. This world of experience is called the 'phenomenal field'. This is a key concept, its essential feature being that it is totally private. No individual can enter into another individual's phenomenal field, except indirectly, when the other individual describes his experience, or by surmise or intuition. Some of the phenomenal field is conscious (symbolised) and some unconscious (unsymbolised). What an individual perceives and how he behaves depends not on any objective reality but on his own perceived (phenomenological) reality as he experiences it. An individual may respond both to conscious and unconscious experiences. Incorrectly symbolised experiences (misperceptions) can lead to inappropriate behaviour. Thus the individual needs constantly to test his phenomenal reality with objective reality if misperceptions are to be avoided, even though he might not always do it. More precisely, since his only contact with reality is through his phenomenal field and he can have no direct access to reality, what the individual does is to test one aspect of his phenomenal field against another to see if they together form a coherent picture of the outside reality. Thus I might test a feeling that Miss *X* loves me by matching it with my perception of what she does when I approach her. If she approaches me and in some way demonstrates her love, then my original feeling is validated, but if she avoids me then the matter is at least open to question. According to Rogers, the phenomenal field operates as a kind of *Gestalt*, or whole, in which a change in one part affects the total configuration.

The self is a particular part of the phenomenal field which is differentiated from the rest. This part involves the experience of the 'I' or 'me' and its relations to various aspects of life (e.g. work, significant people, and ideals), together with the feeling tone of this experience and the value attributed to it.

The central feature of Rogers' theory is the way in which he relates mental health to the degree of congruity between the self and the organism. When the experiences constituting the self reflect closely the experiences of the organism, then the individual can function fully. Thus, if I perceive myself as popular, witty and entertaining (self) and my experience (organism) is of being avoided by people I have bored, there is a lack of congruence which will make me feel threatened and anxious. Two other aspects of congruity reflect the relationship of the phenomenal field to external reality and the relationship of the self to the ideal self. A lack of correspondence between either of these will lead to disturbances of feeling and behaviour.

So far we have only discussed certain structural aspects of Rogers's theory. It is now time to look at the driving dynamic which activates the structure, his concept of 'motivation'. To quote Rogers (1951): 'The organism has only one basic tendency and striving to actualize, maintain, and enhance the experiencing organism.' This idea is very close to the self-actualisation motive of Maslow and to the concept of self-actualising man which we shall meet in the final chapter. Unlike Maslow, however, Rogers believes that this one drive is sufficient to account for all behaviour. As the organism develops, this drive becomes more differentiated and expands until it is capable of generating all the behaviour of the adult. This drive can only operate satisfactorily when the choices before the organism are perceived and symbolised accurately; in this way the path of growth can always be chosen. We have said before that the primary motive expands and becomes differentiated, and two of the differentiations are particularly important, the learnt needs for positive regard and for self-regard. Both of these are established as a result of the baby's experiences. The experience of being loved and cared for produces expectations and a consequent need for positive regard from others. The receiving of positive regard from others enhances the baby's self-regard and in the same way generates an expectation and need for self-regard to be maintained.

During childhood the self and the organism develop together. However, certain actions on the part of the child are evaluated positively by parents and others, whereas other actions are evaluated negatively. What then happens is that the negatively evaluated actions and feelings tend to get excluded from the self concept in the interests of maintaining positive self-regard. However, the organism continues to experience these. This produces incongruity between the self and the organism. The child then tries to bring the organism's experiences into line by behaving only as others and his distorted self want him to. Thus experiences come to be valued because others value them and not because they serve to enhance the organism. An example would be the young child's aggression towards his parents which is excluded from the self because it is disapproved of by the parents but continues to recur in the organism. This causes the child to distort his personality by avoiding feelings and actions involving aggression to the parents. Yet the child's own values are being supplanted by the parents'. Such a child will feel uncomfortable with himself. His wants will not be his own and he will be confused about what he really does want. Life loses its sharpness and meaning.

A constant feeling of incongruity between self and organism results in each organismic experience being at variance with the distorted self-concept, thus generating anxiety. The anxiety, if great enough, causes the organism to distort its own experience by means of mechanisms similar to Freud's defence mechanism. Thus aggression may be denied and seep out in terms of an excessive obsequiousness. This kind of mechanism distorts not only the personality but also the individual's relationships with others. So, as in the above case, this can bring about an exaggerated formality and politeness which gets in the way of intimacy in human relationships.

Rogers's chief clinical concern is with reducing the incongruity between self and organism and enhancing the individual's self-esteem. The method he advocates is called 'non-directive' or 'client-centred' counselling and the technique is described in greater detail in Chapter 11. Here, all that needs to be said is that the role of the interviewer is to offer the client unconditional positive regard and to reflect back to the client what he seems to be saying. In this way, basking in the warm regard of the interviewer, he is able to come to a re-evaluation of his own organismic and self experiences and so feel less incongruity and more enhancement of his self-regard.

The most important aspects of the theory are those which contribute towards its being a viable alternative to psychoanalysis and behaviourism. The aspects of the theory which make it distinctive are its phenomenological standpoint and its humanism. These two are related, for the basic trust in the essential goodness of man and his innate motivation to actualise himself is reflected in the belief that what is important is the way man perceives his world rather than any external objective.

Rogers, like Freud, has chosen a field of study which is particularly inaccessible to scientific investigation. None the less his work has been characterised by empirical attempts to provide evidence for his clinically derived theoretical formulations. The research does not always provide direct proof of the theory but with a few exceptions is certainly compatible with it (for example, a large number of references to clients' utterances at different stages of therapy, illustrating particular self-pictures of clients and the changes that occur as the therapy progresses (e.g. Rogers, 1951, 1967)). However, these do little more than illustrate the theory rather than act as direct evidence either for or against the theory.

More rigorous research using content analysis (a technique allotting the content of utterances of speakers into different categories) of therapy sessions has shown that clients deemed to have most improved showed more positive self-references in later sessions than earlier sessions (Raimy, 1948).

Various researchers have attempted to use content analysis to test the proposition that acceptance of oneself goes together with acceptance of others. Although it seems that a change in one during therapy is not necessarily associated with a change in the other, Wylie (1961), in a survey of twenty-one studies, suggests that the evidence points towards a general tendency for self-acceptance and acceptance of others to go together. Whether one needs the superstructure of Rogers's theory to account for this is debatable. For example, Suinn (1961) has proposed that the learning of a generalised acceptance for both self and others would be sufficient to account for the phenomenon.

Further research compatible with Rogers' standpoint concerns the effectiveness of psychotherapists. Truax and Mitchell (1971), reviewing fourteen studies between 1963 and 1969, report that the therapists with the highest success rates are those scoring high on three attributes: "accurate empathic understanding', 'non-possessive warmth' and 'genuineness'. Since Truax (1963) has shown that therapist behaviour tends to be constant across patients, it seems unlikely that the Truax and Mitchell finding is due to the patient influencing the therapist and not vice versa. Thus it would seem that here we have some evidence that under conditions where the patient experiences 'unconditional positive regard' his self-esteem is enhanced.

Stephenson's (1953) Q-sort technique (in which the subject is asked to sort a number of statements along a continuum ranging from those most characteristic of himself to those least characteristic) has been used to measure the degree of congruity between the self and the ideal self. This was found to increase as a result of therapy, indicating a greater degree of satisfaction with the self and hence, presumably, indicating greater self-esteem.

One of the interesting features of Rogers's work is that it has been under attack from both psychoanalysts and behaviourists. In particular, the psychoanalysts have made the criticism that Rogers pays insufficient attention to the unconscious, and that unconditional regard is unlikely to be sufficient to penetrate the unconscious without analysis and interpretation. The behaviourists hold that to operate entirely from within the phenomenal field is mistaken in that hypotheses derived from such a standpoint are in principle only testable indirectly.

To all this, Rogers replies that the viewpoint has proved extremely fruitful to him and in the meantime he is not prepared to reject it. It is an open question as to whether or not there is any one correct way to look at personality. Certainly Rogers and his associates have made use of a wide variety of methods derived from a number of viewpoints in order to validate his theory. It is in this role as a bridge between viewpoints while firmly remaining rooted in his own that Rogers will perhaps be best remembered.

9.5 Kelly's personal-construct theory

Essentially, in that he is phenomenological in outlook, Kelly has much in common with Rogers. However, the authors are risking a degree of replication in this section in the interests of reviewing a theorist who in a unique way has been able, to an extent greater even than Rogers, to forge links between the nomothetic and idiographic approaches (respectively emphasis on the study of the whole individual and emphasis on traits common to all individuals). At the same time he also attempts to span the gap between the phenomenologists and those who want everything to be measurable and observable. He does this by focusing on human beings as objects for study by scientists, but by making all men equal, investigator *and* his subjects. All are scientists. Not only do investigators hypothesise about the nature of their world, but so does eveyone else. 'Everyman' (the scientist) attempts actively to conceptualise his world and then to test out these conceptualisations in action. Man the scientist is the subject of study of man the scientist. As Kelly (1961) states:

> Abstraction and generalization of human activity are not the exclusive prerogatives of professional psychologists. What they do any person may do. Indeed, every person does! Each individual the psychologists study abstracts and generalizes on his own, for he is even more vitally interested than they can ever be in the task of understanding himself and his relationship to other persons and values. Thus the psychology of personality is not simply a matter of disinterested psychologists assessing a disinterested organism but of psychologists who happen to be professionally and casually interested in their chosen subject matter, assessing a non-professional psychologist who, on his part, is intimately and urgently involved with the job of making sense out of the life upon which his existence depends.

Thus each person's activities are channelled by the ways in which he conceptualises and anticipates. The conceptual framework he uses is called the 'construct system'. A construct is a bipolar concept such as 'black–white', 'kind–cruel' or 'extravert–introvert' which we make use of to interpret our experiences. Clearly there are a large number of possible constructs which a person could use for this purpose. It is the particular set of constructs which a person uses and the way in which they interrelate as a system which determine the individuality of each personality. A construct system is a complex hierarchical system in which each construct may overlap with, subsume or be subsumed by another construct. For example, my father may be kind on the kind–cruel construct, ambitious on the ambitious–unambitious construct and dominant on the dominant–submissive construct. If my experience of other people is that the kind ones also tend to be ambitious and dominant, then these constructs will begin to be seen as related and to form some kind of a system. Essentially Kelly is concerned with such questions as how construct systems develop and change, and the possibility of predicting behaviour from knowledge of a person's construct system. To this end, Kelly makes a number of statements (corollaries) which elaborate upon the basic idea of a construct. There are eleven of these, and they can be summarised as follows:

(i) the 'construction' corollary refers to the fact that man attempts to anticipate events in terms of the constructs which he has evolved and found to be relevant;

(ii) the 'individuality' corollary points out that people differ in their construction of events;

(iii) the 'organisation' corollary states that constructs are organised into a system;

(iv) the 'dichotomy' corollary states that each person has a finite number of bipolar constructs;

(v) the 'choice' corollary states that the individual chooses that alternative in a bipolar construct which enables him better to anticipate events;

(vi) the 'range' corollary states that a construct is convenient for a limited range of events only;

(vii) the 'experience' corollary states that a person's construct system varies as he construes successfully the replication of events;

(viii) the 'modulation' corollary states that the variation in a person's construct system is limited by the extent to which the existing constructs and their interrelationships enable new constructs and events to be subsumed under the system (permeability);

(ix) the 'fragmentation' corollary states that if a person is unable to integrate the construct sub-systems he uses into one, he may employ a number of such sub-systems independently of each other;

(x) the 'commonality' corollary states that constructs and systems employed by different people may be essentially similar and to that extent those two people's processes are similar;

(xi) the 'sociality' corollary states that to the extent that a person construes accurately the construct system of another, he can interact socially with him. (This is the basis of human relationships.)

Apart from those stated above, constructs may have a number of qualities. Some may be pre-verbal, deriving from very early stages of development. Some constructs are core constructs in that any disturbance of these would disturb radically the individual's way of life and even existence. Others are peripheral, in the sense that they are of less crucial importance. Some are comprehensive in that they subsume a wide range of events, whereas others are incidental in that they subsume only a narrow range. As indicated earlier, some are permeable, in that they allow new elements into their sphere of reference; others are impermeable in that they do not. Some relations between constructs are tight and lead to unvarying predictions (this is a table, therefore it is solid), others are loose. These different types of constructs and relationships between constructs serve further to increase the variety of possible construct systems.

A particularly interesting feature of the theory is the way in which emotions are defined. For example, anxiety is simply the recognition that one's constructs are inadequate to handle new events. Fear is the awareness of an imminent change in one's core structures. Hostility is the continued effort to distort validational evidence in favour of a social prediction which has already been recognised as a failure. What is interesting is that each of these is defined in terms of the construct system and the perceived elements involved.

The theory contains, almost built into it, its own measurement device, the role construct repertory test or repertory grid. Essentially it is a method for eliciting a person's constructs in such a way that their interrelationships in the form of a system can also be ascertained. We will describe the method in more detail in the Section 9.7. The repertory grid has enabled considerable validatory research to be carried out, both of an idiographic and nomothetic kind. For example, Bieri (1955, 1961) has used it to study the thought processes of thought-disordered schizophrenics. The suggestion behind the theory is that particular kinds of personality have particular kinds of construct system. Thus schizophrenics with mental confusion should have a large number of disconnected constructs. This idea has been confirmed by several writers (e.g. Bannister, 1960, 1962; Bannister and Fransella, 1966). However, there are individuals who are complex cognitively and are far from schizophrenic in that they operate extremely well simply as a result of the richness of their construct systems. Initial findings indicated that thought-disordered schizophrenics do in fact show similar repertory grids to cognitively complex normals. A way of distinguishing between the two groups which made use of the reliability of the grid with normals was found by Bannister. Fjeld and Landfield (1961) report a retest reliability of 0.79 over a two-week period between the two administrations of the grid. The schizophrenic and normal groups were retested after an interval and it was found that whereas the normal group showed a high retest reliability, the schizophrenic group did not, indicating that the discriminating factor for the latter group was not just that they had a large number of constructs with low intercorrelations but also that these intercorrelations were inconsistent over time. Their construct system was not only patterned weakly, it was also unstable.

Runkel and Damrin (1961) followed a group of student teachers through their training and observed the changes in their construct systems. At the beginning, middle and end of training the investigators faced their subjects with a number of problems they might encounter in relation to their pupils, and asked them to rank order the kinds of information they would require when trying to solve those problems. Statistical analysis of the responses enabled the investigators to identify the number of constructs which were being used in the attempt to achieve a solution. Initially the students started with a considerable variety of constructs, only some of which were relevant. In the middle of training their anxiety level increased and the number of constructs used was reduced markedly. Finally, as the students became more confident and had obtained more experience, their range of constructs widened again. The study also showed some evidence that the most successful students were those who had shown the greatest dip in cognitive complexity during training. This restriction in the number of constructs due to anxiety, which is also a feature of anxiety neurotics, might be responsible for the phenomenon of the plateau in learning a skill (see Chapter 3) and is clearly an important consideration for anyone involved in training.

We cannot leave this discussion of Kelly without reference to the use of his ideas in the study of single individual cases. We shall show how a personal-construct theory approach enabled closer examination of a woman who wished to have a 'sex-change' operation. Salmon (1963), using repertory grids, found that this woman had a highly organised construct system for construing men but virtually no structure in her system for construing women. Probably this indicated a degree of confusion as far as women were concerned. Thus in order to perceive herself as a woman she would have needed an entirely new conceptual framework. Only in this way would it be possible to give some substance to the word 'woman' for her and then possibly for herself as a woman. Advising her to be more feminine, in the same way as advising Runkel and Damrin's students to consider more dimensions at the height of their anxiety, would have been meaningless, as the constructs were just not available. It is pointless to provide advice or ideas to people who do not have a construct system which can contain them. Thus highly anxious people (who operate with few constructs) do better in skill-learning if performance feedback is kept to a minimum.

Enough has been said in this short section to indicate the richness of the possibilities of research which Kelly's theory has stimulated. This in itself is a valuable achievement. The way in which it bridges the gaps between a number of viewpoints is also important. But a word should be said about this. It is not a total bridging that has been achieved. The 'phenomenal field' is still intractably private if the individual chooses not to communicate its contents. However, for those who will settle for accounts of a person's experiences in the absence of the availability of those experiences themselves for study, Kelly's work is in the best scientific tradition.

To date we have focussed upon fairly wide-ranging theories of personality. Much work has gone on, however, outside these broad theoretical frameworks. It is very diverse in terms of approach and has focussed upon various aspects of personality. We shall now touch briefly upon some of this work.

9.6 Other specific areas of personality research

Over the last twenty-five years psychologists have been concerned with the concept of 'authoritarianism'. Initial work on this was carried out by Adorno *et al.* (1950), who found that high scores on the F scale (a measure of authoritarianism) were typically categorical and judgemental in reactions to others, intellectually rigid, depressive of inner life, hostile in response to restraint, deferential to those above them and exploitative of those below them, fearful of social change, distrustful, self-pitying and self-serving. Recently, more subtle and indirect variants of the F scale have been devised, for example Christie's scale for Machiavellianism (Christie and Geis, 1971). There is evidence that Machiavellianism is related to eye-gaze behaviour (Poppleton, 1971). Specifically, high-scoring people tend to look at others more than low scorers when they are lying.

As we remarked at the beginning of this chapter, many of the other chapters are concerned with topics related to personality, if the term is used in its broadest sense. We have discussed already the importance of motivation. We have examined some of the work that has been done, for example, on the need for achievement (see Chapters 6 and 7). Socialisation and moral-judgement measures, stemming from a learning approach, have also been studied (Kohlberg, 1964). Work on social intelligence (e.g. Guilford, 1967) and creativity, dealt with in the next chapter, might also have been dealt with here.

Other approaches to the study of personality take a biological perspective. This shows itself for example, in research aimed at (i) elucidating how biochemical factors affect personality (e.g. Barchas *et al.*, 1971), (ii) estimating the heritability components of various measures of personality characteristics (Lindzey *et al.*, 1971), and (iii) examining the relationship between sleep patterns and personality (Hartmann *et al.*, 1971).

All of the work discussed in this section requires some measure of the personality characteristic concerned, and it is to a discussion of techniques of personality assessment that we now turn.

9.7 Personality assessment

Each of us is constantly making assessments of the personality of others; we need to do this in order to proceed with our lives in an orderly manner. Kelly has produced a whole theory of personality which is based entirely on our tendency to categorise people, objects and events and we have seen that such categorisations are subject to distortion. In this section we shall take a brief look at the attempts psychologists have made to obtain reliable and valid assessments of personality. Certain methods which have been used for personality assessment have been or will be discussed elsewhere, e.g. interviews and attitude scales. We shall not repeat the discussion here. Instead, we shall confine ourselves to the typical methods used by the three kinds of personality theorists we have reviewed so far: the psychoanalyst, the neo-behaviourist and the phenomenologist.

We shall begin by introducing two concepts which will be dealt with in more detail in the next chapter, 'reliability' and 'validity'. Between them they supply the criteria which a personality assessment must meet if it is to be satisfactory. Reliability is defined as being the capability of a measure always to give the same results when applied repeatedly to the same subject under the same circumstances. Essentially it refers to the consistency of a measure. It is said to be valid if it measures what it is supposed to be measuring. There are several types both of reliability and of validity (see Chapter 10).

The three main types of assessment procedure typical of our three types of personality theory are self-report questionnaires (neo-behaviourism), projective techniques (psychoanalysis) and self-rating procedures (phenomenology). In addition, various rating methods are available for use by observers (see Chapter 11).

QUESTIONNAIRES

Examples of self-report questionnaires are the Cattell 16 P.F.Q. and the Eysenck Personality Inventory (E.P.I.). They consist of a number of questions which have to be answered 'Yes 'or 'No'. Some questionnaires have an intermediate category of 'Do not know' or 'Cannot say'. Certain superficial objections arise immediately in connection with these measures. Respondents' answers are likely to be inaccurate for a number of reasons: (1) They may consciously be trying to give a false impression in their answers. Poppleton (1975), for example, suggests that faking occurred on the Cattell 16 P.F.Q. when it was used for the selection of salesmen. Salesmen in employment with life-assurance companies tend to score above average on extraversion and below average on anxiety when compared with the general population. Applicants for jobs, however, scored markedly more extraversion and less anxiety than the already employed groups. An explanation of this might be that both extraversion and low anxiety appear to be desirable qualities in a salesman and job applicants 'fake' their responses accordingly. Cattell *et al.* (1970), also report appreciable motivational distortion (faking) effects with the 16 P.F.Q. (2) Respondents may not have sufficient self-awareness to give a correct answer. (3) They may misperceive the questions for a number of reasons.

Questionnaire constructors have used two main methods to overcome these objections. First, they have tried to disguise the test to look like something else. Second, they have introduced lie scales, of which there are two main kinds. One is the 'faking-good' kind, which consists of a series of such utterly perfect characteristics that no one could possibly possess more than one or two of them. Too high a score on this scale leads the tester to suspect all the other answers in the test. The other kind of lie scale involves repeating individual items, sometimes with opposite evaluative slants and observing whether the respondent gives the same answer to both. What is important is the possibility of using a questionnaire validly for the purpose for which it is being used. There is no such thing as the absolute validity of a test. Its validity can only be determined empirically in respect of the particular situation for which it is employed. Thus if a questionnaire is being used to detect neurotics, it must have been shown previously to discriminate between groups of neurotics and normals. As far as the authors are aware, there is no evidence that the inclusion of a lie scale has been shown generally to increase validity. Its use is in pointing out when a test score should be disregarded. Where the lie scale can be of use is in consideration of a single case, e.g. in the prison service, but even here there is often enough evidence from other sources against which the questionnaire result should be balanced.

Various other measures can be taken in the design of questionnaires to overcome some of the problems mentioned above. See, for example, Cronbach (1946, 1950), Jackson (1967) and Messick (1967) for discussions of response sets (the tendency to respond in particular stereotyped ways to questionnaire items, e.g. the acquiescence response set, the tendency to answer 'yes', which is thought to be typical of the authoritarian personality) and Edwards (1957, 1967) on social desirability.

PROJECTIVE TESTS

Projective tests make use of the Freudian idea of projection. Projection is a defence mechanism by which we reject unacceptable parts of ourselves and project them on to others. An example would be the prim virgin who assumes that an innocent bystander wants to rape her. The suggestion is that projection is a much more pervasive mechanism than its use solely as an ego defence would imply. Every story we tell and every fantasy we have reflects our personality, both conscious and unconscious. The two best-known projective tests are the Rorschach Test and the Thematic Apperception Test (T.A.T.). Each involves the presentation of the test material (in the case of the former a series of ink blots, in the latter a series of pictures of a more or less ambiguous nature) to the subject who is then asked what he sees in each picture or ink blot. The themes with which he responds reflect the underlying aspects of his personality. This method generates a large amount of material and the scoring and interpretation of open-ended verbal or written responses pose considerable problems. Klopfer and Davidson (1962) review this issue for the Rorschach test and Murstein (1963) for the T.A.T. For both tests, and particularly the T.A.T., reliable methods of scoring have been devised which have yielded useful research results. None the less the methods do pose particular problems of reliability and validity, and, as Harris (1960) suggests, their general value in the field of personality assessment remains unproven. However, in the hands of the psychoanalytically orientated clinician they provide valuable information which is likely to be free of the kinds of contamination often found in an individual questionnaire.

SELF-RATING METHODS

Self-rating methods are similar to questionnaires in conception but are less structured and more complex to administer. Usually a more complex activity is demanded of the respondent. In general what they gain in eliciting the most individually relevant aspects of the personality, they lose in any direct comparison between individuals on the same dimensions of personality. Although this is possible in respect of higher-level variables such as the organisation of personality, individuality of the basic responses does prevent direct comparison. In a sense this type of test represents the same kind of middle position between questionnaires and projective tests that phenomenology does between psychoanalysis and behaviourism. They enable quantification of what are, in essence, idiographic measures.

The methods we are talking about now include the 'Q-sort' (Stephenson, 1953), the 'semantic differential' (Osgood, Suci and Tannenbaum, 1957) and the 'role construct repertory test' (Kelly, 1955). Since we focussed on Kelly earlier in the chapter, we shall devote the rest of this section to a consideration of the repertory test. There are several ways of administering the test, but we shall describe only the original version whilst noting some of the other possibilities.

The test starts with the subject being asked to name the twelve or twenty most significant people in his life. If ways of construing people are not being studied, objects or events may be substituted. These are called 'elements', which comprise one side of the matrix or repertory grid (see Figure 9.4).

The tester then works through the elements in threes, asking the subject to say in which way two of them are similar and the third different. The subject's description of the way in which two are similar and one different is

Role titles

	Self	Mother	Father	Brother	Sister	Spouse	Ex-flame	Best-friend	Ex-friend	Rejecting person	Pitied person	Threatening person	Attractive person	Accepted teacher	Rejected teacher	Boss	Successful person	Happy person	Ethical person	Neighbour	Constructs
	1	2	3	4	5	6	7	8	9	10	11	12	13	14	15	16	17	18	19	20	
																	O	O	O		1
						O	O	O													2
	O					O		O													3
		O				O	O														4

Circles indicate triads of figures for eliciting constructs. The two poles of each construct are written alongside the row to indicate which of the figures are allotted to the first (emergent) pole of the construct. Blanks indicate that the figures are seen as characterised by the contrast pole. In the grid form of the test the array of ticks and blanks can be scanned vertically to examine relationships between constructs, and horizontally to examine relationships between role figures.

Figure 9.4   Role-construct repertory test form (Bannister and Mair, 1963)

taken to indicate one of the ways in which he construes his environment, i.e. it is a construct. For example, he may say that his girlfriend is permissive and his mother and father restrictive, then restrictive–permissive goes down as the first construct on the side of the grid, and so on until the subject runs out of constructs. The pattern of crosses on the grid can be analysed statistically to determine the pattern of interrelationships of the constructs. Various measures of patterning are possible and it is these that enable comparisons between subjects and groups of subjects, while the constructs themselves do not. There are several different ways of presenting the elements and the subject may or may not be given a choice of the initial elements. Thus the 'rep' test can move either in the direction of the questionnaire, in the sense that questions asked are relatively fixed, and in the direction of the projective test, in the sense of being more open-ended.

A number of studies (see Bonarius (1965), for a review) report high retest reliability for the 'rep' test. We have already mentioned Fjeld and Landfield's (1961) study in another connection. As to validity, conclusions, as always, are more difficult. As we pointed out earlier, a test is only valid or invalid in relation to some outside criterion which, for example, it is attempting to predict. That said, Bonarius does report some studies which show the 'rep' test to be related significantly to overt behaviour and some others (fewer) not significantly. Payne (1956) (in Bonarius, 1965) has found that subjects with access to 'rep' rest results concerning individuals were better able to predict their behaviour than subjects who only had access to other people's descriptions of those individuals. Other evidence of this type is also available, and seems to indicate that understanding how a person sees or construes his world can help in predicting his behaviour. An important issue in personality assessment concerns the integration of a number of different personality measures into an over-all judgement. Here we shall only make four key points: (i) actuarial prediction tends to give better results than intuition; (ii) the most effective actuarial methods have generally been those involving linear methods of prediction, such as regression (Goldberg, 1969); (iii) a promising approach is a decision-tree method (Kleinmuntz, 1963) which ordinarily is linear at each choice point, but in which systems of choice may be non-linear; (iv) in predicting behaviour it is essential to take into account the context and specifics of a given situation. On this last point, for example, the context can sometimes be viewed as a moderator variable (see Chapter 12), as in Fenelon and Megargee's (1971) studies. They found that dominance was related to the assumption of task leadership only when the task was viewed as relevant to leadership. Assessments of personality are of particular interest to the occupational psychologist when they are related to job performance. Before concluding this chapter, we turn to this relationship.

9.8 Personality and job performance

Much recent research on personality assessment has attempted to predict managerial performance. Most effective in this context have been multiple-assessment programmes which use a wide array of procedures, including interviews, ability tests, situational tasks and personality inventories (e.g. Bray and Grant, 1966). Personality tests alone tend to give both lower and less consistent correlations with performance.

A number of researchers have administered several measures of personality to various groups of business executives. For example, Harrell (1969, 1970) studied business-school graduates. He found that those with the highest salaries in large businesses were higher on the management-orientation scale of the 'Strong Vocational Interest Blank' (S.V.I.B.), the hypomania scale of the 'Minnesota Multiphasic Personality Inventory' (M.M.P.I.), the general activity and social-interest scales of the 'Guildford–Zimmerman Temperament Survey' (G.Z.T.S.), and the initiative, self-assurance and decision-making scales of the 'Ghiselli Self-description Questionnaire'. Those with highest earnings in small businesses, on the other hand, were higher on the personnel-manager scale of the S.V.I.B., psychopathic deviate and paranoia scales of the M.M.P.I., ascendence and thoughtfulness scales of the G.Z.T.S. and consideration for others on the 'Leader Opinion Questionnaire'. They were also lower on authoritarianism.

Rawls and Rawls (1968) found that successful executives in an American utility company were higher on the 'Edwards Personal Preference Schedule' scales of dominance, heterosexuality and aggression and lower on deference and order. On the 'California Personality Inventory' they were lower on self-control and femininity and higher on dominance, capacity for status, sociality, social presence, self-acceptance, intellectual efficiency, psychological-mindedness and flexibility. A number of biographical characteristics were also related to success. Successful executives learnt to swim and drink alcohol at earlier ages and were elected to leadership positions at an earlier age than less successful ones.

Many other studies, mostly in the context of selection, have examined the relationship between personality and job performance. These include personality assessments made on the basis of both interviews and tests, and we shall examine some of this evidence in the two following chapters.

9.9 Conclusion

Most of the discussion in this chapter has been directed at particular theories and their associated methods. It illustrates that there can be no one correct way of looking at personality. Granted that there are at least three main ways, and an infinite number of variations on these, and that one's choice of theory or assessment method cannot be determined by any absolute criteria, it becomes very much a question of trade-offs. The advantages of each theory or method has to be counterbalanced by the disadvantage intrinsic to it and those resulting from the neglect of another. Thus what the Freudians gain in richness they lose in objectivity and quantifiability. The reverse is true of the behaviourists. The phenomenologists can be said to have the best of both worlds (or to fall between two stools!). What is gratifying is that increasingly, investigators are involved in subjecting Freudian theory to scientific study and in looking at the psychodynamic aspects of, for example, the factorial theories of personality. The historical influence of Rogers, Kelly and others has been considerable in this development.

10
Intelligence and Abilities

10.1 Introduction

This chapter is concerned with differences between individuals in their capacity for performing the activities they undertake. It concentrates on the abilities of the individual. Section 10.2 attempts a definition and explanation of some of the main concepts. Section 10.3 tackles the thorny and long-standing debate about the relative contributions of heredity and environment to a person's level of intelligence and ability. Sections 10.4 and 10.5 are related, in that Section 10.4 is an introduction to factor analysis, the statistical technique on which much of the work on the structure of human abilities (Section 10.5) is based. Section 10.6 considers the question of intelligence and age. This is a topic of some importance for the employment of older workers. In Section 10.7 we discuss an area which will also be touched on in Chapter 12, that of the relationship between intelligence and abilities and performance (e.g. in education and work). Finally, we turn in Section 10.8 to the important question of the measurement of intelligence and abilities and this involves consideration of the design and use of psychological tests.

10.2 The nature of intelligence and abilities

The purpose of this section is to familiarise the reader with the concept of 'intelligence'. Any simple attempt to define intelligence is doomed to failure. There are a large number of possible definitions and we propose to submit three for the reader's perusal, not in the hope of a definitive conclusion but to offer the three most commonly held views. Freeman (1962) suggests that most present-day definitions fall into one of these three categories. First, there are those that emphasise the adaptation or adjustment of the individual to his total environment or to parts of it (his ability to cope). Second, there are those that emphasise the individual's ability to learn from experience. Third, there are those that emphasise the capacity for abstract thinking.

Over the years various solutions have been offered to solve this somewhat unsatisfactory situation. They range from pretending it does not exist ('Intelligence is what intelligence tests measure') to combining the three versions above into one broad entity ('Intelligence is the aggregate or global capacity of the individual to act purposefully, to think rationally, and to deal effectively with the environment' (Wechsler, 1958)). The latter has the advantage of comprehensiveness but requires time-consuming tests to cover all aspects adequately, e.g. Wechsler's 'Adult Intelligence Scale' (W.A.I.S.). The former pragmatic approach amounts to saying that since we cannot agree on a definition we must proceed by defining it operationally in terms of a particular test each time we investigate the topic, no matter that the operational definition may be slightly different for each test.

The fact that each test is likely to measure something slightly different has been turned to advantage by means of the use of the mathematical technique of 'factor analysis'. Essentially this is a method for identifying which factors a group of tests measure in common and which are measured by only some of them. It should therefore be possible by administering a number of intelligence tests (a 'battery', as it is usually called) to a sample of people and factor analysing them, to categorise what they are measuring into a number of factors which are sometimes called 'abilities'. In this way it was hoped that the problem of whether intelligence is a unitary entity or consists of a number of factors would be resolved. Time has not wholly justified the early promise of factor analysis but considerable results have been achieved.

Before moving on to the next section we must refer to a distinction which has been made between fluid and crystallised intelligence (Cattell, 1963), as this will be relevant to our discussion of heredity and intelligence. Fluid intelligence, or intelligence *A* (Hebb, 1949), refers to the maximum level of intelligence which a person is capable of attaining. Usually this maximum level is thought of as being determined hereditarily. Crystallised intelligence (or intelligence *B*) refers to the level of intelligence actually attained and usually it is thought of as being the result of interaction between heredity and the environment. The proportions of each in this interaction are the subject of the debate in the next section.

10.3 Heredity and environment

Much work has been done in trying to estimate the relative effects of heredity and various environmental influences on intellectual abilities. A summary of this is presented in Figure 10.1. It should be remembered, however, that the correlations (see Section 10.4) in Figure 10.1 apply to particular groups of subjects who have experienced particular sets of environmental circumstances. Had these circumstances been radically different, the relative contributions of heredity and environment might well have been different. These estimates have been derived from studies of identical twins, fraternal twins and other degrees of relationship obtained in North American and British studies. The value of twin studies derives from the fact that there are two kinds of twins. Identical or monozygotic twins result from the splitting of a fertilised egg into two individuals each consequently possessing the same heredity. Fraternal or dizygotic twins result from the fertilisation of two separate eggs which are not identical and whose heredities are no more similar than those of ordinary brothers and sisters. The environment in which they are brought up is likely to be more similar than that of ordinary siblings, at least because they are brought up at the same time. If hereditary has a part to play in intelligence, one would expect that people of decreasing degrees of relatedness would show less and less similarity in intelligence. This is in fact the case, but such differences in intelligence could equally well be attributable to differences in environment. Twin studies, particularly comparisons of identical twins reared together and reared apart, are helpful in that the hereditary component is held constant and the environment is varied.

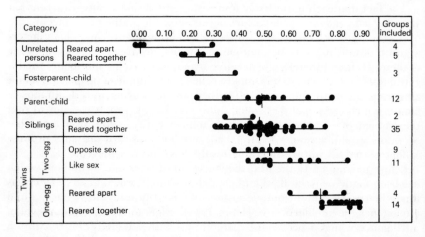

Figure 10.1 Correlation coefficients for 'intelligence' test scores from fifty-two studies. Some studies reported data for more than one relationship category; some included more than one sample per category, giving a total of ninety-nine groups. Over two-thirds of the correlation coefficients were derived from IQs, the remainder from special tests (for example, primary mental abilities). Midparent–child correlation was used when available, otherwise mother–child correlation. Correlation coefficients obtained in each study are indicated by dark circles; medians are shown by vertical lines intersecting the horizontal lines which represent the ranges (Erlenmeyer-Kimling and Jarvik, 1963)

Thus any differences in intelligence should be attributable to environmental factors. However, separated identical twins are likely to be placed in fairly similar environments and may sometimes see each other. This means that the heritability of intelligence is likely to be overestimated by this method. None the less, such studies suggest that heredity plays a considerable part in determining intelligence. Results from fifty-two studies are illustrated in Figure 10.1. The figure shows that as the genetic similarity of people increases so does the correlation between their intelligence test scores. Perhaps most striking is the consistently high correlation for identical twins reared apart from birth onwards, which is greater than that of fraternal twins of the same sex reared together, indicating a considerable hereditary influence. On the other hand, the fosterparent–child correlation is significantly greater than zero, indicating environmental effects.

RACE, CULTURE AND INTELLIGENCE

The debate about the heritability of intelligence has generated particular controversy when discussion has turned to differences in tested intelligence between members of different ethnic groups. In general, early studies show that black Americans score 10–15 IQ (see footnote p. 192) points lower than white Americans (see Klineberg, 1944, for a review). Whether this is attributable to hereditary or environmental influences will affect such questions as the usefulness of remedial education to reduce the difference and the use of tests of intelligence in personnel selection (see Chapter 12).

A major problem in the resolution of this debate is a lack of clarity over what is meant by 'race'. It is generally more of a demographic (and hence environmentally determined) concept than a biological (and hence hereditarily determined) one, for although there are obvious superficial differences, differences in genetic make-up are usually greater within races than between them. None the less we shall review some of the aspects of this controversy.

Although North American studies show that, typically, blacks score less on average than whites, Lee (1951), in a longitudinal study, found that the longer blacks had spent in the North, the higher were their scores on tests of intelligence and primary abilities. Indeed, an early study in the U.S. Army reported by Klineberg (1944) found a superiority of blacks in some North American states over whites in some Southern ones. On the other hand, Lesser, Fifer and Clark (1965) found that differential ethnic patterns of abilities were remarkably stable irrespective of social class.

Vernon (1969) studied children in England, the Hebrides, Jamaica, East Africa as well as Canadian Indian and Eskimo children. He found considerable evidence of environmental effects on abilities in these groups. He suggests that extreme environmental conditions such as early dietary deficiencies can have predominating effects on abilities and personality development. There is also evidence that extreme social deprivation can have extreme effects, as can sensory or perceptual deprivation. Vernon suggests that conceptual and linguistic deprivation from eighteen months onwards throughout childhood may be considerably more important than such sensory or perceptual deprivation. He hypothesises, for example, that the frequent difficulties of African children with the analytic perception of figures and pictures and with three-dimensional interpretation may be due to their comparative lack of visual and kinaesthetic experience, encouragement of play and exploration.

Vernon's studies showed that a democratic and demanding home climate was associated with intelligence more than over-protective autocratic or unconcerned homes. Similar findings come from Witkin et al. (1962), who found that encouragement of resourcefulness and independence in children led to a greater clarity and differentiation in their perceptions and concepts. They found in addition that maternal over-protection was associated with higher verbal abilities.

Home background was also found to be of importance by Douglas (1964), who examined socio-economic class with its associated conditions of child care, neighbourhood morale and schooling quality. He found substantial differences in children's intelligence and achievement. Of most importance in determining these were cultural level of the home and parental interest in, and aspirations for, their children's education. He also found a cumulative deficit in intelligence with age for the lowest social classes, as is found typically in studies of underprivileged communities (e.g. North American blacks, canal-boat children, gipsies).

Vernon (1969) found that amount of schooling even in backward countries with a relatively low standard of education tended to promote school achievement and non-verbal reasoning ability. The formality of schooling received was greater in the less technologically developed countries and tended to be associated with superior memorising ability but lower intelligence. Generalising over several cultures, Vernon found that the purposefulness and rationality of the home was correlated positively with attainments in English and arithmetic. Encouragement of initiative and perceptual-kinaesthetic stimulation was correlated positively with practical and spatial abilities and the latter also with inductive reasoning ability. (Spatial abilities include the abilities to perceive size and shape accurately, to reason about and to manipulate objects in space.) Vernon concludes that intelligence is affected by many factors, including the satisfaction of needs, conceptual stimulation by a varied environment (books, television, travel, etc.), absence of magical beliefs, tolerance of non-conformity in the home and community, emphasis on discovery rather than rote learning, a positive self-concept, realistic vocational aspirations and broad and deep cultural and other leisure interests.

Loehlin, Lindzey and Spukler (1975) have surveyed the whole debate about race and intelligence. Many of the studies support the conclusion of a considerable environmental interaction with genetic factors. Estimates of the heritability coefficient vary from 0.81 to 0.35. These differences are due to different assumptions made by the investigators, largely in the area of excluding the effects of unrecognised environmental influences. There are systematic differences in the upbringing of blacks and whites due to culture, class and other factors which it is very difficult to estimate in such a way that, if excluded, all remaining differences in the intelligence of blacks and whites would be unequivocally due to race. The current situation seems therefore to be that extreme positions are still tenable. Jensen (1969, 1973) has concluded there are genetic differences in intelligence between blacks and whites, particularly in abstract problem-solving ability, which account very largely for the found IQ[†] differences. Kamin (1974) points to methodological and statistical shortcomings in the studies reviewed by Jensen and argues that there is no evidence for a genetic factor in IQ test differences. Due to the problems of estimating accurately the environmental contributions mentioned above, however, the present authors are in agreement with Layzer's (1974) more conservative conclusion that it is not yet possible to draw valid conclu-

[†]IQ, or intelligence quotient, is a means of representing performance on a test of general intelligence. Originally defined as (Mental age/Chronological age) × 100, it is now calculated on the basis of population averages, so that the median of the population, or 50th percentile, obtains an IQ of 100.

sions about genetic racial differences in intelligence from the available data. Certainly no rash conclusions should be drawn and action taken on the basis of these.

10.4 Factor analysis

At this point we need to say a little about factor analysis, for some of the crucial points of the ensuing discussion stem from it. Factor analysis is a mathematical technique which enables the interrelationships between a number of variables to be summarised in terms of a small number of factors which between them represent the information contained in those interrelationships. In general terms, the factors may be said to describe the main threads which run through a particular pattern of interrelationships.

This pattern of interrelationships may be described in the form of a matrix of correlations between a large number of individual personality measurements. These measurements may derive from observation, questionnaires, ratings of physiological measurements. Correlation is a statistical technique for measuring the interrelatedness of two measurements or variables. A correlation of $+1$ represents a perfect positive relationship between the two variables (i.e. a high score on one variable is always associated with a high score on the other, and similarly for low scores – see Figure 10.2). A correlation of 0 represents no correlation between the two variables and a correlation of -1 represents a perfect inverse relationship (i.e. a high score on one variable is always combined with a low score on the other). Intermediate degrees of relationship are shown by intermediate points on the scale from $+1$ via 0 to -1.

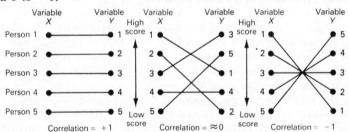

Figure 10.2

A series of interrelationships between such correlated variables is then set out in the form of a correlation matrix, like the one in Table 10.1. The matrix is then factor analysed and a number of factors or dimensions emerge which together can be used to describe the matrix, rather in the way that the dimensions of a box can be multiplied together to discover its volume.

Initially it was hoped that the factors obtained would yield the key to the basic dimensions of intelligence (and a lot of other psychological topics such as personality). Unfortunately this was not to be, for just as the number 12 can be factorised in a number of different ways (6×2, 4×3, $2 \times 2 \times 3$), so also can a correlation matrix be factor analysed in a number of different ways. Thus there is no one best way of obtaining the basic factors in intelligence. Indeed, one of the chief differences between British and American researchers is that they used different factor-analytic methods. None the less much work that is fruitful in other respects has emerged and it is this that we shall now describe.

Table 10.1   A correlation matrix

	a	b	c	d	e	f	g
a		+0.7	+0.8	+0.8	−0.1	0.0	0.0
b			+0.9	+0.7	+0.1	+0.2	0.0
c				+0.8	−0.2	−0.1	−0.1
d					0.0	−0.1	+0.2
e						+0.8	+0.7
f							+0.7
g							

The lower left would, of course, be an image of the upper right and is not entered. By adding together the scores on *a*, *b*, *c* and *d*, we could get an estimate of the underlying source trait *X*, and similarly, but not quite so reliably, of *Y* from *e*, *f* and *g*. Trait *X* covers *a*, *b*, *c* and *d*. Trait *Y* covers *e*, *f* and *g*.

Source: Cattell (1965).

10.5   The structure of human abilities

The argument as to whether or not there is a general intelligence factor has centred around factor-analytic studies. By using factor analysis we can analyse a whole matrix to find out how much of the variation in performance on all the measures can be accounted for by one common factor, and how far supplementary factors are required.

This was first done by Spearman (1904), who found evidence for an important general factor. This was due partly to his limited sampling of performances for study, and led to his two-factor theory; this stated that all branches of intellectual ability have in common one fundamental function (or group of functions), whereas the remaining or specific elements of the ability seem in every case to be wholly different from that in all the others.

Subsequent research, sampling a wider range of performances (Kelley, 1928; Stephenson, 1931; El Koussy, 1935), suggested that in addition to a general ability factor and specific ability factors, group factors were necessary to explain relatively high intercorrelations among particular sets of measures, e.g. verbal (the ability to use and manipulate words) and special tasks. Thus performance on verbal tasks tended to correlate more highly with performance on other verbal tasks than with performance on tasks requiring spatial ability.

On the basis of this evidence, Burt (1940) proposed a hierarchical structure

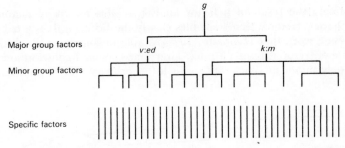

Figure 10.3   Hierarchical structure of human abilities (Vernon, 1950b)

of human abilities, as illustrated in Figure 10.3. Thus for a full description of an individual's abilities (his over-all 'intelligence') what are needed are (i) a measure of general ability (g) which influences his performance on all tasks, (ii) measures of certain group abilities, e.g. $k:m$ or $v:ed$ (see below), specific to certain groups of tasks, and (iii) abilities specific to the particular task or tasks involved.

Vernon (1950b) points out that the exact nature of the above hierarchy depends upon the particular population and performances sampled. Hence the lower echelons are left vague. Research points to at least two major group factors – $v:ed$ (verbal–educational ability) and $k:m$ (spatial–practical–mechanical ability). However, general factor g usually accounts for more variation in performance and provides prediction over a wider range of tasks than measurement of a major or minor group factor. On the other hand, if the range of tasks sampled is narrow and largely mechanical in content and the population sampled are engineers or the like, variations in the $k:m$ group factor are likely to be more important. The Burt/Vernon hierarchy is only likely to hold for the general population and a variety of tasks.

In the United States less importance has usually been attached to a general intelligence factor. Very early studies (Sharp, 1899; Wissler, 1901) found very little intercorrelation between tests of simple sensory abilities. This has led to a tradition among American psychologists of postulating a number of relatively independent ability factors rather than a general factor. In turn this has generated factor-analytic techniques which are less likely mathematically to yield a general factor. The reader will remember that just as the number 12 can be factorised in a number of different ways so too can a correlation matrix. The Americans (e.g. Thurstone, 1938; and Guilford, 1956) prefer to use methods which yield specific factors rather than a general one. These methods have the advantage of enabling relationships to be established between performance of jobs requiring a particular factor and tests measuring it – potentially very useful for personnel selection and occupational guidance. Using university students as subjects, Thurstone (1938) found some seven factors which were relatively independent, though correlated, and which he called 'primary mental abilities'. These were spatial ability (S), perceptual speed (P), numerical ability (N), verbal meaning (V), memory (M), verbal fluency (W) and inductive reasoning (I or R). Since these factors are themselves correlated, it is possible to construct a correlation matrix for them.

Interestingly the result of a factor analysis of this matrix of factors is a 'second-order' factor which resembles closely the British *g*. It is a tribute to Thurstone's work that Dunnette (1976) is able to conclude: 'Remarkably, the years of factorial research since Thurstone's seminal contributions have added only minor modifications to his list of primary mental abilities.'

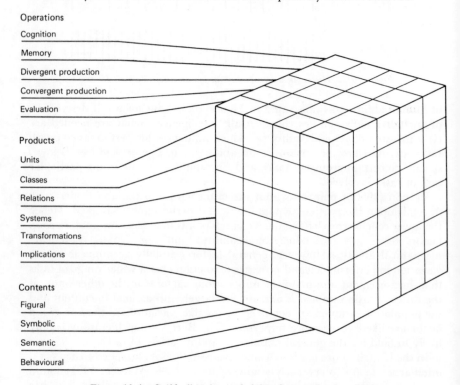

Operations

Cognition

Memory

Divergent production

Convergent production

Evaluation

Products

Units

Classes

Relations

Systems

Transformations

Implications

Contents

Figural

Symbolic

Semantic

Behavioural

Figure 10.4   Guilford's scheme of ability factors (Butcher, 1968)

There is, however, one significant extension of Thurstone's work which it is important to mention; it is that of Guilford (1956, 1959, 1967). Guilford classifies abilities by operation, product and content (as shown in Figure 10.4). There are therefore 120 independent abilities, corresponding to each cell of the cube. He has been attempting to construct tests for each of these abilities, such that abilities are independent of one another (i.e. uncorrelated). Guilford and Hoepfner (1971) claim to have been successful in identifying factors for ninety-eight of these abilities over a twenty-year period. However, there are criticisms of this approach. (1) It does not allow for the positive intercorrelations between abilities demonstrated by the British and American studies cited previously. Haynes (1970) found a general factor with loadings of 0.3 or greater on twenty-eight of thirty-four tests chosen to represent seventeen of the most clearly established structure of intellect factors. (2) The factors which Guilford has isolated have been very little tested in the work situation for their predictive value and when this has been done they have not generally been predictive of performance. (3) Some studies (e.g. Sultan, 1962) have not replicated Guilford's factors. (4) Horn and Knapp (1973) have suggested that it is possible to support almost any kind of *a priori* theory using Guilford's particular methods of factor analysis. One aspect of Guilford's work which cannot be denied, however, is his contribution to the area of intellect called 'divergent thinking' (thinking which requires the production of novel answers to a problem), and it is to this that we now turn.

CREATIVITY

Until about 1960 there was a tendency for tests of intelligence and ability, and for schools and colleges in assessing performance, to emphasise students' capacity to think convergently, i.e. to achieve a single correct answer to a problem (as in mathematics). Yet hovering in the background were the constant anecdotes of highly successful people (such as Einstein) who had been no more than average in school. A study by Getzels and Jackson (1962), which showed that performance on 'creativity' tests (measuring the variety and inventiveness of the solutions offered to various problems) was also related to success at school, was a turning-point in the study of intelligence. Creativity is a term used rather loosely to imply an ability for divergent thinking, and instruments designed to measure various divergent-thinking capacities are often called 'creativity tests'. Guilford (1967), for example, has proposed twenty-four different divergent production operations (see Figure 10.4) and has attempted to find tests to measure each of them. Whether or not creativity is a useful term in this sense depends upon whether such measures appear to have something in common (i.e. are intercorrelated) which is not attributable to some other characteristic (e.g. intelligence of the convergent kind, or motivation).

The evidence for a general creativity factor is mixed. Vernon (1967) suggests that creativity tests may represent a common factor other than general (convergent) intelligence. Some support for this view comes from work by Wallach and Kogan (1965), who used untimed measures of verbal and non-verbal associative fluency (the number and uniqueness of the responses given to a verbal or pictorial stimulus) and obtained a creativity factor relatively distinct from general intelligence.

On the other hand, other studies show rather low intercorrelations between different measures of divergent thinking, suggesting that creativity is not a single entity. Getzels and Jackson (1962) used five tests of word association which we will describe briefly. The first was a test in which meanings and uses are required of common words with multiple meanings, e.g. 'bolt' or 'rack'. The second was a test in which as many uses as possible have to be found for objects such as 'brick' or 'paper clip'. The third involved finding a geometric figure hidden in a more complex pattern. The fourth required the provision of three different endings to each of four stories, one moralistic, one humorous, one sad. The final test comprised four complex paragraphs with a number of numerical statements in them, the object being to make up but not to solve as many mathematical problems from these statements. The intercorrelations between these tests ranged from $+0.1$ to $+0.5$. This was only slightly more than their correlations with general (convergent) intelligence (IQ), suggesting that, in part, the relatively small common factor might be intelligence.] Stronger evidence for this hypothesis comes from a fairly close replication of the Getzels and Jackson study by Hasan and Butcher (1966). Whereas Getzels and Jackson's group of children had a mean IQ greater than 130, Hasan and Butcher studied children unselected for ability, and found much more overlap between the creativity tests and general intelligence.

Another approach to the study of creativity has been to focus upon the characteristics and thought processes of eminent men considered to be creative in their sphere. Such studies are less satisfactory than those described earlier, as there are no obvious criteria of creativity. Furthermore, the determinants of performance of outstanding originality are very complex. It may be that original work of great merit might be more a function of motivation, knowledge and intelligence than of the divergent-thinking capacities referred to earlier. This argument is partially supported by Hudson's (1966) finding that whereas science students are better at convergent thinking, arts students are better at divergent thinking, though both may be equally termed 'creative' individuals. Thus it would not be surprising if the creative thought processes of eminent original thinkers are different in kind from those involved in responding to tests of divergent thinking. We shall now examine in a little more detail some of the characteristics of some creative people who have been studied.

We have presented evidence that tests of creativity may be measuring intelligence. Eysenck (1967) has suggested that the superiority of arts students at divergent thinking can be attributed to their superiority at verbal fluency, which is associated with extraversion (see Chapter 9). Certainly there is much evidence from studies of creative people which suggests that personality is an important factor in their creativity. Roe (1953), Barron (1955) and Cattell (1957) all found that creative people, especially scientists, were high on intellectual autonomy and independence of judgement. Cattell and Drevdahl (1955) and Drevdahl (1956) found that eminent research scientists were significantly more withdrawn and unsociable, intellectually self-sufficient and of a radical temperament. Taylor and Holland (1964) conclude from the evidence that creative people are:

> more autonomous, more self-sufficient, more independent in judgement (they go against group opinion if they feel it is incorrect), open to the irrational in themselves, stable, feminine in interests and characteristics (especially in awareness of their impulses), more dominant and self-assertive, more complex and more accepting of themselves, more resourceful and adventurous, more radical (Bohemian), more self-controlled, and possibly more emotionally sensitive and more introverted but bold. . . . Creative scientists rate themselves as high in professional self-confidence, self-sufficiency, independence and emotional restraint and low in aggressiveness, assertion, social desirability, sociability and masculine vigour.

These studies deal with relatively broad personality characteristics. Other studies using creativity tests to distinguish between more and less creative groups, usually of children, have demonstrated relationships between creativity and more specific characteristics. Getzels and Jackson (1962), in the study of above-average-intelligence children mentioned earlier, found that those scoring in the top 20 per cent on creativity, but not on IQ (mean IQ of 127), did as well in scholastic achievement as those in the top 20 per cent on IQ, but not on creativity (mean IQ of 150). This suggests that creativity may account for scholastic success as much as IQ. However, Hasan and Butcher (1966) failed to confirm this finding with an unselected group of Scottish schoolchildren. Getzels and Jackson also found that the high creativity–low IQ group, when compared with a low creativity–high IQ group, showed the following differences: (i) there was less correspondence (*a*) between qualities they valued for themselves and those they thought to be conducive to adult life success, and (*b*) between the qualities they would have liked to possess and those approved of by teachers; (ii) they valued a sense of humour more highly; and (iii) they received more adverse teacher ratings.

Wallach and Kogan (1965) compared four groups of children with various combinations of creative ability and fluency. They found that children high on both measures showed both control and freedom. Those high in creativity and low in intelligence were in angry conflict with themselves and the school environment, accompanied by feelings of unworthiness and inadequacy. They performed best in a stress-free environment. Those low in creativity and high in intelligence showed a continual striving for academic excellence. Those low in both measures were bewildered and showed defensive behaviour such as regression and psychosomatic symptoms. There is some evidence (Torrance, 1965; Fuqua, 1967) that creativity becomes an important factor in determining scholastic performance at IQs greater than about 120, when IQ is no longer a satisfactory predictor. This would account for the difference in the findings of Getzels and Jackson (1962) and Hasan and Butcher (1965). In general, however, tests of divergent-thinking abilities have not been shown to be good predictors of real-life performance. Two exceptions to this are measures of 'ideational fluency' (i.e. fluency or capacity for generating a large amount of ideational output to various stimuli) and 'preference for complexity–asymmetry over simplicity–symmetry' (Wallach, 1971) which at college student level are predictive of behaviour involving creative production.

What conditions lead to creativity? Reinforcement theorists would say that creative behaviour occurs as a result of instrumental conditioning. Indirect evidence for this hypothesis comes from Torrance's (1965) finding that creative children do better in permissive and flexible kinds of schools. It also receives indirect support from Getzels and Jackson's (1962) study when they found that the families of high-creativity children permitted more divergence in behaviour and accepted behaviour which exhibited risk.

In summary it seems that much of what is commonly considered to be creativity may be attributed to general intelligence and personality factors. Well-controlled studies, such as that of Wallach and Kogan (1965), do suggest that something separate from general (convergent) intelligence might usefully be designated as 'creativity'. However, we know little of its likely relationship to the creative processes of eminent original thinkers, and its predictive value for important real-life behaviour has not been well established. There is, however, some indication that it might be related to scholastic attainment, particularly with IQs of above 120.

10.6 Intelligence and age

The great majority of studies show that intelligence increases with age up to adolescence and that it declines in old age. Typically children show a smooth increase in average scores on intelligence tests with age. Piaget and his collaborators have studied the development of intellectual processes in children over many years (Piaget, 1950; Flavell, 1963; Lunzer, 1968). Piaget sees the growth of intelligence as involving two basic functions, each forming one aspect of adaptation to the environment; these are assimilation and accommodation. In assimilation the child incorporates and uses stimuli from the environment, fitting them to his existing intellectual organisation and reacting on the basis of this as he has done in the past. Accommodation occurs when new reactions to stimuli are required and the child must accommodate by changing his behaviour. According to Piaget, intelligent behaviour requires a state of equilibrium between these two functions, 'in which potentially slavish and naively realistic accommodations to reality are held in check by an assimilating process which can organize and direct accommodations and in which assimilation is kept from being too authentic by sufficient continuing accommodatory adjustments to the real world' (Flavell, 1963). Throughout intellectual development these functions remain unchanged, unlike the structures or organisations of intelligence which change qualitatively during the main periods from birth to adolescence. Succeeding structures develop from and incorporate the preceding structure. The order of development is not variable, though the ages at which structures are attained vary somewhat from individual to individual. These correspond to four main periods: (i) sensori-motor operations (the co-ordination of reflexes, reaching, grasping, exploration, etc.) extending from birth to about 18 months or 2 years; (ii) pre-operational representations from about 2 to 7 years old (e.g. the first signs of inner, symbolic, abstract representation); (iii) concrete operations from about 7 to 11 or 12 (e.g. important changes occur in conceptions of causality, time, space, quantity, chance and morality); and (iv) formal operations from 11 to 12 typically complete at about 15 (i.e. fully developed abstract reasoning ability).

Some backward adults may not reach the final stage of development, and it may be that some primitive and isolated societies do not do so. Many adult studies show that a large percentage of adults display pre-causal thinking typical of earlier periods of development, at least on occasions (e.g. Dennis and Mallenger, 1949). Within each of the main periods, Piaget distinguishes sub-periods. The age at which stages are reached can be affected markedly by both social and other environmental conditions.

Much research has involved the administration of tests of general intelligence and more specific intellectual abilities to large numbers of people from adolescence upwards. These studies have either been cross-sectional (i.e. tests administered to different age groups at the same time) or longitudinal (i.e. tests administered to the same group of people over a long time period). Somewhat different results have usually been obtained from these two types of study.

Usually cross-sectional surveys show a decline in tested intelligence, beginning in the middle to late teens (e.g. Foulds and Raven, 1948; Jones and Conrad, 1933; Wechsler, 1958). In the Jones and Conrad study, which produced typical results, the Army Alpha group intelligence test was administered to 1200 New Englanders aged from 10 to 60. They were selected so as to be relatively homogeneous in economic status and educational opportunity and were all native born of native-born parents. Intelligence scores rose sharply from 10 to 16 years old, when there was a levelling off followed by a slow steady decline, such that 55-year-olds obtained similar scores to 14-year-olds. The typical curve relating age to intelligence is shown in Figure 10.5. It illustrates the greater deterioration found generally on non-verbal tests. At the highest ages where senility is common appreciable declines are likely to arise. Typically studies do not include senile people in their samples, thus underestimating declines in old age.

Jones and Conrad found marked differences in the rates of decline on the different sub-tests of the intelligence scale. General information and vocabulary were almost constant from 20 to 60, with a maximum at 40. There was a fairly sharp decline on numerical problems, particularly on those involving non-routine procedures, and the sharpest decline was on analogies, where 55-year-olds obtained similar scores to 10-year-olds. They found as much decline in power (i.e. untimed test) as in speed, though typically research shows decline with age to be in speed rather than power (e.g. Miles, 1934). Finally, it was found that individual differences at any one age group were appreciably greater than differences between age groups. That is to say, we have been considering averages, and should remember that such averages apply exactly to few individuals. There is evidence (Vernon, 1960) that decline is slowest amongst those of highest intelligence. Nisbet (1957) found

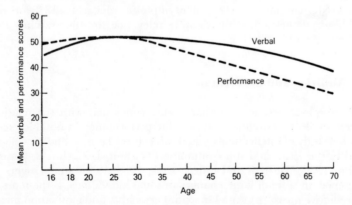

Figure 10.5 Comparative decline of verbal and performance sub-tests on W.A.I.S. with age (ages 16–75 and over; 2052 cases) (Wechsler, 1958)

an increase in intelligence between the ages of $22\frac{1}{2}$ and 47 in people of superior intelligence. However, Burns (1966) found that Nisbet's sample of graduates at 56 years old scored less than they had at 47 though still more than they had at $22\frac{1}{2}$.

In spite of the fact that this sample might have acquired more test sophistication in the intervening period between $22\frac{1}{2}$ and 47, this kind of finding has given rise to the hypothesis that keeping active intellectually reduces the decline in intellectual functioning.

Longitudinal studies, interestingly, have in general shown little or no decline in intelligence to quite an advanced age. For example, Owens (1966) gives evidence from a study over forty-two years (1919–61) using the Army Alpha test of intelligence. Gains were recorded on nearly all the sub-tests, the greatest gain being in general information and verbal ability. The relative performance on sub-tests paralleled those from cross-sectional studies. However, when a correction was made for the general improvement in cultural and educational standards (by comparing 1961 19-year-olds with the tested group's 1919 scores when they were 19 years old) many of the gains disappeared, leaving slight gains only in verbal and general information tests. There was a slight loss on numerical ability and a more substantial one on reasoning ability. This corrected pattern parallels closely that found in cross-sectional studies.

A number of studies point to the increasing importance of verbal comprehension in intellectual functioning with increasing age. Maxwell (1961) found that high performance on intelligence tests in old age was greatly and increasingly a function of verbal comprehension ability. Birren and Morrison (1961) found increases on the verbal comprehension sub-test of the Wechsler 'adult intelligence scale' (W.A.I.S.) up to 65 years old.

Welford (1958) cites evidence to suggest that the decline in abilities with age is explicable in terms of decrements in channel capacity and short-term memory, not in ability to make intellectual leaps and attain insights. A decline in channel capacity for the intake of information with age has been shown by Pont (1963), who found that it increased almost linearly from 10–14 years old, then more slowly to an asymptotic value at 14–18 before declining. This hypothesis has considerable relevance for the training and retraining of the older worker.

10.7 Abilities and performance

There have been few longitudinal studies concerned with the relationship between intellectual abilities and later life performance. A notable exception to this is a study of intellectually gifted subjects by Terman and his colleagues, started in the 1920s and still continuing (Terman, 1925; Burks, Jensen and Terman, 1930; Terman and Oden, 1947, 1959). This study suggests that intelligence, in spite of large changes in some individuals, is the most stable and predictive measure over a life span. Personality and motivation measures, even in combination, typically have lower predictive power than an intelligence test.

They selected over 1500 children from urban schools in California for study. Each child selected had an IQ of at least 140 as measured by the Stanford–Binet intelligence test. When compared with average children, they were heavier at birth, walked earlier, talked on average three months earlier, were larger and heavier at the time of testing, matured earlier physically, appeared to have better general health and at 12 years of age slept on average one hour longer. They showed interests typical of older children, were less involved in social and competitive games, played alone more, preferred older friends and were often described as 'queer' or 'different' by other children.

Many studies have found that intellectual abilities correlate positively with scholastic attainments. Lavin's (1965) American survey, for example, showed an average correlation of about +0.5 between single tests of ability and grade-point average. Average high-school grade was the best single predictor. Interestingly, he also found that the performance of college women was more consistently in line with their measured abilities and more predictable than was the case for men.

Terman's studies also found that the high-intelligence group had superior scholastic achievement and examination performances. For example, in their last year at secondary school they were on average within the top 10 per cent, despite being in classes selected for high ability and being younger than average. Terman and Oden (1947) report that at average age 35, they had lower death, delinquency and crime rates than average. They were also well above average in terms of occupational status and earnings. A group of subjects selected from the gifted groups with IQs over 170 were found to differ significantly from the remainder of the gifted group in only two respects: (i) they obtained more college distinctions; and (ii) they achieved higher occupational status.

Ghiselli (1966) has reviewed studies relating abilities to job performance for over a hundred occupations. He concluded that tests of ability generally predicted training criteria more effectively than they did job performance. Bemis (1968), using the 'United States Employment Services General Aptitude Test Battery', obtained a similar result. Tests of intelligence, verbal, numerical and spatial abilities all correlated more highly with training criteria. Tests of co-ordination and finger dexterity, on the other hand, correlated more highly with job performance. The vast majority of correlations reported were between +0.15 and +0.40.

Intelligence has been found to be correlated with success in many occupations, usually positively (particularly in managerial and higher-level jobs), but also negatively in jobs where people of higher intelligence are likely to get bored easily. Mechanical abilities have been shown by factor-analytic studies (Tyler, 1965) to split into (i) comprehension of mechanical relations, recognition of tools used for various purposes and related cognitive abilities (which appear to be related to mechanical experience), and (ii) the perception and manipulation of spatial relationships. These factors have been found to be related to job performance for craftsmen, mechanics, repairmen, draughtsmen and engineers.

Psychomotor tests (tests of manipulative ability and manual dexterity) have been found to be related to job performance. For example, Wolins and MacKinney (1961) found that the Purdue Keyboard and Minnesota Rate of Manipulation Tests predicted the performance of packers in a handicraft company. However, in spite of the attempts of Fleishman and his co-workers (Theologus and Fleishman, 1971; Levine, Romashko and Fleishman, 1973) to isolate different kinds of psychomotor ability by factor-analytic methods, complex motor tests sampling job behaviour have been more successful at predicting job performance (Dunnette, 1976).

Tests of visual skills have been found to be frequently related to job performance. These include tests of visual acuity, depth perception, colour discrimination and phobias. Six visual job families have been isolated (i.e. groups of jobs with similar visual requirements for successful performance): clerical and administrative, machine operator, inspection, labourer, vehicle operator and mechanic (McCormick and Tiffin, 1974). Two facets of divergent thinking have been found to be related to various performance measures: (i) ideational fluency was related to excellence in art, original writing, winning science prizes, building scientific apparatus and election to leadership positions in school and college (Wallach and Wing, 1969; Csikszentmihalyi and Getzels, 1970; Singer and Whiton, 1971); (ii) preference for complexity—asymmetry was related to ratings of significance of contribution by artists, architects, mathematicians and scientists (Dellar and Saier, 1970).

10.8 The measurement of abilities

Many standardised tests of abilities are available. Tests of abilities differ in a number of ways, the most important being the following: (i) group or individual (a test which can be administered by one person to a number of subjects at the same time or to one person only); (ii) level (the range of ability at which the test is aimed); (iii) speed or power (whether the test measures the speed of the testee or his ability without any time constraint); (iv) aptitude or attainment (measurement of potential or present performance); (v) specificity (ranging from measures of general intelligence to highly specific measures); (vi) verbal or non-verbal; (vii) paper and pencil or performance.

Most measures of intelligence and other abilities approximate to interval scale measures, i.e. there are differences of equal size between units of measurement. However, comparisons of intelligence and abilities are relative rather than absolute, and are related to a given population via test norms (the distribution of test scores in the population in question) and to the kind of test used. Thus each published test usually has an accompanying manual in which norms are given for representative samples of the general population, or relevant parts of it. In this way a particular testee's score may be compared with those of such samples.

Tests of intellectual ability in general have higher reliabilities and validities than tests of practical abilities. Reliability is a measure of test error and is a prerequisite for the validity of a test. Two types of reliability may be distinguished: (i) internal consistency measures of test items, often measured by the split-half correlational method (correlating the two halves of a test with each other), or if parallel forms of a test exist by testing two halves or two forms for statistical equivalence; (ii) stability over time of test scores (the test–retest method). Reliability, like validity, depends not only on test items but also upon the sample of people tested and the testing situation. Reliability may be increased by increasing the number of test items.

The validity of a test may be defined as the extent to which it fulfils its purpose. There are in fact as many validities as there are purposes. However, four main kinds of validity can be distinguished: (i) *content validity* refers to the extent to which measures of attainment sample representatively the domain of knowledge supposed to be learnt; (ii) *predictive validity* is the extent to which a measure predicts a measure of behaviour (the criterion) such as job performance; (iii) *concurrent validity* is similar to predictive validity except that both measures are taken at the same time – like predictive validity it is usually expressed in the form of a correlation coefficient; (iv) *construct validity* is an indication of the extent to which a test actually measures the intended construct. Normally this last will be a judgement expressed on the basis of knowledge about all relationships known between the measure and other types of behaviour and measures. We should also mention *face validity*, the extent to which a measure appears to be measuring what it is purported to measure for those being measured. Face validity can be important to ensure a fully motivated response but it is no substitute for any of the genuine validities we have mentioned. The more reliable and valid a test is, the more useful it will be.

In test construction, therefore, we are concerned with establishing a reliable and valid test. To do this involves a number of steps. For example, to construct a paper-and-pencil ability test, the following stages would be necessary: (i) define clearly the purpose and scope of the test; (ii) define the kinds of item to be used, first broadly, then more specifically, considering the items as being sampled from a large population of some kind; (iii) define the test population in terms of ability level and range of ability, e.g. a test aimed at differentiating between graduates in intelligence would contain all relatively difficult items – a graduate's score on the test (final version) would then be compared with those of a large group of representative graduates (the group norms) to establish his relative score or position compared with other graduates; (iv) draw up a large number of items which seem likely to sample the desired content, using past research where relevant; (v) try out these items on a representative sample of the target population; (vi) analyse items by calculating indices of difficulty and power to discriminate (for a test to discriminate equally throughout its range, the average difficulty of an item should be 50 per cent, i.e. 50 per cent of the population should get the right answer) – this is done by relating the item to internal criteria (e.g. over-all test score) or external criteria.

The reliability, and hence the validity of a test, can be affected by many factors at the time of testing which affect the test-taker's mood and motivation. For example, Heim (1957) found that people who had just taken a difficult test do better on a test of moderate difficulty than those who have started with an easy one, and Wober (1961) found that varying the degree of enthusiasm of the tester also affected test scores. For these reasons, tests are standardised (i.e. given under standard conditions) to reduce such sources of error to a minimum.

Similarly there are many factors which contribute to the relatively low predictive validities of tests, such as a subject's domestic situation, or the exact nature of training and supervision given him. This cannot be foreseen at the time of test administration. Any variation in subsequent environments of tested individuals can serve to reduce test–criterion relationships. These problems will be taken up further in Chapter 12.

11
Person Perception, Interviewing and Staff Appraisal

11.1 Introduction

This chapter contains something of a mixture of topics with a common thread uniting them. In any case we shall spell it out immediately. It is often necessary in the world of work for one individual to make a judgement about another – 'Is he working effectively?', 'Is he satisfied?', 'Is he having problems?', 'Should we promote him?', 'Should we employ him?', 'How will he react to a change in his job?'; and, from the other side, 'Can I trust him?', 'Can I confess to being unable to keep up with the job?', 'Can I ask him for what I want?', 'Can I tell him what I really feel about the job?', 'Will he give me the day off?' In the first part of the chapter (Sections 11.2 and 11.3) we shall look at some of the processes which determine the conclusion reached. In Sections 11.4, 11.5 and 11.6 the different kinds of interview in which these judgements may be made are discussed, with a particular focus on the interviewing techniques which best enable the information on which the judgement is to be based to be elicited. The various purposes to which interviews can be put are also discussed. Finally, in Section 11.7 we take a look at the problems of performance assessment and staff appraisal. The latter has many objectives for which the interview techniques mentioned earlier in the chapter may be used, as well as other methods discussed elsewhere in this part of the book.

11.2 Person perception and communication

Person perception as a subject for study is concerned with the manner in which we perceive the personal characteristics of others, in particular their current mood and their total personality. The inclusion of 'communication' into the heading for this section is perhaps misleading but it is intended simply to refer to the means by which people, intentionally or unintentionally, communicate to others their current mood and their personality as a whole. This will be in contrast to the next section, which will focus on the mental processes in the perceiver which are responsible for the way in which judgements are made about others.

Warr and Knapper (1968) contend that the principles governing our perception of other people are not qualitatively different from those governing our perception of objects in space and their two-dimensional representations. There is no serious problem in saying that we perceive the height, texture of skin, colour of clothes, etc. of a person in just the same way as we perceive the size, colour and texture of cardboard shapes in the experimental psychologist's laboratory. The perception of speech is more complex but also seems to be based on principles which are not intrinsically different from those governing object perception (Osgood and Sebeok, 1965).

What of the perceptual illusions and constancies? Do they have their equivalent in person perception?

Visual illusions are thought generally to be caused by certain cues giving the impression of a characteristic which is not present in reality. The perceiver then draws all kinds of conclusions about the object which cause him to interpret falsely certain other cues. For example, the Müller–Lyer arrow-heads are a false cue of depth which cause the shaft to be handled by our perceptual system as though it is either nearer or further away than in fact it is. Since our retinal images of the two shafts are the same size and our perceptual system tells us that one is nearer than the other, the further one is perceived to be longer than the nearer (see Chapter 2).

In person perception we cannot measure the stimulus accurately enough, so that truth or falsity of perception cannot be clearly assessed. However, analogous changes in perception arising from variations of even minor cues can alter the whole way in which the rest of the person is perceived.

Asch (1946) found that changes of one item in a list of characteristics attributed to a person can result in considerable differences in the manner in which the person is conceived. These differences are not confined to the trait in question but to the attributed characteristics. Asch compared subjects' impressions of imaginary people possessing the two following sets of traits:

Intelligent	Intelligent
Skilful	Skilful
Industrious	Industrious
Warm	Cold
Determined	Determined
Practical	Practical
Cautious	Cautious

Varying only 'warm' in the list of seven traits produced very different impressions of the imaginary person's generosity, shrewdness, happiness, irritability, humour, sociability, popularity, ruthlessness, self-centredness and imaginativeness. Such changes are similar in kind to those effected by making changes to one part of a visual stimulus (e.g. the slope of a line or the angle of a corner). The interesting thing is that the distortions occur not only in related traits (kind–cruel) but also in unrelated ones (imaginative–unimaginative). It would seem that, as in the perception of objects, we impose our own rules of organisation when confronted with incomplete descriptions of people. It may be that modified versions of the *Gestalt* laws of proximity, symmetry, closure, good form, continuation, etc. apply to our perception of people (as implied by the consistency principle discussed in Chapter 8).

Another similarity between object perception and person perception is that subjects adopting a 'whole-perceiving' attitude are much more susceptible to the Müller–Lyer illusion than those with a 'part-isolating' approach. A variation of Asch's experiment has been conducted in which the different traits were presented serially and separately. It was found that this reduced the influence of the trait of warmness on the rest. This experiment can be construed as a 'part-isolating' version of Asch's.

The constancies also have their counterpart in person perception. Warr and Knapper (1968) have shown that there is considerable stability in subjects' judgements of politicians before and after newspaper reports of varying kinds concerning the politician in question. The strongest constancy effect was shown when the tone of the report to which they were exposed was least discrepant from their original judgement. Indeed, it was possible for a discrepant report to reduce constancy to zero in the case where the original judgement had been relatively neutral (Jo Grimmond, former leader of the Liberal Party). In the case of Barry Goldwater, former Republican candidate for President (to whom subjects initially had stronger attitudes) some degree of constancy was maintained even after exposure to discrepant reports.

It is true that the word 'constancy' is used in a less specific way in person perception than in experimental psychology. It is also true that research into constancy in person perception is more designed to demonstrate that the phenomenon exists than to investigate the variables which influence it. However, neither of these two points invalidate the conclusion that there is no discontinuity between the way we perceive people and the way we perceive objects.

The influences of motivation and personality on perception described in Chapter 2 can also be taken to apply to the perception of people as well as objects.

TYPES OF JUDGEMENT IN PERSON PERCEPTION

There are many possible typologies of perceptual judgement. Cook (1971) distinguishes between (i) static judgements about enduring characteristics (things like age, beliefs, ability, manners, personality traits, liking of others, etc.), and (ii) dynamic judgements of changing characteristics (things like specific actions, moods, emotions, intentions, e.g. 'Does he mean to carry on speaking?'). Warr and Knapper (1968) call these (i) dispositional judgements, and (ii) episodic judgements; and they sub-divide further each of these according to whether they are judgements of overt or covert characteristics or facts. However, they say that all this describes only one component of making a judgement of another person – the attributive component, that of attributing some characteristic to him. The two other components are the expectancy component (what we expect of him) and the affective component (what we feel about him). Warr and Knapper distinguish further between direct and indirect perception, i.e. between perception of the person himself and perception of him indirectly through photographs or newspaper articles.

A MODEL OF PERSON PERCEPTION

The model presented here is one which is part and parcel of the social-skill model of Argyle (1969), with which we shall deal in detail in Chapter 13 on group processes. Essentially person perception is seen as a continuing process, an integral part of social interaction as a whole. The model is in two parts: a 'person-perception' part and a 'regulation' (or social-interaction) part. Both are presented here for the sake of completeness, but we shall be focussing on the person-perception part, leaving the question of 'regulation' to Chapter 13. The chief inputs for person perception are from the person to be perceived (the object in Figure 11.1) and from the context. These combine

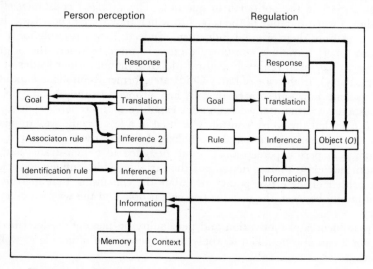

Figure 11.1   The model of Argyle and Kendon (1967) (from Cook, 1971)

with further information from the perceiver's memory and are processed by the perceiver until the perceptual response is complete. This processing consists of a number of stages which enable the object to be identified (identification rule), associated with other information available (association rule) and evaluated in terms of the perceiver's motivation or goal. The result will be the perceiver's perception of the object. To emphasise the fact that the process is not a once and for all thing, the model also indicates that the perception is not the only result. Behaviour is also likely to occur in the perceiver, which in turn will influence the object, who will then be re-examined by the perceiver, a process which will continue for as long as the interaction lasts. The picture is not complete, however, until one realises that the object (who is after all another person) is also perceiving the perceiver and bringing about changes in his state which in turn will influence his perception and behaviour towards the object.

For present purposes the main point to note is that if the model is correct, and the authors feel that it offers a good framework, then there is even more scope for subjectivity, bias and other kinds of error when we turn to the perception of *people* rather than the perception of objects. In the later part of this section this problem will represent an important theme. This is because of the large number of personal factors influencing the perception as well as to the ambiguity of the cues (information) which the perceived person may be exhibiting. It is to this latter point that we now turn.

THE CUES AVAILABLE

In making judgements about others we clearly only make use of certain cues out of the large number available to us. The clues which we shall discuss are (1) verbal, and (2) non-verbal. Contextual cues are also available.

(1) Verbal cues might seem to be the least subject to inaccurate perception; indeed, this is probably the case, but they are not infallible. Ambiguous sentences exist just as ambiguous pictures exist. The situation in person perception is complicated further by the fact that (i) non-verbal cues may provide contradictory information to the verbal information – the 'double bind' (Bateson, 1966), and (ii) statements about intended behaviour and the behaviour itself are not always constant. The study of La Piere (1934) illustrates the latter point. Restaurant owners' stated policy of not serving non-whites was not put into practice when non-whites actually came into the restaurant.

(2) Non-verbal cues include both (i) relatively static enduring features (e.g. the person's face, physique, voice, clothes, make-up, hair style), and (ii) dynamic features (changing features such as posture, gesture, body movement, facial expression, gaze direction, tone of voice, rate, amount and fluency of speech, orientation and distance).

On point (i), in general we can draw the conclusion that judges tend to make stereotyped interpretations of the static features of a person. Secord (1958) asked people to describe the personalities of people on a series of still photographs and found considerable uniformity in the descriptions – widely held identification rules. Other evidence suggests that these judgements are not likely to have validity. The reason why people probably believe they can judge others from their faces is a self-validation effect whereby they look at the person as though they were 'unpleasant', 'deceitful', etc., and as a result the person resents this and indeed does become disagreeable. Similar findings about stereotyped perception are available with regard to physique (Strongman and Hart, 1968) and clothes (Gibbins, 1969). Stereotypes also occur with regard to the voice (Lalljee, 1967). A review by Kramer (1963) suggests that these stereotypes (e.g. with respect to regional, national and social origins and age) are quite accurate. But with personality traits like leadership, though the judges may agree in their ratings, they tend to be quite inaccurate.

On point (ii), there has been a great deal of interesting work on dynamic features such as body movement, posture and gesture. Ekman and Friesen (1969) distinguish five functions of non-verbal cues: (i) emblems (signals specifically translatable into words (e.g. shaking the fist to mean anger)); (ii) affect displays; (iii) illustrators (illustrating the subject's attitude to what he himself is saying); (iv) regulators (indicating how the listener is reacting to the speaker); and (v) adaptors (which are highly individual and consistent but not between individuals). Posture, gesture and body movement play a part in all of these, though other cues such as facial expression are clearly also relevant. Ekman and Friesen consider the face to be the main channel for displays, but Ekman (1965) and Sainsbury (1955) show that anxiety or stress produce identifiable changes of posture and frequency of movement which can be detected by observers. Ekman also suggests that the body indicates the intensity of the emotion while the face identifies it. Kendon (1968) provides some interesting evidence on illustrators as a kind of non-verbal punctuation. For example, shifts in the trunk or legs occur only at the ends of paragraphs while movements of the hands and forearm tend to occur at every phase. Such movements also illustrate content with the gestures moving towards the speaker when first-person pronouns are used and away from him with other pronouns. Regulators indicate such things as whether the speaker is interested or not or wants the speaker to go faster, slower or stop. Head-nods, eyebrow-raising and slight postural shifts fall into this category (Scheflen, 1965). Krasner (1958) has found that head-nods serve as a positive reinforcer, causing the speaker to speak more. On adaptors, Krout (1954) has found that under stress many subjects use consistently gestures which are quite individual.

Certainly people are very good at recognising these kinds of non-verbal cues, particularly together with other concomitant information. Ekman's classification of cues applies to other types of non-verbal cues and in particular to facial expression. Birdwhistell (1973) has put forward the idea of 'kinesics', a kind of non-verbal language based on the changes in the bodily features of a person, in accompaniment to what he is saying and as a reaction to what others say.

Eye-gaze direction is another feature of non-verbal communication which has received some attention. Kendon (1967) reports that people look for more of the time and in longer gazes when they are listening and in shorter but more frequent gazes when speaking. Returning of the other's gaze rarely occurs for more than a few seconds at a time. Kendon (1967) also found that when the speaker is coming to the end of his utterance he looks up and continues to look at the other person who then starts speaking. Looking up seems to be a signal to take over. If the signal is not given, there is a delay before the listener takes over. Exline and Winters (1965) find that people look less at those they dislike and if the topic or conversation is difficult or embarrassing. People also seem to like less those whose gazes are short and frequent than those who look in longer gazes. Poppleton (1971) found that amount of mutual gaze (i.e. when two people look at each other in the region of the eyes simultaneously) was greater in dyads in which there was greater mutual attraction. Amount of gaze was greater in female students than in males, and was related to both dominance (measured by Cattell's 16 P.F.Q.) and perceived dominance in an affiliative situation. The importance of some of these features in interviews and other assessment situations is clear, but as yet only limited recognition has been made of this potentially valuable field of study.

ACCURACY OF JUDGEMENTS

Having considered a number of non-verbal cues available to the perceiver, let us now pursue further the question of how these cues help us to judge accurately certain characteristics of others. In general, two main kinds of methodological problem bedevil this kind of research: (i) the criterion problem; and (ii) artefacts.

The criterion problem

An indication of the nature of this problem is obtained by considering the nature of characteristics to be judged and the types of criteria available. The two main types of characteristic used in research studies have been emotions and personality characteristics. The difficulty has been to obtain criteria for identifying them. Solutions to the problem have included the taking of expert opinions, ratings by other individuals and groups, self-descriptions of the subject and objective data. The first two of these beg the question of the accuracy of perception, the third raises the problem of the validity of self-reports and the last is seldom available for this kind of judgement, except for such traits as intelligence.

Artefacts

These may be divided into two kinds: (i) stereotype accuracy; and (ii) statistical artefacts. In stereotype accuracy, judges tend to perceive the subject as similar to a stereotype, e.g. themselves (Vernon, 1964), or to assume that the subject likes them (Tagiuri, 1958). These tendencies make accurate judgements more likely because they virtually guarantee perception in cases of real similarity or liking, whereas the random guesser does not have this advantage. What happens is that the judges can identify and use a stereotype to judge the subject. The problem is how to distinguish stereotype accuracy from genuine perceptual accuracy (differential accuracy). Statistical artefacts are illustrated by Cronbach (1955). He has shown that when judges are required to rate a series of subjects on a particular trait, a judge who gives each subject an average rating on the trait is likely, over a series of subjects, to obtain a high accuracy score since the majority of subjects are in fact likely to be clustered around the mean rating if the trait is distributed normally.

This said, let us turn to some research findings on accuracy. Toch, Rabin and Wilkins (1962) report that judges could distinguish photographs of Jews from those of Protestants and Catholics and that Jews are better at the task than others. This study does not have the methodological shortcomings of much of the earlier work. Sissons (unpublished research) has shown that social class can be identified quite accurately from photographs and from samples of recorded speech. Cline and Richards (1960) and Crow and Hammond (1957) report that judges can judge accurately on whether subjects will discuss certain topics in public, how subjects would describe themselves and how much they would score on scales such as 'paranoia', 'social contact' and 'hypochondria', and the vocabulary sub-test of the 'Wechsler adult intelligence scale' (W.A.I.S.). Both of these studies used as their material filmed interviews with the subjects. Woodworth (1938) and Schlosberg (1954) report that judges can judge the emotions intended in posed photographs with some accuracy. The trouble with posed photographs is that the actor may simply be portraying a stereotype. Tagiuri (1969) reports inferior accuracy using photographs taken from real-life situations.

CONCLUSION

We might conclude from the above review that accuracy in person perception is hard to find with certainty. This is a justifiable conclusion if one considers evidence from the literature on the selection interview which shows highly variable validity coefficients for different interviewers (Handyside and Duncan, 1954). However, Warr and Knapper (1968) point out that we rarely need to perceive individual characteristics in isolation, and Argyle and McHenry (1971) offer evidence that the effect of exposing the judge to larger samples of the subject's behaviour is to reduce the importance of at least some cues. Thus when we take into account the undoubted ability of some judges to judge accurately (Ghiselli, 1966) and the evidence that interviewers and psychiatrists can improve their accuracy by concentrating on particular items (Vernon and Parry, 1949; Wing, 1961), we need not be quite as sceptical about man's ability to perceive his fellow man accurately as the general tone of this review might have indicated. However, we should not rely too much on it.

11.3   Attribution theory

Up till now we have concentrated on a particular kind of model of person perception and particular aspects of that. We have been talking mainly about what might be called the 'tips' of the problem, the nature of the perceptual response, the nature of the perceptual cues and the way in which they are related. What has been missing from our discussion has been any real consideration of what kind of processing or mediation occurs between the reception of the cues and the perceptual response. Little attention is paid to this aspect in Argyle and Kendon's model. A model designed for the processing (translation and inference) aspects of person perception has been put forward by Jones and Davis (1965) (see Figure 11.2).

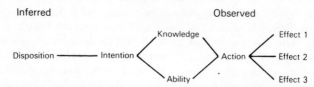

Figure 11.2   Jones and Davis's model for inferring disposition from action

The model attempts to explain how a perceiver (*P*) attributes dispositional characteristics to another person (*O*). *P* starts by observing a particular action on the part of *O*. At this stage a whole inference process comes into operation based on a number of questions which *P* asks himself about the action. Reading from right to left in Figure 11.2, *P* asks himself first whether *O* has the knowledge and the ability to carry out the action of taking into account all the implications of the action. If he has this knowledge and ability, *P* holds *O* responsible for his action, and on the basis of this *P* will attribute a different kind of disposition to a person who is responsible for his action to one who is not. A further question remains to be answered and this is whether his action is intentional or accidental. Clearly if it is the former we are more likely to hold him responsible and consequently attribute to him a different kind of disposition.

Let us illustrate this with an example. If I am at a party and I (P) observe O spill his drink over X's best suit, what kind of disposition am I likely to attribute to O? Clearly, spilling the drink had several effects. For present purposes we shall focus on two of these: (i) O has messed X's suit; and (ii) O has lost his drink. Both of these outcomes may be regarded as unsatisfactory. The first is unsatisfactory to X, the second to O. The next question I may ask is 'Did O act intentionally (did he *throw* his drink over X), or accidentally (was he perhaps jolted by a third party)?' Alternatively, he may just not have been looking at what his hand was doing in the heat of the conversation. I am likely to make a different kind of attribution in each of these three cases. I am only likely to make an attribution where I can see that O was responsible for his actions. Thus in the first case I am likely to come to a fairly strong conclusion about someone who throws his drink over someone else intentionally. In the second case, since O was not, properly speaking, the agent and the action was accidental, I shall be unlikely to attribute anything to him on the basis of it. In the third, intermediate, case I may not feel able to attribute any disposition to O but may be tempted to attribute some non-dispositional characteristic to him, e.g. 'clumsiness'.

The question of intentionality has been studied in depth by De Charms and his co-workers. Their contribution has been to identify the origin–pawn dimension which identifies the extent to which an individual is acting by his own intent (i.e. as an origin), or in response to external pressure (i.e. as a pawn). De Charms, Carpenter and Kuperman (1965) used a paper-and-pencil test to investigate the conditions under which the agent is likely to be seen as either origin or pawn. Subjects were asked to study a series of stories about seven different agents who were influenced by either another individual, a small group, or a large organisation. The agent either liked or disliked the persuader. The results showed that there was a general tendency for the agent was seen more as a pawn if he was responding to a large organisation or if the persuader was responding, and more of an origin if he was responding to a small group.

When we turn to the question of individual differences between subjects, de Charms *et al.* (1965) provide us with another interesting finding, namely that subjects who perceive themselves as pawns have a greater tendency to perceive the agent in the stories as a pawn. Likewise, subjects who perceive themselves as origins tend rather to see the agents as origins.

To summarise so far, inferences made by P about O's disposition are a function of the perceiver's personality, the nature of the influencing situation or person, the nature of the agent and the agent's relationship to the influencing situation or person. Further work in this field has investigated the effects on the inference process of variables such as O praising or criticising P, the effects of O's actions on the environment, the effects of O martyring himself for P and the effects of P having acted in some way towards O. The results of this work have produced the following broad conclusions: (i) with regard to praise, P receives it as genuine if O's status is higher than his or if O is not dependent on him, but if the reverse is true he perceives it as ingratiation;

(ii) with regard to criticism, P forms a positive impression if O and P are peers or if O is superior to P or in an informal situation, but forms a negative impression of O if O is of lower status or the context is a formal one; (iii) if O martyrs himself for P, P forms a negative impression of O; (iv) with regard to P being responsible in some way for O's suffering, P forms a negative impression of O and the same applies if P fails to prevent O's suffering; and (v) if P manages to save O from suffering, then he is likely to form a favourable impression of O.

This has been a quick excursion through some of the ramifications of attribution theory in order to give the reader an appreciation of the kind of research which has been carried out and the kind of conclusions drawn as to the nature of the inference process in person perception. Clearly the manner in which the mechanisms of attribution work has an influence on how people interpret the actions of others. Although discussion of accidents at work is beyond the scope of this book, the reader may care to speculate on how the observer might attribute blame for an accident depending on whether he perceives himself to be either an origin or a pawn. (For a very readable discussion of attribution theory, see Sampson (1976).)

A final word is needed on the relationship between the Argyle approach and the attribution-theory approach. We feel that Argyle's approach is very much complementary to attribution theory in that whereas the former concentrates on the information available for person perception, the latter is concerned with the manner in which the information is processed.

11.4 Interviewing

There are many purposes to which interviews are put and in this section we shall discuss some of them. It is convenient first, though, to make a general distinction between two main purposes: (i) to gather information; and (ii) to be, broadly speaking, therapeutic (to help the interviewee with some difficulty). Information-gathering interviews are used for personnel selection, market research, opinion surveys and any other situation in which the interviewer attempts to obtain information from the interviewee in the interest of furthering his (the interviewer's) aims. Therapeutic interviews are used for psychotherapy (the treatment of people with personal or emotional problems), the resolution of work grievances, and counselling of various kinds. Two kinds of interview, however, do not fit clearly into either category. One is the occupational guidance interview (aimed at helping a person choose a career) and the other is the appraisal interview (where superior and subordinate meet in order to discuss the latter's work performance, his feelings about his work and future). The reason for this is that to some extent they fall into both camps. In occupational guidance the interviewer requires information about the interviewee in order to assess realistically what kinds of work he is capable of doing and interested in. On the other hand, it is quite likely that the interviewee has come for guidance on account of some problem of a personal kind. Thus the interviewer needs both to gather information and be therapeutic. A similar conflict of objectives exists in the case of appraisal interviewing when the interviewer needs to inform the interviewee of where he stands, and, if there is something wrong with his job performance, to gather information about the reasons. Yet at the same time the interviewer may need to help the interviewee resolve any problems he has concerning his work. It is difficult to play the roles of judge and helper at the same time.

Broadly speaking, different kinds of interview technique have been used for information-gathering and therapeutic interviews; these are directive and non-directive interviews respectively. They differ in the extent to which the interviewer determines what will be discussed. In the directive interview the interviewer asks more questions and, in general, structures the content more than in the non-directive interview, where the interviewee is encouraged to explore his feelings about whatever is on his mind at the time. This said, it should be pointed out that there is evidence that in directive information gathering interviews the less interviewer speaks in proportion to the interviewee, the better the interview is likely to be (Cavanagh, Drake and Taylor, 1962). In most kinds of interview the focus is, or should be, on what the interviewee has to say.

In the next two sections we shall be looking at the actual techniques used in directive and non-directive interviewing with a view to discovering whether and how they achieve their aims.

11.5   The directive interview

As suggested earlier, the directive interview is used mainly for gathering information. This is not to say that a well-placed question or statement on the part of the interviewer may not be helpful or therapeutic. Indeed, there has been an increasing tendency for interviewing techniques to move out of their traditional areas of use and for techniques to be combined within the same interview, for example in staff appraisal. Still, directive interviews are used mainly for information-gathering and it is on this that we shall concentrate in this section.

The directive interview is an important tool in the work situation. However, a lot of research has indicated what our study of person perception has led us to suspect, that it is both unreliable and invalid; that is to say that different interviewers are likely to form different impressions of the same interviewee and the same interviewer may form different impressions on different occasions (unreliability). Further, it may not do the job it is intended to do (invalidity).

Let us look at a few classical research studies in the field. Hollingworth (1929) reports that when twelve sales managers interviewed fifty-seven candidates, there was very little consistency between the interviewers in their ratings. One candidate was ranked first by one interviewer, fifty-seventh by another, second by another, fifty-third by another, and so on. This seems pretty damning for the interview. However, two points need to be made: (i) these were not systematic, well-planned interviews of the kind we are about to describe; and (ii) Laird (1937), using Hollingworth's original data, found that although there was a great deal of inconsistency between interviewers, some pairs of interviewers showed a very high degree of agreement with each other. This does not imply that the interview is unreliable in itself but that interviewers are variable. A reasonable conclusion may still be that, provided appropriate steps are taken, reliable and valid interviews are possible.

One of these steps seems to be not to expect the interviewer to make too many fine discriminations. For example, Hunt *et al.* (1944) report that when psychiatrists in the British armed forces were required to designate recruits into specific personality categories, they achieved rather poor agreement, but when asked to decide simply whether they were fit or unfit for service, 95 per cent agreement was reached.

Another step to be taken is to ensure that the interview is being used for a purpose suitable for it. Vernon and Parry (1949) conclude that for predicting success at tradesman jobs in the British Army, tests of various kinds had greater validity than interviews. Kelly and Fiske (1951) came to a similar conclusion about the prediction of success for clinical psychologists. However, the reverse was true in selection for the administrative and executive grades of the Civil Service (Vernon, 1950a).

Two more variables need to be considered before we are in a position to assess the true value of the interview. These are the training of the interviewer and the systematic planning of the interview. McMurry (1947) reports rather high validities (0.48 to 0.68) of systematic interviews by trained interviewers in predicting the job performance of employees in three companies. Other studies (Handyside and Duncan, 1954; Hovland and Wonderlic, 1939; Grant and Bray, 1969; Yonge, 1956) show similar but less spectacular results. In this rather under-researched field the interview is not yet dead. Quite apart from the debate as to its reliability and validity, perhaps its greatest strength lies in its greater flexibility and comprehensiveness than any of its rivals in personnel assessment (see Section 11.7).

CHARACTERISTICS OF THE DIRECTIVE INTERVIEW

The usual purpose of the directive interview is to enable the interviewee to be as informative about himself as possible in the areas which interest the interviewer. To this end a number of points need to be borne in mind. They are widely made by experienced interviewers and receive some (usually indirect) support from the research literature. However, we should stress that there is little direct supportive evidence for them.

Perhaps the most important prerequisite is a clear view of what information is required. In the case of selection interviewing, this will take the form of a personnel specification (a list of the requirements the candidate must possess). It is often helpful if the items on the specification are used as headings for note-taking. Systematic coverage of these items is most important.

In order to ensure a systematic and thorough coverage, a basic interviewing technique is required; we shall mention some aspects of this in the following paragraphs.

It is important to collect facts as far as possible. Thus questions such as 'How good a handy-man are you?' should be avoided in favour of the more precise 'What is the most difficult job you have taken on at home yourself?'

In a similar vein the interviewer should be careful that he is not simply collecting labels. Thus 'What do you do in your spare time?' 'Photography' needs to be followed up with further questions designed to discover the extent of the interest.

A typical error on the part of the directive interviewer is to ask questions which restrict the possible answers which may be given. Thus questions like 'Did you empty the till yourself?', 'Did you count the money?' and 'Then did you check the totals?' only leave limited scope to the interviewee to expand on the basic 'Yes' or 'No', whereas 'Tell me exactly what you did' might produce a lot more information. Another way in which the answer may be restricted artificially by the interviewer is if he asks questions which suggest that one answer is expected more than another, e.g. 'How many days' holiday did you have – fourteen?'

Further errors on the part of the interviewer are simply to do with making the candidate feel uncomfortable. These include acting like a judge and evaluating the interviewee's answers, asking two questions at once so the interviewee does not know which to answer first, not waiting long enough for an answer (silences are not bad), interrupting the interviewee, talking unnecessarily, asking catch questions and being aggressive, all of which make it less likely that the candidate will talk freely.

Finally, there are things like assessing knowledge and ability which are probably best done by other methods such as psychological tests, though Wagner (1949) does cite evidence suggesting that intelligence is one of the most accurately judged characteristics in a selection interview. These relatively simple points are often ignored by interviewers and yet a relatively small amount of planning and training for the interview could well do much towards improving the low reliability and validity of the interviews reported in many studies.

11.6   The non-directive interview

The non-directive interview is totally different in conception and style from the directive interview, outlined in the last section. It originated in the clinical work of Rogers (see Chapter 9). He was a clinical psychologist who took the view that a large number of people, as a result of a lack of belief in their own worth and ability, give up trying to solve the problems in their lives and resort to a kind of non-rational behaviour. This may vary in its nature, but a typical pattern is for the individual to feel sorry for himself, angry and resentful, yet unable to express it directly 'because one doesn't do these things in public'. Consequently he will feel guilty for feeling that way and suspicious that people might see through him and condemn him for the way he is feeling. He might feel that people are trying to do him down and is thus consequently prone to disliking them. He will resent any indication that they *might* be criticising him. Such individuals often find their outlet by expressing their hostility towards various aspects of their work, and, indeed, the non-directive interview has been made much use of in the handling of such grievances.

An indication of how common the above pattern is may be gained by considering the common experience of finding one's job or studies more irksome on some days than on others. In all probability nothing much has changed in the job or studies and the most likely explanation would seem to be that the change has been in one's life outside work or in one's general personality. Who has not been tempted to take it out on their nearest and dearest if something has gone wrong at work? In one form or another very many of us are prone from time to time to the kind of behaviour we have been describing and in the heat of the moment are unable to recognise the real nature of what we are doing. If tackled directly about it, the result would be a flat denial that anything else apart from the ostensive cause of the complaints was the matter.

The fact is that human beings are very much inclined to catch themselves in this sort of a trap. Repeated failure can lead to the individual feeling angry and sorry for himself. This he cannot express directly so he finds some other outlet for his feelings, say at work. Being able to find successfully a scapegoat for his feelings directs his attention away from the need to do something about solving the original problem or to be constructive about his work situation. Although it is not too comfortable to be continually aggrieved, it is a lot more comfortable than to remain face to face with continual failure in some other aspect of one's life (e.g. an unhappy marriage or love affair, a problem child, difficulties with parents, loneliness).

As suggested earlier, the interviewer attempting to resolve this problem has a difficult task on his hands if he tries to approach it directly. Such an individual may be prickly at best. If the interviewer agrees with his grievance, he may feel that here is someone who will solve his problem for him and he will become highly dependent. If he disagrees, it will be seen as criticism and reinforce the aggrieved feelings. Either way the individual is unlikely to return to rational, problem-solving behaviour.

The main requirement in this kind of interview is for the interviewer to maintain a consistent attitude towards the interviewee. This attitude must be one of unconditional acceptance of the individual, combined with a belief in the person's ability to solve the problem himself. This means he must not show shock, boredom, criticism, agreement or disagreement. At the start of the interview this may be very difficult. The opening gambits are usually smoke-screens, and any contradiction may freeze the interview at this point. In a word, the interviewer makes no value judgements and the whole interview is conducted in the context of acceptance of the individual. Only under these conditions will the person feel safe enough to express his feelings and to confront the real problem. The interviewee will seize upon any opportunity to become dependent or feel criticised and it is for this reason that the interviewer must underpin his activities with the belief (but not a sermon!) that the person can solve the problem himself. It is only when the state of frustration has been relieved through expression of feelings that the interviewer may take the opportunity of being helpful without danger of dependency.

The chief skill required to enable individuals to express their feelings are those of listening and reflecting the person's feelings. Listening is not as easy as it may sound. It may often require the interviewer not to react spontaneously when he is needled, frightened, verbally abused or witnesses another individual in tears. All he does is to show that he has understood and accepts the feelings that the person has expressed: 'I can see your feelings have been hurt'; 'You feel you have been let down.' This encourages him to talk further, does not agree or disagree and enables the person to re-examine his own words and feelings. Only in the final stage of the interview when the person is over his frustration should an ordinary discussion take place. Some of the practical steps towards a solution may require action on the part of the organisation. Alternatively the person may conclude that he needs more counselling or therapeutic treatment and this is something which can be discussed.

In recent years there has been a tendency for non-directive interviewing to be used outside its traditional areas of use, i.e. counselling psychotherapy and grievance interviewing. Its value has turned out not only to be in therapy but also in the field of gathering information. As we have suggested, the non-directive approach enables a person to express feelings and attitudes which otherwise he would conceal. Thus, although it is rather time-consuming it has been used in personnel selection, occupational guidance and market research in cases where information is required concerning the deeper levels of people's feelings. A discussion of research into the non-directive interview will be found in Section 9.4.

We shall now turn to two areas – performance assessment and staff appraisal – in the latter of which the non-directive approach is coming to have an increasing influence.

11.7 Performance assessment and staff appraisal

Assessment and appraisal are two words very loosely used, often taken to mean the same thing. We have chosen the terms 'performance assessment' and 'staff appraisal' carefully both to reflect the general view that appraisal is a somewhat wider term than assessment and to indicate the way in which this is so. Usually assessment is taken to mean the assessment of the work performance of a subordinate by a superior – hence performance assessment. Generally appraisal means a review of the current relationship between worker and organisation including an assessment of the worker's performance as well as his development, his attitude to his job, his grievances and his hopes and plans for the future – hence staff appraisal.

PERSONNEL ASSESSMENT AND APPRAISAL

The purposes of introducing appraisal schemes are numerous, and may be broadly classified as (i) administrative, and (ii) developmental. The administrative purposes aim at producing greater organisational efficiency by obtaining an inventory of manpower skills such that best use can be made of the work-force, e.g. by transfers and promotion. The developmental purposes aim at developing individuals in their present jobs, developing them for other jobs, planning their careers and resolving any current work problems. The purpose of a scheme determines the form it takes. Broadly speaking, schemes with administrative aims are primarily evaluative, obtaining detailed information on abilities and performance. Those with developmental aims are more concerned with helping an employee to improve his performance, and are problem-solving in orientation rather than evaluative. If the organisation wishes to achieve both aims, then it may be better to have separate systems for each purpose. A common reason for the failure of appraisal schemes is the requirement for a manager both to evaluate and help a subordinate at the same interview. The resulting conflict of roles is often more than the manager or subordinate can handle and both often try to avoid such confrontations. Another reason for failure is that participants either do not know or do not agree with the objectives of the appraisal.

In evaluating an individual's performance, we must be aware of the many determinants of job performance. These are illustrated in Figure 11.3. Since

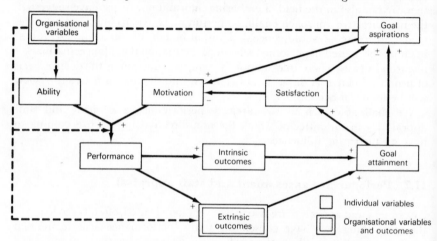

Figure 11.3   An integrated model of the determinants of performance (Cummings and Schwab, 1973)

each of these may enter into the determination of performance, it may well be that a certain amount of diagnostic and counselling work will be required even in the simplest performance-improvement scheme.

It is important not only to evaluate performance, but even more important to understand the relative contributions to various aspects of it. In our view this should be a primary aim of an appraisal interview. First, however, we must consider a number of the more common methods of assessing performance.

METHODS OF PERFORMANCE ASSESSMENT

We shall review six main types of assessment methods.

(1) *Direct indices,* such as productivity and absenteeism, are sometimes used. The difficulty with such indices is that it is often difficult to assess what is an individual's contribution to such a measure. For example, general staff morale may also be responsible as well as his own personal attitude and the

characteristics of any equipment being operated. Direct indices do not make it clear which of many variables contribute to an individual's level of performance.

(2) *Rating scales* are perhaps the most widely used method. A number of worker characteristics are selected, ideally on the basis of a job analysis aimed at isolating the most important aspects of the job for the purpose(s) of the scheme. Characteristics should be relatively independent of one another to avoid duplication and aid clarity. That this is often not the case is illustrated by a study by Ewart, Seashore and Tiffin (1941), who found that factor analysis of twelve characteristics revealed only two basic factors, ability to do the present job and quality of job performance. Employees are then rated on each characteristic either on a graphic or multiple-step scale. In the former type the rater places a tick at a point on a line which he considers represents the degree of the characteristic possessed by the ratee. A problem with this scale is that different raters may have different conceptions about what a particular point along the scale means. This problem can be overcome, at least to some extent, on the multiple-step scale; this consists of a discrete number of categories, each one corresponding to a certain amount of the characteristic. For each point on the scale, an explanation can be provided of the kinds of behaviour exemplifying such a rating.

Nevertheless, many studies of rating behaviour show that it is susceptible to various forms of error, the most important of these being the four listed below:

(i) *The halo effect.* This is the tendency to rate a person high or low on many factors because of his high or low score in one specific factor. This might explain such findings as that of Ewart *et al.* (1941). For example, a supervisor may like the way a worker relates to his fellow workers and this may cause him to ignore his untidiness or his slowness.

(ii) *Errors of central tendency.* These refer to a commonly found tendency to rate most people about the middle of a scale. Recently one of the authors came across a case where forty-eight out of fifty ratings on a particular characteristic were at the middle point of a five-point scale. This error can be overcome by using a forced-choice distribution, i.e. making the rater use all the categories in some specific proportion.

(iii) *Errors of leniency.* These refer to the tendency of raters to be reluctant to be critical of a subordinate and to assess with differing degrees of leniency. This effect can be allowed for by converting ratings to standard scores (see any basic statistical text). Fiedler's (1967) research on leadership suggests that this rating tendency is related to other aspects of leadership behaviour (see Chapter 14).

(iv) *Errors due to criterion contamination.* These refer to errors due to the rater not allowing for the effects of various variables extraneous to the individual being rated which have nothing to do with him, e.g. a particularly efficient secretary or being a member of a highly respected department.

(3) *Comparison methods.* We have so far mentioned the forced-distribution system, which is particularly useful when a person has to rate a large number of people. Two other comparison methods are paired comparisons and ranking: (i) paired comparisons, where each ratee is paired with every other one

for purposes of comparison, have not been used much in performance appraisal, but there has been some success (Lawshe, Kephart and McCormick, 1949). It is, of course, only feasible for relatively small numbers of employees; (ii) ranking, where the rater simply ranks the ratees, raises the problem that the ratees may compete with each other by being deliberately uncooperative.

(4) *Behavioural check-lists and scales* consist of descriptive statements of job-related behaviour. The rater indicates which of these statements describe the ratee. Such scales are difficult and lengthy to develop, but they can make a most valuable guide for an interview of a job-improvement kind, for they require description rather than evaluation by the rater. An accurate description of behaviour is a necessary prerequisite for a useful analysis of performance, which in turn is essential before performance can be improved.

(5) Flanagan and Burns's (1955) *critical incident technique* requires the recording of behaviour that is particularly desirable or undesirable. The technique is very useful for a performance-improvement interview but suffers from the same disadvantages as behavioural check-lists.

(6) *Management by objectives* (M.B.O.) is based essentially on two related concepts (Wilkstrom, 1968): (i) the clearer the idea of what is to be achieved, the better the chance of achieving it; (ii) progress can only be measured in terms of what is trying to be achieved – usually this involves a four-step process: (*a*) defining the goals to be achieved; (*b*) the subordinate carries out the objectives established; (*c*) evaluation of performance against the goals initially established with an emphasis on self-evaluation and; (*d*) establishing new goals. Its main characteristic is that it allows unique goals to be set for each subordinate. This is of great benefit in obtaining performance improvement but it does not lend itself to an effective or fair system of evaluation across individuals. When the achievement of objectives *per se* is used as a means of evaluating personnel, a common result is an attempt by the subordinate to get for himself objectives which are easily attainable. We see the value of objectives as lying primarily in their ability to direct and motivate people. Whether or not they are achieved provides relatively little information. An interview which focusses upon *why* an objective was achieved, not achieved or exceeded can be of great value in performance improvement. M.B.O. schemes also emphasise the importance of participation in goal-setting. We would suggest that not only should participation be encouraged in the interview but that its aim should be to improve the performance of the interviewer, the department and the organisation as well as of the subordinate. There is some empirical support for the benefits of participation in the appraisal interview. For example, Meyer, Kay and French (1965) found that participation in goal-setting resulted in higher performance. Most important appears to be whether goals are set at all (Locke, 1968). Another consequence of the objective-setting approach is that the interviews arise as and when necessary in terms of the time scales required by particular objectives. Such interviews are part of on-going job activities, rather than being at fixed intervals when they tend to become increasingly ritualistic and removed from important day-to-day considerations. This can be illustrated by objective-setting simply designed to satisfy the requirements of the scheme (or

training board!) and which receives no further review until the subsequent appraisal.

THE APPRAISER

Who does the appraising is a matter which varies with the scheme. There may be benefits in including additional personnel to the supervisor in the evaluation (e.g. Bayroff, Haggerty and Rundquist, 1954). However, Whitla and Tirrell (1954) found that raters closest to ratees in terms of organisational level produced better ratings than raters at higher organisational levels. In the British Civil Service the immediate superior does the rating while his superior (i.e. the grandparent) conducts the appraisal interview! To some extent this avoids the problem of the same person being both judge and helper. Although such an arrangement can pose problems like the undermining of the authority of the superior (or protection of the superior by his superior), the system seems to have proved to have been generally satisfactory. However, if performance improvement is a major objective, a one-to-one interview between immediate superior and subordinate of a 'problem-solving' kind is quite appropriate.

When evaluation is the sole purpose of appraisal, then assessment centres are sometimes used, usually to spot management potential. Typically a small group of managerial personnel participate over several days in various individual and group activities under the observation of assessment-centre staff. Activities often include business games, problem-solving tasks, group discussions, various psychological tests and interviews. The advantage of this method is that assessments are not limited to those displayed in job performance.

THE APPRAISAL INTERVIEW

The rationale for an appraisal interview stemmed originally from the various studies of learning which suggest the feedback or knowledge of results can play an important role in improving performance. Research (Kay *et al.*, 1965), however, shows that such feedback often evoked more negative than positive consequences. In particular, statements made by superiors which appeared (to trained observers) to be critical, to threaten the subordinates self-esteem, impaired subsequent goal achievement in subordinates low in occupational self-esteem as measured by questionnaire (Kay *et al.*, 1962). Other studies (e.g. Mayfield, 1960) have found that the majority of employees express satisfaction with evaluation interviews.

There is evidence from various sources that subordinate satisfaction with the interview is related to the subordinate's desire to improve performance (Burke and Wilcox, 1969). The various studies we have cited point clearly to the fact that different individuals with different relationships with their superiors will find different kinds of interview satisfying. It is therefore impossible to be generally prescriptive about the form any such interview should take. However, the discussion of interviewing in the previous sections should indicate the range of possibilities available granted that appraisal has various purposes, evaluative, developmental, diagnostic and therapeutic. (For a detailed discussion, see Poppleton and Salaman (1978).)

12
Personnel Selection

12.1 Introduction

Personnel selection is one of the aspects of the world of work for which the industrial psychologist's contribution is best known. It is clearly in the interest of the employer that the employee should be satisfactory in his work. A successful selection procedure will select from among the candidates those who are both able (have the capacity) and willing (have the inclination) to perform the required job satisfactorily. Likewise, it is clearly in the interests of the employee to have a job and working conditions which will satisfy him. Probably this is also in the interest of the employer since dissatisfied employees are particularly subject to high rates of voluntary absenteeism and turnover.

The personnel selector's job comprises three aspects. First, he must recruit enough suitable candidates from which to choose: not too few, since this will give him only a limited perspective of what is available; not too many, since this is uneconomical and laborious. Second, he must undertake an exercise in prediction: which of the candidates is most likely to be both satisfactory and satisfied in the job in question. To this end he makes use of a number of possible methods such as interviews, psychological tests and group discussions. Finally, he has to ensure that the procedure is both reliable and valid. Reliability involves the procedure being consistent in what it does. Its validity is determined by whether it does what it is required to do, i.e. select candidates who turn out later to be both satisfactory and satisfied in their work.

In this chapter we shall begin with a description of the traditional predictive validity model of personnel selection (Section 12.2). (We are excluding the truly traditional model which is based largely on the personal preference of the interviewer and is so dependent for its success on the interviewer's intuitive skills that reliability between interviewers is bound to be extremely low.) The model has its limitations and we shall discuss these before presenting some modern refinements and modifications in Section 12.3. This is followed in Section 12.4 by a discussion of some of the main 'tools of the trade', such as interviewing and other assessment procedures, used in personnel selection. Finally, Section 12.5 discusses the relationship between personnel selection and occupational guidance and counselling and indicates the contribution of the latter approach to personnel selection.

12.2   The predictive validity model

This is the traditional systematic approach to personnel selection which is based on determining the capacity of certain measures administered at the time of selection to predict whether a candidate will later become a successful employee. To this end a number of steps have to be taken and we shall outline these here.

JOB ANALYSIS

This is simply a careful description of the job. It is the first stage in many personnel activities, including training, method study and job evaluation for the determination of payment rates. However, the type of analysis required for personnel selection differs from that required for other purposes in that it concentrates specifically on those aspects of the job which are relevant to the success, failure, satisfaction and dissatisfaction of employees and may therefore leave out other aspects of the job. A number of methods are available, such as observation, interviews, questionnaires, check-lists, and work diaries. Observation may be carried out either directly or via film. Interviews with workers doing the job, with their supervisor, and with any other working personnel coming into contact with them at work, are particularly important in classifying the more subtle aspects of the work and in eliciting how the workers feel about their job (see the job-analysis form in Table 12.1). Interviews may have various degrees of structure and can be conducted on a one-to-one basis or in the form of a group discussion. Check-lists of job activities

Table 12.1   A job-analysis form

Job...

Stage ....

Department ....

Firm ....

Entry age............   Age range...............

Number, sex of workers M......   F......

Classification of job ....

Duties and responsibilities
(1) Main routine duties

(2) Responsibility for the safety, health, work of others

Responsibility for equipment, materials

(3) Duties and responsibilities most prominent in employers' accounts of common difficulties of workers

Working conditions and rewards not recorded elsewhere
(4) Is the work place
      dark
      damp
      dusty
      drab
      noisy
      stuffy
      hot
      cold?

(5) Is the work itself
      heavy
      dirty
      unvaried
      finnicky
      dangerous
      solitary?

(6) Does it offer
      companionship
      teamwork
      independence
      rivalry
      prestige?

(7) What do workers say they like about the work?

(8) What do they say they dislike about it?

(9) Is there anything else to be noted about the working conditions and rewards?

and structured questionnaires concerning aspects of the jobs can be used by the job analyst himself or can be administered to employees. These will often be based on some preliminary interview and/or observational study. Work diaries are used to record work activity, by the workers themselves, as the work occurs. Usually some combination of these methods will be used.

Each of these methods can be extremely laborious if the job is at all complicated and if detailed descriptions are obtained. To overcome this difficulty particular attention is paid to those aspects of the job which are of importance in determining good or bad job performance, at the expense of some of the more detailed and less relevant job behaviour. Rodger and Cavanagh (1962) have called these the difficulties (since these may cause poor performance through the worker's inability to handle them) and distastes of the job (since these may cause dissatisfaction on the part of the worker. Typically the end result of this procedure is a list of job activities organised under major headings and sub-headings, along with other relevant job information such as training received, working conditions (physical, social and economic) and opportunities for transfer and promotion (see for example, Reeves *et al.*, 1951). We should note that this procedure is very difficult to follow for jobs in which behaviour cannot always be specified in advance (e.g. high-level managerial jobs).

DERIVING A PERSONNEL SPECIFICATION

On the basis of the job analysis hypotheses are derived concerning the worker characteristics necessary to perform the job adequately or successfully. The personnel specification is a description of these characteristics. Sometimes acceptable standards of performance will be clearly evident from the job analysis, and sometimes labour-market conditions (i.e. who is available) will dictate acceptable performance standards. Frequently both of these aspects will play a role in hypothesis formation. They will also determine whether the required workers are to be recruited by means of personnel selection at all. It may be more appropriate to train or retrain existing workers for the job. If the labour market has a glut of suitably trained workers, personnel selection is usually the answer; but if there is a great shortage of suitable workers, then the provision of appropriate training (see Chapter 4) will also be needed since untrained workers may have to be selected or recruited from inside the organisation. There is evidence that trained raters derive the required personnel characteristics from the job analysis with high reliability and validity (Trattner, *et al.*, 1955; Marquardt *et al.*, 1972). However, the derivation of intellectual and perceptual abilities was more successful than that of practical and physical skills.

Perhaps the most important point concerning personnel specifications is that they are only hypotheses, and as such should be tested empirically, using statistical techniques, for their validity.

It can be a help in constructing personnel specifications to use a check-list of characteristics which may be of relevance for job performance. One of the most commonly used is presented in Table 12.2. Other similar plans are Munro-Fraser's (1966) five-point plan and Sidney and Brown's (1961) nine-

Table 12.2   N.I.I.P. seven-point plan

(1)   Physical characteristics
(2)   Attainments
(3)   General intelligence
(4)   Special aptitudes
(5)   Interests
(6)   Disposition
(7)   Circumstances

point plan. The plan shown in Table 12.2 is regularly used in conjunction with the job-analysis form shown in Table 12.1 and the reader might care to test his skill in deriving a personnel specification from the job analysis of a particular job with which he is familiar. He will then see that the process of derivation is not automatic and hence not totally reliable in the sense that there is room for divergences of opinion. However, the method is a considerable improvement over armchair guesses as to what the personnel specification ought to be. This is because it forces the prospective personnel selector to think in detail about the nature of the job and the characteristics of the person who will do it.

THE CHOICE OF CRITERIA

A criterion is a standard by which we judge the value, success or failure, of a given activity. One of the activities of the personnel selector is to evaluate his selection system. To do this he needs a criterion against which to judge it. Idealists in the field of personnel selection usually make use of the two criteria referred to in the introduction to this chapter, the satisfactoriness of the employee and his satisfaction. A more pragmatic, and some would say less human, approach is to use only the satisfactoriness of the employee to his employer as the criterion against which the success of a personnel-selection procedure is judged.

Thorndike (1949) has divided criteria into three kinds: immediate, intermediate and ultimate. They differ according to how close they come to measuring what the user of the criterion wants to measure. In the present case he wishes to measure the total worth of the selection procedure in terms of both the satisfaction and the satisfactoriness of the employee over the long term. This would be the ultimate criterion, a combined measure of satisfaction and satisfactoriness a given number of years after selection. Unfortunately ultimate criteria are very rarely used. They take a long time to obtain and many things, including the job itself, might have changed over that period. For this reason intermediate and immediate criteria are usually used for personnel selection. Immediate criteria are simply those available immediately (see the discussion of the 'concurrent validity model' later in this chapter), in the sense that there is no waiting involved. Intermediate criteria are perhaps those most commonly used. Typically these involve some kind of approximation to the ultimate criterion and usually involve a relatively short wait until they are available. Thus examples of intermediate criteria would be work performance after six weeks on the job, i.e. before any really long-term evaluation can be made, or in the case of a college degree course the first-year examination results as opposed to the final results. As suggested earlier, for selection purposes the criteria used are likely to be measures of job effectiveness. These measures may be behavioural, subjective (e.g. ratings), status (e.g. job tenure), or accident indices, or any combination of these. These may be divided into (i) job-performance criteria, such as quantity of work, quality of work, a job sample, learning criteria, ratings and promotions, and (ii) job-attendance criteria, i.e. job tenure, absenteeism and lateness.

In selection, criteria are needed which reflect individual differences. In so far as they measure situational variables, a source of bias is introduced, known as 'criterion contamination'. For example, we might assess the performance of sales personnel by number of products sold. This would be a contaminated criterion if it was easier to sell products in some territories than in others. A frequent source of contamination in selection occurs when the person selecting later evaluates the performance of the same personnel. His judgements are often biased by his judgements at the time of selection, or else both judgements show a systematic bias.

Not only selection procedures as a whole but also the criteria themselves need to be both reliable and valid. The reliability of a criterion refers to its consistency. We can distinguish between intra-rater reliability (i.e. ratings by the same rater at different times) and inter-rater reliability (ratings by different raters at the same time). Both types of reliability are necessary though not sufficient for a valid criterion. However, intra-rater reliability may itself be contaminated by changes in performance, particularly if the interval between measures is appreciable. In fact there is evidence that people's performance can change considerably over time, even week by week (Rothe and Nye, 1961). Indeed, Klemmer and Lockhead (1962) found that there were individual differences in consistency of performance from day to day. This evidence suggests that criterion measures should be taken over as lengthy time periods as possible to increase reliability.

We mentioned earlier that jobs may have a number of purposes. Often, therefore, we may need several measures of different aspects of job performance. Further, performance on one job dimension may not be related to performance on other dimensions. For example, Seashore, Indik and Georgopoulos (1960) found low intercorrelations between the job dimensions of productivity, effectiveness, accidents, absences and errors in delivery-men. This suggests that no general dimension of job success exists, but only dimensions of success for particular aspects of jobs. The possibility of combining these dimensions into a composite measure of success means that the same composite score can be made up from different combinations. This has led some psychologists to argue against the use of composite measures. However, although this argument may be valid for research purposes, in personnel selection proper decisions have to be made on the basis of some kind of concept of over-all worth. Hence in evaluating selection procedures we feel that there is a place for an over-all criterion. Finally, we should note that Ghiselli and Haire (1960) cite evidence to show that criteria may be dynamic, i.e. the dimensions of job performance may change as a result of experience. For example, a group of investment salesmen showed a continuing change in performance over ten years such that sales increased by more than six times and no levelling-off in performance was apparent. Once again this emphasises the desirability of approximating as closely as possible to the ultimate criterion for selection purposes.

PREDICTOR DEVELOPMENT

Once the criteria for the successful employee have been selected, the next task is to choose those measures available at the time of selection which on the basis of previous experience or research may be expected best to predict whether the candidate will later reach the criteria. There is evidence that job-specific measures are often better predictors of job performance than tests of more general characteristics. Examples of job-specific tests are: work-sample tests, written and oral achievement tests and the 'in-basket' test, which simulates a typical management activity. Wernimont and Campbell (1968) argue that we should use samples of behaviour similar to the behaviour to be performed on the job as predictors. One of the authors is at presenr (1978) constructing a test for the selection of salesmen by using items which indicate such samples of behaviour in the applicants' previous work and educational backgrounds. A study by Campion (1972) suggests that such an approach holds considerable promise.

ADMINISTRATION OF THE SELECTION PROCEDURE

Ideally all predictors are administered to a representative sample of relevant job applicants without being used for selection and all applicants should be taken on. This enables later evaluation of the procedure. Employers, under-standably, are rather loth to permit this rather risky procedure to take place and prefer to insist on the new selection procedure being used in the normal way (i.e. to employ only those candidates who do best). This prevents the selection procedure from being tested properly since there is no real way of discovering whether the rejected candidates would have been successful or not had they been employed. Current practice therefore represents a de-parture from the true predictive validity model and there is always the risk that the cut-off point below which candidates are rejected may be too high or too low so that too many suitable candidates may be rejected or unsuitable ones selected.

ESTABLISHMENT OF PREDICTOR–CRITERION RELATIONSHIPS

Two main statistical methods are available for determining the relationship between a predictor and a criterion in personnel selection. These are the correlational and cut-off methods. The correlation coefficient has been des-cribed elsewhere (see Chapter 10). Essentially it is a method of giving a numerical value from $+1$ to -1 to the relationship between two variables. Thus two variables so strongly related that any change in one involves an equivalent change in the other have a correlation coefficient of $+1$. If they have no relationship at all, the coefficient is zero, and if their relationship is such that a change in one involves an equivalent negative change in the other, the coefficient of correlation is -1. So if the score on a particular psychological test correlates $+0.6$ with successful work performance a year later, the test in question could be said to be quite a good one, for in practice correlation coefficients of 0.6 between a single predictor and the criterion in selection are quite rare. To improve this situation a number of predictors may be used and a multiple correlation coefficient is calculated reflecting their combined predictive value.

Essentially cut-off systems are expectancy charts or tables relating the level of job performance expected to each possible predictor score. Such charts facilitate the choice of a cut-off score on a predictor below which a candidate will not be selected. When predictors are combined, the term 'multiple cut-off system' is used. Korman (1971) suggests that the most satisfactory method of proceeding is likely to be to use the multiple cut-off method initially for those variables where a minimum level is considered necessary (a kind of hurdle requirement) and then to apply the multiple correlation method after the initial cut-off has been made.

The arguments for and against the two methods are beyond the scope of this book. The cut-off method is certainly easier to understand and operate for the layman but is less flexible in some ways. It is often difficult to determine the practical significance of a correlation coefficient, but a minimum level of statistical sophistication in the user enables a more flexible use to be made of it. (For a fuller discussion, see Korman (1971).)

CROSS-VALIDATION

If some useful predictor–criterion relationships have been established, the procedure should be repeated using another representative population sample. Commonly, relationships which hold for one sample fail to appear in another due to chance factors. If similar results are obtained on cross-validation, we can then have confidence that the relationships found are real ones, and not due to chance alone. The predictors in question may then be incorporated into the selection procedure.

IMPLEMENTING THE SELECTION PROCEDURE

Whether or not a predictor should be incorporated into the selection procedure depends upon its predictive validity (and hence reliability), the selection ratio (the number of posts available in proportion to the number of applicants) and the proportion of present employees who are satisfactory on the job. For individual prediction (e.g. where there is one candidate for an important job), or in occupational guidance (when the most accurate analysis for each individual is required), then high predictive validities are strongly desirable. If, on the other hand, it is desired to select a sub-group from a larger group, e.g. where twenty candidates are applying for three jobs, quite small validities can be useful, provided that the proportion of successful placements is higher with tests than without them. As suggested earlier, there are problems in determining the practical significance of a coefficient of validity (correlation) but the essential point to note is that the relationship between predictor and criterion needs to be less strong to be useful when a large number of candidates are available for a given job (low selection ratio). Thus, to sum up, the usefulness of tests of low validity depends upon the selection ratio (i.e. the ratio of those selected to those applying). A reduction in the selection ratio has the same effect as an increase in predictive validity, and hence a low selection ratio may be used to compensate for low validities.

The usefulness of a test also depends upon the percentage of employees considered satisfactory without tests. Other things being equal, the smaller the percentage of present employees satisfactorily placed without tests, the larger is the percentage increase of satisfactory employees when placement is by test results.

It is possible, for a given percentage of present employees considered satisfactory, to estimate from the Taylor–Russell tables (see, for example, McCormick and Tiffin, 1974) the improvement in placement resulting from a test of given predictive validity for a particular selection ratio, provided test validity is expressed as a correlation coefficient. Similar results can be obtained from a cut-off method developed by McCollum and Savard (1957) which does not require the computation of a correlation coefficient to measure validity.

SOME POINTS ON THE TRADITIONAL PREDICTIVE VALIDITY MODEL

The chief and not insignificant advantage to this model is that it forces the personnel selector to be systematic and pragmatic about the procedures he adopts. At all stages the emphasis is on using reliable and valid measures of the job, the candidate and employee performance. Each component of the procedure is justified in terms of its contribution to the predictive validity of the whole procedure.

Unfortunately there are limitations, some of which have been touched on already. However, it will be convenient to list them here for easy reference.

(i) The procedure is a long and laborious one. Consequently, managements are inclined to fight shy, particularly since a successful method of selection is not necessarily the outcome (e.g. in the event of no effective predictors being found).

(ii) In view of the lengthy time required for validation, the job for which it is designed might have changed due to advances in related fields, organisational change, etc. An allied point is that it is in the nature of many jobs for them to evolve over time or for the individual occupant to devise his own methods. In this kind of situation, the predictive validity model is unsuitable.

(iii) The model is inappropriate for situations in which there are very few positions in a particular category of job. The reason for this is that in order to compute correlation coefficients or cut-off points, a sufficient number of candidates have to be followed up. Clearly this rules out the use of the model for many of the higher-level posts in organisations, and for posts in very small organisations.

(iv) There is evidence (Green and Farquhar, 1965; Kirkpatrick, Ewen, Barrett and Katzell, 1968) that different groups of workers may make use of different personal characteristics in order to achieve effective performance on a job. Take, for example, the case of an intelligent but idle student achieving the same performance as a less intelligent one who is well motivated and persistent. Kirkpatrick *et al.* (1968) report a numerical test predicting performance best for whites in a particular job whereas a coding test predicted best for blacks in the same job. We shall return to this problem and a way of overcoming it when we describe the 'moderator variable model' in the next section.

Lest the reader is left with the feeling that we have written the obituary of the traditional model, we shall end this section with the statement that it is still valuable in the situations in which the limitations above are not telling or do not apply. Certainly variations on this model will prevail in the field of personnel selection for some time to come. But now it is time to turn to some of the more systematic recent modifications which attempt to overcome some of the difficulties listed above.

12.3   Modifications to the predictive validity model

In this section we shall discuss (i) the concurrent validation model, (ii) the moderator variable model, (iii) the suppressor variable model, (iv) the synthetic validity model, and (v) the clinical judgement model.

THE CONCURRENT VALIDITY MODEL

In this method, sometimes also called the 'present employee method', the proposed selection procedure is administered to people already employed on the job in question. The proposed predictors are then related to measures of job performance of these employees obtained at the same time. The apparent advantage of this method is that we do not have to wait for what may be a period of some years before we can relate the predictors to job performance. However, the procedure involves three problems. (1) The range of individual characteristics among present employees (an already selected group) is likely to be less than in the applicant population. Hence, due to the manner in which correlation coefficients are calculated, relationships between these characteristics and job performance will tend to be underestimated. (2) The attitude of present employees to the selection measures is likely to be different from that of applicants, and hence so is their performance on these. In general, we would expect job applicants to try harder on ability tests, and to fake or distort answers to personality measures rather more. (3) Scores of present employees on individual characteristic measures may be differentially affected by job experience. For example, Poppleton (1975), in a concurrent validation study of life-assurance representatives, found that anxiety measures and sales success were related inversely. However, it is not clear from a concurrent (simultaneous) study whether the more successful salesmen were less anxious at the time of selection, or became less anxious because of their job success, or some combination of both occurred. Hence a predictive validation study had to be done in order to find out whether these anxiety measures predicted job performance. Because of these problems, we must agree with Guion (1965) when he argues that the concurrent procedure should only be used to suggest hypotheses which should then be tested by a predictive procedure.

THE MODERATOR VARIABLE MODEL

A moderator variable is one which divides the applicant population into a number of sub-groups for which there are different correlation coefficients between predictor variables and later performance. Thus, in the case of Kirk-patrick *et al.* (1968), the study mentioned at the end of Section 12.2, race is a moderator variable. Once the moderator variable has been identified, the normal predictive validation procedure is followed, but by treating each sub-group separately. Variables which most frequently have been found to moderate predictor performance correlations are sex, ethnic group and some personality factors. For example, Ferguson (1958) found that sales aptitude 'moderated' the relationship between an interest measure and job perform-ance for life-assurance salesmen. He found that for applicants scoring over a certain level on the sales aptitude test there was a significant correlation be-tween the interest test score and job performance. There was, however, no significant relationship for applicants with scores below this level. In carrying out the traditional procedure we should always look out for possible modera-tor variables, and treat the resulting sub-groups separately. For different sub-groups we may need to measure different characteristics or treat the same measure differently if we want to obtain maximum prediction of performance.

If we fail to isolate significant moderator variables, then prediction will be impaired and significant characteristic performance relationships may even fail to appear. For example, for men there might be a positive correlation between, say dominance and ability to do job X, whereas for women the correlation could be negative. If we do not divide the population by sex, then it is quite possible that no dominance–performance correlation would emerge.

One problem posed by the application of moderator variables is that we need larger applicant samples to obtain significant results for each sub-group. Thus, although the method succeeds in overcoming one of the problems associated with the predictive validity model, it actually intensifies another while not really touching two more (see the end of Section 12.2). None the less it has a greater sensitivity to the complexity of human behaviour which must be valuable in the long term.

THE SUPPRESSOR VARIABLE MODEL

We shall start by explaining the term 'suppressor variable' by means of an example. Suppose a measure A has no correlation with later job performance. Suppose a predictor B correlates significantly with later job performance. Suppose, further, that A and B are correlated. That part of B which is com-mon to A bears no relationship to job performance, and acts as a source of error. This source of error may be removed by statistical methods, thus enhancing the predictive power of *B*. This is a sophisticated modification to the predictive validity model which has not as yet been much used. However, it does share with the moderator variable model the ability for teasing out relationships between possible predictors and job performance which would not otherwise be possible, as well as making those predictors potentially more powerful.

THE SYNTHETIC VALIDITY MODEL

This approach was first advocated by Lawshe (1952) for situations in which applicant numbers are too small for predictive validation. It requires the division of jobs into dimensions (e.g. technical expertise, good human relations, etc. for a managerial job), where each dimension represents a fairly specific kind of behaviour. Lawshe argues that jobs with similar dimensions will require similar worker characteristics for successful performance. If we can find a test to measure each dimension, and we are able to classify each job in terms of its dimensions, then we should be in a position to choose appropriate tests for a particular job. Ideally such an approach requires that all jobs be analysed into a number of common dimensions. Towards this goal, McCormick, Jeanneret and Mecham (1972) factor analysed job behaviour from 536 jobs and arrived at twenty-seven job dimensions. Ultimately, what are required are tests or other measures which predict successful performance on each of these job dimensions. Until this ideal is reached, however, synthetic validity must rely on the judgement of experts in isolating job components and on their knowledge of test–component relationships. As yet, the only systematic studies have been with lower-level occupations, and it seems unlikely that top-level jobs will yield easily to this kind of analysis.

THE CLINICAL JUDGEMENT MODEL

All the methods reviewed so far have, as we have seen, considerable limitations either in flexibility or laboriousness. One method which has received a certain amount of attention recently is potentially highly flexible and easy to operate. It involves, very simply, selecting the selector. The aim is to find an individual or individuals who have the (perhaps intuitive) skills to select accurately. Korman (1968), in a review of prediction of managerial performance, reports somewhat more support for the clinical–judgemental model than for the statistical models we have been discussing. However, evidence can be found for the success of both (e.g. Ghiselli, 1966). Clearly some people are good interviewers. If we can identify them, they seem likely to provide a possible answer to the difficulties of selection in the case of higher-level jobs, unique jobs, new jobs, small samples of applicants, all of which have posed problems for the other methods.

12.4   The tools of personnel selection

Thus far we have referred generically to the actual tools and techniques of personnel selection as tests, measures, variables or predictors. It is now time to look at some of the specific tools and techniques in more detail. It may help the reader if he keeps in mind the typical stages of a selection procedure as shown in Figure 12.1.

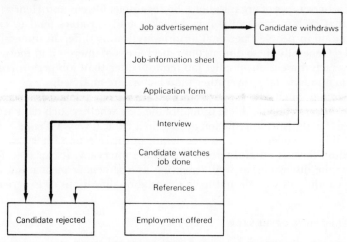

Figure 12.1 Steps in a selection procedure

THE ADVERTISEMENT AND JOB-INFORMATION SHEET

The purpose of the advertisement is to recruit a suitable number of suitable candidates: not too many, as this will involve a lot of work processing the applications; not too few, as this does not give sufficient choice to the selector. The advertisement should contain a clear but unglamorised description of the job derived from the job analysis, mentioning in particular any difficult or distasteful features. The purpose of this is to discourage enquiries from all but serious applicants. Similar considerations apply to the job-information sheet which is sent out to all respondents to the advertisement together with the application form. Only serious candidates should be encouraged to apply and they will be those in possession of a realistic idea of what the job is. The job-information sheet aims to inform the candidate about this and to provide additional information about conditions of service, career prospects, and so on. If it is possible for the candidate to see the job being done, this is another means by which his idea of the job can be made more realistic. It is certainly better that he withdraws at this stage rather than later after he has been employed. Often, for example in the case of mental-health nurses, there is such a shortage of candidates that the organisation is reluctant to discourage any. Yet this is precisely what was done by a Sheffield Hospital recently. They told the truth about the tough work, the long hours and the poor hospital facilities and managed to employ four new nurses as a result, quite an achievement in this very tight market.

THE APPLICATION FORM

Application forms (i.e. questionnaires asking for information about life history) play a large part in the initial screening of applicants. There is evidence, however, that groups of interrelated life-history items tend to reflect relatively basic patterns of previous experience which can result in predictive validity, and that sometimes these validities can be general for related jobs or types of organisations. For example, Owens and Henry (1966) found that certain types of personal-background variables tend to exist in combination in people's personal histories, reflecting different dimensions of life style. Generally these dimensions reflect areas of interest and motivation. Usually such dimensions predict job tenure better than job performance, at least when individual items rather than factors are analysed.

Research on such data shows that application-form data can be of considerable value in selection. This is probably the case whether such data are used as a basis for statistical prediction or used in a clinical way. Of course similar data should be collected, in greater detail, in the selection interview. If the application form is administered prior to the interview, it can then form a basis for the discussion, as well as serving as a screening mechanism for rejecting candidates who do not have essential qualifications or experience.

THE SELECTION INTERVIEW

The selection interview is by far the most commonly used means of obtaining information about job applicants. This is the case in spite of the fact that there is little really good evidence concerning its validity (Wagner, 1949; Mayfield, 1964; Ulrich and Trumbo, 1965). Its widespread use is doubtless attributable to its apparent simplicity, flexibility and, probably most importantly, its 'face validity' (i.e. the extent to which it *appears* to the participants to be capable of providing valid evidence). People have more confidence in the interview than might be expected from research evidence (given the lack of it!). There are, however, other reasons for its widespread use which do not concern its qualities as a predictor. It may be used for providing the interviewee with information, persuading him to accept the job and advising him as to possible alternative employment, quite apart from the public-relations benefits to the organisation of an apparently fair and systematic interview. None of these should be underestimated. Indeed, there is very much to be said for an elaborate selection procedure which has no predictive validity if it enhances the reputation of the organisation and improves recruitment!

An early review by Wagner (1949) of selection-interview research covering ninety-six individual characteristics assessed over a wide range of situations revealed marked differences in both the reliability and the validity of the interview from situation to situation. Similar conclusions come from the later reviews of Mayfield (1964), Ulrich and Trumbo (1965) and Wright (1969). In addition, Webster (1964), on the basis of a number of experimental studies, has found that judgements by a number of interviewers examining the same applicants differed markedly.

It is not surprising that validity of interview judgements has been reported to be so different in different studies, for the studies have differed widely with respect to the type of job involved, the information sought, the length of the interview, the purpose(s) of the interview, the use of other sources of information prior to the interview, and a large number of interviewer, interviewee and situational variables. Depending upon which studies are given greatest credence, the conclusions vary accordingly. For example, Wagner concludes that only intellectual qualities can be assessed with relatively high validities, whereas Ulrich and Trumbo cite only career motivation and social skills as characteristics which can be predicted from the interview.

Mayfield suggests that, in spite of the large variation in results, interviews involving more than one interviewer result generally in better predictive validities. Support for this view comes from Vernon and Parry's (1949) report of the war-time selection of British Admiralty psychologists, involving an interview board of trained interviewers and using a structured interview (one in which certain specific areas of content are covered consistently with each interviewee).

There is also some evidence that structured interviews have more predictive validity than semi-structured or unstructured ones in which the coverage is not so systematic (Hovland and Wonderlic, 1939). Certainly, in the field of psychiatric diagnosis, Wing (1961) has shown that reliability can be improved considerably by training the different interviewers to seek the same information before making their judgements.

There are probably two main reasons why selection interviews generally have low predictive validities and why assessments of specific individual characteristics are usually of poor validity. The first is the accuracy of the information elicited from the interviewee. One of the major reasons for incorrect information is probably a general tendency to display an acceptable and impressive personality (Goffman, 1956). Evidence supporting this hypothesis comes from studies by Weiss and Dawis (1960) and Weiss *et al.* (1961) which showed persistent and important differences between interview data and that obtained from previous employers. In the latter study there was least agreement concerning pay increases (38 per cent) and most agreement concerning reason for leaving a previous job (83 per cent) for a group of physically handicapped people. In addition, interviewees presented information fairly consistently in a more favourable light than the more 'objective' source. The generality of this finding is in doubt, though, as Keating, Paterson and Stone (1950) found high agreement between the same two sources of information for wages, job duration and duties.

The second reason for lack of interview validity lies in various kinds of errors of person perception (see Chapter 11), for example the use of stereotypes. Stereotyping refers to the tendency to see people as examples of personality types and to attributing all characteristics of the type to a particular individual. Prejudice involves a stereotyped view of the group toward which a person is prejudiced and can lead to inaccurate perception. For example, Allport and Postman (1947) found that white Americans prejudiced against blacks tended to misperceive pictures and incidents involving white and blacks. Webster (1964) presents evidence which suggests that selection interviewers develop a stereotype of a good candidate and then match applicants with the stereotype. Rowe (1963) found evidence that such a stereotype was shared by a group of Canadian Army interviewers as items describing applicants were rated reliably as clearly favourable or unfavourable. A study by Mayfield and Carlson (1966) of life-assurance sales managers suggested that two kinds of stereotype operated in the selection of salesmen, one common to most of the managers, the other specific to each interviewer. However, the use of stereotypes in interviewing need not always be harmful. If the interviewer hits upon the right stereotype for the job, the validity of his judgements is likely to be very high.

Interpretation of information
We would expect that some judgemental differences in the interview stem from individual differences in the weighting of various pieces of information. Evidence for this comes from research by Carlson (1967), who found that the tendency of life-assurance sales managers to place more weight on factual information than on photographs increased with interviewing experience. However, there is also evidence that interviewers show similarities in weightings. For example, Bray and Grant (1966) found that situational measures of simulated job behaviour were given greater importance than ability tests, which were in turn weighted more heavily than personality tests.

First impressions
There is evidence that first impressions in the interview are of particular importance. Springbett (1958) found that interviewers could typically have made the same selection decision after four minutes of a fifteen-minute interview as they would at the end of it. This is what we would expect given a general tendency of people to oversimplify, to exaggerate consistencies. This over-simplification shows itself in a 'set' (or orientation) during the interview. Springbett suggests that the set in the selection interview is towards caution, and is primarily a search for negative information. Springbett's study showed that interviewers placed more confidence in application-form data than in appearance or the interview and that initial ratings from the application form correlated highly with final ratings. This suggests a strong 'set' prior to the interview. He found that if appearance or personal history were rated first, then a favourable first impression led to an intensification of the search for negative information, whereas an unfavourable impression confirmed the 'set' to reject the applicant. Some support for these ideas comes from a study by Miller and Rowe (1967), who found that interviewers were more influenced by unfavourable than favourable information. The interviewer's 'set' is likely to be affected by the context of the interview. Rowe (1967) found that the order in which candidates were seen affected judgement of them. Seeing poor candidates first resulted in a greater number of acceptances than seeing good candidates initially.

Other individual differences in interviewers
The kinds of perceptual error we have discussed, such as stereotyping and prejudice, are present in varying degrees from individual to individual, as are other perceptual tendencies such as egocentricity (i.e. the tendency to evaluate people in terms of how they affect us and assume most of their

actions are directed towards us) and projection (attributing our own feelings and characteristics to others). The two latter tendencies have been found to be strongest in the less educated and in children. Frenkel-Brunswick (1949) has suggested that an important source of individual differences in perceptual styles is tolerance of ambiguity. Intolerance of ambiguity is shown by rigidity and insistence on the use of definite categories in perception and thinking. It is thought to be associated with authoritarian prejudice and racial intolerance and is related to particular kinds of insecurity in the person's personality make-up. There is evidence that motivation, personality and perception are related (see Chapter 2) and clearly these can affect interview judgements.

What evidence there is, then, concerning the predictive validity of the interview suggests that it is likely to be very low indeed unless an agreed structure, such as that of the seven-point plan (see Section 12.2), is used by trained interviewers. Unfortunately, studies of such methods are still very scarce.

GROUP-SELECTION PROCEDURES

These procedures originated in the German Army and were adopted by the British Army during the Second World War for officer selection, in the form of War Office Selection Boards (W.O.S.B.s). Typically they consisted of a number of tasks analogous to those required by the job, involving various kinds of social situation. Vernon (1953) cites fairly low correlations between W.O.S.B. judgements and subsequent assessments of performance, but presents evidence for the superiority of W.O.S.B. methods to previous ones. Furthermore, in general W.O.S.B. methods appeared fair to the selectors and candidates.

Similar selection methods were adopted soon after by the Civil Service for the selection of administrative-grade staff. Typically the procedure would include group discussions as well as task situations in which a leadership role was sometimes assigned, sometimes not. Vernon (1950a) states that the leaderless-group test did not result in judgements of very high reliabilities, but they were nevertheless superior to those of interview ratings and ratings based on acquaintance or casual observation. Each part of the procedure added something to its over-all predictive validity, though there was no way of assessing independently the precise contributions of exercises as successive gradings were affected by previous impressions. The whole selection procedure had correlations of the order of $+0.5$ to $+0.6$ with performance criteria, which, given the highly selected nature of the applicants and the difficulty of obtaining reliable and valid criteria, is quite impressive.

Similar group procedures have been adopted by various organisations, usually for the selection of high-level managers or management trainees. Occasionally they have also been used for the selection of salesmen (e.g. Higham, 1952).

Evidence on their validity comes from a number of studies. Handyside and Duncan (1954) followed up an earlier National Institute of Industrial Psychology (N.I.I.P.) study concerning promotion to supervisory positions in a Scottish engineering works which had found a correlation of +0.63 between group-session ratings and job-performance ratings. The validity coefficient of the whole selection procedure was +0.68 as compared with +0.23 for the traditional selection method. A follow-up study showed a correlation of +0.58 between group-discussion ratings and job-performance ratings.

A South African study (Arboue and Maris, 1951) of a leaderless-group discussion and an original leadership situation found (i) low correlations between judgements by observers of a group discussion and intelligence as measured by a paper-and-pencil test, (ii) high correlations between ratings of social skill and intellectual ability for each judge, (iii) a high correlation between combined social-skill and ability scores, (iv) that both of these types of judgement had a high correlation with a person's over-all job-suitability rating, with the assigned leadership score giving a slightly higher correlation, and (v) when all selected and non-selected candidates were followed up, correlations between +0.3 and +0.6 were found between combined group situation ratings and supervisor job performance ratings.

Confirmation of finding (ii) comes from several studies by Poppleton (1970) conducted at the N.I.I.P. Judges rated each of six candidates in a group discussion on intelligence and acceptability displayed in the group. The measures were correlated highly with one another. Furthermore, they each correlated highly with amount of talking; that is to say, the candidates rated most intelligent talked most, and were rated as being most influential and most acceptable to the group. Clearly judges' ratings are very much influenced by the amount of talking done by candidates in a group discussion. Thus, although we may conclude that the use of group discussions can be valuable, it is clear that many of the considerations applied to the interview apply here also. In particular, systematic observation and recording are necessary.

PSYCHOLOGICAL TESTS AND QUESTIONNAIRES

We have considered many of the important issues concerning tests earlier in this chapter as well as in the chapters on motivation, intelligence and abilities, and personality. Here we shall summarise briefly the ground already covered, elaborating on it as necessary. The reasons for measuring people's characteristics via tests are many: to help in decisions about transfers from one job to another, promotions, training needs, evaluation, selection, placement and occupational guidance. When tests are used they are administered usually in combination with other selection tools.

Tests may be sub-divided into types on the basis of such characteristics as whether they can be administered to groups of people or to individuals only. They may also be broadly distinguished in terms of content, as we have done in Chapter 2 on motivation (tests of motivation, attitude, interests and values), Chapter 10 on intelligence and abilities (where we also distinguished between aptitude tests designed to predict performance and achievement or attainment tests designed to measure what has been learnt) and Chapter 9 on personality (measures of personality and temperament). Other tests which might be used in selection are various kinds of medical and physiological tests, tests of physical capacities and tests and questionnaires of heterogeneous content such as application forms which are designed to have maximum predictive validity for a specific job. The weakness of such application forms are (i) they only provide limited information about the applicant, i.e. whether he has a 'good score', but we do not know exactly what the questionnaire is measuring, and (ii) if the questionnaire loses its predictive validity over time, we do not know why, and hence do not know how to modify the questionnaire to increase predictive validity.

We have discussed at length the importance of reliability and validity for any selection instrument and tests should be constructed so as to have the maximum validity possible. Given the predictive validity of a test, the selection ratio, and the percentage of employees satisfactory in a job prior to the use of a selection test, it is possible, via the Taylor–Russell tables, to estimate the improvement in selection which would take place on using the test. If more than one test is used, these may be combined into a test battery.

Tests should be administered under standardised conditions, so that all testees have an equal chance, e.g. the time allowed on speed tests should be identical for all applicants. All applicants should understand test instructions clearly and should approach tests with as little anxiety as possible, given that they want to do their best. Usually test instructions are standardised to achieve this. Test scores, like other selection information, should be confidential and applicants should know this prior to testing.

Finally, an aspect of increasing importance has been the fairness of test use for different racial groups. We feel, along with McCormick and Tiffin (1974), that test use is only unfair when people with an equal probability of job success do not have an equal probability of being hired. Very few tests are entirely free of cultural influences, and hence great care has to be taken to avoid the use of psychological tests in such a way that they operate against any particular group.

REFERENCES

It is likely that the validity of references will vary widely, depending upon the referee's knowledge of the applicant with respect to the job-relevant characteristics, his motivation to give an honest opinion and his ability to express those opinions such that he can be understood accurately. There is considerable evidence from studies of performance appraisal that people do not like making public negative judgements about other people's job performance. This is likely to be the case with references, particularly when the referee, for whatever reason, very much wishes the applicant to obtain a particular job. Conversely, negative references have doubtless been used to try to ensure an individual staying in his present job. Another reason for referees' reluctance to give frank opinions is the fear that a judgement might be presented to someone other than the selector, most commonly the job applicant. A number of selectors have told the authors that an oral evaluation by telephone will generally lead to a more honest evaluation than the standard letter. Another approach which is used quite commonly is to ask the referee to complete a questionnaire asking a number of specific questions. This, at least, can get over the main problem of the open letter, when what the referee does not say (often deliberately) is the information required.

What little research evidence there is concerning references suggests that the problems we have raised have substance. Mosel and Goheen (1958) administered the 'employment recommendation questionnaire' to obtain ratings of occupational mobility, character and reputation for over 1000 workers in skilled trades. These ratings only had very low correlations with subsequent supervisor ratings of job performance. Similarly Browning (1968) found only a low correlation between pre-employment ratings by references of over 500 applicants for teaching posts and evaluations of their performance after one year of teaching.

12.5 The placement and counselling approach

So far we have implied that it is the organisation which selects the candidate. It is also the case that the candidate selects the organisation. This aspect of selection is one to which the counselling approach attaches great importance. We are not talking here of occupational guidance or counselling in which the individual goes to a counsellor for help in the choice of a career. Rather, we are referring to an approach to personnel selection and placement in which the decision is viewed as one where the organisation and individual attempt to see whether both can be, or have the capacity to be, mutually beneficial to one another. This approach is exemplified by a consultancy job done by one of the authors for a firm which was closing down one of its operations. The author was asked to counsel a number of employees, to help them choose another job in a different part of the organisation which would most suit them. The author was free to counsel the employees to take up alternative employment or a training or educational course if the employees did not wish to take up any of the jobs available within the organisation.

OCCUPATIONAL GUIDANCE

The effectiveness of the counselling approach just described, as well as of occupational-guidance techniques, will depend very much upon the prevailing economic and social factors, which can limit greatly the choices available to individuals and organisations. Within these constraints psychologists have been interested in how occupational decisions are reached, as well as with designing procedures aimed at improving that choice. The latter approach has been the concern of both researchers and occupational practitioners, who until the last twenty-five years almost invariably used what has been described as the 'differentialist' approach. This was first formulated explicitly by Parsons (1908) and rests on the following assumptions: (i) people have different abilities and personalities; (ii) jobs have different requirements, which can be specified in terms of ability and personality (i.e. a personnel specification) for effective job performance and satisfaction; (iii) ability and personality characteristics are sufficiently stable over time to give useful predictions concerning job performance and job satisfaction; and (iv) it is possible and desirable for an individual to match his own ability and personality profile with job-requirement profiles and so obtain the best match. In essence this is the same approach as the traditional selection procedure. Thus, in this country, vocational guidance was pioneered by the National Institute of Industrial Psychology using the seven-point plan as a basis for matching individuals with jobs. Furthermore, N.I.I.P. studies on school-leavers suggested that occupational guidance along these lines resulted in greater job satisfaction and better job performance for those taking the advice given compared with those not taking such advice, and compared with pupils not receiving such guidance.

Much research has been conducted which has shown that various kinds of abilities, interests and personality characteristics are related to both job satisfaction and job performance for many jobs. Whereas the main focus of concern in selection is job performance, the main focus in occupational guidance is satisfaction. Consequently measures of interest are likely to be of particular importance, and many studies show this to be so. A particular difficulty in evaluating occupational guidance is obtaining adequate criteria, i.e. measures of satisfaction. This is made even more difficult when time considerations are taken into account, i.e. should we be measuring satisfaction after one year, ten years, twenty-five years, or some combination of the three? Another approach to the problem of occupational choice has been termed the 'developmental' approach. Ginzberg *et al.* (1951) first emphasised the sequential aspect of occupational decisions. They saw occupational choice as a sequence of decisions making up a largely irreversible process in which compromise plays an essential part. Thus the individual develops through a series of stages, from the early fantasy period of childhood, which is modified first by interests and then abilities, via the development in adolescence of an increasingly clear value system, a realistic period involving exploration, crystallisation of ideas and the emergence of a career plan in adulthood.

The relevance of this approach to occupational guidance was suggested by Super (1957), who emphasised the importance of an individual's self image in making an adequate job decision. There is a parallel here with Rogers' phenomenological approach (see Chapter 9) where an individual's perceptions, particularly of himself, are seen as key determinants of his behaviour. Rogers' counselling techniques have had considerable impact on the techniques of occupational guidance, so much so that counselling has come increasingly to replace the term 'guidance'. Thus in an occupational counselling situation the major focus of concern is the individual's perception of himself, and emphasis is placed on ways of helping him to become more accurate in his perceptions.

Of course, the traditional matching idea (selection and guidance through matching personal characteristics with job requirements) is not incompatible with an emphasis on a person's perceptions. The counsellor could and should be concerned that the client obtains an accurate perception of himself through use of test information, and should also provide him with accurate information about job requirements. Having the right answer is not enough; the client must perceive it to be the right answer for him before he will act on it.

Part V

SOCIAL ASPECTS OF ORGANISATIONS

So far this book has examined the behaviour of people largely as individuals in terms of their motivations, cognitive processes and personality as a whole. The vast majority of people, however, work not as individuals but in some kind of social relationship to others. The manner in which this social aspect of work has its influence is the focus of this final part. Chapter 13 looks at the interaction of individuals in small groups of up to about twenty. Here we consider the influences of social groups on individuals. One of the most common features of social groups is the emergence of leadership roles within the group. The topic of leadership is treated separately in Chapter 14. This has been done for two main reasons. First, it is perhaps the most widely researched aspect of social groups, and as such merits special treatment. Second, it is a topic of particular importance for those concerned with the work situation. The last chapter of the book (Chapter 15) attempts to relate what has been learnt about individual and social behaviour to the organisation as a whole. This chapter not only indicates current thinking on organisations but also relates different managerial strategies to organisational structure.

13
Group Processes

13.1 Introduction

In this chapter we shall consider a number of issues concerning social groups. In particular we shall be interested in aspects of the subject which are of particular relevance to the world of work. This topic lies at the heart of our social life as well of at least some approaches to the study of work organisations.

In Section 13.2 we shall clarify certain problems of definition and answer the question 'What is a group?' We shall also consider what is meant by certain related terms such as 'primary group', 'secondary group' and 'reference group'. In Section 13.3 we shall move on to a discussion of the way in which groups form and develop. In Section 13.4 we shall discuss group norms, one of the essential features and processes of a group. In three sections we shall discuss three aspects of group activity which are relevant to the field of business and administration: (i) communication networks (Section 13.5); (ii) group resistance to change (Section 13.6); and (iii) intergroup relations (Section 13.7). Finally, in Section 13.8 we shall discuss and evaluate theoretical contributions to the field, and point the way to the next chapters on leadership and organisations.

13.2 Definitions

'A group consists of a number of people who interact with each other on the basis of a common set of values (norms) in a given context more than they do with anyone else.'

This definition contains two main ideas, those of interaction and norm (to be discussed in Section 13.4). There are more restrictive and less restrictive definitions available. Golombiewski (1962) has noted that researchers into social-group phenomena have tended to use the term 'group' in one or other of three senses, sometimes rather indiscriminately. This has led to a number of findings about groups which seemed contradictory until it was realised that the different findings were about different types of 'groups'. Golombiewski has put forward three definitions, or, as he calls them, designations of the word 'group'.

Designation I: (i) 'A small number of individuals in more or less interdependent status and role relations'; and which (ii) 'Has an indigenous set of values or norms which regulates the behavior of members, at least in matters of concern to the group.' This is the traditional definition and bears a rather close resemblance to ours.

Designation II: 'Any number of persons engaged in a single face-to-face meeting or group of meetings in which each member receives some impression of the others as a distinct person, even though it was only to recall that the other was present' (Bales, 1950).

Designation III: 'A group involves simply a collection of people who have something in common, e.g. being college students.

Our definition and Designation I refer clearly to a number of people, their interactions and the values which unite them.

The reader might have come across a number of terms which refer to groups of different kinds. We shall now attempt to clarify these. They are primary group, secondary group, reference group, large group and small group.

Primary groups are face-to-face groups in which everyone knows everyone else to some extent. More or less our definition is a definition of a primary group. Examples of primary groups are the immediate family and work groups.

Secondary groups are groups which are larger than the basic primary group, with which people interact and share common values, but not to the extent that they do in a primary group. Examples of secondary groups are hospitals or department stores, in which the primary groups are wards, departments or sections. We shall leave it to the last chapter to discuss the question of whether an organisation is simply a very large secondary group or whether it is something over and above that.

Reference groups are groups which can influence people even though the person is not in any clear sense a member of them. They are groups with which a person identifies or aspires to but which he need never meet. An example might be a board of directors of a company for someone who is seeking rapid progress in the company.

On the size of groups, it is generally accepted that the dynamic forces which characterise social groups and which we are about to describe lose much of their intensity beyond a certain number of members. This number varies considerably with the context, but traditionally the dividing line between 'large' and 'small' groups has been placed between fifteen and twenty. Certainly, sports teams and similar associations do not seem to exceed this number and it is likely that the reason would be the difficulty in co-ordinating the activities of the members if they did.

We may now move on to a discussion of some of the characteristics of groups in the processes of their formation and their development.

13.3 Formation and development of groups

Most of the research in this area has been done on two main sorts of groups: psychotherapy groups (concerned with helping people with personal problems) and T-groups (a device for training people in human relations: see Chapter 4). However, it may be possible to generalise from such groups to other kinds of groups. Tuckman (1965) reviews a large number of studies and identifies four main phases of development: forming, storming, norming and performing. Each phase is recognisable in terms of its characteristic group structure and task activity, as can be seen from Table 13.1.

Table 13.1   Summary of Tuckman's (1965) scheme

Stages	Group structure	Task activity
(1) Forming	There is anxiety, dependence on a leader, testing to find out the nature of the situation and what behaviour is acceptable	Members find out what the task is, what the rules are, what methods are appropriate
(2) Storming	Conflict between sub-groups. Rebellion against leader, opinions are polarised, resist control by group, conflicts over intimacy	Emotional resistance to demands of task
(3) Norming	Development of group cohesion, norms emerge, resistance overcome and conflicts patched up, mutual support and development of group feeling	Open exchange of views and feelings: co-operation develops
(4) Performing	Interpersonal problems are resolved, interpersonal structure is the tool of task activity, roles are flexible and functional	Emergence of solutions to problems, constructive attempts at task completion, energy is now available for effective work, this is major work period

Source: Argyle (1969).

These stages may take quite different amounts of time in different kinds of groups. Indeed, some groups may never get beyond stages (1) or (2). Thus it is possible to put together combinations of members which will never succeed in becoming a cohesive group. Schutz (1953) identified the motivations of his subjects before placing them in groups. By putting in the same group two members high in dominance or members with widely different degrees of affiliative motivation (see Chapter 6) incompatible groups were formed which were particularly poor at tasks requiring co-operation. In the first case the two members in question vied with each other for dominance, thus preventing any other activity, and in the second people with strong needs to be with others probably felt rejected by people with low levels of this need. Further, Haythorn *et al.* (1956) found that in groups of four consisting of an authoritarian leader and followers with democratic values and vice versa there was lower morale, less effective communication, more conflict and less co-operation than in alternative combinations of leaders and followers.

In the next section we shall continue our discussion of how groups develop, but at this point we must interrupt this in order to introduce a new concept which is crucial to the question, that of 'norm'.

13.4   Group norms

Probably the central concept in the psychology of groups is the norm. To some extent members of all groups behave in ways which are required by the other members, i.e. they conform to certain norms within the group. This phenomenon is apparent everywhere people meet, from the 'uniform' of the city gent to the customs and taboos of primitive societies. Norms have been studied intensively by psychologists, sociologists and anthropologists, and in this book we can only discuss this research illustratively using a limited number of investigations in the interests of at least doing some justice to the theoretical issues involved.

A norm may be defined as something which (i) influences the behaviour, beliefs and perceptions of members through processes of communication within the group, and (ii) is associated with the hierarchical structure of the group. Part (i) of the definition means that various forms of pressure and persuasion are brought to bear on individual members to conform to the standards of the group. A clear example of this comes from the Bank Wiring Room study of the Hawthorne Investigations (Roethlisberger and Dixon, 1939). Here, workers were found to be restricting their output to a certain level for various reasons. Workers who deviated either above or below this level were subjected initially to friendly explanations, later to name-calling ('speed king' for the over-producer, 'chiseller' for the under-producer) and finally, if this did not bring the deviant into line, to the more physical method of 'binging'. This involved striking the victim's upper arm with the protruding knuckle of the middle finger in such a way that the bone was bruised, causing immediate and briefly incapacitating pain. The bruise, of course, rendered the arm more sensitive to future binging. If this did not work, the final method used was rejection and isolation. These findings are paralleled by those of Schachter (1959), who introduced stooges into already formed groups to play a deviant role. The pattern observed was for there to be an increase in communication to the stooge followed by rejection and isolation when it was realised that the attempts at persuasion were not going to work.

Part (ii) of our definition of norm refers to group structure and is connected with part (i). Leaders tend to emerge and form the top part of the status hierarchy. The process described under part (i) is responsible for the deviates being consigned to the bottom part of the hierarchy. Thus norms are likely to be concerned with who are leaders, followers and deviates.

Therefore, norms are standards which influence members in connection with almost any relevant area of activity or thought, and we have singled out for emphasis the hierarchical structure of the group. The work of Bales and his co-workers (see Chapter 14) is an illustration of the emergence of hierarchical aspects of the group, as is that of Sherif (see Section 13.8).

Essentially two kinds of conditions are required for the establishment of group norms. We shall call them 'communicational' and 'motivational'. The former refer to the setting up of minimum requirements concerning the extent to which communication between the members is necessary for norms to form. The second concerns the minimum requirements for members to want to continue to interact long enough for norms to form (see Table 13.2).

Table 13.2 Conditions required for norm establishment

Communicational factors	Motivational factors
Interdependence	Similar interests
Possibility of monitoring other members	Appropriate and just rewards

The communicational factors concern the requirements for norm emergence that (i) there is some need for the members to communicate, and (ii) members should be able to monitor others both to check up on them and to discover what kinds of behaviour and beliefs are acceptable.

The motivational factors concern requirements that the individuals' motivations for joining the group are compatible (see Schutz, 1953; and Haythorn *et al.*, 1956) and that those motivations are in some way satisfied by the group.

We shall discuss the communicational factors further in the next sections. Some of the evidence for the motivational factors has been produced already. The theoretical section, particularly in connection with exchange theory, will include further discussion of the issue.

It is certainly not true that unless all four factors are present, no formative features will emerge. What seems to be the case is that the extent to which they are present determines the speed and degree of norm formation. Norms emerge most strongly when all these conditions exist, but they can emerge even when some do not exist at all. What seems to happen is that the more these conditions are present, the stronger the norms are likely to be, and the more likely the group is to approach Golombiewski's Designation I.

A group member's likelihood of conforming to a particular group norm will depend upon (i) the strength of group pressures to conform, (ii) expectations of rewards and punishments contingent on norm-related behaviours, and (iii) the congruence between the norm and the member's value system.

Two experiments, one by Sherif (1947) and the other by Asch (1958), show how in the most rudimentary group settings, where the four above conditions (Table 13.2) are present only to the barest degree, the mere presence of others engaged ostensibly in the same activity can influence the judgements of individuals.

Sherif's experiment is based on the fact that a stationary point of light in a completely dark room will appear to the observer to move erratically (the autokinetic effect). His subjects were told: 'When the room is completely dark, I shall give you the signal "Ready" and then show you a point of light. After a short time the light will start to move. A few seconds later the light will disappear. Then tell me the distance it moved.'

At first subjects' judgements varied widely, but settled down eventually to a rather narrow range around a central value. This value varied quite widely from subject to subject. Sherif then combined subjects who had established individual ranges in private sessions into groups of three and asked them to report their judgements aloud.

The result was that their judgements converged. It would seem, therefore, that the mere expression of an opinion by a subject influenced the expressed judgements of others. Sherif has demonstrated some of the minimum conditions required for social forces to have an effect, using people who do not know each other and limiting their communication to the statement of a distance and direction.

Asch (1958) demonstrated even more clearly the influence a group can have on people. He, like Sherif, used a situation well short of Golombiewski's Designation I. He asked volunteers in a series of trials to judge which of three lines was equal in length to a standard. This involves the judgement of physical reality and no strange perceptual effects as in the case of Sherif's experiment. Unknown to the subject, however, the other subjects with whom he was participating were collaborators of the experimenter. They were sitting in a semi-circle and he always had to take a position second from the left because that was the only position left when he came into the room. This meant that he was always the second from last to express his opinion on the lines. The first few trials proceeded in an uneventful manner. Suddenly the subject found that his fellow 'subjects' would sometimes unanimously report a judgement that was incorrect. The result was that about one-third of the judgements made by subjects in the Asch situation were not correct but were in accordance with the group judgement. Some subjects conform frequently, others seldom. The majority of subjects conform on some trials but are independent on others. Questioning the subjects later showed that, for the most part, they respected the genuineness of the judgements expressed by the majority and that they had great doubt about their own judgements when they disagreed with the majority, i.e. they agreed not merely for the sake of agreement but because they had rejected their original beliefs as being caused by some sort of optical illusion. In other experiments of this kind, Asch placed two naive subjects in the group or instructed one of the majority to agree with the subject. This tended to reduce the influence of the group. In research designed to investigate the effects of the size of the majority, it was found that influence increased as the majority increased from one to four but remained about constant thereafter.

We can summarise the experiments of Asch and Sherif by saying that yielding may occur (i) when the conditions lack clarity, (ii) when a majority is in disagreement with the subject. It will depend upon (iii) the size and unanimity of the opposition, and (iv) individual differences. The mere assertion of majority opinion without any effort to persuade may lead susceptible individuals to agree with the majority even on a factual matter on which individual judgement would lead to opposite conclusions.

As yet very little work of a quantitative kind has been carried out on group norms. An exception to this is Jackson (1965), who has proposed the 'return potential model', which is applicable to any group norm. A return potential curve is obtained by plotting the degree of approval by group members of

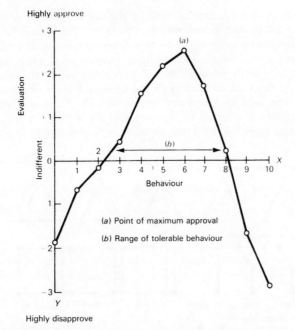

Highly approve

Highly disapprove

(a) Point of maximum approval

(b) Range of tolerable behaviour

Figure 13.1   Schematic representation of the return potential model (R.P.M.) of normative structure (the ordinate is an axis of evaluation; the abscissa is an axis of behaviour) *(Jackson, 1965)*

the norm-relevant behaviour against the extent of that behaviour (see Figure 13.1).

For example, Figure 13.1 could apply to a group member's productivity over a specific time period. Over- or under-production would meet with disapproval, the intensity of which would be greater for over-production than under-production. Theoretically such a curve could be of any shape depending on the situation it describes.

Having seen how the presence of others can influence the judgements of individuals, in the next three sections we shall illustrate how these dynamic forces in a group can influence its behaviour when engaged on tasks of different kinds.

An aspect of group functioning which has received considerable attention concerns the structural properties of the communication process. This is related to group effectiveness, the emergence of leadership of the adaptability of the group. It is to a discussion of these relationships that we now turn, via experimental studies of communication networks.

13.5   Communication networks

Bavelas (1948, 1950) was the first to suggest an experimental method which has stimulated a vast amount of research in this field. Subjects are placed in cubicles connected by means of slots in the walls through which written messages can be passed to one another. Slots may be closed to create any given communication structure. The experimenter can monitor and time the passing of messages through a signal light which flashes when messages are passed. Normally free communication is permitted within the structure, but some investigators have limited both the time and the content of messages and others have used an 'intercom' system instead of slots and written messages. The reader is referred to Shaw (1964) for a detailed review of such studies (see also Figure 13.2). Here we shall confine ourselves to some general conclusions.

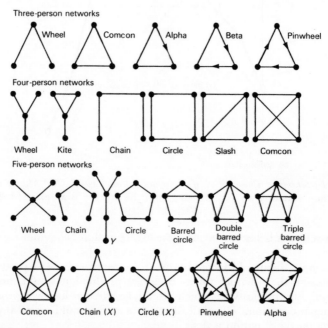

Figure 13.2   Some communication networks used in experimental investigations (dots represent positions, lines represent communication channels and arrows indicate one-way channels (Shaw, 1964)

The general conclusions to which studies of communication networks lead may be stated as follows: (i) the major differences in group performance and satisfaction are between the centralised, e.g. (wheel, Y and chain) and decentralised networks, e.g. (comcon and circle); (iii) the more complex the problem, the more effective is the decentralised network.

Table 13.3 summarises the numbers of investigations leading to this conclusion, as well as several others: (i) centralised networks result in quicker solutions for simple problems, whereas decentralised ones are faster for complex problems; (ii) decentralised networks involve the reading of more messages; (iii) centralised networks result in more errors for complex problems, whereas decentralised networks result in more for simple problems, and (iv) satisfaction is greater in decentralised networks.

Table 13.3 Number of comparisons showing differences between centralised (wheel, chain, Y) and decentralised (circle, comcon) networks as a function of task complexity

	Simple problems*	Complex problems†	Total
Time			
Centralised faster	14	0	14
Decentralised faster	4	18	22
Messages			
Centralised sent more	0	1	1
Decentralised sent more	18	17	35
Errors			
Centralised made more	0	6	6
Decentralised made more	9	1	10
No difference	1	3	4
Satisfaction			
Centralised higher	1	1	2
Decentralised higher	7	10	17

*Simple problems: symbol-, letter-, number- and colour-identification tasks.
†Complex problems: arithmetic, word arrangement, sentence construction and discussion problems.
Source: Shaw (1964).

Shaw (1964) suggests that two main concepts are required to explain the results shown in Table 13.3: 'independence' (Leavitt, 1951; Shaw, 1954); and 'saturation' (Gilchrist, Shaw and Walker, 1954).

Independence is the degree of freedom with which an individual may function in the group, and is clearly far more restricted in centralised than in non-centralised networks. In the wheel, for example, the central person (high dependence) controls the rest of the group (low independence) but in the circle the members are not so clearly controlled by others (moderate to high independence) since there is less tendency for clearly defined roles to emerge. Morale is greater, with greater possibilities for autonomy and independence in the latter kind of network.

Saturation refers to the load of information to be processed by an individual and is determined by the number of channels with which a person has to deal and the amount of information these channels are carrying. Thus the central person in a centralised network, occupied on a complex task, is more highly saturated than a member of a non-centralised network, whatever the task.

While independence is the primary cause of satisfaction, Shaw (1964) holds that saturation is the most significant network factor in performance. It interacts with the complexity of the task in three ways. First, a more complex task requires more communication and hence more use of the central person's channel space, making him oversaturated. Second, members are less likely to accept the dictates of the central person on a complex task which engages their interest and their need for achievement and recognition more than on a simple task. Third, the data-processing load on the central person is increased on a complex task. All these factors serve to bring about a reduction in the effectiveness of centralised networks as the task becomes more complex.

It is interesting to speculate on the extent to which the general conclusions outlined above may be relevant to real-life situations, and indeed to organisations as a whole rather than to small groups. Some evidence in this connection may be found in work on organisations which we shall review in Chapter 15.

From our earlier discussion of group norms and group pressures for conformity, we might expect considerable resistence by group members to any change which might make adherence to group norms more difficult. Certainly we see many examples of this in the work situation, where, for example, changes may be seen as leading to the break up of valued work groups, or as threatening standards of work valued by the group. A good deal of research work, particularly recently, has concerned itself with trying to find ways of overcoming such resistance to change.

13.6 Group resistance to change

One way of approaching this problem is to recognise that some group members are more influential than others, and probably have higher status within the group. Because of this higher status, they may be less concerned with rejection by the group, and hence be more likely to go against or attempt to change group norms. Group resistance might therefore be overcome by first persuading these 'opinion leaders', who in turn are then able to influence other group members.

Another approach, and one which has been the subject of an increasing amount of research, is a participative one. Lewin (1958) showed that housewives participating in discussion groups which came to a consensus concerning the use of less popular foods were more likely to change their use of them than a comparable group lectured on the desirability of the change. According to Lewin, the dynamics of the participative approach to changing group norms are: (i) free discussion with no pressure to come to a quick conclusion; which leads to (ii) a reduction in hostility to new ideas; which may eventually give rise to (iii) an unfreezing of group norms if all ideas of threat or attack have been dispelled; paving the way for (iv) mobility in group thinking; and (v) consensus and the refreezing of the new group norm(s).

One of the first studies in which a participative approach was tried in industry was in the Harwood Corporation, a manufacturer of pyjamas (Coch and French, 1948). The work-force was composed mainly of women and labour relations were generally good except for a difficulty arising from the need to make frequent changes in products and methods. Employees tended to resist these changes. Grievances, labour turnover and hostility towards management increased while efficiency went down. The usual pattern was that morale would go down immediately following a change, and although the average learning time for the new skills for new workers might be, say, five weeks, experienced workers might take eight weeks to reach standard production rates. The possibility of negative transfer from previous jobs was ruled out by studies showing little evidence of errors after the first week of work on the new job. It was concluded that low morale and restriction of output on a group basis were responsible for the failure of production to pick up after a change.

In order to overcome this resistance to change, Coch and French selected four groups of workers involved in changes in job methods and rates. Group 1 was a control group and the usual factory routine was followed. The production department modified the job and a new piece-rate was set. The workers were told of this at a meeting in which everything was explained carefully by the time-study man, who answered questions arising from what he had said. Group 2 employed a system of participation through representation. The management's case was presented to them in a meeting at which it was agreed in principle that greater efficiency could be achieved without putting an additional burden on the workers. Operatives were then selected by the group to act as representatives and to learn and help design the new jobs. They met as a group and made many suggestions that were incorporated into the new methods. After they had learned the new jobs, piece-rates were set on the basis of how they performed. At a later meeting these representatives explained the jobs to the other workers and trained them in the new methods. Groups 3 and 4 were small, and all members, not just the representatives, helped design the new jobs.

The results showed clearly that all the experimental groups did better after the change was instituted than did the control group, who immediately dropped below the standard rate of sixty units as expected and remained at about fifty units until conditions were changed after two and a half months. Group 2 dropped initially but recovered gradually so that after about thirteen days it was back at sixty units, and after thirty two days it was nearly seventy. Groups 3 and 4 did even better, exceeding sixty units after only four days and going beyond seventy shortly after. When the control group was permitted full participation in designing their jobs, they too immediately increased their production, reaching seventy units within a week. Morale also increased in all groups after participation with a concomitant decrease in aggression towards the management.

Although many studies have shown similar beneficial effects for participation, this has not always been the case. Its success depends on a number of characteristics such as personality (Vroom, 1960), organisational climate and cultural practices, values and attitudes.

The next section will move away from the theme of within-group phenomena and consider the between-group phenomena which arise under the influence of inter-group competition.

13.7 Inter-group relations

A particularly illustrative study in this context is that of Sherif (1966). Sherif's subjects were all boys aged 11 to 12, from stable, white, Protestant middle-class families. They did not know each other previously and were selected in such a way that any results obtained could not be explained in terms of their emotional instability or difference of background. The experiment took place at holiday camp sites. As far as the boys were concerned, they were attending a summer camp and the experimenters played the roles of camp director, senior counsellors, handy-men, etc. They recorded their observations only when they were out of the boys' sight and produced their reports in the evenings. The boys' friendship choices had to be elicited in 'casual conversations' and their attitudes were assessed through judgement tasks presented as games.

The experiments covered four stages: (i) spontaneous interpersonal friendship choices; (ii) group formation; (iii) inter-group conflict; and (iv) inter-group co-operation and reduction of inter-group conflict. Not all the experiments covered all four stages.

Stage (i) was the stage of introduction to the site where all the boys were housed in one large bunk-house. This ended after they had begun to be consistent in their friendships and each boy was asked who his best friends were. The main purpose of this stage was to reduce the possibility that groups formed in stage (ii) would be formed according to initial friendships. Accordingly the next experimental manipulation was to split the boys into two groups. Repeated soundings after the new groups had been allowed to form on an overnight 'camp-out', hike and other activities showed that friendship choices shifted to their new groups for about 90 per cent of choices, whereas before the split the figure had been about 35 per cent.

Stage (ii) lasted approximately a week, during which time group norms and structure emerged. The two groups gave themselves names, 'The Rattlers' and 'The Eagles'. The formation of structure was illustrated by the following experiment. Before an important baseball game, a target board was set up in order to make practice in pitching more interesting. It was not possible to measure the distance from the bull's-eye from the front of the target, but the back was wired with electric lights to make accurate measurement possible. It was found that the boys tended to overestimate consistently the accuracy of those whom the experimenters had observed to be the leaders and whom the boys had chosen in informal sociometric soundings as leaders. Thus, not only had a leadership formed, but so also had consistent ways of behaving towards them. The same was also true of low-status members. There was also evidence that those who did not support group activities or who tried to bully others were subjected to pressure from the rest.

Stage (iii) was the first occasion that the two groups came into contact with each other. A tournament was set up including baseball, touchball, football, tug of war and a treasure hunt, with prizes for the winning group. The good sportsmanship which had characterised the start of the tournament soon disappeared with the groups stealing each other's banners and burning them, and with fights and name-calling being a constant activity. Eventually they wanted to have nothing to do with each other.

Another experiment illustrates this stage. A bean-collecting game was introduced. Each boy had to collect as many beans as possible, in a set time, from a large number scattered on the ground. The beans were collected in a bag with a narrow opening so that the number in it could not be checked. The boys were then shown through an opaque projector the number supposedly collected by each of them, and were asked to write down their esti-mate. In fact the same number of beans were shown each time, yet they consistently overestimated the number collected by their own group and underestimated the number collected by the others.

Not only were there changes in attitude towards the other group but there were also changes within their own group. The groups became immensely more cohesive and unaware of outsiders, apart from the enemy. Leadership changed if the existing leader was reluctant to take the offensive. A bully who had been put in his place now emerged as a hero fighting against the enemy.

Stage (iv) started with an attempt to investigate the 'contact as equals' hypothesis of conflict resolution. The groups went to films and firework parties together and ate in the same room, but hostilities continued. The joint activities continued, but crises requiring co-operation between the two groups were now engineered. The water supply which came from a tank about a mile away broke down and the groups co-operated to check the pipe-line for faults. They clubbed together to pay for a film that was too expensive for one group only, then watched it together. On an excursion the food truck broke down and the two groups pulled together using the tug-of-war rope to get it started. None of these incidents by themselves did more than reduce hostility temporarily, but a combination of them brought the groups together and friendships began to form again between them.

Clearly this series of experiments does not offer a way of reducing inter-group conflict. Rather, it points out how difficult such conflict reduction is. First the crisis leading to co-operation had to be engineered, and second there had to be several of them before any continuing change in attitude occurred. We should of course be wary in generalising from this study to other conflict situations, such as those which occur typically in the work situation. How-ever, there may be theoretical threads in common.

We have so far focused upon a number of important but specific aspects of groups. We turn next to more general theoretical issues.

13.8 Theory in the psychology of social groups

As we suggested in Chapter 1, theory in psychology, and even more so in social psychology, bears only a fleeting resemblance to its counterpart in the physical sciences. We shall introduce four theories of which two can by now be called 'classical', the others being more recent. The classical theories are balance theory (Newcombe, 1961; Heider, 1958) and exchange theory (Homans, 1961), while the social-skill model of Argyle (1967) and the group-influence models of Hackman (1976) are more recent. As we shall see, it is not a question of which is the best theory but rather a question of the extent to which each can illuminate the scene. It is comparatively easy to point out their inadequacies, and this we shall do. However, this activity must be seen in the context of the complexity of the field under investigation.

BALANCE THEORY

We have already discussed balance theory, in connection with attitudes, at some length in Chapter 8. According to the theory each individual seeks to establish a situation in which certain cognitive elements (elements in his mind) form a system in balance.

The balance principle can account for one kind of social phenomenon – the Asch (1956) experiment (see Section 13.4). In Figure 13.3 the naive subject is A, the group is G and the group judgement is represented by X. The

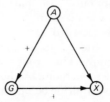

Figure 13.3   The Asch (1956) experiment in balance-theory terms

unbalanced situation of disagreeing with a group to which, as a fellow student, A feels some degree of affiliation is felt as uncomfortable by almost all subjects. On some 30 per cent of occasions subjects resolve the imbalance by conforming with the group, but on 70 per cent of occasions they maintain an independent judgement. In general, those who conform explain this by indicating that they believe the solution they and the group have produced really is the correct one. This gives three positive signs in the diagram, a balanced situation (see Figure 8.1). Usually those who maintain an independent line indicate that they are severing their positive bond with the group, thus producing two negative signs in the diagram which are also an indication of balance.

Newcombe (1961) tested this theory on college students who came to live in a hostel. He predicted that most friendships would form among those who held initially similar attitudes on matters of common relevance and importance. Their orientation towards a variety of objects – including each other – and their patterns of attraction were measured from the time they entered the hostel for a sixteen-week period. Attitudes did not change over this period, but friendships formed to a greater extent among those who held initially similar views. Another result from this study was that attraction occurred where one student believed that the other liked him. In addition it was found that students were attracted to others whom they perceived as seeing them in the same way as they saw themselves in respect of both faults and virtues. These findings have been confirmed by others (Tagiuri, 1958; Backman and Secord, 1959, 1962; Broxton, 1963) and all are in line with the theory.

A different kind of experiment also supports Newcombe's theory. Sampson and Insko (1964), using a stooge, engineered two balanced and two unbalanced situations on a perceptual task (the autokinetic effect). Pairs of subjects, one of whom was the stooge, had independently to make judgements about the task. The balanced situations were those in which the subject was led to like his partner and to perceive his judgements as similar to his own and to dislike his partner and to perceive his judgements as dissimilar. Imbalance was created by having the liked partner make dissimilar judgements and the disliked one produce similar ones. The prediction that the imbalance would tend to be resolved by a change of judgement was confirmed. However, on the debit side of the balance model, the following comments do need to be made.

(1) While it is clear that the balance model accommodates the facts of the Asch experiment, it does little more. Certainly it does not enable prediction of which of the bonds is likely to change under conditions of imbalance. It would be better equipped to do this if it made provision for the degrees of positiveness and negativeness of the bonds, and this might be an indicator of which was most likely to be changed under conditions of imbalance. The congruence model of Osgood, Suci and Tannenbaum (1957) does in fact ascribe numerical values to the bonds by measuring them on a generalised attitude scale with values from $+3$ to -3. While this does enable a greater precision of prediction, it also produces some highly unlikely predictions. (There are also other mathematical formulations of the balance principle (Cartwright and Harary, 1956; Abelson and Rosenberg, 1958).)

(2) There is considerable evidence of individual differences in the tendency to conform over a wide variety of tasks. Blake, Helson and Mouton (1956) report that conformity is related to pronounced feelings of inadequacy and inferiority. The balance model requires extension to incorporate the factor of individual differences in the tendency to conform.

(3) The simple model presented is clearly inadequate to fit many common phenomena. It has, however, been developed to encompass the much more usual situation where an individual relates to more than one object or person at a time. It is possible to envisage a multidimensional balance model which includes several people and objects in a total configuration of forces (see Figure 13.4). Hence it could not be a question of balance or imbalance but of degrees of total imbalance within the system.

(4) If the particular issue or person involved is not important for either of the two people in the interaction, problems arise with the theory. For example,

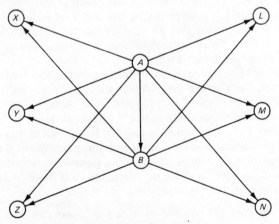

Figure 13.4   Expanded balance model

A's dislike for a politician and *B*'s liking for him may not be particularly important to either of them. Yet the model in its simple form would still predict that this would cause them to dislike each other, or change their attitude to the politician. However, it seems likely that the unimportance of the issue might cause it not to have any effect on their friendship; that is to say, the importance of an issue to a person is a factor influencing the strength of the strain towards balance.

(5) Certain kinds of liking for a third party or object seem to have a different quality to others. Whereas a liking for Leeds United, or photography, or a particular very charming or loving person, might be accepted generally as tending to draw people together, there are other likings that could be expected to do the opposite. For example, if someone shows an undue (in your eyes) liking for your marital partner, your liking for them would be most likely to decrease. It is nice to have people show approval for one's choice of partner, but distinctly not nice for this to go beyond a certain point. It seems necessary to introduce some modification to accommodate the intervening variable of 'jealousy'. This example provides some idea of the amount of sophistication needed to begin to do justice to the whole field of human interaction along balance-theory lines. (For a good review see Sampson (1976).)

HOMANS' EXCHANGE THEORY

Homans' (1950) sees social groups as comprising an 'external system' and an 'internal system'. The external system is 'the behavior of a group so far as that behavior represents one possible answer to the question: How does the group survive in its particular environment?' The internal system is 'the elaboration of group behavior that simultaneously arises out of the external system and reacts upon it'. This distinction has elements in common with that made between formal and informal systems and between technical and social systems (see Chapter 15). The basic point is that there is a system of interaction necessary for the survival of the group in the context in which it operates, e.g. the task it is undertaking (the external system). The informal social interaction occurring around the task and interacting with it is called the internal system. These systems interact and both operate on the basis described by social-exchange theory.

The essence of Homans' exchange theory lies in the five basic propositions listed below through which he believes the empirical findings of social-psychological research can be explained. The influence of Skinner (see Chapter 3) and elementary economics is apparent, for they both envisage human behaviour as a function of its pay-off. In amount and kind, behaviour depends on the amount and kind of reward and punishment it fetches. Thus the set of general propositions Homans uses envisages social behaviour as an exchange of activity, tangible or intangible, and more or less rewarding or costly, between at least two persons:

(i) 'If in the past the occurrence of a particular stimulus situation has been the occasion on which a man's activity has been rewarded, then the more similar the present stimulus situation is to the past one, the more likely he is to emit the activity, or some similar activity now' (Homans, 1950, p. 55).

(ii) 'The more often within a given period of time a man's activity rewards the activity of another, the more often the other will emit the activity' (Homans, 1950, p. 53).

(iii) 'The more valuable to a man a unit of the activity another gives him, the more often he will emit activity rewarded by the activity of the other' (Homans, 1950, p. 55). ('Value' here refers to the degree of reinforcement that is received from a unit of another's activity. 'Cost' refers to the value obtainable through an alternate activity which is forgone in emitting the present activity. Profit equals reward minus cost.)

(iv) 'The more often a man has in the recent past received a rewarding activity from another, the less valuable any further unit of that activity becomes to him' (Homans, 1950, p. 55).

(v) 'The more to a man's disadvantage the rule of distributive justice fails of realization, the more likely he is to display the emotional behavior we call "anger" ' (Homans, 1950, p. 75). (The rule of distributive justice is stated thus: 'A man in an exchange relation with another will expect that the rewards of each man be proportional to his costs – the greater the rewards, the greater the costs – and that the net rewards, or profits, of each man be proportional to his investments – the greater the investments, the greater the profit.') The similarity between this rule and equity theory (see Chapter 3) is clear. Equity theory (Adams, 1963) also proposes that the reward/cost ratio should be interpreted in the light of comparison other(s), and applies to feelings of 'profit' as well as 'loss'.

These propositions are used to explain many aspects of social behaviour. The basic suggestion is that interaction of any kind will not continue unless all parties are making profits from the interaction – profits to be defined as rewards minus costs. Rewards may be of any kind – approval, agreement, change of opinion to conform with the opinion of the other, esteem, similarity, help, status congruence or cohesiveness. Likewise, costs may include such things as disapproval, disagreement, failing to convince, humiliation, demonstration of inadequacy and spending of time. Profits need not be maximised but they must occur.

The rule of distributive justice implies that individuals expect their profits to be in proportion to their investments or social status. Thus a high-status person will expect greater profits from interaction with a low-status person than will the latter. The profits of each should be in proportion to his status for interaction to occur:

As a practical matter, distributive justice is realized when each of the various features of his investments and his activities, put into rank-order in comparison with those of other men, fall in the same place in all the different rank-orders. This condition, which we call status congruence, is not only the condition of distributive justice but also that of social certitude; the status of a man in this condition is secure, established, unambiguous in the eyes of his fellows.... Congruence facilitates social ease in the interaction among men and ... should encourage their joint efficiency (Homans, 1961, p. 264).

Certain comments may be made about exchange theory as stated by Homans:

(i) In spite of the undoubted influence of Skinner's ideas about reinforcement (see Chapter 3), it is clear that Homans has not done justice to the sophistication of some of Skinner's work. For example, in proposition (ii) Homans states that the more often an activity is rewarded, the more often it will be emitted. Yet one of Skinner's most important contributions was to show the resistance to extinction of responses which have been only intermittently reinforced. It is, however, a moot question as to who is right in the field of social interaction.

(ii) Homans refers to reward and not anticipated reward. The theory could perhaps be modified by using an incentive framework instead of a reinforcement one (see Chapters 6 and 7).

(iii) The two main variables in Homans' theory are the value of a unit of activity and the number of such units received within a period. It is these which are supposed to enable rewards and costs to be measured. The need for computation of rewards minus costs implies a common unit in which each of these can be measured, which, as we have noted earlier (Chapters 6 and 7), creates a difficulty in testing this kind of theory. With what unit of measurement can one compare a pint of beer with a kiss?

(iv) The formula 'profit = reward − cost' implies a simple additive or subtractive manner of interaction between rewards and costs. Human beings are more complex than this. It is, for example, possible for an interaction to be both rewarding and expensive to an individual and for this to create 'a conflict within him whose tension may be either rewarding or costly to him, depending on his personality make-up. Such considerations complicate immensely the computation of profit.

Having so far raised some criticisms of Homans' theory, certain strengths should be noted. The defects of vagueness, incompleteness and lack of adequate conceptual and empirical definitions are no more characteristic of Homans's than most other theories in social psychology.

The theory has a very wide area of application, and although it does not enable accurate prediction of all major research findings in the area, it does provide a valuable viewpoint from which to examine and understand them. The analogy of the market-place has been most fruitful in this way. The rule of distributive justice, too, has been valuable, together with the concept of 'status congruence', in suggesting one of the central conditions of group equilibrium.

ARGYLE'S SOCIAL-SKILL MODEL

Argyle's skill model of social interaction differs from traditional theories such as exchange and balance theories in that it focusses on the way in which the participants attempt to bring about desired outcomes rather than on the outcomes themselves.

Argyle (1967) puts forward the suggestion that social interaction is a skill rather like, though perhaps in some ways different from, a motor skill like driving a car (see Chapter 3). He assumes that the ways in which social skills differ from perceptual and motor skills are not crucial and do not detract from the value of this way of looking at social interaction. Skilled activity means an economical organisation of perceptions and responses such that the minimal amount of stress and capacity are taken up. This means that the individual always has surplus capacity and time to meet any unpredictable demands the task might thrust upon him.

The basic model for a perceptual-motor skill is as shown in Figure 13.5.

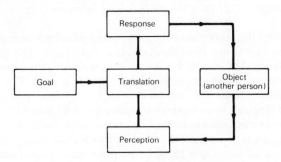

Figure 13.5 Basic perceptual-motor skill model

For example, if it is your intention to try to get a pint of beer from someone (goal), you will first look at him (perception), evaluate your perceptions in the light of your goal and translate the conclusion into your next action. The cycle is then repeated until success ensues or the attempt is given up. A wealth of experience and practice will progressively render the activity more smooth and effective!

To indicate the complexity of the model we shall now present an expanded version (see Figure 11.1, p. 210). Essentially what this does is to separate the perceptual and response parts of the model and to enlarge upon these. The goal and translation processes are common to both.

There are three main components to the model: (i) a motivational component (see Chapter 6 for a review of relevant motives) to be found in Figure 13.5 in the box labelled 'goal'); (ii) a skill component which is learnt in order to achieve satisfaction of the motive or motives (the 'regulation' part of Figure 11.1); and (iii) a person-perception component which enables the effects of behaviour to be monitored. We shall confine ourselves here mainly to the skill (regulation) component, for it is this which makes Argyle's model distinctive.

Argyle's skill (regulation) component requires (i) an input (the person-perception model), (ii) an output (behaviour), and (iii) a translation process which converts the input into an output. The output is monitored continuously for its effects. This monitoring provides a new input, which in turn modifies the output.

The model is seen as applying to two or more people in interaction and whose behaviour is enabled to mesh by the manner in which they exercise their social skills. For the sake of simplicity only one person's situation is illustrated in Figure 11.1 above. Anyone interacting with this person features in the box labelled 'object', and he in turn possesses a whole apparatus of perception, information-processing and motor-skills' boxes.

Norms are regarded as comparison models or expectations about the system of relationships between group members. When an individual learns the norms of a group he builds such a comparison model or programme (to use a computer analogy), which presumably then becomes part of the translation process.

A considerable body of experimental material is compatible with the model, but there are certain comments which should be made:

(i) The model fits successfully the conception of norms as expectations of behaviour, but norms are also expectations about values. The latter are not solely a specification of what behaviour is required but also a specification of what more distant goals the behaviour is expected to lead to. This second type of norm, therefore, must also have a feedback loop into the motivational component of Argyle's total model, or some similar adjustment.

(ii) Usually perceptual-motor skills involve a man and a machine with a predictable response repertoire. Social skills involve the interaction of a man with someone who has a less predictable repertoire. Thus norms must be regarded not simply as a programme for behaviour but as a programme whose functioning is dependent on the functioning of an interdependent and inter-acting programme in another person. Thus the successful exercise of skill by one person depends on its successful exercise by another. Breakdowns in social relations may therefore arise from a failure of programmes to mesh.

(iii) The translation process poses a problem, for it requires the individual to compare his feedback input with a comparison model of expected results (which are in line with attainment of his goal) before the output can be ap-propriately modified. Much of the translation process must remain, for the time being, no more than hypothetical.

(iv) The model is complementary rather than contradictory to older theories. Argyle's criticism of these may be taken in two ways, (*a*) as criticisms of the capacity of the theories to account for the facts they attempt to account for, and (*b*) as a statement of the inability of these theories to account for the phenomena towards which his model is directed specifically, e.g. certain kinds of behaviour like altruism (Sahlins, 1965), and the means people use to achieve their goals.

Exchange theory and balance theory, if they are taken to postulate drives either to obtain social profits or to achieve cognitive balance, clearly fit into the box labelled 'goal' together with the other kinds of social motive Argyle suggests. These older theories, in spite of their limitations, might serve to generate hypotheses about the motivation concerned in the choice of goals.

It follows that matters of exchange and balance do indeed enter into determining the course of interaction and group formation and continuation but that they are not the only determinants. A necessary condition would be that the social skills of the participants were sufficient for interaction to continue, through the meshing of their responses to each other. Surely it would be wrong to argue that successful meshing by itself is more than a prerequisite for continued equilibrium conditions in interaction.

(v) It is perhaps in the provision of a perspective from which to view the whole process of interaction that Argyle may turn out to have made his greatest contribution, rather than through his considerable empirical work designed to elicit the component parts of social skills, valuable though this emphasis has been.

(vi) It has been argued that the model operates primarily from a consensus rather than a conflict approach to social interaction and that as such it is unable to account for the interaction involving continuing interpersonal conflict, since the essence of successful conflict is to make one's behaviour unpredictable to the other. However, it might also be argued that some implicit understanding of social skills and of making oneself predictable is necessary before a person may enter into both co-operative and conflict situations and that a person who finds himself constantly in conflict situations can be explicable in terms of his failure to master the appropriate skills, or by the breakdown of those skills, for example through stress.

HACKMAN'S GROUP-INFLUENCE MODELS

Recently Hackman (1976) has proposed two group-influence models. One of them is concerned with how the group influences the behaviour of an individual member. Table 13.4 illustrates the variables in the model.

Table 13.4   The availability and impact of group-supplied stimuli

Availability of stimuli	Impact of stimuli		
	Informational (i.e. on member beliefs and knowledge)	Affective (i.e. on member attitudes, values, and emotions)	Behavioural (i.e. directly on individual or social behaviour in the group)
Ambient (pervades the group-setting) Discretionary (availability at the discretion of other group members)			

Source: Hackman (1976).

He distinguishes between ambient stimuli which pervade the group setting (e.g. other group members, equipment and working conditions) and discretionary stimuli which are made available at the discretion of other group members (e.g. praise, criticism, instructions and various rewards and punishments such as financial ones). These stimuli are seen as influencing the individual in three ways: (i) his informational state via beliefs and knowledge;

(ii) his affective state via attitudes, values and emotions; and (iii) his behaviour. Hackman then organises much of the research literature which we have just cited within the framework of this model.

His second model is concerned with the major determinants of group-member behaviour and performance effectiveness (see Figure 13.6). The

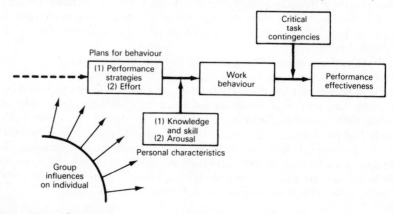

Figure 13.6 Major determinants of group-member behaviour and performance effectiveness (Hackman, 1976)

model indicates that the group influences the individual work behaviour of its members through its impact on four classes of variables: (i) the knowledge and skill of the individual; (ii) the level of psychological arousal which the individual experiences while working; (iii) the approaches or 'performance strategies' which the individual uses in doing his work; and (iv) the level of effort an individual exerts in doing his work.

A FINAL COMMENT

We are not very impressed by the explanatory force and scientific standing of any of the theories outlined above. What we are impressed by is the way in which a range of different ways of looking at social interaction is introduced. Each theory, in its turn, while doing very little to provide precise prescriptions for action in a given situation as would be required if it were to be used as a piece of management technology, does, if studied carefully, open up a new way of thinking about social interaction. Each one could provide the individual with a range of possibilities for action in the light of his own make-up and creative abilities.

14
Leadership

14.1 Introduction to basic concepts

Typically definitions of leadership satisfy certain criteria but do no justice to others. On the other hand, comprehensive definitions tend to subsume far too many things.

Examples of definitions are: (i) 'Leadership is that quality which enables X to get Y to do what X wants him to do'; (ii) 'Leadership is that which occurs when A persuades B that B wants to do what A wants him to do'; or (iii) 'Leadership is the process of A and B coming to an agreement about what needs to be done and then A arranging the situation so that B can do it.' The question of whether a leadership attempt is successful or not complicates the issue further, for one might ask whether only successful attempts are leadership or whether unsuccessful attempts are also leadership, but of an ineffective kind. One could go on *ad infinitum*, but this would be pointless. The crucial element in all of these definitions seems to be an attempt to persuade another person to behave in the way in which the leader wishes him to behave. This element (which is sometimes called 'leadership' or 'leadership ability') is seen typically as an individual characteristic which seems to involve a motivational component (the attempt to persuade) and an ability component (ability to persuade). A leader's effectiveness in persuading others is of course not only a function of this hypothetical characteristic but also of situational factors (e.g. the rewards at his disposal). We shall call this type I leadership.

This kind of usage of the term 'leadership' should be distinguished from the 'role' of leader, i.e. type II leadership. For example, a manager in a department of an organisation, an armed-forces officer and the President of the Students' Union all occupy roles which can be considered to be leadership roles. Each could therefore be described as a 'leader'. A leadership role in this sense has a formal character, in that a particular individual is appointed formally or elected to the position. Such a leader will often be, and is usually expected to be, a leader in the first sense (i.e. should be influential and persuasive). However, this is not always the case, as is illustrated by the occurrence in everyday life of some leadership posts in which the occupant is merely a figure-head and where the real power lies 'behind the throne'. On the whole occupying a formal leadership role makes leadership in the first sense easier, because such roles often give the occupant special powers of reward and punishment (e.g. a manager may often be able to promote or sack people) over other group members. Thus, in many situations, 'leadership ability' may only become apparent when a person has a formal role and hence has power over rewards and punishments, or when at least such power is relatively weak amongst other group members. The failure to make this distinction has caused some confusion in discussion of leadership. In this chapter, we shall therefore be concerned with both leadership ability (when it arises, how it reveals itself, an analysis of its dimensions and of its effects on group performance) and with the behaviour exhibited by people occupying leadership roles, and in particular that behaviour which is most associated with effectiveness of group functioning. A major concern will be with the impact of various situational variables on leader behaviour and effectiveness. The chapter will begin (Section 14.2) with a historical background so that the reader is able to detect trends and locate each of the particular types of investigation reviewed in relation to particular approaches to leadership which have been used in the past. These approaches will then be discussed in greater detail. Section 14.3 covers the search for leadership as a personality quality or characteristic. The search for leadership behaviour characteristics as opposed to particular personality qualities is discussed in Section 14.4. These approaches paid insufficient attention to situational variables. In response to this two types of model have been proposed: Fiedler's contingency model (Sections 14.5 and 14.6) and Vroom and Yetton's situational models (Section 14.7). Fiedler's (1967) model attempts to take account of both the leader's characteristics and situational variables. Vroom and Yetton (1973), on the other hand, are concerned primarily with the variability of a leader's behaviour and with the role of situational variables in this.

14.2 Historical background

Early research into leadership started with the roots of a controversy which is still with us today. The 'great man' theory held that it was the personality characteristics of the individual which rendered him likely to be a leader, no matter what the circumstances, and his personality would impose itself on the situation and cause other people to follow his wishes and direction. The second kind of theory, the 'times' theory, holds that different times, different tasks and different situations require different characteristics in a leader. This kind of theory holds that there are no universal personality characteristics associated with leadership, i.e. there is no 'leadership quality'. There is only a specific situation which requires a particular kind of person to be leader. It can be seen that there are certain political implications to these kinds of theories. For example, the 'great man' theory sees advancement, development and progress as being the result of the action of a relatively select few. These people have leadership qualities that make them likely to be followed. (This is the general thesis on which Plato's *Republic* is based.) The 'times theory' is a much more democractic kind of theory in which the mass of the subordinates and the situation in which they find themselves are responsible for the choice of a particular kind of leader. During this chapter a constant theme will be the swing from one of these two approaches to the other.

14.3 The search for leadership characteristics

Early systematic research into leadership was concerned entirely with those personal qualities and abilities (i.e. those characteristics common to all men in greater or lesser degree) which for some reason or other, if present in a larger quantity or in a particular combination, were thought to amount to 'leadership quality'. Stogdill (1948), reviewing some 124 published papers on leadership, summarised them in the following way:

(i) The average leader (either elected or appointed) is above average (compared with group members) on the following characteristics: intelligence, educational attainments, dependability in exercising responsibilities, activity, social participation, socio-economic status, sociability, initiative, persistence, knowing how to get things done, self-confidence, alertness to and insight into situations, co-operativeness, popularity, adaptability, verbal facility.

(ii) The characteristics required of a leader are determined to a large extent by the demands of the situation.

(iii) Leaders have been found to be above average on a number of factors specific to well-defined groups, e.g. athletic ability and physical prowess in boys' gangs and play groups, intellectual fortitude and integrity for eminent leaders in maturity.

(iv) In order of decreasing size of average correlation coefficient, the characteristics correlating with leadership are: originality, popularity, sociability, judgement, aggressiveness, desire to excel, humour, co-operativeness, liveliness and athletic ability.

(v) The results suggest low positive correlations between leadership and age, height, weight, physique, energy, appearance, dominance and mood control.

(vi) The evidence suggests that leadership exhibited in various school situations may persist into college, vocational and community life.

It should be emphasised that although the above generalisations are supported by a considerable number of studies, those specific characteristics related to leadership vary from study to study, and in particular from one type of situation to another. The size of the relationship between each characteristic and leadership in any specific study is generally small. We should expect this to be the case in a review of this nature, when the range of situations studied is very wide, and when leadership includes both elected leaders and those appointed by authorities outside the group. Further, some of the studies were concerned simply with how leaders (elected or appointed) differed from followers, others with characteristics associated with leadership effectiveness.

In more specific situations there is evidence that good predictions of leader behaviour can be obtained from measures of personality characteristics (Cattell and Stice, 1954).

However, the generally small magnitude of relationships between individual characteristics and leadership measures, along with the finding that the situation played an important role in leadership, led to a general rejection of the 'trait approach to leadership'.

More recently, this approach has re-emerged to some extent, mainly through the work of Ghiselli (1963). His research, largely on supervisors and managers, suggested that, at least in the work situation, effective leaders possess certain characteristics to a greater extent than less effective leaders and non-leaders. Specifically they tend to be higher on intelligence (verbal and symbolic reasoning, see Chapter 10), initiative (willingness to strike off in new directions), supervisory ability (ability to direct others), self-assurance (favourableness of self-evaluation) and self-perceived occupational level (the degree to which a person sees himself as belonging with 'high' rather than 'low' socio-economic status individuals). Similarly Miner (1965) has found quite good correlations between a drive for power and various criteria of effective leadership in managerial and supervisory positions. Such correlations tend to be greater the higher the level of the manager in the organisational hierarchy. The instrument used by Miner, a sentence-completion scale, measures a drive for power involving a positive attitude toward authority figures, competitive situations, the masculine role, competitive games, imposing wishes on others, standing out from the group and the routine administrative function.

These findings suggest that a trait approach can be both valid and useful, provided that measures are designed to predict specific aspects of leadership behaviour (e.g. group productivity, *or* group satisfaction, *or* whether a person is likely to be elected or appointed to leadership roles) within a fairly narrow range of situations. It is probable that Ghiselli and Miner's results were significant and useful because they concentrated on one type of leadership role, i.e. that of manager/supervisor in fairly large business enterprises. They also focused primarily on one aspect of leadership effectiveness, group productivity. Better predictions could almost certainly be achieved by focusing on a narrower range of situations (e.g. those in which managers have the same kinds of power over rewards and punishments), though the findings, of course, would have less generality.

There is therefore a considerable body of evidence that certain people are much more likely to become leaders than others. For example, the leadership prospects of an unintelligent, working-class, unreliable recluse are slim, whereas those of an intelligent, reliable, socially adept member of the middle class are much better.

14.4   Focus on leadership behaviour

Shortly after Stogdill's review on characteristics associated with leadership, there emerged a number of investigations concerned with detailed analyses of leadership behaviour. The first of these were first conducted in laboratory settings (Bales, 1950) and later in work situations. The latter studies were conducted mainly by two groups of researchers, one at the Survey Research Centre at Michigan, the other at Ohio State University. We shall consider the significance of each of these research programmes in turn.

LABORATORY STUDIES

In laboratory experimentation the work of Bales and his associates plays a key role. Bales was concerned with the evolution of leadership in groups who met only on a small number of occasions, usually four, who rarely knew each other previously and who met for the purpose of discussing a business case study. His results suggest that there is a tendency for groups to develop in such a way that certain people fall into leadership roles. Although this was by no means universal, most groups did behave in this way in Bales's laboratory and it is interesting that although Bales's work has been taken generally as lending support for the idea that leadership is a role which is determined situationally, i.e., by the group and the task, his research also provides evidence for leadership traits or characteristics.

In this part of the chapter we shall describe not only the results of his research but also his methodology, since it represents an interesting combination of techniques which give a 'richness' to his work.

The starting-point for the research we are about to discuss is the 'interaction process analysis' developed by Bales (1950) for the classification of acts of communication in groups. Our discussion will be confined to his studies of paid undergraduates in groups of three to seven people at a time.

The interaction process analysis is a classification system which consists of four main categories and twelve sub-categories (see Table 14.1). Further explanation of these categories can be found in Bales and Slater (1955).

Table 14.1   The interaction process analysis system

	Qualitative type	Communicative act	
(A)	Positive reactions	(1) Shows solidarity (2) Shows tension release (3) Agrees	Social-emotional area
(B)	Problem-solving attempts	(4) Gives suggestion (5) Gives opinion (6) Orientation	Task area
(C)	Questions	(7) Asks for orientation (8) Asks for opinion (9) Asks for suggestion	
(D)	Negative reactions	(10) Disagrees (11) Shows tension increase (12) Shows antagonism	Social-emotional area

In the typical Bales experiment the subjects enter the room and have pointed out to them the microphones and the one-way screen through which the observer will record their activities.

Each subject is given a summary of facts about a human-relations or administration problem of the case-study type. They study this individually and then it is taken away. They are then asked to reach a group decision in the form of a report to a senior administrative officer on why the persons behaved as they did and asked to make their recommendations as to what to do about the problem. Forty minutes is allowed for discussion, with the last two set aside for dictation of the decision.

The observer makes his recordings on a horizontally moving paper tape. Every act which occurs is classified as to its quality, who performed it, towards whom, and when. Using this data the interaction process analysis is used to describe the activities of each person in a group as a twelve-dimensional profile. After each meeting each member is asked to fill out a questionnaire with the following questions:

(i) Who contributed the best ideas for solving the problem?
(ii) Who did most to guide the discussion and keep it moving effectively?
(iii) How well did you personally like each of the other members?

Usually subjects were asked to rank or rate all the members, including themselves, where appropriate. After the final session the subjects were asked additionally the following question:

(iv) Considering all the sessions, which member of the group would you say stood out most definitely as leader in the discussion (include yourself)?

In some of the studies the California F-scale (a measure of authoritarianism) was also administered to the subjects.

The purpose of the typical experiment (e.g. Bales and Slater, 1955) is to observe the formation of group structure.

Taking the answers to questions (i), (ii) and (iii) on the questionnaire, it was found that there was a significant tendency for the 'best-liked man' to be progressively differentiated from the 'best-ideas man' as time went on over the four sessions. Summarising the findings, we can say that the most active person initially was likely to be perceived as both the best-ideas and the best-liked man, but progressively the role ceases to be held by one person and the most active and best-ideas man ceases to be also best-liked. Another member takes over this role.

What of the relations between these two? Taking the groups as a whole, (i) they interacted with each other more than the other members, and (ii) they agreed with each other more than with anyone else. This seems to indicate that they may have operated to some extent as a team.

However, when we examine separately those groups in which there was greatest agreement as to who was best liked and who gave the best ideas (high-status consensus groups) and those in which there was least agreement (low-status consensus groups), separate pictures emerge. In the low-status consensus groups the relationship described fails to reach statistical significance, unlike the high-status consensus groups.

We have so far considered the evidence for the differentiation of roles. The question now arises: Who did the group consider to be their leader? The answer was that leadership coincided 78.6 per cent with 'most guidance', 60.7 per cent with 'receiving communications', 59.3 per cent with 'best ideas',

50 per cent with 'talking' and 14.3 per cent with 'best liked'. Bales and Slater suggest that leadership is a generalised role which, depending on the group, will be made up of varying proportions of these elements. In these groups, the heavy task element brought about the emphasis on guidance and the lesser importance of likeability.

In general, the top men on the various preference scales derived from the questionnaire tended to score higher on authoritarianism in the low-consensus groups than in the high-consensus groups. Further, in the high groups the ideas men scored lower than the best-liked men, but in the low groups there was no difference between these. In summary, in these groups there emerged, particularly in the high-consensus groups, two types of 'specialist': the task specialist (the 'ideas *cum* guidance' man); and the social-emotional specialist (the 'best-liked' man). In general, groups regarded the former as their leader most often, the latter rarely. The leader tended to be low on authoritarianism. Taking the high-status consensus groups, the relatively low authoritarian scores of the ideas men suggest them to be more flexible than the best-liked men. Bales and Slater suggest that the latter may be expressing their rigidity in a compulsive need to be liked, whereas the former are better able to adjust their behaviour to the conflicting and varying demands of the task. They are therefore likely to be chosen as leaders, except in those instances where an ideas *cum* guidance man turns out to be inflexible and unable to deal effectively with the social-emotional aspects of leadership (i.e. to be disliked).

Bales and Slater suggest that the poor differentiation in the low-consensus groups is due to a low degree of similarity in the basic values of members. They are therefore unable to agree on such things as who has the best ideas. Individual participation is likely to be governed not by an adjustment between the various specialists and the other members but by the various rigid tendencies of individuals.

There are a number of points which emerge from this work. One of them is that, in the situation described, typically no formal leader (elected or appointed) emerges. Only type I leadership (see Section 14.1) appears. Attempts at influence are shown at some stage by most subjects in such a situation, though it is true that some people show more than others, and some people are more likely to be successful in their attempts. In some groups Bales found considerable disagreement among group members as to how much influence people showed, in others less. Even in these latter groups, where agreement is high, who is considered to be the leader appears to be a function of other characteristics in addition to influence. In this context we would question the meaning and usefulness of the term 'leadership'. 'Best-ideas man' and 'best-liked man' seem more appropriate as a description of people's behaviour.

We believe that the term 'leadership' is only necessary when some kind of formal role differentiation occurs between group members (i.e. they are given different tasks and means to carry them out), and then only when one of these roles involves one person (the leader) being given certain powers which the others do not have. Usually these powers give him higher status and greater ability to persuade and control the behaviour of group members than other group members.

Bales's studies, nevertheless, have relevance to the formal leadership situation. They illustrate that some people, by virtue of loquacity, self-confidence, task competence or whatever (type I leadership), tend to play a more influential role than other group members, at least in certain types of task and situation. The 'best-ideas' man' may or may not be the formal leader. If he is not, then a possible occurrence might be a battle for dominance between the two leaders (i.e. type I *versus* type II) which Schutz (1953) has demonstrated can lead to a lack of group cohesiveness and efficiency.

It is also interesting to speculate on the situation where leaders emerge through election by group members, whether the best-liked or best ideas man would be chosen. This, of course, would probably vary with circumstances. Stogdill (1948), in summarising the research, suggested that popularity is an important characteristic in leadership, though it is not clear whether he is referring to the attainment of a formal leadership position or to leadership effectiveness. It seems likely that popularity would be related positively to attaining leadership positions, and also to effectiveness, at least to the extent that being unpopular might lead to group discontent and hence lower effectiveness, although the relationship between satisfaction and productivity varies considerably from situation to situation (Brayfield and Crockett, 1955).

THE MICHIGAN STUDIES

These studies, which were done by the Survey Research Center at Michigan, investigated supervisory behaviour in a number of large organisations, from the Chesapeake and Ohio Railroad to the Prudential Assurance Company. The investigators were concerned with eliciting relationships between supervisory behaviour as described by subordinates and performance of the work group (obtained from company records). Miner (1963) summarises the findings as follows:

1. Supervisors who spend most of their time doing non-supervisory tasks are likely to be less effective.
2. Delegating tasks to subordinates so that they may carry them out in their own way was facilitative of performance.
3. Having concern for the subordinate as a human being increased performance.
4. The effectiveness of the previous three characteristics as a determinant of performance increases the more the supervisor has influence with his own superiors.
5. The effective supervisor assumes an active leadership role rather than a passive one (in Korman, 1971).

Concerning delegation, Tannenbaum (1966) argues that to give subordinates increased control over what they do and how they do it will increase the motivation with which they do it. If a supervisor expects his subordinates to be able to exercise autonomy and responsibility in the job, they will be more likely to do so than if the supervisor is standing over them the whole time waiting for the mistake he is bound to make, and such close supervision could lead to the failure to act responsibly through having no practice at, or inclination for, doing so. Certainly there is an abundance of evidence from level of aspiration studies (see Chapter 6 on motivation), as well as from other laboratory and industrial studies, to support the argument that people do as well as you expect them to do. However, a study by Morse and Reimer (1956) (see Chapter 15) indicated that although increasing autonomy increased output, it did not do so to such a great extent as increasing hierarchical control did. However, there was more satisfaction among the groups subjected to the former treatment. Hence the autonomy programme could perhaps be justified on these grounds and possibly in terms of a likely advantage through less labour turnover. The fact remains, however, that performance can be improved through methods other than that advocated by the Michigan researchers.

THE OHIO STATE UNIVERSITY STUDIES

The early studies isolated two main dimensions of leadership behaviour using factor analytic techniques. These dimensions were consideration (behaviour indicating mutual trust, sensitivity, respect and *rapport* between the leader and his group) and structure (behaviour involving the definition of roles of the members, forward planning and pushing for production). They indicated that production supervisors rated high in proficiency by plant management tended to have leadership patterns high in structure and low in consideration, particularly if they felt pressures to meet dead-lines. Such supervisors also tended to have subordinates amongst whom there were more labour turnover, absenteeism, accidents, union grievances and dissatisfaction. Fleishman and Harris (1962) investigated the relationships between structure, consideration and two measures of group satisfaction: (i) labour grievances; and (ii) labour turnover.

Leader behaviour was measured by the 'Supervisory Behaviour Description Questionnaire' as answered by three or more workers drawn randomly from each foreman's department. Mean consideration and mean structure scores were obtained for each foreman. The correlation coefficient between the two in this case was -0.33, i.e. there was a tendency for the two not to go together.

Fifty-seven foremen and their work groups in a motor-truck manufacturing plant took part in the study. The results indicated curvilinear relationships between both aspects of leader behaviour and both criteria. Generally speaking, low consideration and high structure were related positively to high grievances and turnover. However, while extremely high structure and extremely low consideration are most related to high grievances and turnover, there is a certain point beyond which reducing structure or increasing consideration does not serve to reduce turnover or grievances. Turnover begins to increase steeply at a higher level of structure and a lower level of consideration than do grievances. This follows if we assume that people complain before they actually leave. It was also found that if consideration was low there would be high turnover and grievances no matter what the degree of structure. Likewise, foremen showing high consideration could show fairly high structure without unduly influencing turnover or grievances.

These results might have been different had the performance criteria been related more closely to productivity. Indeed, earlier studies had shown that plant managers tended to rate most highly foremen high in structure. One wonders whether this was in spite of turnover and grievance figures. It is likely that effective leadership behaviour differs depending on the measures of group performance taken.

One further result of these studies has been the formulation of programmes designed to change members' 'leadership styles' so as to be high in both consideration and structure (e.g. Blake and Mouton, 1964). This emphasis on leadership behaviour and style has frequently been accompanied by the assumption that such behaviour or style is less 'fundamental' than basic personality traits or characteristics. They are assumed to be less fundamental in two ways: (i) they are specific to certain kinds of situation only (i.e. those requiring leadership behaviour); and (ii) they are capable of radical change through various learning experiences. It is further assumed that such change is not difficult, and can be accomplished in a relatively short time period.

We are most sceptical about this latter assumption, for the evidence on such change studies is most difficult to evaluate as so many variables may be operating (Harris and Fleishman, 1955; Warr, Bird and Rackham, 1970). Certainly there is evidence that supervisors adopt characteristic styles (Argyle *et al.*, 1958). Ghiselli's work (1963) would strongly suggest that these styles are related to more fundamental aspects of personality which do not lend themselves readily to change.

We suggested earlier that leadership effectiveness will be determined by both type I and type II leadership. In particular, we noted that type II leadership (i.e. the allocation of a leadership role) involves the allocation of certain specialised role behaviour which varies with the group, and that usually it involves some special powers of reward and punishment over group members. Fiedler (1967) has proposed a contingency model of leadership, which proposes that the nature of the situation will affect greatly what kind of leadership style will be effective, and it is to this that we now turn.

14.5 Fiedler's contingency model of leadership

Earlier we indicated that studies of leadership and supervision had shown that both democratic and autocratic styles of leadership can be effective in the sense of producing high levels of performance in subordinates. It is also likely that both styles of leadership can be responsible for depressing productivity in subordinates. The difficulty is to discover when and how. Fiedler (1967) examined the previous research concerning autocratic or democratic leadership with the aim of explaining the conflicting findings of different researchers. He then proposed that the effectiveness of a particular style of leadership is contingent upon the situation. Those aspects of the situation upon which Fiedler focussed initially were the leader–group-member relations, the power of the leader and the degree of structure in the task on which the group was engaged. In later refinements of the model, factors such as stress were taken into account. The hypothesis upon which the contingency model is based is as follows. That style of leadership which tends to be more controlling and active (autocratic) is most effective in group/task situations which are either very favourable or very unfavourable to the leader. A leadership style which is more permissive and passive (democratic) is more appropriate in group/task situations of intermediate favourableness. The model is illustrated in Figure 14.1.

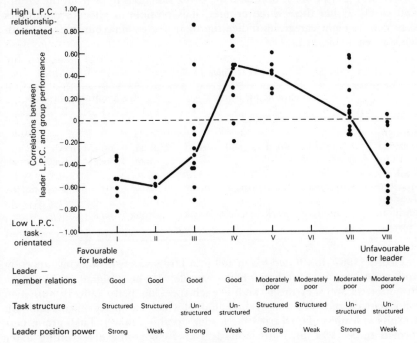

Figure 14.1   Correlations between leaders' L.P.C. scores and group effectiveness plotted for each cell (from Fiedler, 1967)

The vertical axis takes the form of correlation coefficients, ranging from +1 to −1 with a zero point in the middle. On it are plotted correlations between 'leadership style' (L.P.C. score, to be discussed later) and effectiveness of the group's performance as measured by the success with which the task in question is completed. Leadership style is measured on a scale (the L.P.C. scale) going from 'controlling, active' at the low end to 'permissive, passive' at the high end. Thus a positive correlation between leadership style (L.P.C.) and effectiveness means that permissive, passive leadership is most effective and a negative correlation means that controlling, active leadership is most effective. The correlations found in the experimental studies of Fiedler were plotted against the situation favourableness scale on the horizontal axis. This scale, in its simplest form, is a compendium of three elements which describe significant aspects of the situation. Task structure is defined in terms of the extent to which the solution is verifiable empirically and objectively, the extent to which a clear statement of the goal is possible, the number of possible ways of completing the task and the number of possible solutions. Thus solving a mathematical problem is a structured task, while making a flower arrangement is comparatively unstructured. Leader–member relations are ascertained by getting the leader to fill in a questionnaire about the extent to which he gets on with the group. Finally, the power position of the leader is assessed by a questionnaire indicating the extent to which he is able to hire and fire, promote and demote, bring sanctions to bear on the group, and so on. Using these three criteria, it is possible to allocate group/task situations to eight categories indicating their degree of favourableness to the leader (see Table 14.2).

Table 14.2

	Favourable for leader				Unfavourable for leader			
	8	7	6	5	4	3	2	1
Leader–member relations	good	good	good	good	mod. poor	mod. poor	mod. poor	mod. poor
Task structure	structured	str.	unstr.	unstr.	str.	str.	unstr.	unstr.
Leader position power	strong	weak	strong	weak	strong	weak	strong	weak

Fiedler (1967) has tested his model in a large variety of working, sporting and experimental situations. For example, in his Belgian Navy study the subjects were Flemish- and French-speaking petty officers and men who were assigned to teams of three, half of which had petty officers and half recruits as leaders. This varied the leader's position power. Each group performed three tasks, an unstructured task of composing a recruiting letter aimed at persuading 16- and 17-year-olds to join the navy, and two structured tasks involving computing the shortest route for ships through ten and twelve ports respectively. Group atmosphere scores (to determine leader–member relations) were obtained from the leader after each task. Two further aspects of group/task difficulty were also introduced: homogeneity (all French-speaking, all Flemish-speaking or mixed French and Flemish groups); and the recency of formation of the group (the first task they worked on presumably involving more difficulty than the second or third).

Ninety-six three-man groups were used, all on the same day to prevent communication between them. There were forty-eight homogeneous and forty-eight heterogeneous groups, half with petty officers and half with recruits as leaders, half beginning with a structured task and half with an unstructured task. They were matched on the basis of L.P.C. scores, intelligence and attitude towards the other language group. L.P.C. (leadership style) was correlated with the group's performance for each of the forty-eight group-task conditions in the study, graded in terms of favourableness to the leader. The results of the study give a reasonably close fit to the hypothesised curve illustrated in Figure 14.1.

Thus in this study, as well as in others (e.g. Insko and Schopler, 1972), the contingency model is confirmed. However, not all the evidence supports the model and there are a number of problems associated with it:

(i) A considerable lack of precision is involved in the measurement of the favourableness scale on the horizontal axis, and what constitutes favourableness may vary from situation to situation. For example, considering the aspect of task structure, different measures will need to be used according to the particular task. A similar problem applies to the leader's power position. By itself this lack of comparability between tasks makes the favourableness scale into an ordinal scale for each occasion it is used. There is therefore no way of knowing in the case of non-confirmation of Fiedler's results whether this is due to a genuine contrary instance or simply to the fact that favourableness has been measured inadequately. In addition, Fiedler (1967) himself recognises that there are other factors concerned in favourableness apart from those in the basic model.

(ii) Graen *et al.* (1970) have reviewed experimental tests of Fiedler's model and report that while the model accounts quite well for some studies, particularly the early ones, a number of later studies do not fit into Fiedler's predicted pattern. This may be due to the limitations outlined in (i) above or to a number of other reasons. For example, the broad idea of favourableness as a relevant dimension may be correct but the particular mixture of components may not be. In this context, as a more recent development, Fiedler has added a measure of stress to the original components.

(iii) Ashour (1973) makes a number of methodological criticisms of Fiedler's research.

(iv) From the practical point of view, Fiedler's model, which carries the implication that certain styles of leadership are suitable for certain kinds of group/task situation, is as yet less than useful in view of the impossibility of comparing group/task situations in order to discover precisely where on the continuous each new situation lies. Thus a leader entering a new situation is unable to know in advance which style of leadership is most suitable. All he can do is bear in mind the likelihood that he might have to switch 'styles' as he sorts out in his mind precisely what situation confronts him.

(v) There is a static element in the model which suggests that each situation is favourable, or unfavourable, or in between the two, for the foreseeable future. Clearly the interaction between the leader and the group can influence the favourableness of the leader–follower relations. Also, it is quite common that groups are involved in tasks of varying degrees of structure at different times either through the natural evolution of the task or through organisational change. Fiedler recognises this, and certainly recognition of the changing nature of many group/task situations could be incorporated into the model without destroying its basic nature.

(vi) As indicated earlier, leadership effectiveness can be measured according to two main criteria: the performance of the subordinates, and their satisfaction. Fiedler's studies may be said to be lacking in that they neglected the satisfaction or morale of the subordinates and concentrated on their performance. His model portrays leadership effectiveness in terms of subordinate performance.

(vii) Korman (1971) suggests that the contingency model may be unnecessarily complex and that evidence (e.g. Ghiselii, 1963; Miner, 1965; Fiedler and Meuwese, 1963; Dunnette, 1967; Nash, 1965) supports the personality trait hypothesis that at least in typical work situations effective leaders possess certain characteristics.

Our hypothesis is that effective leaders in certain types of similar situations will tend to have particular characteristics in common. We also believe that some kind of contingency theory of leadership (the idea that leadership effectiveness is a function both of the leader's behaviour/personality and the situational demands) can be the only type of theory to explain all the evidence we have presented in this chapter. Far from Fiedler's model being unnecessarily complex, we believe it will be necessary to include more variables. We shall now present an expanded contingency approach.

14.6   An expanded contingency approach

We believe that Fiedler's model is not only oversimplified but that some of the variables should be changed. This is the case for Fiedler's measure of leadership style, the L.P.C. score. This score is determined by asking the leader about the person with whom he has least enjoyed working in his working life. The description is made on twenty items such as friendly or unfriendly, co-operative or unco-operative. A high L.P.C. score means a relatively favourable, accepting description of the 'least preferred co-worker' (hence L.P.C.). Fiedler cites a number of studies which have shown that high L.P.C. score leaders tend to be permissive, non-directive and considerate in their reactions to group members, whereas low L.P.C. leaders tend to be directive, managing and task-controlling in their leadership behaviour.

It is notable that these two leadership styles appear to have much in common with autocratic or democratic styles and also seem to be related to the Ohio dimensions of leadership behaviour (initiating structure and consideration). Initiating structure reflects the extent to which an individual is likely to define and structure his role and those of his subordinates towards goal attainment. A high score on this dimension characterises leaders playing an active role in directing group activities through planning, communicating, information, scheduling, etc. Consideration reflects the extent to which the individual is likely to have job relationships characterised by mutual trust, respect for subordinates' ideas and consideration of their feelings. A high score is indicative of a climate of good *rapport* and two-way communication. A low score indicates that the supervisor is likely to be more impersonal in his relations with group members. Thus high L.P.C leaders would appear to resemble closely those high in consideration and low in initiating structure and vice versa for low L.P.C. leaders. If this is the case, then L.P.C. score does not appear to distinguish between other combinations of leadership style.

For example, where would a high-structure and high-consideration leader lie on the L.P.C. scale?

Furthermore, the use of the L.P.C. score as a global measure of leadership style appears to us to be highly questionable, for it is actually a measure of judgement style, and then of a rather specific kind. Although we can conceive of some correlation between it and leadership behaviour in many situations, and research has shown this to be the case, to use it as the only measure of leadership style seems to be going too far. We have also argued that the term 'leadership' style should not be used to imply that personality characteristics of some stability are of no importance in leadership behaviour. In fact we believe that the L.P.C. score should be replaced by a desciption of the leader's personality. For example, Ghiselli (1963) has demonstrated that such measures may be related to success in the work situation. Cattell and Stice's (1954) study suggests that the relationships can be very strong for a specific situation.

We feel that the exact nature of the personality measures taken should depend on the specific situational demands, though some list of more general characteristics like that of Ghiselli (1963) could be useful for important and large classes of leadership situations. For more specific situations, then other characteristics such as those cited by Stogdill (1948) in his review would have to be added or substituted. These characteristics would be wide-ranging, covering the fields of intelligence and abilities, motivational characteristics (one aspect of these would be the extent to which the leader identifies with 'organisational goals') and temperamental ones. In addition, characteristics not directly related to personality may need to be included. These relate to the way a leader is likely to be perceived by his subordinates (e.g. his educational and work history, his social-class and ethnic status) and might all influence group members' reactions to him, regardless of his personal attributes and qualities. Such reactions might be considered to be prejudiced in that they are not based on the leader's behaviour, but rather on the fact that in some sense he appears to belong to another 'group' of people. Fiedler's Belgian Navy study uses this variable as an index of leader–member relations. Finally, we should emphasise that, although we believe that a fairly comprehensive description of individual characteristics will be necessary to predict leader effectiveness in a specific type of situation, such personality characteristics can be modified to a greater or lesser extent through experience and training.

These individual characteristics of the leader, which are related to effectiveness, will depend upon the situation. We do not believe that it is possible to describe adequately the situation in terms of its favourableness to the leader. What is favourable depends upon the particular group and its situation. For example, the fact that a leader has a great degree of power (type II leadership) may be unfavourable for the leader if the group of members have very democratic values and resent this imposition of power.

Again, as for individual characteristics, we believe it is necessary to describe the situation on a fairly large number of dimensions. It should then be possible to generalise about types of situations which are similar on these dimensions. For each type of situation, an ideal leader profile will exist. At least the following variables need to be taken into account: (i) the nature of the task; (ii) the group (characteristics of group members); and (iii) the external situation. We shall consider each of these variables in turn.

The nature of the task

Fiedler (1967) selects the aspect of structure of a task as being all important. By this he means the degree to which the task is spelled out step by step and the extent to which it can be done according to a detailed set of standard operating instructions. We would differentiate further between whether a task *is* spelled out in such a way and whether it *can* be. Sometimes it may be possible yet undesirable to so structure a task (e.g. because the task would be too boring or innovation would be stifled). If a task is structured already, then a leader must cope with that, but if it is not he is faced with more alternatives. This is not necessarily less favourable, but it is different. Another important task variable is its difficulty, defined as the ability requirements of group members to perform it successfully. Very difficult tasks may require a different but not necessarily more demanding leadership role from very easy ones. In the former case the role may involve developing subordinates' skills, increasing their self-confidence and best utilising members' abilities, whereas in the latter case the great problem may be in motivating subordinates to work and remain in the job.

Of particular importance may be the extent to which a task requires careful allocation of roles (i.e. subordinates must be selected and trained for appropriate tasks) and co-ordination of people in these roles. This co-ordination activity may involve the setting up of communication systems, as well as fostering team spirit, so that members want to and do help each other. Again, we believe that tasks having these requirements to a great degree will need different kinds of leaders from other tasks.

The group

Fiedler singles out leader–member relations as being the important 'group' variable in determining which leadership style will be most effective. Intra-group relationships between group members other than the leader (as in the Belgian Navy study) will also bear on the above problem. Clearly these relationships are again not simply of a favourable–unfavourable kind for the leader. They are of many different kinds, and for effectiveness different kinds of leadership style/characteristics will be required. First, the individual characteristics of each of the group members, including the leader, will be important. This is so for abilities (and hence whether the task will be easy or difficult), motivational and other personality characteristics. The personality 'mix' will be a factor, (see Chapter 13). This will help to determine the degree of intra-group conflict, dependence and cohesiveness, and these in turn will help to determine the type of leadership most likely to be effective.

Also of importance will be the values of the group members and any existing group norms. In so far as members have values and goals in common, the group will be more cohesive and have stronger norms. The leader's task will depend upon how well these group norms fit in with organisational goals. In so far as the leader has been able to select his subordinates or they to elect him, then greater cohesiveness should exist, and there should be greater compatibility in their goals. Further, member satisfaction is likely to depend upon the extent to which individual goals are satisfied within the group. Such goals may be satisfied by mere membership of a group and/or by joining in the group task. If they are not satisfied, the leader wishing to preserve the group membership must do something about satisfying such goals, for example by changing the manner in which a task is done, giving people different sub-tasks, and so on.

The external situation

By the external situation we mean those factors outside the group which influence its effectiveness. One of these is Fiedler's concept of 'position power', or, as we have called it, type II leadership. Higher authority in the organisation gives a leader certain powers over his subordinates to select them; dismiss them, reward and punish them. Whether this is weak or strong should have implications for effective leadership behaviour – also important is actual power as opposed to that which is given formally. Actual power will be in part a function of individual characteristics. The precise nature of the 'reward' and 'punishment' is also important in relation to the needs of the subordinates. For example, if subordinates do not want promotion, then the leader's power to promote will be unimportant.

Other relevant factors here might be how the leader was appointed and whether group members perceive the appointment as fair. Another factor may be more general organisational factors such as organisational structure, goals and values. Thus the leader may be expected to behave in a certain way by his superiors (role requirements), thus constraining his behaviour. He will be rewarded and punished by his superiors depending on how well he carries out these role requirements. In some situations role requirements and group norms may be in conflict, thus resulting in role strain. The leader is under pressure to adhere to group norms *and* outside organisational pressures – which may be in conflict. If they are, then the situation is very different from the case where they are not.

What we have proposed, then, is that leadership effectiveness is a function of the leader's individual characteristics, various group characteristics, and some factors of organisational functioning which impinge on group activities. We believe that groups can be divided into types using the variables we have outlined above, and that these types of groups can be further sub-divided by type of organisation, again using the variables outlined above. For each of these types of groups, we believe that a specific type of individual will be able to achieve the greatest effectiveness. Clearly the construction of a model to do justice to the wealth of variables discussed so far is a monumental task.

One further point is in order here, namely an elaboration of the concept of 'leader effectiveness'. We have suggested that group norms and larger organisational objectives may be in conflict. Now, this means that what a leader's superiors consider to be effective may not be the same as his sub-ordinates view. Broadly speaking his superiors are likely to be most concerned with task accomplishment, results and productivity, whereas subordinates might be more concerned with satisfaction, achieving their own objectives and being in a happy and stimulating work group. Sometimes effectiveness in the sense of productivity might take place at the expense of member satisfaction. This may then result in absenteeism or leaving the organisation, which in turn may lower productivity. Thus, although we noted earlier (Brayfield and Crockett, 1955) that there is no consistent relationship between satisfaction and productivity, such a relationship is quite conceivable in a specific situation. The point we are making is that effectiveness can be measured in the long or short term, and that different leadership styles may be involved in each of these. Over all, it seems reasonable to suggest that leader-ship is most effective when larger organisational goals, group norms and individual goals are all satisfied at the same time. Depending on all the variables we have outlined in our model, different situations will require different behaviour to achieve this objective. It is quite conceivable that in some situations these objectives cannot all be achieved because of incompatibility amongst them. In these cases, no individual, no matter what his super-human qualities, could be fully effective in terms of both superiors and subordinates.

In this section, therefore, we have pointed the way towards a complex contingency model of leadership. We believe that this is necessary because Fiedler's clear and simple model does not cope adequately with research evidence. This is because many important individual and situational variables need to be included in a satisfactory model.

Any kind of contingency model assumes that leaders operate according to some basic model style, which we have suggested depends on personality characteristics. However, Vroom and Yetton (1973) have emphasised the variability in the behaviour of individual leaders and the importance of the situation in determining this variability. It is to their approach to leadership that we now turn.

14.7   Recent developments

The starting-point of Vroom and Yetton's (1973) approach is the schematic representation of variables (depicted in Figure 14.2). They suggest that we need two complementary models of leadership: (i) a descriptive model (comprising items (1), (2) and (3)) in which leader behaviour is seen as a function of both personal attributes and situational variables; and (ii) a normative model (comprising items (1a), (3) and (4)) in which organisational outcomes are seen as a function of leader behaviour and situational variables.

Their descriptive model aims to describe those variables which in combina-tion generate leadership behaviour of different kinds. Their normative model is concerned with identifying those kinds of leadership behaviour which lead to a desired organisational outcome when particular sets of situational variables prevail. The normative model is in the nature of a device for choos-ing appropriate leadership styles for particular situations with particular

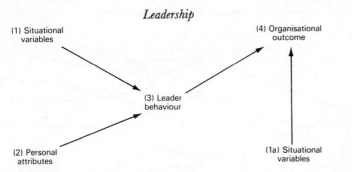

Figure 14.2   Schematic representation of variables used in leadership research (Vroom, in Dunnette, 1976)

outcomes in view. As a step towards such a normative model, Vroom and Yetton focus on one aspect of leadership behaviour, that of participation in decision-making.

They start with six assumptions which guide the development of the model: (i) leadership behaviour should be specified unambiguously; (ii) no one leadership method is applicable to all situations; (iii) the analysis of the situation should be in terms of the problem to be solved and its context; (iv) leadership methods should be changeable in relation to situation; (v) the leader can choose between a range of participative and non-participative social processes for solving organisational problems; and (vi) different leadership methods or social processes are appropriate depending on whether individual or group problems are involved.

They then go on to list five different leadership methods (decision processes) of the kind mentioned in (v) above and varying in participativeness. These range from a non-participative method ($A1$ in Figure 14.3), through gathering information from subordinates but making the decision alone ($A11$), sharing the problem with individuals but making the decision alone ($C1$), sharing the problem with the group but making the decision alone ($C11$), to sharing the problem with the group and making the decision as a group ($G1$).

Problems mentioned in (iii) above are described in terms of seven attributes. These are identified by means of the questions A–G in Figure 14.3. It has been found that managers can diagnose situations quite quickly on the basis of these seven questions. Figure 14.3 is a decision tree illustrating the process of diagnosis.

A set of seven decision rules, three protecting the quality of leadership decisions and four protecting the acceptance of the group, are then applied to the rest of the diagnosis in order to determine a feasible set of leadership methods and exclude inappropriate ones. The results of this process are shown on the right of Figure 14.3 ($A1$, $A11$, $C1$ etc.).

When there is more than one leadership method in the feasible set, other decision rules can be used, such as the number of man-hours used in problem solution, in order to arrive at the one best leadership method.

Vroom and Yetton examined the behaviour of managers by asking them to recall work problems which they had had to solve and asking them how

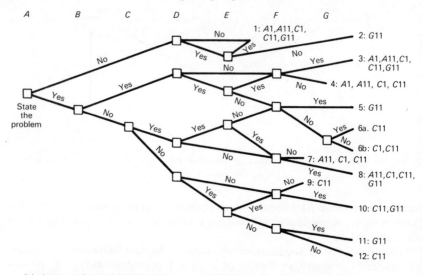

A Is there a quality requirement that one solution is likely to be more rational than another?
B Do I have sufficient information to make a high-quality decision?
C Is the problem structured?
D Is acceptance of decision by subordinates critical to effective implementation?
E If I were to make the decision by myself, is it reasonably certain that it would be accepted by my subordinates?
F Do subordinates share the organisational goals to be attained in solving this problem?
G Is conflict among subordinates likely in preferred solutions?

Figure 14.3   Decision process flow chart for group problems (Vroom, in Dunnette, 1976)

they had approached the problems with respect to the five leadership methods. From the problems recalled by the managers, Vroom and Yetton produced a standardised set of problems. They then gave the standardised set to all the managers and asked them which leadership method they would use to solve the problems. The leadership methods chosen in connection with the recalled problems were consistent with the feasible set of methods derived from the application to the problem of the decision tree of Figure 14.3 in about two-thirds of the situations, i.e. in one-third of the cases the managers broke the decision rules suggested by the model. In particular, the decision rules protecting group acceptance were prone to violation. One startling finding in this study which is contrary to common belief is that, on the standardised problems, individual differences between managers in the participativeness of the decisions chosen accounted for only about 10 per cent of the total variance in decision processes observed, and these differences were small when compared with differences within managers, i.e. individual managers use a range of decision processes but in fact differ relatively little in this connection from each other. The implication is that leader behaviour is influenced more by situational variables, such as the problem attributes, than it is by personal attributes of the leader.

The normative model has been used by Vroom and Yetton for management training by using it as a device for encouraging managers to examine their leadership styles, and for coming to a conscious appreciation of their own choice in relation to the model.

Fiedler, too, has moved his research thrust away from pure research and the elaboration of his contingency model in the direction of applying what is known so far to leadership training. He has produced a self-administered programmed manual called *Leader Match* which attempts to teach managers and others how to diagnose their leadership style and situation. The purpose is to obtain the best match between the situation and their personal style. This is done largely by modifying the situation, since Fiedler believes that personal styles of leadership are relatively firmly entrenched in the personality (Fiedler, 1976).

Validation studies of the Vroom and Yetton decision-tree approach and of Fiedler's Leader Match are now available and seem promising though they do still seem to be prey to the usual problems of validation in this field (problems of criterion, stability of results over time and lack of adequate controls).

However, lest we seem to be too disparaging, it must be said any approach which causes managers to think about the way in which they carry out their leadership role is to be welcomed as being infinitely preferable to merely instructing them in an ideology of leadership (be it task- or person-oriented) irrespective of the circumstances.

15
Organisations

15.1 Introduction

This chapter, in addition to providing an examination of various views of organisations, has as a subordinate aim the task of drawing together some of the threads which have been woven in earlier parts of the book. In particular, material will be drawn from the chapters on perception, motivation, learning and social groups. Our opinion, in company with others, e.g. Schein (1965), is that there is a direct connection between the model one adopts of basic human psychology (particularly in its motivational and perceptual aspects) and (i) the type of preferred managerial strategy in an organisation, and (ii) the kind of theoretical standpoint to be adopted in the study of the organisation. Table 15.1 indicates this.

Table 15.1   Motivation models and organisational approach

Motivational model	Rational economic man	Social man	Self-actualising man	Complex man
Managerial strategy	Scientific management	Human relations	Job enrichment, enlargement	Diagnostic
Organisational theory	Classical hierachical	Systems approach	Action approach	?

Schein (1965) argues that, historically, organisational theorists have, so to speak, moved from left to right across Table 15.1. Thus in the early part of this century Taylor (1911) emphasised the idea that money acted as a motivator, and derived from this assumption (backed up by his own studies in the U.S. Bethlehem Steel Company) that the important tools in management were the selection of money-motivated people, efficient organisation of work and the payment of high financial rewards. Certainly, by these methods Taylor was able to reduce the number of wagon loaders in the steel works from 500 to 140, while only raising the level of wages by 60 per cent. Thus from a simple assumption about human nature there evolved a particular style of management. With that came the development of concomitant techniques such as the use of financial incentives, systematic personnel selection and a hierarchical chain of command in the organisation. These ideas are discussed in more detail in Section 15.2.

Industry began to move away from this approach under the influence of the Hawthorne investigations (Roethlisberger and Dixon, 1939), in which the influence of social factors in the performance of workers was demonstrated. These studies, together with the work of the Tavistock Institute in London and the Survey Research Center at Michigan, were responsible for a new conception of the organisation as a combined social and technical system with social and technical factors influencing each other mutually. The implications for management were felt to be a concern for the social needs of the individual and the recognition of the importance of groups in the organisation. Great emphasis was laid on the concept of 'employee-orientated leadership' as opposed to the task-orientated emphasis in Taylor's 'scientific management'. On to the traditional hierarchical organisation chart (see Figure 15.1 later) were superimposed various new lines, rings and triangles indicating the social interrelationships within the organisation (e.g. Likert's (1961) overlapping group model; see Figure 15.3 later). The idea of 'social man' with its implications for management and organisation is pursued in Section 15.3.

The 1950s heralded the introduction into organisational psychology of the motivational concept of self-actualisation, derived originally from Maslow (1943) (see Chapters 6 and 7). The idea was that the highest level of motive in man was a need to extend and develop himself to his limits in his activities. This kind of activity, epitomised by the work of the creative artist in any field, is held to be uniquely satisfying. If the worker can be enabled to find this kind of meaning in his work, this should create the ideal conditions for satisfaction and productivity. So the argument went. One kind of managerial technique which was designed to meet this need involved the idea that employees should be provided with as much autonomy and responsibility as they could manage, so as to enable them to develop and 'actualise' themselves. The particular methods used involved job enlargement (the introduction of a larger number of activities into the job), job enrichment (the introduction of more challenging activities into the job) and job rotation (allowing alternation between different jobs). The aim of all of these was to keep the employee stimulated and the work from being boring and repetitive, i.e. the work should be meaningful. The equivalent theoretical formulation of the nature of the organisation can be seen in the form of a derivation from sociological symbolic interaction theory, namely action theory (see Silverman, 1970). Here, an attempt is made to get away from the idea of the organisation as a concrete entity which can in any way be seen from the outside. The way in which the organisation is conceptualised is as a function of the meaning it has for the individuals in it. Only to the extent that these meanings have something in common can the organisation be said to 'exist'. Thus, if the shared meaning it has for its employees is as a place where you have to go through some kind of ritual of working in order to be paid enough money to live comfortably, it will be one kind of organisation, and if it is generally considered an exciting and stimulating place to work, it will be another kind of organisation. It might be noted here that Vroom's (1964) expectancy theory of motivation also fits in well with this formulation, in the sense that a worker's expected outcomes in terms of organisational reward are one of the factors determining his performance. Section 15.4 is concerned with 'self-actualising man' and its implications for management and organisation theory.

These three main types of theory are still paramount in the field of organisational theory. However, currently the movement is away from single theories and towards a study of the particular determinants of organisational behaviour (e.g. Payne and Pugh, 1971). This is in line with Schein's characterisation of man as complex in his motivations. Schein suggests that the role of the manager working from this kind of conception of his employees' motivations is to be a diagnostician. His job is to diagnose which kind of motivation is predominantly operative and then to employ the appropriate managerial technique, a skill requiring considerable flexibility. It is difficult to characterise the kind of organisational model which fits this. Hence, the question mark in Table 15.1. However, what we can do at this stage is to indicate some of the difficulties in order to give an inkling of the kind of model which would be required. Burns and Stalker (1961) distinguished two kinds of organisation in terms of the manner in which they adapted to their environments. They found that 'mechanistic' organisations (ones which more or less fitted the 'Taylorian' model described above) seemed to function best in a relatively fixed and stable technological, social and economic environment, and that 'organismic' organisations (which are characterised by multiple and flexible communication channels survive best in changing environments. If we consider the internal environment (i.e. the employees' motivations) as being fixed, then clearly one of the simple models should be satisfactory, but if we view man's motivations as complex and changing, then some kind of continually changing 'organismic' model is required. Section 15.5 will indicate some of the characteristics this model needs to possess.

15.2 Rational economic man, scientific management and classical organisation theory

The idea of man as a rational animal seeking to maximise his profits is a familiar one from classical economics. The conception is of an essentially idle, passive worker who needs to be induced to work and who will not spontaneously further the ends of anyone but himself, least of all the organisation for which he is working. The only motivation he has from management's point of view is a basic motivation to earn money for his own benefit. Management, in its turn, can take advantage of this by offering the carrot of financial gain in return for labour of the kind it desires. The scientific application of this was developed in the increasingly sophisticated use of financial incentive schemes. On the grounds that the worker is unlikely to devise particularly efficient methods of working, he has to be paid more for producing more and he has to be helped by the newly developing techniques of work study and equipment design to achieve this management goal of high productivity. As a complement to these two methods of work study and financial incentives, a further technique was suggested, namely the use of systematic methods of personnel selection. Thus recognition was given to the fact that individuals differed in their work capacity. For the efficient running of the enterprise, it was important that only the most suitable were employed. This brief outline, though something of a caricature, reflects in considerable part the writings of Taylor (1911). The idea is that managers do the work for which they are best fitted, namely the fixing of work methods, pay rates, quality control, supervision and control of workers. Workers in turn do the job they are paid to do. Management and workers have the common goal of increased prosperity. Taylor goes on to speculate as to why it is that there was so much discord between the 'two sides' of industry. He suggests three main causes: (i) the mistrust of management by the workers, in particular the belief that any increase in productivity will automatically lead to unemployment; (ii) the workers' protection of their interests in this connection by restricting output; and (iii) inefficient methods of work. The solutions are those mentioned above: the development of work-study methods (or, as Taylor called them, a 'true science of work'), the selection and training of workers so that they may develop to be able to do the highest and most interesting work congruent with their abilities and the continuous close co-operation of management and workers. In present day terms this is highly simplistic. However, what does make Taylor's thinking different from that of later writers is that this co-operation is based on adherence to the ideology of 'the scientific study of work'. Both parties see constantly that their own and the others' behaviour and decisions are subject to the same discipline. This is different from a concern for human relationships at work or the personal development of the worker as an end in itself as well as a means.

There has been much criticism of Taylor's work, particularly from those with a human-relations or 'self-actualisation' orientation. Clearly it is possible to see the approach as inhuman, mechanical and showing a lack of concern or even recognition of the fact that human beings have other characteristics than those upon which Taylor focussed. Thus the approach has been criticised on the grounds that the assumptions behind the model are untrue factually (man is not solely a rational economic animal), that morally the prescriptions of scientific management show a lack of regard for the essentially human aspects of man and, finally, that the consequences of scientific management can often be that the much vaunted increased efficiency often does not materialise for the social, personal and economic reasons to which Taylor paid little or no attention. We feel that these criticisms are valid to a large extent but equally strongly we feel that this should not be allowed to undermine the positive aspects of his work, namely the recognition of the importance of work design and working methods, the importance of personnel selection and training and the beginning of the serious study of the relationship between pay and work. Perhaps the greatest testimony that can be paid to him is that he was to be the forerunner of a number of theorists and practical workers in the field of management and organisation who formed the school of 'classical' organisation theorists (e.g. Fayol, 1949; Urwick, 1947; Brech, 1957; Weber, 1947). (For a review, see Pugh, Hickson and Hinings (1971).)

What kind of organisation structure is implied by the classical theorists? In order to answer this question it is necessary to look at four variables: span of control, economies of scale, co-ordination and nature of activity. Span of control refers to the number of subordinates reporting directly to a superior. Urwick (1947) suggested that the ideal number of subordinates for a manager is four, but that at the lowest level of the organisation where the responsibility is only for performance of specific tasks, and not for the over-all supervision of others, this number may be increased up to about twelve. Brech (1957), who in general shows much greater concern for individual differences and the social aspects of work, suggests that the span of control should vary with the capacity of the particular manager. Span of control determines the number of levels in the organisation. The smaller it is, the larger is the number of of levels. Simon (1960) suggested that the number of levels in the organisation should be as few as possible, as an organisation with a large number of levels becomes cumbersome in many ways. Economies of scale (the idea that it is more economical to produce large quantities at a time than small since this reduces the portion of the unit cost attributable to overheads, etc.) can also have an influence in that as these tend towards the institution of larger units, this tends to result in an increase in the span of control. An alternative way of solving the problem could be to increase the number of units, each being looked after by a supervisor with a smaller span of control. This, however, would increase problems of co-ordination.

These kinds of issues were the life-blood of the classical organisation theorists. It can be seen that they did not propose one ideal organisational structure, though all their thinking lay within one particular conceptualisation of what the structure of business organisations was supposed to be. This structure is the hierarchical one (see Figure 15.1).

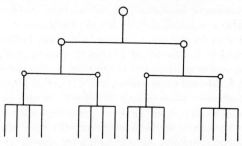

Figure 15.1　Hierarchical organisation structure

The emphasis is on the activities which need to be carried out in order to achieve the objectives of the organisation. Thus at the lowest level are the individual jobs required for production of the organisation's output. These are grouped into sections which are in turn grouped into departments. (The terminology varies from one organisation to another). These parts of the organisation are linked for purposes of co-ordination into a chain of command in such a way that each person knows what his responsibilities or job description(s) are and to whom he is responsible.

One of the advantages of this type of organisation is that so long as the organisation's environment remains the same, or at least is not subject to undue change, everyone in it knows what is required of him. This kind of organisation, which Burns and Stalker (1961) have termed 'mechanistic', is geared specifically to high production in an unchanging environment over the long term, and for this purpose it can be most effective. However, Burns and Stalker's conclusion was that in times of change another kind of organisation, the 'organismic' one, was more adaptive. Mechanistic organisations are characterised by predominantly vertical lines of communication which tend to produce a 'well-grooved' communication pattern which may have all the advantages of a successful routine but which is inflexible to the extent that it tends not to be open to new ideas and is not designed for making changes. On the other hand, the organismic type of organisation, may lack these smooth-running qualities, but the lateral communication patterns enable greater cross-fertilisation of ideas which is an asset in times of change. This is what makes the organismic organisation more likely to survive in such times. Of course, the main criticism levelled at the hierarchical view of organisations is that it does not take into account sufficiently all those aspects of human beings which are not mechanical or rational–economic. It is to these aspects that we shall now turn.

15.3 Social man, the human-relations school of management and systems theory

The evidence for man's social motivation at work comes from a variety of sources. Historically the first clear recognition emerged in the series of investigations (Roethlisberger and Dixon, 1939) which have come to be known as the Hawthorne investigations after the name of the plant where they were carried out – the Hawthorne plant of the Western Electric Company, Chicago, Illinois. In the first investigation a group of girls working in the plant were chosen to be placed in a separate room under a supervisor and their work performance was observed. The initial purpose of the research was to discover the effects of changes in variables in the working environment, in this case illumination. As the rather dull level of illumination was brightened, the girls' production went up. It continued to rise up to the point where the experimenters decided to reverse the process. As the level of illumination was reduced, production showed no signs of dropping off. Indeed, it maintained its rise to the extent that it was still high when the level of illumination was reduced below the original level. If production levels were not related to illumination, the independent variable in this experiment, to what were they related? Follow-up work in the Hawthorne plant suggested that the unrecognised independent variable was the social recognition accorded to the girls by being placed apart from the rest and being taken an interest in by the investigators. This effect, the raising of performance in response to an increase in recognition and interest from outsiders or from an unaccustomed source within the organisation, has come to be called the 'Hawthorne effect'. This conclusion arises not as direct deduction but rather by scouring the evidence for alternative explanations and concluding that this was the only factor which could account consistently for all the fluctuations in performance found in response to the other independent variables which were manipulated. For example, in the Relay Assembly Test Room (a later part of the Hawthorne investigations) for a number of aspects of the working enrivonment (e.g. rest pauses, tea breaks and length of working day), no clear-cut relationship was found between any of these and performance except that each major change had a tendency to lead to an increase in production. The only factor left, it seemed, which could account for the results had to be some kind of social factor. Further experiments in the Hawthorne series, notably the Relay Assembly Test Room, the Bank Wiring Observation Room and the Counselling Programme, testified further to the importance of these social factors in determining work performance (Roethlisberger and Dixon, 1939).

To illustrate the way in which these social factors were investigated, we shall describe the Bank Wiring Observation Room (B.W.O.R.) study.

Fourteen men were placed in a separate room where they were studied by an observer who was present in the room. Their work was to wire up banks of electrical equipment which other members of the group then soldered. The final product was then inspected by two inspectors. After initially getting used to the presence of the observer in the room, the group began to settle down to a normal working routine. Five main results emerged from this study.

(1) There was no 'Hawthorne effect'. Indeed, as we shall see, the social forces in this situation acted in a different direction. Many reasons for this have been put forward, and it is likely that a combination of factors was involved, but here we shall mention a few only. The subjects of investigation in the earlier experiments were women, whereas those in the B.W.O.R. were men. The part played by work in the lives of women was probably different from that for men. It was certainly the case for young women, work was very often a necessary evil to be suffered until they got married, and for the married women work took a subordinate place to their households. For only a small proportion of women did work have the integral position in their life style that it does for men. On these grounds, therefore, it might be expected that extraneous influences like the presence of an observer and being singled out for observation might have a disproportionate influence. For the men, other considerations had more influence, e.g. a fear that to increase production would threaten their current pay rates, and, in the final instance, their jobs, for these experiments were carried out in times of deepening economic depression. Thus the fact that work has been less anchored in the way of life of women might make them more amenable to the Hawthorne effect. We are not saying that this is necessarily the primary cause of the results. Indeed, it is possible that if the B.W.O.R. had been studied first, i.e. at a less economically depressed time, the results might have been similar to those for the girls. What we are suggesting is that the Hawthorne effect has important implications for leadership in that a feeling of participation in something new does seem to make people work harder, provided that other factors are not restraining them.

(2) The B.W.O.R. group did feel a certain identity as a group, but a particularly interesting feature was the way in which it formed into two cliques who differentiated themselves in terms of status. The clique at the front felt

itself to be of higher status than the clique at the back because the banks of equipment on which they were working were more difficult. Each clique had its own ways of interacting and spending the breaks. There was a certain amount of competitition between the groups in the form of verbal sparring.

(3) The entire group resistricted its output below what it could have achieved had it tried to produce more. There was a norm of 6000 units per day which was enforced to prevent 'rate-busting' (producing too much) and 'chiselling' (producing too little). The means of enforcement ranged from mild warnings and looks to physical violence. A particurlar delicacy in this connection was the procedure of 'binging'. This involved a blow to the sensitive part of the side of the upper arm adjacent to the biceps with the protruding clenched knuckle of the middle finger of the fist. The effect was to immobilise the arm temporarily, which could be expected to slow down the rate-buster, and bruise bone and muscle sufficiently to make it more sensitive for the next time. In learning-theory terms, an 'avoidance-conditioning' procedure was used.

Another norm of the group was that inspectors must not pull rank or act officiously. One inspector, who infringed this norm, was ostracised and had all kinds of tricks played on him. In the end he asked for a transfer. The other inspector conformed and was accepted.

(4) It has been said that a norm of 6000 units was established and this is the figure that the men reported as their daily production figure. In fact this was seldom what they actually produced on any one day. Their habit was to average 6000 units, and therefore to produce more on some days than others. For example, they would often produce a lot more one day in order to have a slack day the next, or have a slack day and then catch up the next. Other acts of disobedience to company policy included the trading of jobs (wiremen doing soldering and vice versa) and the supervisor allowing the men to do their own production reporting instead of doing it himself.

(5) The high-status group produced more than the low-status group, and viewed the low-status group as chisellers, whereas the low-status group resented being looked down upon and the only way they could 'get their own back' was by irritating the others by producing less. This helped further the existing restrictions of output.

Sufficient has been said by now to indicate the variety of social forces which were observed in action in the Hawthorne investigations. Obviously this short review cannot do justice to the seminal influence of these important investigations, which, because of their complexity and the lack of clarity of their conclusions, have been criticised for the way in which they failed to control important variables.

The other, now classical, evidence for social man comes from the Tavistock coal-mining studies (Trist and Bamforth, 1951). The latter investigated the effects on the social structure of an existing organisation of introducing technological change. The existing method of mining coal, known as the 'short-wall method', involved small groups of up to eight men working very closely together on a small area of the coal face. In the team were face-cutters, their mates and the labourers, whose job was to get the coal away from the face in tubs. The strong interdependence of these men continued not only at the face but also in their outside lives. Coal-mining is a dangerous job and these small groups served to contain all the ensuing emotions, from frustrations leading to hostility and fights between members to emotional support in times of anxiety, death and injury. Competition and hostility between groups also served as an emotional outlet after, for example, one group had taken possession of the best part of the coal face, or more than its fair share of tubs.

The new method, which theoretically should have produced more coal in a shorter time, failed rather quickly. It involved the use of mechanical coal-cutting equipment which required the miners to work in teams of about forty to fifty spread out over some 200 yards in low narrow tunnels in such a way that supervision was virtually impossible, and the close relationships between the men working together in close proximity on a regular basis which had previously sustained efficiency could be maintained no longer. In addition, such a high level of co-ordination was required within these large groups that it was not possible to maintain it. Deficiencies in one part of the group had their effect in reducing the output of the entire group, with no possibility of adequate communication. The dangers of the work still provoked the same emotions but without the possibility of release in the small group. The consequence was a norm of restricted output and feelings of meaninglessness on the part of the miners. The so-called 'human-relations school' of management theorists derived their philosophy from the kind of evidence found in the Hawthorne and Tavistock investigations.

The assumption that man is an animal with social needs is seen to imply that management must recognise this in the way it manages. Bales and Slater (1955) distinguished the task-orientated leader from the social-emotional leader. Many others have produced similar if not equivalent classifications (see Chapter 14). The recognition of man's social needs implies not only attention to the task but to the needs of employees. Instead of concern of the classical theorists for motivating and controlling employees, the human-relations school is concerned with the workers' feelings of identity with the organisation through the satisfaction of their social needs. In exchange-theory terms (see Chapter 13) the reward to the employee from this satisfaction offsets the cost of harder work. The stress is on involvement with the organisation.

The human-relations school does not neglect money. However, the approach is different to that of the 'scientific managers'. No longer is the individual incentive of money stressed, but instead the emphasis is on group incentives. In this way it is felt that the group is recognised for its contribution in being more than the sum of the individuals which comprise it. Hence the social forces are stimulated further in the direction of organisational goals.

Thus the manager takes on a far more sympathetic role. He is now, if not yet the friend of the worker, then something approaching it. Payne and Pugh (1971) call it 'bureaucracy with a smile'. Instead of being a motivator and controller, he becomes a facilitator of the desire of the worker to play his part in a kind of psychological contract to which he has consented.

The Tavistock studies show how it is possible for management to alienate employees through the imposition of, for example, new technology, which disrupts their social relationships and leads them to form norms which run contrary to those of management. Coch and French (1948) (see Chapter 13) have shown how it is possible to overcome resistance to new work methods and anti-management norms through participation and recognition of the feelings of the workers. The ideology of the human-relations school is that if management can satisfy the social needs of workers, then workers will respond by identifying with organisational goals. In other words, their norms will be in line with, as opposed to being against, those of management.

We are now in a position to derive an organisational theory from the kinds of issues which have emerged in connection with seeing man as a social animal. The way in which work and social relationships are seen to interact must cast doubt on the adequacy of the type of straight-line hierarchical model put forward by the classical theorists. This need for some reference to factors other than the purely technical aspects of the organisation seemed to require immediately devised appendages to the basic model. A distinction had long been made between the formal and informal aspects of the organisation (e.g. getting what you want through the regular channels or through influence with a particular friend, the tendency for messages not to be passed through a particularly difficult person). The systems approach to organisation was to be the answer to these difficulties.

Basically the systems approach is very simple. However, like all good simple ideas, it is capable of many refinements in order to take account of the untidiness of the real world. Basically a system has an input, a processing system and an output (see Figure 15.2). In the case of, say, a biscuit factory the inputs are flour, sugar, butter and the other raw materials which go into the

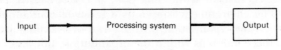

Figure 15.2   A simple system

making of biscuits. The processing system includes both the equipment used to make the biscuits and the people who operate the equipment and inspect the process as well as the managers. The product is the finished biscuit.

Most of the systems models put forward by human-relations theorists have in common the idea of organisations comprising two overlapping systems. In the case of what Schein (1965) has called the 'Tavistock model (after the Tavistock Institute where the model was conceived), these are called the social system, which is the system of social relationships prevailing between all those involved in the processing system, and the technical system, which inclues raw materials, equipment, machinery and the work environment. Trist *et al.* (1963) call this combination of systems a 'socio-technical system'. The social system influences and determines the technical system and vice versa.

A very similar conceptualisation is put forward by Homans (1950), except that he calls his interdependent systems the 'external' and 'internal' systems. These are slightly different from social and technical systems in that the external system includes not only technical aspects of the organisation but also the social interactions directly required by the technical system. The internal system comprises the informal interrelationships thrown up by the external system which in turn influence it.

We shall end this section with a discussion of what has been a very in-fluential model. Likert's overlapping work group model (1961). This is a development of the Homans–Tavistock thinking in that Likert conceptualises organisations as systems of interlocking groups superimposed on, and reacting with, a formal hierarchical system (as in Figure 15.3). An interesting feature

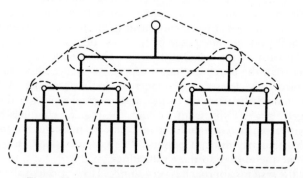

Figure 15.3   Likert's (1961) overlapping group structure

is his emphasis on the individuals who are members of two overlapping groups. For example, the foreman is both part of management and part of the shop-floor. As such he is the 'link pin', as Likert calls it, between these two groups. The environment is seen as a series of overlapping groups or systems of which the organisation, with its own overlapping groups, is part. Not only are there link pins within the organisation, but also link pins who connect the organisation with the outside environment. An example of these might be the public-relations officer who is, say, a member of Parliament or a journalist as well. Likert's view is that in the ideal organisation the link pins use a facilitative and supportive style of leadership (best human-relations style) in the interests of meeting the needs of the subordinates or the public and hence fostering an identification with the organisation. Dubin (1961), however, argues that participative management carried to an extreme can involve so much participative activity in the form of committees and meetings that it is often slow and wasteful. Yet Likert does state that care should be taken that people should not be asked to participate beyond their need and expectation to do so. Indeed, Tannenbaum *et al.* (1961) suggest further limitations to group decision-making in that they feel that where time is pressing or where it is not cost effective it is inapplicable (see also Vroom and Yetton's approach, Chapter 14).

We have not done justice to the full nature of the systems approach, in particular in its mathematical and communication theory aspects (see, for example, Berrien, 1976). However, the interested reader might care to read or reread the section on communication networks (Chapter 13) and speculate on the way in which communication systems in the organisation as a whole might affect morale and performance.

15.4 Self-actualising man, work design and the action approach

After Jung the psychologist who really gave the term 'self-actualisation' wide usage was Maslow (1954, 1962) (see Chapter 6). Here, we shall have a look at some of the experimental work carried out by Maslow and others concerning the concept. What Maslow (1954) did was to study a large number of students and pick out those who best represented what he had in mind as self-actualisers. He also made a study of famous people such as Lincoln, Einstein and Eleanor Roosevelt. Having studied both samples he arrived at a composite picture of what a self-actualising person was. Fifteen main items were involved, such as good reality contact and perception, a comfortable relation with it, acceptance of self and others, spontaneity and continued freshness of appreciation, a resistance to being totally absorbed by one's culture and the ability to see beyond it and act accordingly.

Maslow suggested that his self-actualising students were healthier mentally than the rest of the population, and there is evidence that people who score high on a dogmatism scale (who are too inflexible to be self-actualising) also seem to be less perceptive in certain respects. Kaplan and Singer (1963) found a -0.61 correlation between dogmatism and sensory actuity as measured in the laboratory. Knapp (1965), using a self-actualisation questionnaire, found that the self-actualisers tended to score low on a neuroticism questionnaire, supporting Maslow's idea that self-actualisers are healthier mentally. Maslow's (1959) later attempts at identifying self-actualisers centred around the idea he developed that self-actualisers have more 'peak experiences' than other people. Peak experiences are characterised by happiness and fulfilment. They are temporary, non-striving, non-self-centred, purposeful, self-validating personal events which are perfectly and totally satisfying. They have qualities such as wholeness, effortlessness, aliveness, perfection, goodness, beauty and truth. They can occur in any sphere of human activity and endeavour.

Writers on self-actualisation in relation to work are referring to something less exotic and certainly much less interesting. The evidence, it must be said, for the existence of self-actualisation of Maslow's kind in the world of work is scarce. Certainly it is interesting that none of Maslow's sample found it in an organisation, unless the United States can be said to be an organisation. It is probably no accident that the main study which provides evidence for self-actualisation at work (Herzberg *et al.*, 1959) was carried out on professional workers, engineers and accountants (see Chapter 8). To recap briefly, Herzberg *et al.*, in their study of engineers and accountants, found different kinds of factors to be responsible when people felt good about their work from when they felt bad about it. The 'motivators' (responsibility, achievement, autonomy, and so on) were involved when people felt good about their jobs. These factors are clearly related to personal growth and self-actualisation. The 'hygiene factors' (things like salary, working conditions, security, supervision, and so on) were involved when they felt bad about their jobs. The presence of a satisfactory level of the hygiene factors was enough to remove dissatisfaction, but not to create positive satisfaction. What interests us here are the motivators. Clearly they have an important part to play in working life for at least some people. Pelz and Andrews (1966) report that for scientists in research organisations productivity and creativity go closely together with challenge, job accomplishment and autonomy. As Schein (1965) says, 'some degree of autonomy is probably crucial because it permits a person to set some of the dimensions of his task and thus to provide for himself an appropriate level of challenge'.

The reader will see that the self-actualising man thesis is much less well established than that of the social-man theory. In any case the concept has been attenuated from Maslow's original version. Yet it is still worth noting that all the evidence used to support the social-man thesis can also be used indirectly to support that of self-actualising man. Participation in an organisation can satisfy self-actualisation needs as well as social ones.

If we can accept the assumption of man as a self-actualising being, what does this mean for the manager? It means several different things and certainly a shift away from the techniques advocated under both the rational economic man and social-man assumptions. The possibility of self-actualisation in work means a shift away from the idea that management has to offer certain kinds of extrinsic rewards (e.g. financial and social ones), as under the two other ideologies, in exchange for work. Instead, the rewards are to be found in the work itself. The manager is therefore concerned primarily with making the work as interesting and satisfying as possible and arranging for it to have meaning for the individual worker. This will mean a constant effort to discover what has meaning and challenge for a particular worker and the attempt to introduce this into his work situation. More than ever, the manager becomes a facilitator providing for the employee a path to self-fulfilment through work. A corollary is that if management attempts to operate in a different way (e.g. by 'motivating and controlling'), the individual's self-esteem will be threatened and he will feel that he is not trusted to exercise the kind of autonomy and responsibility he would like. Like the child who is frustrated in the attempt to explore and develop, he will behave in an infantile, or at least less mature, manner and will show his hostility by acting as though he has no initiative, waiting to be led, restricting output or by dumb insolence.

This is a management ideology which more than any of the others so far mentioned, requires trust on the part of management. For more even than in the case of the human-relations approach, the manager must give up some of his traditional authority. If autonomy and responsibility are to be exercised by the worker, the manager must give up at least some of his controlling functions. The implication is that, though the amount of power in the organisation remains the same, it is not concentrated in the hands of management but shared between management and workers. Leavitt (1963) calls this 'power equalisation'. This aspect of the approach has been one of the major obstacles to its implementation. A manager does not like to give up the power he has even though he may be more likely to achieve his goals through the voluntary, autonomous co-operation of his subordinates.

Although the true flavour of this approach lies in the general readiness of the manager to be sensitive to the self-actualisation needs of his subordinates on a more or less individual basis, some more generalised methods of introducing meaning into work have been attempted. These go under the headings of 'job enlargement', 'job enrichment' and 'job rotation'. Division of labour, brought about by mass-production techniques, causes workers to repeat the same activities. Various researchers have noted the human cost of this in terms of lower job satisfaction, poor performance or both (e.g. Walker and Guest, 1952; Wyatt and Marriott, 1956; Argyris, 1964; Friedman, 1961; Kornhauser, 1965). Fiske and Maddi (1961) have even noted the similarities between highly restricted assembly-line jobs and sensory-deprivation experiments in which the subjects are cut off from all sensory stimulation (blindfolded, ears plugged, hands muffed with fingers separated and kept in a blood-temperature bath). Fiske and Maddi recognise similarities in the adverse psychological reactions of both groups. Ways of introducing meaning can be to enlarge the job, thus providing more variety, to rotate workers round jobs and increase variety on a longer time scale, or to enrich the job by making it more meaningful and giving it more depth. Friedman (1961), reporting on several job-enlargement projects, notes various positive benefits including improvements in quality, increased satisfaction, increased productivity and decreased absenteeism. Lawler (1969) suggests, however, that an increase in quality is a more likely consequence than an increase in quantity, and, in his review, can find only four studies where increases in quantity are reported. Increasingly, however, research (e.g. Alderfer, 1967) is showing that job-enlargement programmes can produce a deterioration in relationships (e.g. between superiors and subordinates). This may be because the superiors felt their jobs to be threatened by the increase in power of the subordinates to determine their own fate. The current conclusion can only be that where such programmes actually do increase the meanignfulness of the work (as opposed to simply giving people more boring work or another boring job to do in addition to their own), there can be considerable benefits. However, care must be taken to look out for any consequent disturbances in the social relationships in the organisation and these must then be dealt with. Good reviews of this field are to be found in Argyris (1973), Birchall and Wild (1973) and Warr and Wall (1975).

It is in principle possible to advocate a systems-type model of organisation which would take into account the relationship between management and workers advocated by the human-growth school (self-actualisation) outlined above. However, it would not directly do justice to the major concept here, that of the 'meaningfulness' of the work situation to the worker. The only kind of model which actually deals in terms such as 'meaningfulness' is some kind of action model (e.g. Silverman, 1971). The action approach derives from symbolic interactionism, a sociological approach in which the essential feature is that all events, institutions and relationships are seen in terms of what they mean to the perceiver. Reality consists of the interactions of the worlds of symbolisation and meaning of the individuals concerned. Thus an organisation may only be said to exist in the sense that the individuals concerned with it actually perceive it as an organisation, and the characteristics it possesses may only be said to exist in the sense that they are the shared perceptions of the perceivers, i.e. that the perceivers attribute the same meaning to them. This may seem vague, and, indeed, does not constitute a theory of organisation. Both Silverman (1971) and Cohen (1968) stress this. As Silverman states, 'it is best understood as a method of analysing social relations within organisations'. He goes on to suggest a path along which the analysis of organisations might proceed. He suggests an examination of six interrelated areas in the following order:

1. The nature of the role-system and pattern of interaction that has been built up in the organisation, in particular the way in which it has historically developed and the extent to which it represents the shared values of all or some or none of the actors.
2. The nature of involvement of ideal-typical actors (e.g. moral, alienative, instrumental) and the characteristic hierarchy of ends which they pursue (work satisfaction, material rewards, security). The way in which these derive from their biographies outside the organisations (job history, family commitments, social background' and from their experience of the organisation itself.
3. The actors' present definitions of their situation within the organisation and their expectations of the likely behaviour of others with particular reference to the strategic resources they perceive to be at their own disposal and at the disposal of others (degree of coercive power or moral authority; belief in individual opportunity).
4. The typical actions of different actors and the meaning which they attach to their action.
5. The nature and source of the intended and unintended consequences of action, with special reference to its effects on the involvement of the various actors and on the institutionalisation of expectation in the role-system within which they interact.
6. Changes in the involvement and ends of the actors and in the role-system, and their source both in the outcome of the interaction of the actors and in the changing stock of knowledge outside the organisation (e.g. political or legal changes; the varied experiences and expectations of different generations) (Silverman, 1971).

It can be seen immediately that there is a clear philosophical split between the action approach and the earlier approaches referred to. The key point of conflict is, as can be seen from the following quotation from Dawe (1970), whether action is the derivative of systems or vice versa:

'There are . . . two sociologies: a sociology of social system and a sociology of social action. They are grounded in the diametrically opposed corners with two central problems, those of order and control. And, at every level, they are in conflict. They posit antithetical views of human nature, of society, and of the relationship between the social and the individual. The first asserts the paramount necessity for societal and individual well-being of external constraint; hence the notion of a social system ontologically and methodologically prior to its participants. The key notion of the second is that of autonomous man, able to realise his full potential and to create a truly human social order only when freed from external constraint. Society is thus the creation of its members; the product of their construction of meaning, and of the action and relationships through which they attempt to impose that meaning on their historical situations. In summary, one views action as the derivative of system, whilst the other views system as the derivative of action' (Dawe, 1970).

Silverman (1971) criticises systems theory on the grounds that it involves the reification (the objectification) of something which is in fact no more than a conceptual construct. The conceptualisation of an organisation as a system does not confer upon that conceptualisation the characteristics of an object which thinks, moves and acts in the real world. Many other conceptualisations are possible. Can they also have the same characteristics? If so, which one is *the* organisation? It is not the conceptualisation which is the subject of study but the organisation. Silverman criticises the view which he attributes to Bennis (1966) and Schein (1965) that organisations are natural systems subject to health and disease and undergoing unconscious processes to ensure survival and adaptation. What is, after all, only (in action-theory terms) a social construct cannot think and act. The only sense in which it can be said to do so is in so far as what the organisation means to the individuals concerned forms some kind of consensus and their actions have some kind of common interlocking unity.

15.5 Complex man and diagnostic management

The paradigm of natural science requires as much economy of explanation as possible. Regrettably the search so far for a simple yet comprehensive model of man in organisation has not yielded any view which turns out to be better than the rest. Each applies very well to its own particular area of relevance: rational economic man to the field of incentive schemes, where it is found that, other things being equal, people do work harder for more money; social man to the field of social relationships at work, where it is found that social factors, other things being equal, do influence productivity and satisfaction at work; self-actualising man to the field of job design, where other things being equal, it is found that the more meaningful the job, the more likely are job satisfaction and improved quality, if not necessarily greater productivity, to ensue. The operative phrase is 'other things being equal'. If the other factors in man's make-up are not engaged, or in some other way are held constant, then each one of these is likely to be influential. However, other things rarely are equal. Thus it is that we are left with the conclusions that all of the 'men' so far presented represent but part of man the complex being.

As with the other 'men' we shall now look for the evidence which directly points to complexity. The fact that there is positive evidence for all the earlier conceptualisations goes some way to enabling us to draw such a conclusion.

However, over and above this we have evidence that men differ, both from each other in their predominant motivations and within themselves, depending on the time and place. Thus Zalesnik *et al.* (1958) report that, in a study of some fifty workers in a medium-sized organisation, deviants producing above the mean for the group tended to be somewhat lower in social motivation than the conformers, or else their main motivations lay elsewhere. In any case this group of workers did not aspire to group membership. This was contrasted with deviants and isolates who did aspire to group membership. These people tended to produce at a level below the group norms. Similar findings are reported by Whyte (1955). Actual behaviour seems to depend on which particular kind of motivation is dominant. Vroom (1964), in a study of motivation in management, found that sales and personnel managers have strong social and affiliative needs, whereas production managers tend to have strong needs to work with mechanical things. Also, the higher the level of management, the more likely that self-actualisation and personal-growth needs are to be involved. A further line of thought which opens the subject up even wider derives from Gellerman (1963). He has pointed out that a particular kind of reward may have different meanings for different people. Thus money may represent security, achievement, power, luxury or social opportunities, depending on the individual. Even the fact that a person responds to a particular kind of incentive is insufficient evidence that a particular motive is operating. A combination of factors may be responsible.

Man is complex in his motivation. Schein (1965) suggests that 'perhaps the most important implication is that the successful manager must be a good diagnostician and must value a spirit of inquiry'. If his work-force is such a mixture of motivations and abilities, he must be able to identify these. He must then have the flexibility to alter his behaviour to suit the situation he finds. In a word, he needs all the skills of the scientific manager, the human-relations manager and the personal-growth and development manager combined.

If the manager has to have a variety of skills then both the prescibed model of organisation and the conceptual framework need to be able to contain this flexibility. The point is that, even though an organisation may have all the hallmarks of a traditional hierarchical one of a mechanistic kind, and though the role played by 'informal' motivations, communication processes, and so on may not be playing a great part, in that employees are satisfied, producing well and the organisation is doing well in its environment, these factors still exist, and we need an analytical model to contain them. Two possible solutions exist: (i) the action approach, which as we have noted already makes no claim to constituting a general theory of organisations; and (ii) some highly sophisticated form of systems approach, which for reasons already suggested is likely to fall well short of satisfactoriness. Quite apart from the arguments of the action theorists against the systems approach, it seems likely that such are the complexities of the interactions between human motivation, organisational and environmental variables that even the most sophisticated system model is unlikely to be satisfactory. Paradoxically both systems and action approaches seem at present to have reached very similar points in that their research efforts are not directed towards testing any kind of general theoretical propositions; rather, their respective theoretical frameworks determine simply the kinds of empirical research to be undertaken. Thus Payne and Pugh (1971) present what they call 'a framework for conceptualising behaviour in organisations' (see Figure 15.4).

Each unit of analysis is a separate open system which acquires inputs such as raw materials or clients (in the case of a service organisation), processes these in some way by the use of an appropriate combination of labour and equipment and produces an output in the form of some product or service. These outputs in turn feed back into the organisation in the form of reputation, environmental hazard, or whatever. As can be seen from Figure 15.4, each unit contains boxes labelled 'aims and resources' and 'structure and processes'. These interact with each other constantly, as do the variables within each box. The interested reader might care to identify some of the features of earlier systems approaches – socio-technical systems, internal and external systems and overlapping groups – within this more complex framework. An interesting point to note here is that the organisation is seen as comprising a series of inter-reacting sub-systems each of which contains its own 'micro systems'. Payne and Pugh (1971) argue that in this way the need is shown for explanatory propositions which combine both sociological and psychological frameworks. Thus psychological factors would seem to play most part in the lower-level units of analysis, whereas sociological factors might play a greater part in the higher-level units, even though each continue to play their role at the other levels.

As can be seen, this 'framework' owes much to systems theory, but the interests of simplicity and generality prevent it from providing any tight hypothetico-deductive basis from which to make detailed predictions which can be tested empirically. Such a model simply presupposes that each part will have an influence on other parts, and inasmuch as this is so the model is validated. However, the exact nature of these interrelationships is not specified and it is left to the individual researcher to specify what his hypothesis is, to test it and then to fit the conclusions into the framework. The framework itself is not a theory of organisation in the same sense that the action approach is not a theory of organisation. It provides, however, a way of thinking about organisations which does stimulate the kind of research needed to fill the various boxes and lines in it with empirical generalisations. As such, it does fulfill, as does action theory, one of the minimum criteria for a theory put forward in Chapter 1.

If everything is as complex and changing as all this, perhaps there is only one kind of organisation from which fits the needs of both complex man and complex environment, Burns and Stalker's organismic types. This, viewed from a different angle, might easily provide the significant meaning for the individuals concerned which, for the action theorist, determines the satisfactoriness of an 'organisation'. Yet, as Burns and Stalker show, mechanistic organisations do well if the conditions under which they operate are relatively static. Further, the work of various authors indicates that there are likely to be individuals who might not fit well into an organismic type of organisation. For example, Vroom (1960) has shown that people with authoritarian personalities do not fit in well with participative leadership. They prefer to be

Social aspects of organisations

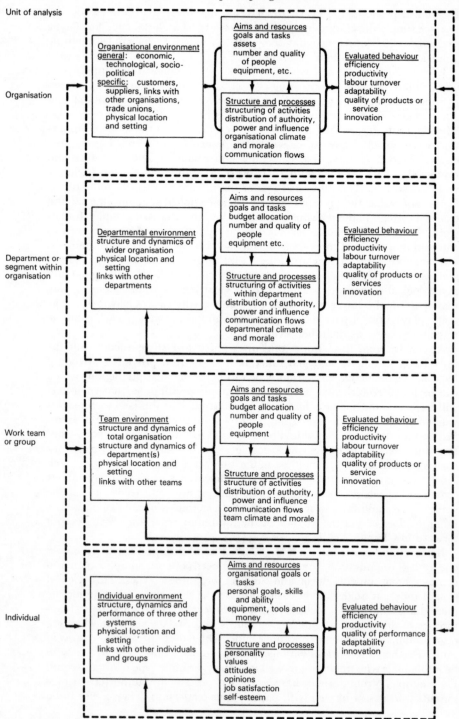

Unit of analysis

Organisation

Department or segment within organisation

Work team or group

Individual

Figure 15.4   A framework for the study of behaviour in organisations (Payne and Pugh, 1971)

told what they have to do in a clear manner. They need to know where they stand.

As Payne and Pugh suggest, there is no universally best organisation model. The need is to identify which type of organisation fits best into which environmental slot. Similarly, we need to determine into which type of organisational slot each individual best fits. (The reader who is interested in a fuller review of this whole area is directed to Payne and Pugh (1976).)

Bibliography

Abelson, R. P. and Rosenberg, M. J. (1958) 'Symbolic Psycho-logic: a model of attitudinal cognition', *Behavioral Science*, vol. 3, pp. 1–13.

Adams, J. S. (1963) 'Toward an Understanding of Inequity', *Journal of Abnormal and Social Psychology*, vol. 67, pp. 422–36.

Adams, J. S. (1965) 'Injustice to Social Change', in *Advances in Experimental Social Psychology*, ed. Berkowitz, L., vol. 2 (New York, Academic Press).

Adams, J. S. and Rosenbaum, W. B. (1962) 'The Relationship of Worker Productivity to Cognitive Dissonance about Wage Inequalities', *Journal of Applied Psychology*, vol. 46, pp. 161–4.

Adorno, T. W., Frenkel-Brunswik, E., Levinson, D. J. and Sanford, R. N. (1950) *The Authoritarian Personality* (New York, Harper & Row).

Alderfer, C. P. (1969) 'An Empirical Test of a New Theory of Human Needs', *Organizational Behavior and Human Performance*, vol. 4, pp. 142–75.

Alderfer, C. P. (1972) *Existence, Relatedness and Growth: human needs in organizational settings* (New York, Free Press).

Allport, G. W. and Postman L. P. (1947) *The Psychology of Rumor* (New York, Holt).

American Society of Heating, Refrigeration and Air-Conditioning Engineers Handbook of Fundamentals (1967) (New York, A.S.H.R.A.E.)

Anastasi, A. (1956) 'Intelligence and Family Size', *Psychology Bulletin*, vol. 53, pp. 187–209.

Anastasi, A. (1968) *Psychological Testing*, 3rd edn. (New York, Macmillan).

Andrews, I. R. (1967) 'Wage Inequity and Job Performance: an experimental study', *Journal of Applied Psychology*, vol. 51, pp. 39–49.

Annett, J. (1966) 'Training for Perceptual Skills', *Ergonomics*, vol. 9, pp. 459–68.

Annett, J. (1969) *Feedback and Human Behaviour* (Harmondsworth, Penguin).

Annett, J. (1970) 'Notes and Comments: the role of action feedback in the acquisition of simple motor responses', *Journal of Motor Behavior*, vol. 2, pp. 217–21.

Annett, J. (1971) 'Acquisition of skill', *British Medical Bulletin*, vol. 27 (3), p. 266.

Annett, J. and Duncan, K. D. (1967) 'Task Analysis and Training Design', *Occupational Psychology*, vol. 41, pp. 211–21.

Annett, J. and Duncan, K. D. (1970) 'Breaking down the Task' *Personnel Management*, n.s., vol. 2 (5), pp. 28–34.

Annett, J., Duncan, K. D., Stammers, R. B. and Gray, G. J. (1971) *Task Analysis*, Training Information Paper No. 6, Department of Employment (London, H.M.S.O.).

Annett, J. and Kay H. (1956) 'Skilled Performance', *Occupational Psychology*, vol. 30, pp. 112–17.

Arbous, A. G. and Maree, J. (1951) 'Contributions of Two Group Discussion Techniques to a Validated Test Battery', *Occupational Psychology*, vol. 25, pp. 73–89.

Argyle, M. (1967) *The Psychology of Interpersonal Behaviour* (Harmondsworth, Penguin).

Argyle, M. (1969) *Social Interaction* (London, Methuen).

Argyle, M., Gardner, G. and Cioffi, F. (1958) 'Supervisory Methods Related to Productivity, Absenteeism and Labour Turnover', *Human Relations*, vol. 11, pp. 23–40.

Argyle, M. and Kendon, A. (1967) 'The Experimental Analysis of Social Performance', *Advances in Experimental Psychology*, vol. 3, ed. Berkowitz, L. (New York, Academic Press).

Argyle, M. and McHenry, R. (1971) 'Do Spectacles Really Affect our Judgements of Intelligence?', *British Journal of Social and Clinical Psychology*, vol. 10, pp. 27–9.

Argyris, C. (1964) *Integrating the Individual and the Organisation*, (New York, Wiley).

Argyris, C. (1968) 'Some Unintended Consequences of Rigorous Research', *Psychology Bulletin*, vol. 70, pp. 185–97.

Argyris, C. (1973) 'Personality and Organisation Theory Revisited', *Administrative Science Quarterly*, vol. 18, pp. 141–67.

Aronfreed, J. M., Messick, S. A. and Diggery, J. C. (1953) 'Re-examining Personality and Perceptual Defense', *Journal of Personality*, vol. 21, pp. 517–28.

Aronson, E. and Carlsmith, J. M. (1963) 'Effect of the Severity of Threat on the Valuation of Forbidden Behavior', *Journal of Abnormal and Social Psychology*, vol. 66, pp. 584–88.

Aronson, E., Carlsmith, J. M. and Darley, J. M. (1963) 'The Effects of Expectancy on Volunteering for an Unpleasant Experience', *Journal of Abnormal and Social Psychology*, vol. 66, pp. 220–24.

Aronson, E. and Mills, J. (1959) 'The Effect of Severity of Initiation on Liking for a Group', *Journal of Abnormal and Social Psychology*, vol. 59, pp. 177–81.

Aronson, E., Turner, J. and Carlsmith, J. M. (1963) 'Communicator Credibility and Communication Discrepancy', *Journal of Abnormal and Social Psychology*, vol. 67, pp. 31–6.

Arvey, R. D. (1972) 'Task Performance as a Function of Perceived Effort–Performance and Performance–Reward Contingencies', *Organizational Behavior and Human Performance*, vol. 8, pp. 423–33.

Asch, S. E. (1946) 'Forming Impressions of Personality', *Journal of Abnormal and Social Psychology*, vol. 41, pp. 258–90.

Asch, S. E. (1952) *Social Psychology* (Englewood Cliffs, N.J., Prentice-Hall).

Asch, S. E. (1958) 'Effects of Group Pressure upon the Modification and Distortion of Judgments', in *Readings in Social Psychology*, 3rd edn, ed. Maccoly, E. E., Newcombe, T. M. and Hartley, E. L. (New York, Holt, Rinehart & Winston).

Aschoff, J. (1969) 'Desynchronization and Resynchronization of the Human Circadian Rhythm', *Aerospace Medicine*, vol. 40, pp. 844–9.

Ashour, A. S. (1973) 'The Contingency Model of Leadership Effectiveness: an evaluation', *Organizational Behavior and Human Performance*, vol. 9, pp. 339–55.

Atkinson, J. W. (1953) 'The Achievement Motive and the Recall of Interrupted and Completed Tasks', *Journal of Experimental Psychology*, vol. 46, pp. 381–90.

Atkinson, J. W. (1958) 'Towards Experimental Analysis of Motives, Expectations and Incentives', in *Motives in Fantasy, Action and Society*, ed. Atkinson, J. W., (New York, Van Nostrand).

Atkinson, J. W. (1964) *An Introduction to Motivation* (New York, Van Nostrand).

Atkinson, R. C. (1974) 'Teaching Children to Read Using a Computer', *American Psychologist*, vol. 29, pp. 169–78.

Ayllon, T. and Haughton, E. (1964) 'Modification of the Symptomatic Verbal Behavior of Mental Patients', *Behavior Research and Therapy*, vol. 2, pp. 87–97.

Backman, C. W. and Secord, P. F. (1959) 'The Effect of Perceived Liking on Interpersonal Attraction', *Human Relations*, vol. 12, pp. 379–84.

Backman, C. W. and Secord, P. F. (1962) 'Liking, Selective Interaction and Misperception in Congruent Interpersonal Relations', *Sociometry*, vol. 25, pp. 321–35.

Baddeley, A. D. and Levy, B. A. (1971) 'Semantic Coding and Short-term Memory', *Journal of Experimental Psychology*, vol. 89, pp. 132–6.

Bales, R. F. (1950) *Interaction Process Analysis: a method for the study of small groups* (Reading, Mass., Addison-Wesley).

Bales, R. F. and Slater, P. E. (1955) 'Role Differentiation in Small Decision-making Groups' in *Family, Socialization and Interaction Process*, ed. Parsons, T. and Bales, R. F. (New York, Free Press).

Bandura, A. (1965) 'Vicarious Processes: a case of no-trial learning', in *Advances in Experimental Social Psychology*, ed. Berkowitz L., vol. 2 (New York, Academic Press).

Bandura, A. (1973) *Aggression: a social learning anaylsis* (Englewood Cliffs, N.J., Prentice-Hall).

Bandura, A., Ross, D. and Ross, S. A. (1961) 'Transmission of Aggression through Imitation of Aggressive Models', *Journal of Abnormal and Social Psychology*, vol. 63, pp. 575–82.

Bandura, A., Ross, D. and Ross, S. A. (1963*a*) 'Imitation of Film Mediated Aggressive Models', *Journal of Abnormal and Social Psychology*, vol. 66, pp. 3–11.

Bandura, A., Ross, D. and Ross, S. A. (1963*b*) 'A Comparative Test of the Status-envy, Social Power and Secondary Reinforcement Theories of Identificatory Learning', *Journal of Abnormal and Social Psychology*, vol. 67, pp. 527–34.

Bandura, A. and Walters, R. H. (1963) *Social Learning and Personality Development*, (New York, Holt, Rhinehart & Winston).

Bannister, D. (1960) 'Conceptual Structure in Thought Disordered Schizophrenics', *Journal of Mental Science*, vol. 101, pp. 230–49.

Bannister, D. (1962) 'The Nature and Measurement of Schizophrenic Thought Disorder,' *Journal of Mental Science*, vol. 108, pp. 825–42.

Bannister, D. and Fransella F. (1966) 'A Grid Test of Schizophrenic Thought Disorder', *British Journal of Social and Clinical Psychology*, vol. 5, pp. 95–103.

Bannister, D. and Mair, J. M. M. (1968) *The Evaluation of Personal Constructs*, (London, Academic Press).

Barchas, J. D., Stolk, J. M., Ciaranello, R. D. and Hamburg D. (1971) 'Neuroregulatory Agents and Psychological Assessment', in *Advances in Psychological Assessment*, vol. 2, ed. McReynolds, (Palo Alto, Calif., Science Behaviour Books).

Barnes, R. M. (1968) *Motion and Time Study*, 6th edn (New York, Wiley).

Barron, F. (1955) 'The Disposition toward Originality', *Journal of Abnormal and Social Psychology*, vol. 51, pp. 478–85.

Bateson, G., Jackson, D., Haley, J. and Weakland, J. (1956) 'Towards a Theory of Schizophrenia', *Behavioral Science*, vol. 4, p. 251.

Bavelas, A. (1948) 'A Mathematical Model for Group Structures', *Applied Anthropology*, vol. 7(b), pp. 16–30.

Bavelas, A. (1950) 'Communication in Task-oriented Groups', *Journal of the Acoustical Society of America*, vol. 22, pp. 725–30.

Bayroff, A. G., Haggerty, H. R. and Rundquist, E. A. (1954) 'Validity of Ratings as Related to Rating Techniques and Conditions', *Personnel Psychology*, vol. 7, pp. 93–113.

Beach, F. A. (1960) 'Experimental Investigations of Species Specific Behavior', *American Psychologist*, vol. 15, pp. 1–18.

Bechterev, V. M. (1932) *General Principles of Human Reflexology* (New York, International).

Beer, M. (1976) 'The Technology of Organisation Development' in *Handbook of*

Industrial and Organisational Psychology, ed. Dunnette, M. D. (Chicago, Rand Mc-Nally).

Beier, E. G. and Cowan, E. L. (1953) 'A further Investigation of the Influence of Threat Expectancy on Perception', *Journal of Personality*, vol. 22, p. 254.

Belbin, E. and Belbin, R. M. (1968) 'Retraining and the Older Worker' in *Industrial Society*, ed. Pym, D. (Harmondsworth, Penguin).

Belloff, H. (1957) 'The Structure and Origin of the Anal Character', *Genetic Psychology, Monograph*, vol. 55, pp. 141–72.

Bem, D. J. (1972) 'Self-perception Theory', in *Advances in Experimental Social Psychology*, ed. Berkowitz, L., vol. 6 (New York, Academic Press).

Bemis, S. E. (1968) 'Occupational Validity of the General Aptitude Battery', *Journal of Applied Psychology*, vol. 52 (3), pp. 240–4.

Bennis, W. G. (1966) *Changing Organizations* (New York, McGraw-Hill).

Berger, A. (1968) 'The Relationship of Self-perception and Job Component Perception to Overall Job Satisfaction: a 'self appropriateness' model of job satisfaction', unpublished Ph.D. dissertation, New York University.

Berne, E. (1963) '*The Structure and Dynamics of Organizations and Groups* (New York, Grove Press).

Bernstein, A. (1955) 'Some Relations between Techniques of Feeding and Training during Infancy and Certain Behavior during Childhood', *Genetic Psychology, Monographs*, vol. 51, pp. 3–44.

Berrien, F. K. (1976) 'A General Systems Approach to Organizations', in *Handbook of Industrial and Organizational Psychology*, ed. Dunnette, M. D. (Chicago, Rand McNally).

Bexton, W., Heron, W. and Scott, T. (1954) 'Effects of Decreased Variation in the Sensory Environment', *Canadian Journal of Psychology*, vol. 8, pp. 70–6.

Bhatia, N. and Murrell, K. F. H. (1969) 'An Industrial Experiment in Organised Rest Pauses', *Human Factors*, vol. 11(2), pp. 167–74.

Bieri, J. (1955) 'Cognitive Complexity–Simplicity and Predictive Behavior', *Journal of Abnormal and Social Psychology*, vol. 51, pp. 263–8.

Bieri, J. (1961) 'Complexity–Simplicity as a Personality Variable in Cognitive and Preferential Behavior', in *Functions of Varied Experience*, ed. Fiske, D. W. and Maddi, S. (New York, Dorsey).

Bilodeau, E. A. (1953) 'Speed of Acquiring a Simple Motor Response as a Function of the Systematic Transformation of Knowledge of Results', *American Journal of Psychology*, vol. 66, pp. 409–20.

Bilodeau, E. A. (1955) 'Motor Performance as Affected by Magnitude of Error Contained in Knowledge of Results', *Journal of Psychology*, vol. 40, pp. 103–13.

Bilodeau, E. A. (1969) 'Supplementary Feedback and Instructions', in *Principles of Skill Acquisition*, ed. Bilodeau, E. A. and Bilodeau, I. M. (New York, Academic Press).

Bilodeau, E. A. and Bilodeau, I. M. (1958) 'Variable Frequency of Knowledge of Results and the Learning of a Simple Skill', *Journal of Experimental Psychology*, vol. 55, pp. 379–83.

Bindra, D. (1969) 'The Interrelated Mechanisms of Reinforcement and Motivation and the Nature of their Influence on Response', in *Nebraska Symposium on Motivation*, ed. Arnold, W. J. and Levine, D. (University of Nebraska Press).

Birchall, D. and Wild, R. (1973) 'Job Restructuring among Blue-collar Workers', *Personnel Review*, vol. 2, pp. 40–55.

Birdwhistell, R. L. (1973) *Kinetics in Context* (Harmondsworth, Penguin).

Birren, J. E. and Morrison, D. F. (1961) 'Analysis of WAIS Sub-tests in Relation to Age and Education', *Journal of Gerontology*, vol. 16, pp. 365–8.

Bjerner, B., Holm, A. and Swensson, A. (1955) 'Diurnal variation in Mental Performance', *British Journal of Industrial Medicine*, vol. 12, pp. 103–10.

Blackwell, H. R. (1959) 'Development and Use of a Quantitative Method for Specification of Interior Illumination Levels', *Illumination Engineering*, vol. 54 (6), pp. 317–53.

Blake, R. R. and Mouton, J. (1964) *The Managerial Grid* (Houston, Texas, Gulf Publishing).

Blake, R. R., Helson, H. and Mouton, J. S. (1956) 'The Generality of Conformity Behavior as a Function of Factual Anchorage, Difficulty of Task and Amount of Social Pressure', *Journal of Personality*, vol. 25, pp. 294–305.

Blood, M. R. and Hulin, C. L. (1967) 'Alienation, Environmental Characteristics and Worker Responses', *Journal of Applied Psychology*, vol. 51, pp. 284–90.

Blum, G. S. and Miller, D. R. (1952) 'Exploring the Psychoanalytic Theory of the "Oral Character"', *Journal of Personality*, vol. 20, pp. 287–304.

Bolles, R. C. (1967) *Theory of Motivation* (New York, Harper & Row).

Bolles, R. C. (1970) 'Effects of Escape Training on Avoidance Learning', in *Aversive Conditioning and Learning*, ed. Brush, F. R. (New York, Academic Press).

Bonarius, J. C. J. (1965) 'Research in the Personal Construct Theory of George A. Kelly', in *Progress in Experimental Personality Research*, vol. 2, ed. Maher, B. A., (London, Academic Press).

Boocock, L. (1966) 'Toward a Sociology of Learning: a selective review of existing research', *Sociology of Education*, vol. 39, pp. 1–45.

Bower, G. H. (1962) 'An Association Mood for Response and Training Variables in Paired Associate Learning', *Psychological Review*, vol. 69, pp. 34–53.

Bower, G. H. (1972) 'Mental Imagery and Associative Learning', in *Cognition in Learning and Memory*, ed. Gregg, L. (New York, Wiley).

Bowlby, J. (1952) *Maternal Care and Child Health* (Geneva, W.H.O.).

Bransford, J. D. and Franks, J. J. (1971) 'The Abstraction of Linguistic Ideas' *Cognitive Psychology*, vol. 2, pp. 331–50.

Bray, D. W. and Grant, D. L. (1966) 'The Assessment Center in the Measurement of Potential for Business Management', *Psychology Monographs*, vol. 80 (17), no. 625.

Brayfield, A. and Crockett, W. (1955) 'Employee Attitudes and Employee Performance', *Psychology Bulletin*, vol. 52, pp. 396–424.

Brech, E. F. L. (1957) *Organisation: The Framework of Management* (London, Longman).

Brehm, J. W. and Cohen, A. R. (1962) *Exploration in Cognitive Dissonance* (New York, Wiley).

Brickman, P. and Horn, C. (1973) 'Balance Theory and Interpersonal Coping in Triads', *Journal of Personality and Social Psychology*, vol. 26, pp. 347–55.

Briggs, G. E. and Naylor, J. C. (1962) 'The Relative Efficiency of Several Training Methods as a Function of Transfer Task Complexity', *Journal of Experimental Psychology*, vol. 64, pp. 505–12.

Broadbent, D. E. (1957) 'Effect of Noise on Behavior', in *Handbook of Noise Control*, ed. Harris, C. M. (New York, McGraw-Hill).

Broadbent, D. E. (1958) *Perception and Communication* (Oxford, Pergamon).

Broadbent, D. E. (1966) 'The Well Ordered Mind', *American Educational Research Journal*, vol. 3, 281–95.

Broadbent, D. E. (1971) 'Relation between Theory and Application in Psychology', *Psychology at Work*, ed. Warr, P. B. (Harmondsworth, Penguin).

Brock, T. C. and Becker, L. A. (1965) 'Ineffectiveness of "Overheard" Counter Propaganda', *Journal of Personality and Social Psychology*, vol. 2, pp. 654–60.

Bronfenbrenner, U. (1961) 'The Changing American Child – a Speculative Analysis', *Journal of Social Issues*, vol. 17, pp. 6–18.

Brown, J. S. (1953) 'Problems Presented by the Concept of Acquired Drives', in

Current Theory and Research in Motivation: A Symposium. (University of Nebraska Press).

Brown, J. S. (1961) *The Motivation of Behavior* (New York, McGraw-Hill).

Brown R. (1965) *Social Psychology* (New York, Free Press).

Brown, R. and McNeill, D. (1966) 'The "Tip-of-the-Tongue" Phenomenon', *Journal of Verbal Learning and Verbal Behavior*, vol. 5, pp. 325–37.

Browning, R. C. (1968) 'Validity of Reference Ratings from Previous Employers', *Personnel Psychology*, vol. 21(3), pp. 389–93.

Bruner, J. S. and Postman, L. (1947) 'Emotional Selectivity in Perception and Reaction', *Journal of Personality*, vol. 16, pp. 69–77.

Bruner, J. S., Goodnow, J. J. and Austin, G. A. (1956) *A Study of Thinking* (New York, Wiley).

Bryan, W. L. and Harter, N. (1897) 'Studies on the Telegraphic Language: the acquisition of a hierarchy of habits', *Psychological Review*, vol. 6, pp. 346–75.

Burke, R. J. and Wilcox, D. S. (1969) 'Characteristics of Effective Performance Review and Development Interviews', *Personnel Psychology*, vol. 22(3), pp. 291–305.

Burks, B. S., Jensen, D. S. and Terman, L. M. (1930) *The Promise of Youth. Genetic Studies of Genius*, vol. III (Stanford University Press).

Burns, R. B. (1966) 'Age and Mental Ability: Re-testing with Thirty-three Years' Interval', *British Journal of Educational Psychology*, vol. 36, p. 116 (thesis abstract).

Burns, T. and Stalker, G. M. (1961) *The Management of Innovation* (London, Tavistock).

Burt, C. (1940) *The Factors of the Mind* (University of London Press).

Burt, C. (1949) 'The Structure of the Mind: a Review of the Results of Factor Analysis', *British Journal of Educational Psychology*, vol. 19, pp. 100–14, 176–99.

Burt, C. (1966) 'The Appropriate Uses of Factor Analysis and Analysis of Variance', in *Handbook of Multivariate Experimental Psychology*, ed. Cattell, R. B. (Chicago, Rand McNally).

Butcher, H. J. (1968) *Human Intelligence: its nature and assessment* (London, Methuen).

Butler, R. A. (1953 'Discrimination Learning by Rhesus Monkeys to Visual Exploration Motivation', *Journal of Comparative Physiological Psychology*, vol. 46, pp. 95–8.

Campbell, D. P. (1971) *Handbook for the Strong Vocational Interest Blank*, (Stanford University Press).

Campbell, J. P. and Dunnette, M. D. (1968) 'Effectiveness of T-group Experiences in Managerial Training and Development, *Psychology Bulletin*, vol. 70 (2), pp. 73–104.

Campbell, J. P., Dunnette, M. D., Lawler, E. E. and Weick, K. E. (1970) *Managerial Behavior, Performance and Effectiveness* (New York, McGraw-Hill).

Campbell, J. P. and Pritchard, R. D. (1976) 'Motivation Theory in Industrial and Organisational Psychology', in *Handbook of Industrial and Organizational Psychology*, ed. Dunnette, M. D. (Chicago, Rand McNally).

Campion, J. E. (1972) 'Work Sampling for Personnel Selection', *Journal of Applied Psychology*, vol. 56 (1), pp. 40–4.

Cannon, W. B. (1918) 'The Physiological Basis of Thirst', *Proceedings of the Royal Society*, series B, vol. 90, pp. 283–301.

Carlson, R. E. (1967) 'Selection Interview Decision: the relative influence of appearance and factual information on an interviewer's final rating', *Journal of Applied Psychology*, vol. 51, pp. 461–3.

Cartwright, D. and Harary, F. (1956) 'Structural Balance: a generalization of Heider's theory', *Psychological Review*, vol. 63, 277–93.

Cartwright, D. and Zander, A. (1960) *Group Dynamics: research theory*, 2nd edn (Evanston, Ill., Row, Peterson).

Cattell, R. B. (1953) 'Research Design in Psychological Genetics with Special Reference to the Multiple Variance Analysis Method', *American Journal of Human Genetics*, vol. 5, pp. 76–93.

Cattell, R. B. (1957) *Personality and Motivation Structure and Measurement* (New York, World Book Co.).

Cattell, R. B. (1963) 'Theory of Fluid and Crystallized Intelligence: a critical experiment', *Journal of Educational Psychology*, vol. 54, pp. 1–22.

Cattell, R. B. (1965) *The Scientific Analysis of Personality* (Harmondsworth, Penguin).

Cattell, R. B. and Child, D. (1975) *Motivation and Dynamic Structure* (New York, Holt, Rinehart & Winston).

Cattell, R. B. and Drevdahl, J. E. (1955) 'A Comparison of the Personality Profile of Eminent Researchers with that of Eminent Teachers and Administrators and of the General Population', *British Journal of Psychology*, vol. 46, pp. 248–61.

Cattell, R. B., Eber, H. W. and Tatsuoka, M. M. (1970) *Handbook of the Cattell 16 P.F. Questionnaire*, (Institute of Personality and Ability Testing, Champaign, Illinois).

Cattell, R. B. and Kline, P. (1977) *Scientific Study of Personality and Motivation*. (New York, Academic Press).

Cattell, R. B. and Stice, G. F. (1954) 'Four Formulae for Selecting Leaders on the Basis of Personality', *Human Relations*, vol. 7, pp. 493–507.

Cavanagh, P. W. W., Drake, R. I. and Taylor, K. F. (1962) 'Youth Employment Service Interviews: Part 2. Differences between interviews', *Occupational Psychology*, vol. 36, pp. 232–42.

Chapanis, A. (1965) 'Words, Words, Words', *Human Factors*, vol. 7 pp. 1–17.

Chapanis, A. (1967) 'The Relevance of Laboratory Studies to Practical Situations', *Ergonomics*, vol. 10, pp. 557–77.

Chapanis, A. (1974) 'National and Cultural Variables in Ergonomics', *Ergonomics*, vol. 17, pp. 153–75.

Chapanis, A. (1976) 'Engineering Psychology', in *Handbook of Industrial and Organisational Psychology*, ed. Dunnette, M. D. (Chicago, Rand McNally).

Chapanis, A. and Mankin, D. A. (1967) 'Tests of 10 Control–Display Linkages', *Human Factors*, vol. 9 (2), pp. 119–26.

de Charms, R., Carpenter, V. and Kuperman, A. (1965) 'The "Origin–Pawn" Variable in Person Perception', *Sociometry*, vol. 28, pp. 241–58.

Christie, R. C. and Geis, F. (eds) (1971) *Studies in Machiavellianism* (New York, Academic Press).

Cline, V. B. and Richards, J. M. (1960) 'Accuracy of Interpersonal Perception – a General Tract', *Journal of Abnormal and Social Psychology*, vol. 50, pp. 183–92.

Coch, L. and French, J. R. P., jr (1948) 'Overcoming Resistance to Change', *Human Relations*, vol. 1, pp. 512–32.

Cofer, C. N. (1972) *Motivation and Emotion* (Glenview, Ill., Scott, Foresman).

Cofer, C. N. and Appley, M. H. (1964) *Motivation: theory and research* (New York, Wiley).

Cohen, A. (1968) 'Noise Effects on Health, Production and Well-being', *Transactions of the New York Academy of Sciences*, series II, vol. 30 (7), pp. 910–18.

Cohen, A. (1972) 'The Role of Psychology in Improving Worker Safety and Health under the Occupational Safety and Health Act', paper given at the meeting of the American Psychological Association, Honolulu, Hawaii, September 1972.

Cohen, P. S. (1968) *Modern Social Theory* (London, Heinemann).

Colquhoun, W. P., Blake, M. J. F. and Edwards, R. S. (1968a) 'Experimental Studies of Shift Work I: a comparison of "rotating" and "stabilized" 4-hour shift systems', *Ergonomics*, vol. 11, 437–53.

Colquhoun, W. P., Blake, M. J. F. and Edwards, R. S. (1968b) 'Experimental

Studies of Shift Work II: stabilized 8-hour shift systems', *Ergonomics*, vol. 11, pp. 527–46.

Colquhoun, W. P., Blake, M. J. F. and Edwards, R. S. (1968c) 'Experimental Studies of Shift Work III: stabilized 12-hour shift systems', *Ergonomics*, vol. 12, pp. 865–82.

Comrey, A. L. and Jamison, K. (1966) "Verification of Sex Personality Factors', *Educational Psychological Measurement*, vol. 26, pp. 945–53.

Conrad, R. (1966) 'Short-term Memory Factor in the Design of Data-entry Keyboards', *Journal of Applied Psychology*, vol. 50 (5), pp. 353–6.

Cook, M. (1971) *Interpersonal Perception* (Harmondsworth, Penguin).

Cook, S. W. and Selltiz, C. (1964) 'A Multiple Indicator Approach to Attitude Measurement', *Psychological Bulletin*, vol. 62, pp. 36–55.

Cook, T. D. and Campbell, D. T. (1976) 'The Design and Conduct of Quasi-experiments and True experiments in Field Settings', in *Handbook of Industrial Organizational Psychology*, ed. Dunnette, M. D. (Chicago, Rand McNally).

Craik, F. I. M. (1970) 'The Fate of Primary Memory Items after Free Recall', *Journal of Verbal Learning and Verbal Behavior*, vol. 9, pp. 143–8.

Craik, F. I. M. and Lockhart, R. S. (1972) 'Levels of Processing: a framework for memory research', *Journal of Verbal Learning and Verbal Behavior*, vol. 11, pp. 671–84.

Crano, W. D. and Cooper, R. E. (1973) 'Examination of Newcombe's Extension of Structural Balance Theory', *Journal of Personality and Social Psychology*, vol. 27, 344–53.

Crockett, W. H. (1974) 'Balance, Agreement and Subjective Evaluations in the P–O–X Triads', *Journal of Personality and Social Psychology*, vol. 29, pp. 102–10.

Cronbach, L. J. (1946) 'Response Sets and Test Validity', *Educational Psychological Measurement*, vol. 6, pp. 475–94.

Cronbach, L. J. (1950) 'Further Evidence on Response Sets and Test Design' *Educational Psychological Measurement*, vol. 10, pp. 3–31.

Cronbach, L. J. (1955) 'Processes Affecting Scores on "Understanding of Others" and "Assumed Similarity"', *Psychological Bulletin*, vol. 52, pp. 177–93.

Cronbach, L. J. and Gleser, G. C. (1965) *Psychological Tests and Personnel Decisions* (University of Illinois Press).

Crow, W. J. and Hammond, K. R. (1957) 'The Generality of Accuracy and Response Sets in Interpersonal Perception', *Journal of Abnormal and Social Psychology*, vol. 54, pp. 384–90.

Crowne D. P. and Marlowe, I. D. (1964) *The Approval Motive: studies in evaluative dependence* (New York, Wiley).

Crutchfield, R. S., Woodworth, D. G. and Albrecht, R. E. (1958) 'Perceptual Performance and the Effective Person', Lackland AFB, Texas, Personnel Lab. Report WADC-TN-58-60, ASTIA Doc. No. AD 151 039.

Csikszentmihalyi, M. and Getzels, J. W. (1970) 'Concern for Discovery; an attitude component in creative production', *Journal of Personality*, vol. 38, 91–105.

Cummin, P. (1967) 'TAT Correlates of Executive Performance', *Journal of Applied Psychology*, vol. 5II, pp. 78–81.

Cummings, L. L. and Schwab, D. P. (1973) *Performance in Organizations: determinants and appraisal* (Glenview, Ill., Scott, Foresman).

Dabbs, J. M. L. and Leventhal, H. (1966) 'Effects of Varying the Recommendations in a Fear-arousing Communication', *Journal of Personality and Social Psychology*, vol. 4 (5), pp. 525–31.

Dachler, H. P. and Mobley, W. H. (1973) 'Construct Validation of an Instrumentality–Expectancy–Task–Goal Model of Work Motivation: some theoretical boundary conditions', *Journal of Applied Psychology*, vol. 58, pp. 397–418.

Davies, D. R. (1970) 'Monotony and Work', *Science Journal*, vol. 6 (8), pp. 26–31.

Davies, D. R. and Shackleton, V. J. (1975) *Psychology and Work* (London, Methuen).

Davies, D. R. and Tune, G. S. (1970) *Human Vigilance Performance* (London, Staples).

Dawe, A. (1970) Book Review, *Sociology*, vol. 3 (1), pp. 115–17.

Day, R. H. (1972) 'Visual Spacial Illusions: a general explanation', *Science*, vol. 175, pp. 1335–40.

Delgado, J. M. R., Roberts, W. W. and Miller, N. E. (1954) 'Learning Motivated by Electrical Stimulation of the Brain', *American Journal of Physiology*, vol. 179, pp. 587–93.

Dellar, M. and Saier, E. L. (1970) 'Identification of Creativity: the individual', *Psychological Bulletin*, vol. 73, pp. 55–73.

Dennis, W. and Mallenger, B. (1949) 'Aminism and Related Tendencies in Senescence', *Journal of Gerontology*, vol. 4, pp. 218–21.

Deutsch, J. A. and Deutsch, D. (1963) 'Attention: some Theoretical Considerations', *Psychological Review*, vol. 70, pp. 80–90.

Di Cara, L. and Miller, N. E. (1968) 'Instrumental Learning of Systolic Bloodpressure Responses by Curarized Rats: dissociation of cardiac and vascular changes', *Psychosometrical Medicine*, vol. 30, pp. 489–94.

Digman, J. M. (1959) 'Growth of a Motor Skill as a Function of Distribution of Practice', *Journal of Experimental Psychology*, vol. 57, pp. 310–16.

Dixon, N. F. (1958) 'The Effect of Subliminal Stimulation upon Autonomic and Verbal Behavior', *Journal of Abnormal and Social Psychology*, vol. 57, pp. 29–36.

Dollard, J., Doob, L. W., Miller, N. E., Mowrer, O. H. and Sears, R. R. (1939) *Frustration and Aggression* (Yale University Press).

Dollard, J. and Miller, N. E. (1950) *Personality and Psychotherapy: an analysis in terms of learning, thinking and culture* (New York, McGraw-Hill).

Doob, L. W. (1947) 'The Behavior of Attitudes', *Psychological Review*, vol. 54, pp. 135–56.

Douglas, J. W. B. (1964) *The Home and the School* (London, McGibbon & Kee).

Drevdahl, J. E. (1956) 'Factors of Importance for Creativity', *Journal of Clinical Psychology*, vol. 14, pp. 107–11.

Dubin, R. (ed.) (1961) *Human Relations in Administration* (Englewood Cliffs, N.J., Prentice Hall).

Duffy, E. (1962) *Activation and Behavior* (New York, Wiley).

Dunnette, M. D. (1972) 'Validity Study Results for Jobs Relevant to the Petroleum Refining Industry' (Washington D.C., American Petroleum Institute).

Dunnette, M. D. (1976) 'Aptitudes, Abilities and Skills', in *Handbook of Industrial and Organizational Psychology*, ed. Dunnette M. D. (Chicago, Rand McNally).

Dunnette, M. D., Campbell, J. and Hakel, M. (1967) 'Factors Contributing to Job Satisfaction and Job Dissatisfaction in Six Occupational Groups', *Organizational Behavior and Human Performance*, vol. 2, pp. 143–74.

Dusek, E. R. (1957) *Manual Performance and Finger Temperature as a Function of Skin Temperature*, USA Research and Engineering Center, TR EP-68, October.

Ebbinghaus, H. (1885) *Memory*, trans. Ruger, H. A. and Bussenius, C. E. (New York Teachers College, 1913).

Edwards, A. L. (1957) *The Social Desirability Variable in Personality Assessment and Research* (New York, Dryden).

Edwards, A. L. (1967) 'The Social Desirability Variable: a review of the evidence', in *Response Set in Personality Assessment*, ed. Berg, I. A., (Chicago, Aldine).

Ekman, P. (1965) 'Communication through Non-verbal Behavior: a source of information about an interpersonal relationship', in *Affect, Cognition and Personality*, ed. Tomkins, S. S. and Izzard, C. (New York, Springer).

Ekman, P. and Friesen, W. V. (1969) 'Origin, Usage and Coding: the basis of five categories in non-verbal behavior', *Semiotica*, vol. 1, pp. 49–98.

El Koussy, A. A. H. (1935) 'The Visual Perception of Space', *British Journal of Psychology*, Monograph Supplement, no. 20.

England, G. W. and Stein, C. (1961) 'The Occupational Reference Group – a Neglected Concept in Employee Attitude Studies', *Personnel Psychology*, vol. 14, pp. 299–301.

Eriksen, C. W. (1951) 'Some Implications for T.A.T. Interpretation Arising from Need and Perception Experiments', *Journal of Personality*, vol. 19, 282–8.

Erlenmeyer-Kimling, L. and Jarvik, L. F. (1963) 'Genetics and Intelligence', *Science*, vol. 142, pp. 1477–9.

Estes, W. K. (1972) 'Learning', in *New Horizons in Psychology 2*, ed. Dodwell, P. C. (Harmondsworth, Penguin).

Ewart, E., Seashore, S. E. and Tiffin, J. (1941) 'A Factor Analysis of an Individual Merit Rating Scale', *Journal of Applied Psychology*, vol. 25, pp. 481–6.

Exline, R. V. and Winters, L. C. (1965) 'Affective Relations and Mutual Gaze in Diads', in *Affect, Cognition and Personality*, ed. Tomkins, S. and Izzard, C. (New York, Springer).

Eysenck, H. J. (1947) *Dimensions of Personality* (London, Routledge & Kegan Paul).

Eysenck, H. J. (1952) *The Scientific Study of Personality* (London, Routledge & Kegan Paul).

Eysenck, H. J. (1953) *The Structure of Human Personality* (London, Methuen).

Eysenck, H. J. (1954) *Psychology of Politics* (London, Routledge & Kegan Paul).

Eysensk, H. J. (1955) 'Cortical Inhibition, Figural After-Effect and Theory of Personality', *Journal of Abnormal and Social Psychology*, vol. 54, pp. 94–106.

Eysenck, H. J. (1967) 'Intelligence Assessment: a theoretical and experimental approach', *British Journal of Educational Psychology*, vol. 37, pp. 81–98.

Farmer, E. and Bevington, S. M. (1922) 'An Experiment in the Introduction of Rest Pauses', *Journal of the National Institute of Industrial Psychology*, vol. 1, pp. 89–92.

Fayol, H. (1949) *General and Industrial Management*, trans. Storrs, C. (London, Pitman).

Fenelon, J. R. and Magargee, E. I. (1971) 'Influence of Race on the Manifestation of Leadership', *Journal of Applied Psychology*, vol. 55, 353–8.

Ferguson, L. W. (1958) 'Life Insurance Interest, Ability and Termination of Employment', *Personnel Psychology*, vol. 11, pp. 189–93.

Festinger, L. (1954) 'Theory of Social Comparison Procedures', *Human Relations*, vol. 7, pp. 117–40.

Festinger, L. (1957) *A Theory of Cognitive Dissonance* (Evanston, Ill., Row, Peterson).

Festinger, L. and Carlsmith, J. (1959) 'Cognitive Consequences of Forced Compliance', *Journal of Abnormal and Social Psychology*, vol. 58, pp. 203–10.

Festinger, L. and Maccoby, N. (1964) 'On Resistance to Persuasive Communications,' *Journal of Abnormal and Social Psychology*, vol. 68, pp. 359–66.

Fiedler, F. E. (1967) *A Theory of Leadership Effectiveness* (New York, McGraw-Hill).

Fiedler, F. E. and Meuwese, W. (1963) 'Leaders' Contribution to Task Performance in Cohesive and Non-cohesive Groups', *Journal of Abnormal and Social Psychology*, vol. 67, 83–7.

Fishbein, M. (1967a) 'Attitude and the Prediction of Behavior', in *Readings in Attitude Theory and Measurement*, ed. Fishbein, M. (New York, Wiley).

Fishbein, M. (ed.) (1967b) *Readings in Attitude Theory and Measurement*, (New York, Wiley).

Fisher, G. H. (1968) 'An Experimental and Theoretical Appraisal of the Inappropriate Size–Depth Theories of Illusions', *British Journal of Psychology*, vol. 59, pp. 373–83.

Fiske, D. W. and Maddi, S. (1961) *Functions of Varied Experience* (New York, Dorsey).

Fitts, P. M. (1962) 'Factors in Complex Skill Training', in *Training Research and Education*, ed. Glaser, R. (University of Pittsburgh).

Fitts, P. M. (1964) 'Perceptual Motor Skill Learning', in *Categories of Human Learning*, ed. Melton, A. W. (New York, Academic Press).

Fitts, P. M. and Deininger, R. L. (1954) 'S–R Compatibility: correspondence among paired elements within stimulus and response codes', *Journal of Experimental Psychology*, vol. 48, 483–92.

Fitts, P. M. and Switzer, G. (1962) 'Cognitive Aspects of Information Processing 1. The Familiarity of S–R Sets and Subsets', *Journal of Experimental Psychology*, vol. 63, pp. 321–9.

Fjeld, S. P. and Landfield, A. W. (1961) 'Personal Construct Consistency', *Psychological Reports*, vol. 8, p. 127.

Flanagan, J. C. (1954) 'The Critical Incident Technique', *Psychological Bulletin*, vol. 51, pp. 327–58.

Flanagan, J. C. and Burns, R. K. (1955) 'The Employee Performance Record: a new appraisal and development tool', *Harvard Business Review*, vol. 33, pp. 95–102.

Flavell, J. A. (1963) *The Development Psychology of Jean Piaget* (Princeton, N.J., Van Nostrand).

Fleishman, E. A. (1962) 'The Description and Prediction of Perceptual Motor Skill Learning', in *Training Research and Education*, ed. Glaser, R. (University of Pittsburgh Press).

Fleishman, E., Harris, E. and Burtt, H. (1955) 'Leadership and Supervision in Industry: an evaluation of a supervisory training program (Bureau of Educational Research, Ohio State Uhiversity).

Fleishman, E. A. and Harris, E. F. (1962) 'Patterns of Leadership Behavior Related to Employee Grievances and Turnover' *Personnel Psychology*, vol. 15, pp. 43–56.

Fleishman, E. A. and Parker, J. F., jr (1962) 'Factors in the Retention of and Re-learning of Perceptual-motor Skill', *Journal of Experimental Psychology*, vol. 64, pp. 215–26.

Fleishman, E. A. and Rich, S. (1963) 'Role of Kinaesthetic and Spatial–Visual Abilities in Perceptual-motor Learning', *Journal of Experimental Psychology*, vol. 66, pp. 6–11.

Flexman, R. E., Matheny, W. G. and Brown, E. L. (1950) 'Evaluation of the School Link and Special Methods of Instruction', *University of Illinois Bulletin*, vol. 47, no. 80.

Form, W. H. and Geshwender, J. A. (1962) 'Social Reference Basis of Job Satisfaction: the case of manual workers', *American Sociological Review*, vol. 27, pp. 228–36.

Foulds, C. A. and Raven, J. C. (1948) 'Normal Changes in the Mental Abilities of Adults as Age Advances', *Journal of Mental Science*, vol. 94, pp. 135–42.

Fournet, G. P., Distefano, M. K., jr and Pryer, M. W. (1966) 'Satisfaction: issues and problems', *Personnel Psychology*, vol. 19 (2), pp. 165–83.

Fox, W. F. (1967) 'Human Performance in the Cold', *Human Factors*, vol. 9, pp. 203–20.

Fox, P. W. and Levy, C. M. (1969) 'Acquisition of a Simple Motor Response as Influenced by the Presence or Absence of Active Visual Feedback', *Journal of Motor Behavior*, vol. 1, 169–80.

Freeman, F. S. (1962) *Theory and Practice of Psychological Testing*, 3rd edn (New York, Holt, Rhinehart & Winston).

Freedman, J. L. Carlsmith, J. M. and Sears, D. O. (1974) *Social Psychology*, 2nd edn (Englewood Cliffs, N.J., Prentice Hall).

Freedman, J. L. and Sears, D. O. (1965) 'Warning, Distraction and Resistance to Influence', *Journal of Personality and Social Psychology*, vol. 1, 262–6.

Freedman, J. L. and Steinbruner, J. D. (1964) 'Perceived Choice and Resistance to Persuasion', *Journal of Abnormal and Social Psychology*, vol. 68, pp. 678–81.

French, J. R. P., jr (1956) 'A Formal Theory of Social Power', *Psychological Review*, vol. 63, pp. 181–94.

French, J. R. P., jr, Kay, E. and Meyer, H. H. (1966) 'Participation and the Appraisal System', *Human Relations*, vol. 19, pp. 3–20.

Frenkel-Brunswick, E. (1949) 'Intolerance of Ambiguity as an Emotional and Perceptual Personality Variable', *Journal of Personality*, vol. 18, pp. 108–43.

Freud, S. (1920) *Beyond the Pleasure Principle*, standard edn 1961, vol. 18 (London, Hogarth Press).

Freud, S. (1940) *Outline of Psychoanalysis*, standard edn 1969, vol. 23 (London, Hogarth Press).

Friedman, G. (1961) *The Anatomy of Work*, (New York, Free Press).

Fryer, D. H. (1951) 'Training with Special Reference to its Evaluation', *Personnel Psychology*, vol. 4, pp. 19–37.

Fuchs, A. H. (1962) 'The Progression–Regression Hypothesis in Perceptual-motor Skill Learning', *Journal of Experimental Psychology*, vol. 63, pp. 177–82.

Fuller, C. H. (1974) 'Comparison of Two Experimental Paradigms as Tests of Heider's Balance Theory', *Journal of Personality and Social Psychology*, vol. 30, pp. 802–6.

Funkenstein, D. H., King, S. H. and Drolette, M. E. (1957) *Mastery of Stress* (Harvard University Press).

Fuqua, N. (1967) Referred to in Ogletree, E. 'IQ as an Index of Creativity', *The Times Educational Supplement*, no. 2715, p. 1859, 2 June 1967.

Furlong, V. A. (1969) 'T-Groups for Management Development', unpublished B.A. (Business Studies) project, Enfield College of Technology (now Middlesex Polytechnic).

Gagné, R. M. (1965) 'The Analysis of Instructional Objectives for the Design of Instruction', in *Teaching Machines and Programmed Instruction II*, ed. Glaser, R. (Washington, D.C., National Education Association).

Garcia, J. and Koelling, R. A. (1966) 'Relation of Cue to Consequence in Avoidance Learning', *Psychonomic Science*, vol. 4, pp. 123–4.

Gardner, R. W. (1961) 'Cognitive Controls of Attention Deployment as Determinants of Visual Illusions', *Journal of Abnormal and Social Psychology*, vol. 62, pp. 120–7.

Gavin, J. F. (1970) 'Ability, Effort and Role Perception as Antecedents of Job Performance', *Experimental Publication System*, vol. 5, MS. no. 190A, pp. 1–26.

Gellerman, S. W. (1962) *Motivation and Productivity*, (New York, American Management Association).

Georgopoulos, B. S., Mahoney, G. M. and Jones, N. W. (1957) 'A Path–Goal Approach to Productivity', *Journal of Applied Psychology*, vol. 41, pp. 345–53.

Getzels, J. W. and Jackson, P. W. (1962) *Creativity and Intelligence* (New York, Wiley).

Gewirtz, J. L. (1961) 'A Learning Analysis of the Effects of Normal Stimulation, Privation and Deprivation on the Acquisition of Social Motivation and Attachment', in *Determinants of Infant Behaviour*, ed. Foss, B. M. vol. 1 (London, Methuen).

Ghiselli, E. (1963) 'The Validity of Management Traits Related to Occupational Level', *Personnel Psychology*, vol. 16, pp. 109–13.

Ghiselli, E. (1966) *The Validity of Occupational Aptitude Tests* (New York, Wiley).

Ghiselli, E. E. (1973) 'The Validity of Aptitude Tests in Personnel Selection', *Personnel Psychology*, vol. 26, 461–77.

Ghiselli, E. E. and Haire, M. (1960) 'The Validation of Selection Tests in the Light of the Dynamic Character of Criteria', *Personnel Psychology*, vol. 13, pp. 225–31.

Ghiselli, E. E. (Undated) *The Self-Description Inventory Manual,* available from the author, University of California, Berkeley, U.S.A.

Gibbins, K. (1969) 'Communication Aspects of Womens' Clothes and their Relation to Fashionability', *British Journal of Social and Clinical Psychology,* vol. 8, pp. 301–12.

Gibson, J. J. (1950) *The Perception of the Visual World* (Boston, Houghton Mifflin).

Gibson, J. J. (1960) 'The Concept of Stimulus in Psychology', *American Psychologist,* vol. 15, pp. 694–703.

Gilbert, T. F. (1969) 'Mathetics: An Explicit Theory for the Design of Teaching Programmes', *Recall: Review of Educational Cybernetics and Applied Linguistics, Supplement I* (New York, Longmac).

Gilchrist, J. C., Shaw, M. E. and Walker, L. C. (1954) 'Some Effects of Unequal Distribution of Information on Wheel Group Structure', *Journal of Abnormal and Social Psychology,* vol. 49, pp. 554–6.

Ginzberg, E., Ginsberg, S. W., Axelrad, S. and Herma, J. L. (1951) *Occupational Choice: an approach to a general theory* (Columbia University Press).

Goffman, E. (1956) *The Presentation of Self in Everyday Life* (London, Allen Lane).

Goldberg, L. R. (1969) 'The Search for Configural Relationships in Personality Assessment: the diagnosis of psychosis versus neurosis from the M.M.P.I.', *Multivariate Behavioral Research,* vol. 4, pp. 523–36.

Goldberg, M. H., Dawson, R. I. and Barrett, R. S. (1964) 'Comparison of Programmed and Conventional Instruction Methods', *Journal of Applied Psychology,* vol. 48, pp. 110–14.

Goldberg, S. C. (1954) 'Three Situational Determinants of Conformity to Social Norms', *Journal of Abnormal and Social Psychology,* vol. 49, pp. 325–9.

Goldfarb, W. (1955) 'Emotional and Intellectual Consequences of Psychological Deprivation in Infancy: a reevaluation', in *Psychopathology of Childhood,* ed. Hock, P. H. and Zubin, J. (New York, Grune & Stratton).

Goldthorpe, J. H., Lockwood, D., Bechhofer, F. and Platt, J. (1968) *The Affluent Worker: industrial attitudes and behavior* (Cambridge University Press).

Golembiewski, R. T. (1962) *The Small Group* (University of Chicago Press).

Graen, G. (1969) 'Instrumentality Theory of Work Motivation: some experimental results and suggested modifications', *Journal of Applied Psychology,* monograph, vol. 53, pp. 1–25.

Graen, G., Alvares, K., Orris, J. B. and Martello, J. A. (1970) 'Contingency Model of Leadership Effectiveness: antecedent and evidential results', *Psychology Bulletin,* vol. 74, pp. 285–96.

Graham, D. and Sluckin, W. (1954) 'Different Kinds of Reward as Industrial Incentives', *Research Review,* Durham, vol. 5, pp. 54–6.

Grant, D. L. and Bray, D. W. (1969) 'Contributions of the Interview to Assessment of Management Potential', *Journal of Applied Psychology,* vol. 53 (1 pt. 1), pp. 24–34.

Gray, J. A. and Wedderburn, A. A. I. (1960) 'Grouping Strategies with Simultaneous Stimuli', *Quarterly Journal of Experimental Psychology,* vol. 12, pp. 180–4.

Green, R. L. and Farquhar, W. (1965) 'Negro Academic Motivation and Scholastic Achievement', *Journal of Educational Psychology,* vol. 56, pp. 241–3.

Gregory, R. L. (1966) *Eye and Brain* (London, Weidenfeld & Nicolson).

Gregory, R. L. (1971), *The Intelligent Eye* (London, Weidenfeld & Nicolson).

Griffith, J. W., Kerr, W. A., Mayo, T. B., jr and Topal, J. R. (1950) 'Changes in Subjective Fatigue and Readiness for Work during the Eight-hour Shift', *Journal of Applied Psychology,* vol. 34, pp. 163–6.

Gruneberg, M. M., Colwill, S. J., Winfrow, P. and Woods, R. W. (1970) 'Acoustic Information in Long-term Memory: an extension of previous findings', *Acta Psychologica,* vol. 32, pp. 394–8.

Grunefeld, L. N. (1966) 'Personality Needs and Expected Benefits from a Management Development Program', *Occupational Psychology*, vol. 40, pp. 75–81.

Guilford, J. P. (1956) *Fundamental Statistics in Psychology and Education*, 3rd edn (New York, McGraw-Hill).

Guilford, J. P. (1959) 'The Structure of Intellect', *Psychological Bulletin*, vol. 53, pp. 267–93.

Guilford, J. P. (1967) *The Nature of Human Intelligence* (New York, McGraw-Hill).

Guilford, J. P. and Hoepfner, R. (1971) *The Analysis of Intelligence*, (New York, McGraw-Hill).

Guilford, J. P. and Zimmerman, W. S. (1949) *The Guilford–Zimmerman Temperament Survey*, (Beverly Hills, Calif., Sheriden Supply Co.).

Guion, R. M. (1965) *Personnel Testing* (New York, McGraw-Hill).

Guthrie, E. R. (1952) *The Psychology of Learning* (New York, Harper & Row).

Guttman, L. (1950) 'The Basis for Scalogram Analysis' in *Measurement and Prediction*, ed. Stouffner, S. A., Guttman, L., Suchman, E. A., Lazarsfeld, P. F., Star, S. A. and Gardner, J. A. (Princeton University Press).

Hackman, J. R. (1976) 'Group Influences on Individuals' in *Handbook of Industrial and Organizational Psychology*, ed. Dunnette M. D. (Chicago, Rand McNally).

Hackman, J. R. and Porter, L. W. (1968) 'Expectancy Theory Predictions of Work Effectiveness', *Organizational Behavior and Human Performance*, vol. 3, pp. 417–26.

Hall, C. S. and Lindzey, G. (1970) *Theories of Personality*, 2nd edn (New York, Wiley).

Hall, D. T. and Nougaim, K. E. (1968) 'An Examination of Maslow's Need Hierarchy in an Organizational Setting', *Organizational Behavior and Human Performance*, vol. 3, pp. 12–35.

Handyside, J. D. and Duncan, D. C. (1954) 'Four Years Later: a follow up on an experiment in selecting superiors', *Occupational Psychology*, vol. 28, pp. 9–23.

Harlow, N. F. (1959) 'Learning Set and Error Factor Theory', in *Psychology: a study of a science*, ed. Koch, S. vol. 2 (New York, McGraw-Hill).

Harlow, H. F. and Harlow, M. K. (1962) 'Social Deprivation in Monkeys', *Scientific American*, vol. 207, pp. 136–46.

Harrell, T. W. (1969) 'The Personality of High Earning M.B.A.s in Big Business', *Personnel Psychology*, vol. 23, pp. 457–63.

Harrell, T. W. (1970) 'The Personality of High Earning M.B.A.s in Small Business', *Personnel Psychology*, vol. 24, pp. 369–75.

Harris, E. F. and Fleishman, E. A. (1955) 'Human Relations Training and the Stability of Leadership Patterns', *Journal of Applied Psychology*, vol. 39, pp. 20–5.

Harris, J. G. (1960) 'Validity', in *Rorschach Psychology*, ed. Rickers-Ovsiankina, M.A. (New York, Wiley).

Hartmann, E., Baekeland, F., Zwilling, G. and Hay, P. (1971) 'Sleep Need: how much sleep and what kind?', *American Journal of Psychiatry*, vol. 127, pp. 1001–8.

Hasan, P. and Butcher, H. J. (1966) 'Creativity and Intelligence: a partial replication with Scottish children of Getzels and Jackson's study', *British Journal of Psychology*, vol. 57, pp. 129–35.

Haynes, J. R. (1970) 'Hierarchical Analysis of Factors in Cognition', *American Educational Research Journal*, vol. 7, pp. 55–68.

Haythorn, W., Couch, A. S., Haefner, D., Langham, P. and Carter, L. F. (1956) 'The Effects of Varying Combinations of Authoritarian and Equalitarian Leaders and Followers', *Journal of Abnormal and Social Psychology*, vol. 53, pp. 210–21.

Hebb, D. O. (1949) *The Organization of Behaviour* (New York, Wiley).

Heider, F. (1944) 'Social Perception and Phenomenal Causality', *Psychological Review*, vol. 51, pp. 358–74.

Heider, F. (1946) 'Attitudes and Cognitive Organization', *Journal of Psychology*, vol. 21, pp. 107–12.

Heider, F. (1958) *The Psychology of Interpersonal Relations* (New York, Wiley).

Heim, A. W. (1957) 'Psychological Adaptation as a Response to Variations in Difficulty', *Journal of Genetic Psychology*, vol. 56, pp. 193–211.

Herbert, M. J. and Jaynes, W. E. (1964) 'Performance Decrement in Vehicle Driving', *Journal of Engineering Psychology*, vol. 3, pp. 1–8.

Herzberg, F. (1966) *Work and the Nature of Man* (Cleveland, World Publishing Co.).

Herzberg, F., Mausner, B., Peterson, R. O. and Capwell, D. F. (1957) '*Job Attitudes. Review of Research and Opinion*, (Pittsburgh, Psychological Service of Pittsburgh).

Herzberg, F., Mausner, B. and Snyderman, B. (1959) *The Motivation to Work* (New York, Wiley).

Higham, M. H. (1952) 'Recent Work with Group Selection Techniques', *Occupational Psychology*, vol. 26, pp. 170–5.

Hilgard, E. R. (1962) *Introduction to Psychology*, 3rd edn (New York, Harcourt Brace Jovanovich).

Hilgard, E. R., Atkinson, R. C. and Atkinson, R. L. (1975) *Introduction to Psychology* (New York, Harcourt Brace Jovanovich).

Hilgard, E. R. and Bower, G. H. (1967) *Theories of Learning* (New York, Appleton).

Hilgendorf, L. (1966) 'Information Input and Response Time', *Ergonomics*, vol. 9 (1), pp. 31–7.

Hochberg, J. (1964) *Perception* (Englewood Cliffs, N.J., Prentice-Hall).

Holding, D. H. (1965) *Principles of Training* (Oxford, Pergamon).

Holding, D. H. and Macrae, A. W. (1964) 'Guidance, Restriction and Knowledge of Results', *Ergonomics*, vol. 7, pp. 289–95.

Hollingworth, H. L. (1929) *Vocational Psychology and Character Analysis* (New York, Appleton).

Homans, G. C. (1950) *The Human Group* (New York, Harcourt Brace).

Homans, G. C. (1961) *Social Behavior: its elementary forms* (New York, Harcourt Brace & World).

Hoppock, R. (1935) *Job Satisfaction* (New York, Harper & Row).

Horn, J. L. and Knapp, J. R. (1973) 'On the Subjective Character of the Empirical Base of Guilford's Structure of Intellect Model', *Psychological Bulletin*, vol. 80, pp. 33–43.

House, R. J. and Wigdor, L. A. (1967) 'Herzberg's Dual Factor Theory of Job Satisfaction and Motivation: a review of the evidence and a criticism', *Personnel Psychology*, vol. 20, pp. 369–90.

Hovland, C. I., Harvey, O. J. and Sherif, M. (1957) 'Assimilation and Contrast Effects in Reactions to Communications and Attitude Change', *Journal of Abnormal and Social Psychology*, vol. 55, pp. 244–52.

Hovland, C. I. and Janis, I. L. (eds) (1959) *Personality and Persuasibility* (Yale University Press).

Hovland, C. I. and Pritzker, H. A. (1957) 'Extent of Opinion Change as a Function of Amount of Change Advocated', *Journal of Abnormal and Social Psychology*, vol. 54, pp. 257–61.

Hovland, C. I. and Weiss, W. (1952) 'The Influence of Source Credibility on Communication Effectiveness', *Public Opinion Quarterly*, vol. 15, pp. 635–50.

Hovland, C. I. and Wonderlic, E. F. (1939) 'Prediction of Industrial Success from a Standardized Interview', *Journal of Applied Psychology*, vol. 23, pp. 537–46.

Howarth, E. (1972) 'A Source of Independent Variation: Convergences and Divergences in the Work of Cattell and Eysenck', in *Multivariate Personality Research*, ed. Dreger, R. M. (Baton Rouge, La., Claiton).

Hubel, H. D. and Wiesel, T. N. (1962) 'Receptive Fields, Binocular Interaction and

Functional Architecture in the Cat's Visual Cortex', *Journal of Physiology*, vol. 165, pp. 559–68.

Hudson, L. (1966) *Contrary Imaginations*, (London, Methuen).

Hulin, C. L. (1966a) 'Effects of Community Characteristics on Measures of Job Satisfaction', *Journal of Applied Psychology*, vol. 50, pp. 185–92.

Hulin, C. L. (1966b) 'Job Satisfaction and Turnover in a Female Clerical Population', *Journal of Applied Psychology*, vol. 50, pp. 280–5.

Hull, C. L. (1943) *Principles of Behavior* (New York, Appleton).

Hull, C. L. (1952) *A Behavior System: an introduction to behavior theory concerning the individual organism* (Yale University Press).

Humble, J. (1966) *Improving Management Performance* (London, British Institute of Management).

Hunt, W. A., Watson, C. L. and Harris, H. L. (1944) 'The Screen Test in Military Selection', *Psychological Review*, vol. 51, pp. 37–46.

Hyden, H. (1969) 'Biochemical Aspects of Learning and Memory', in *On the Biology of Learning*, ed. Pribram, K. (New York, Harcourt Brace Jovanovich).

I.E.S. Lighting Handbook, 5th edn (1972) (New York, Illuminating Engineering Society).

Insko, C. A. and Schopler, J. (1967) 'Triadic Consistency: a statement of affective cognitive–anative consistency', *Psychological Review*, vol. 74, pp. 361–76.

Insko, C. A. and Schopler, J. (1972) *Experimental Social Psychology* (New York, Academic Press).

Irion, A. L. (1969) 'Historical Introduction', in *Principles of Skill Acquisition*, ed. Bilodeau, E. A. and Bilodeau, I. M. (New York, Academic Press).

Iris, B. and Barrett, G. V. (1972) 'Some Relations Between Job and Life Satisfaction and Job Importance', *Journal of Applied Psychology*, vol. 56, pp. 301–4.

Jackson, D. N. (1967) *Personality Research Form Manual*, (New York, Research Psychologists' Press).

Jackson, J. (1965) 'Structural Characteristics of Norms', in *Current Studies in Social Psychology*, ed. Steiner, I. D. and Fishbein, M. (New York, Holt, Rinehart & Winston).

Janis, I. L. and Feshbach, S. (1953) 'Effects of Fear-arousing Communications', *Journal of Abnormal and Social Psychology*, vol. 48, pp. 78–92.

Janis, I. L. and Field, P. B. (1959) 'Sex Differences and Personality Factors Related to Persuasibility', in *Personality and Persuasibility*, ed. Hovland, C. I. and Janis, I. L. (Yale University Press).

Janis, I. L., Kaye, D. and Kirschner, P. (1965) 'Facilitating Effects of "eating while reading" on Responsiveness to Persuasive Communications', *Journal of Personality and Social Psychology*, vol. 1, pp. 131–6.

Jensen, A. R. (1969) 'How Much Can We Boost I.Q. and Scholastic Achievement?', *Harvard Educational Review*, vol. 39, pp. 1–123.

Jensen, A. R. (1973) *Educability and Group Differences*, (New York, Harper & Row).

Jones, E. E. and Davis, K. E. (1965) 'From Acts to Dispositions: the attribution process in person perception', in *Advances in Experimental Social Psychology*, ed. Berkowitz, L., vol. 2 (New York, Academic Press).

Jones, H. E. and Conrad, H. S. (1933) 'The Growth and Decline of Intelligence: a study of a homogeneous group', *Genetic Psychology*, monographs, vol. 13, 223–98.

Jones, M. B. (1969) 'Differential Processes in Acquisition', in *Principles of Skill Acquisition*, ed. Bilodeau, E. A. and Bilodeau, I. M. (New York, Academic Press).

Jones, M. B. (1970) 'A Two Process Theory of Individual Differences in Motor Learning', *Psychological Review*, vol. 77, pp. 353–60.

Jordan, N. (1966) 'Experimenting with a P–O–Q Unit: complications in cognitive balance', *Journal of Psychology*, vol. 64, pp. 3–22.

Jordan, N. (1968) 'Cognitive Balance as an Aspect of Heider's Cognitive Psychology', in *Theories of Cognitive Consistency: a source book*, ed. Abelson, R., Aronson, E., McGuire, W., Newcombe, T., Rosenburg, M. and Tannenbaum, P. (Chicago, Rand McNally).

Jorgenson, D. O., Dunnette, M. D. and Pritchard, R. D. (1973) 'Effects of the Manipulation of a Performance-Reward Contingency on Behavior in a Simulated Work Setting', *Journal of Applied Psychology*, vol. 57, pp. 271–80.

Kagan, J. (1964) 'Acquisition and Significance of Sex-Typing and Sex Role Identity', *Review of Child Development Research*, vol. 1, pp. 137–67.

Kagan, J. and Moss, H. H. (1962) *From Birth to Maturity* (New York, Wiley).

Kamin, L. J. (1974) *The Science and Politics of IQ*, (Potomac, Md., Erlbaum Association).

Kaplan, M. F. and Singer, E. (1963) 'Dogmatism and Sensory Alienation: an Empirical Investigation', *Journal of Consulting Psychology*, vol. 27 (6), pp. 486–91.

Katz, D. I., Sarnoff, I. and McClintock, C. G. (1956) 'Ego Defence and Attitude Change', *Human Relations*, vol. 9, pp. 27–46.

Katzell, R. A., Barrett, R. and Parker, T. (1961) 'Job Satisfaction, Job Performance and Situational Characteristics', *Journal of Applied Psychology*, vol. 45, pp. 65–72.

Kaufman, H. (1962) 'Task Performance, Expected Performance and Responses to Failure as Functions of Imbalance in the Self-concept', unpublished doctoral dissertation, University of Pennsylvania.

Kay, E., French, J. R. P., jr and Meyer, H. H. (1962) 'A Study of the Performance Appraisal Interview', Behaviorial Research Service Report No. EBR-11, General Electric Company.

Kay, E., Meyer, H. H. and French, J. R. P., jr (1965) 'Effects of Threat in a Performance Appraisal Interview', *Journal of Applied Psychology*, vol. 49 (5), pp. 311–17.

Kay, H. (1951) 'Learning of a Serial Task by Different Age Groups', *Quarterly Journal of Experimental Psychology*, vol. 3, pp. 166–83.

Keating, E., Paterson, D. G. and Stone, H. C. (1950) 'Validity of Work Histories Obtained by Interview', *Journal of Applied Psychology*, vol. 34, pp. 6–11.

Kelley, C. R. (1968) *Manual and Automatic Control*, (New York, Wiley).

Kelley, H. H. and Volkart, E. H. (1952) 'The Resistance to Change of Group-anchored Attitudes', *American Sociological Review*, vol. 17, pp. 453–65.

Kelley, T. L. (1928) *Crossroads in the Mind of Man* (Stanford University Press).

Kelly, E. L. and Fiske, D. W. (1951) *The Prediction of Performance in Clinical Psychology* (University of Michigan Press).

Kelly, G. A. (1955) *The Psychology of Personal Constructs*, vols I and II (New York, Norton).

Kelly, G. A. (1961) 'The Abstraction of Human Processes', *Proceedings of the 14th International Congress of Psychology, Copenhagen*, pp. 220–9.

Kelman, H. C. and Hovland, C. I. (1953) '"Reinstatement" of the Communication in Delayed Measurement of Opinion Change', *Journal of Abnormal and Social Psychology*, vol. 48, pp. 327–35.

Kendon, A. (1968) 'Temporal Aspects of the Social Performance in Two Person Encounters', D.Phil. thesis, Oxford University.

Kirkpatrick, W., Ewen, R. B., Barrett, R. S. and Katzell, R. A. (1968) *Testing and Fair Employment* (University of London Press).

Klein, S. M. and Maher, J. R. (1966) 'Education Level and Satisfaction with Pay', *Personnel Psychology*, vol. 19, pp. 195–208.

Kleinmuntz, B. (1963) 'MMPI Decision Rules for the Identification of College

Maladjustment. A Digital Computer Approach', *Psychological Monographs*, vol. 74 (14), no. 577.

Kleitman, N. (1963) *Sleep and Wakefulness*, 2nd edn (University of Chicago Press).

Klemmer, E. J. and Lockhead, G. R. (1962) 'Productivity and Errors in Keying Tasks. A Field Study', *Journal of Applied Psychology*, vol. 46 (6), pp. 401–8.

Kline, P. (1972) *Fact and Fantasy in Freudian Theory*, (London, Methuen).

Klineberg, O. (ed.) (1944) *Characteristics of the American Negro*, (New York, Harper).

Klinger, E. (1966) 'Fantasy Need Achievement as a Motivational Contract', *Psychological Bulletin*, vol. 66, pp. 291–308.

Klopfer, B. and Davidson, H. H. (1962) *The Rorschach Technique: An Introductory Manual*, (New York, Harcourt Brace & World).

Knapp, R. R. (1965) 'Relationship of a Measure of Self-Actualisation to Neuroticism and Extroversion' *Journal of Consulting Psychology*, vol. 29 (2), pp. 168–72.

Kohlberg, L. (1963) 'The Development of Children's Orientations Toward a Moral Order: I. sequence in the development of moral thought', *Vita Humana*, vol. 6, pp. 11–33.

Kohlberg, L. (1964) 'The Development of Moral Character and Moral Ideology', in *Review of Child Development Research*, ed. Hoffman, M. L. and Hoffman L. W., vol. 1 (New York, Russell Sage Foundation).

Köhler, W. (1925) *The Mentality of Apes*, trans. Winter, E. (New York, Harcourt, Brace & World).

Kolb, D. A. (1965) 'Achievement Motivation Training for Under-achieving High School Boys', *Journal of Personality and Social Psychology*, vol. 2, 783–92.

Korman, A. (1967) 'Self-esteem as a Moderator of the Relationship between Self-perceived Abilities and Vocational Choice', *Journal of Applied Psychology*, vol. 51, 65–7.

Korman, A. (1968) 'Self-esteem, Social Influence and Task Performance. Some Tests of a Theory', paper presented at the meeting of the American Psychological Association, San Francisco.

Korman, A. (1971) *Industrial and Organizational Psychology* (Englewood Cliffs, N.J., Prentice-Hall).

Kornhauser, A. W. (1965) *Mental Health of the Industrial Worker* (New York, Wiley).

Kossoris, M. D., Kohler, R. F. *et al.* (1947) 'Hours of Work and Output', U.S. Dept of Labor, Bureau of Labor Statistics, *Bulletin*, no. 917.

Kraft, J. A. (1970) 'Status of Human Factors and Biotechnology in 1968–69', *Human Factors*, vol. 12, pp. 113–51.

Krasner, L. (1958) 'Studies of the Conditioning of Verbal Behavior', *Psychological Bulletin*, vol. 55, pp. 148–70.

Kramer, E. (1963) 'Judgment of Personal Characteristics and Emotions from Non-verbal Properties of Speech', *Psychological Bulletin*, vol. 60, pp. 408–20.

Krout, M. H. (1954) 'An Experimental Attempt to Determine the Significance of Unconscious Manual Symbolic Movements', *Journal of Genetic Psychology*, vol. 51, pp. 121–52.

Kuder, G. F. (1965) *Manual for General Interest Survey, Form E* (Chicago, Science Research Associates).

Kuder, G. F. (1970) *Manual for Occupational Interest Survey, Form DD* (Chicago, Science Research Associates).

La Benz, P., Cohen, A. and Pearson, B. (1967) 'A Noise and Hearing Survey of Earth-moving Equipment Operation', *American Industrial Hygiene Association Journal*, vol. 28, pp. 117–28.

La Piere, R. T. (1934) 'Attitudes versus Actions', *Social Forces*, vol. 13, pp. 230–7.

Laird, D. (1937) *Psychology of Selecting Employees* (New York, McGraw-Hill).

Lalljee, M. (1967) 'On the Classification of Voices', mimeo., Oxford Institute of Experimental Psychology.

Lashley, K. (1951) 'The Problems of Serial Order in Behavior', in *Cerebral Mechanisms in Behavior*, ed. Jefross, A. (New York, Wiley).

Lauru, L. (1952) 'The Measurement of Fatigue', *Manager*, vol. 22, pp. 299–303, 369–75.

Lawler, E. E. *see* Campbell, J. P. *et al.* (1970), Porter, L. W. and Lawler, E. E. (1968), Porter, L. W. *et al.* (1975).

Lawler, E. E. (1967) 'Secrecy about Management Compensation: are there hidden costs?', *Organizational Behavior and Human Performance*, vol. 2, pp. 182–9.

Lawler, E. E. (1968) 'Equity Theory as a Predictor of Productivity and Work Quality', *Psychological Bulletin*, vol. 70, pp. 596–610.

Lawler, E. E. (1969) 'Job Design and Employee Motivation', *Personnel Psychology*, vol. 22, p. 426.

Lawler, E. E. and Porter, L. W. (1967) 'Antecedent Attitudes of Effective Managerial Performance', *Organizational Behavior and Human Performance*, vol. 2, pp. 122–42.

Lawler, E. E. and Suttle, J. L. (1973) 'Expectancy Theory and Job Behavior', *Organizational Behavior and Human Performance*, vol. 9, pp. 482–503.

Lawshe, C. H. (1952) 'Employee Selection', *Personnel Psychology*, vol. 5, pp. 31–4.

Lawshe, C. H., Bolda, R. A. and Brune, R. L. (1959) 'Studies in Management Training Evaluation: Chapter II. The Effects of Exposure to Role Playing' *Journal of Applied Psychology*, vol. 43, pp. 287–92.

Lawshe, C. H., Kephart, N. C. and McCormick, E. J. (1949) 'The Paired Comparison Technique for Rating Performance of Industrial Employees', *Journal of Applied Psychology*, vol. 33, pp. 69–7.

Layzer, D. (1974) 'Heritability Analyses of IQ Scores: Science or Numerology', *Science*, vol. 183, pp. 1259–66.

Leavitt, H. J. (1951) 'Some Effects of Certain Communication Patterns on Group Performance', *Journal of Abnormal and Social Psychology*, vol. 6, pp. 38–50.

Leavitt, H. J. (ed.) (1963) *The Social Science of Organizations* (Englewood Cliffs, N.J., Prentice-Hall).

Lee, E. S. (1951) 'Negro Intelligence and Selective Migration: a Philadelphia test of the Klineberg hypothesis', *American Sociological Review*, vol. 16, pp. 227–33.

Leibowitz, H. W. and Judisch, J. M. (1967) 'The Relation between Age and the Magnitude of the Ponzo Illusion', *American Journal of Psychology*, vol. 80, pp. 105–9.

Lesser, G. S., Fifer, G. and Clark, D. H. (1965) 'Mental Abilities of Children from Different Social-class Cultural Groups', *Social Research on Child Development, Monographs* vol. 30, no. 4.

Levine, J. and Butler, J. (1952) 'Lecture versus Group Decision in Changing Behavior', *Journal of Applied Psychology*, vol. 36, pp. 29–33.

Levine, J. R., Romashko, T. and Fleishman, E. A. (1973) 'Evaluation of an Abilities Classification System for Integrating and Generalising Human Performance Research Findings: An Application to Vigilance Tasks', *Journal of Applied Psychology*, vol. 58, pp. 149–57.

Levine, R., Chein, I. and Murphy, G. (1942) 'The Relation of Intensity of a Need to the Amount of Perceptual Distortion', *Journal of Psychology*, vol. 13, pp. 283–93.

Lewin, K. (1958) 'Group Decision and Social Change', in *Readings in Social Psychology*, 3rd edn, ed. Maccoby, E. E., Newcombe, T. M. and Hartley, E. L., (New York, Holt, Rinehart & Winston).

Likert, R. (1932) 'A Technique for the Measurement of Attitudes', *Archives of Psychology*, no. 140.

Likert, R. (1961) *New Patterns of Management* (New York, McGraw-Hill).

Linder, D. E., Cooper, J. and Jones, E. E. (1967) 'Decision Freedom as a Determinant of the Role of Incentive Magnitude in Attitude Change', *Journal of Personal and Social Psychology*, vol. 6, pp. 245–54.

Lindzey, G., Loehlin, J., Manosevitz, M. and Thiessen, D. (1971) 'Behavioral Genetics', *Annual Review of Psychology*, vol. 22, pp. 39–94.

Locke, E. A. (1968) 'Toward a Theory of Task Motivation and Incentives', *Organizational Behavior and Human Performance*, vol. 3, pp. 157–89.

Loehlin, J. C., Lindzey, G. and Spukler, J. N. (1975) *Race Differences in Intelligence*, (San Francisco, Freeman).

Lorenz, K. (1966) *On Aggression* (New York, Harcourt Brace Jovanovich).

Loveless, N. E. (1962) 'Direction of Motion stereotypes: a review', *Ergonomics*, vol. 5, pp. 357–83.

Lunzer, E. A. (1968) 'Children's Thinking' in *Educational Research in Britain*, ed. Butcher, H. J. (University of London Press).

Luria, A. R. (1968) *The Mind of a Mnemonist* (New York, Basic Books).

McClelland, D. C. (1961) *The Achieving Society* (New York, Van Nostrand).

McClelland, D. C. (1965) 'Toward a Theory of Motive Acquisition', *American Psychology*, vol. 20, pp. 321–33.

McClelland, D. C., Atkinson, J. W., Clark, R. A. and Lovell, E. L. (1953) *The Achievement Motive* (New York, Appleton).

McClelland, D. C. and Liberman, A. M. (1949) 'The Effect of Need for Achievement on Recognition of Need-related Words', *Journal of Personality*, vol. 18, p. 236.

McCollom, I. N. and Savard, D. A. (1957) 'A Simplified Method of Computing the Effectiveness of Tests in Selection', *Journal of Applied Psychology*, vol. 41, pp. 243–6.

McCormick, E. J. (1970) *Human Factors Engineering*, 3rd edn (New York, McGraw-Hill).

McCormick, E. J., Jeanneret, P. R. and Mecham, R. C. (1972) 'A Study of Job Characteristics and Job Dimensions as based on the Position Analysis Questionnaire (PAQ)', *Journal of Applied Psychology*, vol. 56 (4), pp. 347–68.

McCormick, E. J. and Tiffin, J. (1974) *Industrial Psychology*, 6th edn (London, Allen & Unwin).

McDougall, W. (1908) *An Introduction to Social Psychology* (London, Methuen).

McGehee, W. (1958) 'Are We Using What We Know About Training? – Learning theory and training', *Personnel Psychology*, vol. 11, pp. 1–12.

McGehee, W. and Owen, F. B. (1940) 'Authorized and Unauthorized Rest Pauses in Clerical Work', *Journal of Applied Psychology*, vol. 24, pp. 605–14.

McGehee, W. and Thayer, P. W. (1961) *Training in Business and Industry* (New York, Wiley).

McGinnies, E. (1949) 'Emotionality and Perceptual Defence', *Psychological Review*, vol. 56, pp. 244–51.

McGrath, J. J. (1968) 'An Exploratory Study of the Correlates of Vigilance Performance', in *Studies of Human Vigilance. An Omnibus of Technical Reports* (Goleta, Calif., Human Factors Research Inc.).

McGuire, W. J. and Papageorgis, D. (1961) 'The Relative Efficiency of Various Types of Prior Belief-defence in Producing Immunity against Persuasion', *Journal of Abnormal and Social Psychology*, vol. 62, pp. 327–37.

McGurk, E. (1965) 'Susceptibility to Visual Illusions' *Journal of Psychology*, vol. 61, pp. 127–43.

McKenney, J. L. (1962) 'An Evaluation of a Business Game in an MBA Curriculum', *Journal of Business*, vol. 35 (3), pp. 278–86.

Mackworth, N. H. (1950) 'Researches on the Measurement of Human Performance', Medical Research Council, Special Report Series 268 (London, H.M.S.O.).

McMurry, R. N. (1947) 'Validating the Patterned Interview', *Personnel*, vol. 23, pp. 263–72.

Maddi, S. (1972) *Personality Theories: a comparative analysis* (Homewood, Ill., Dorsey).

Malinovski, B. (1927) *Sex and Repression in Savage Society* (New York, Harcourt Brace).

Mandler, G. (1974) 'Organization and Recognition', in *Organization of Memory*, ed. Tulving, E. and Donaldson, W. (New York, Academic Press).

de la Mare, G. and Walker, J. (1968) 'Factors Influencing the Choice of Shift Rotation', *Occupational Psychology*, vol. 42, pp. 1–21.

Marquardt, L. D. and McCormick, E. J. (1972) 'Attribute Ratings and Profiles of the Job Elements of the Position Analysis Questionnaire (PAQ)', Department of Psychological Sciences, Purdue University, June, ONR Contract NR 151-231.

Maslow, A. H. (1942) 'A Theory of Human Motivation', *Psychological Review*, vol. 50, pp. 370–96.

Maslow, A. H. (1954) *Motivation and Personality* (New York, Harper & Row).

Maslow, A. H. (1959) 'Cognition of Being in the Peak Experiences', *Journal of Genetic Psychology*, vol. 94, pp. 43–66.

Maslow, A. H. (1962) *Toward a Psychology of Being* (New York, Van Nostrand).

Maxwell, J. (1961) *The Level and Trend of National Intelligence* (University of London Press).

Mayfield, E. C. (1964) 'The Selection Interview: a re-evaluation of published research' *Personnel Psychology*, vol. 17 (3), pp. 239–60.

Mayfield, E. C. and Carlson, R. E. (1966) 'Selection Interview Decisions: first results of a long-term project', *Personnel Psychology*, vol. 19 (1), pp. 41–53.

Mayfield, H. (1960) 'In Defense of Performance Appraisal' *Harvard Business Review*, vol. 38 (2), pp. 81–7.

Meyer, H. H., Kay, E. and French, J. R. P., jr (1965) 'Split Roles in Performance Appraisal', *Harvard Business Review*, vol. 43, pp. 123–9.

Miles, C. C. (1934) 'The Influence of Speed and Age on the Intelligence Scores of Adults', *Journal of General Psychology*, vol. 10, pp. 208–10.

Miles, G. H. and Skilbeck, O. (1944) 'An Experiment on Change of Work', *Occupational Psychology*, vol. 18, pp. 192–5.

Miller, G. A. (1964) *Psychology: the science of mental life* (Harmondsworth, Penguin).

Miller, G. A., Galanter, E. and Pribram, K. H. (1960) *Plans and the Structure of Behavior* (New York, Holt, Rinehart & Winston).

Miller, J. and Rowe, P. M. (1967) 'Influence of Favorable and Unfavorable Information upon Assessment Decisions', *Journal of Applied Psychology*, vol. 51 (5), pp. 432–5.

Miller, N. E. *see* Delgado, J. M. R. *et al.* (1954), Di Cara, L. and Miller, N. E. (1968), Dollard, J. *et al.* (1939), Dollard, J. and Miller, N. E. (1951).

Miller, N. E. (1948) 'Studies of Fear as an Acquired Drive. 1. fear as motivation and fear-reduction as reinforcement in the learning of new responses', *Journal of Experimental Psychology*, vol. 38, pp. 89–101.

Miller, N. E. (1969) 'Learning of Visceral and Glandular Responses', *Science*, vol. 163, pp. 434–45.

Miller, N. and Campbell, D. T. (1959) 'Recency and Primacy in Persuasion as a Function of the Timing of Speeches and Measurements', *Journal of Abnormal and Social Psychology*, vol. 59, pp. 1–9.

Miller, N. E. and Dollard, J. (1941) *Social Learning and Imitation* (Yale University Press).

Miller, R. B. (1953) 'Handbook on Training and Training Equipment Design', Wright Air Development Center, Technical Report WADC-TR-53-136.

Miller, R. B. 'Task Taxonomy: science or technology?', *Ergonomics*, vol. 10, pp. 167–76.

Milner, B. (1964) 'Some Effects of Frontal Lobotomy in Men', in *The Frontal Granular Cortex and Behaviour*, ed. Warren, J. M. and Akert, K. (New York, McGraw-Hill).

Milner, B. (1966) 'Amnesia Following Operations on the Temporal Lobe', in *Amnesia*, ed. Whitty, C. W. M. and Zangwill, O. L. (London, Butterworth).

Miner, J. B. (1963) *The Management of Ineffective Performance* (New York, McGraw-Hill).

Miner, J. B. (1965) *Studies in Management Education* (New York, Springer).

Mitchell, T. R. and Albright, D. W. (1972) 'Expectancy Theory Prediction of the Satisfaction, Effort, Performance and Retention of Naval Aviation Officers', *Organizational Behaviour and Human Performance*, vol. 8, pp. 1–20.

Mitchell, T. R. and Nebeker, D. M. (1973) 'Expectancy Theory Predictions of Academic Effort and Performance', *Journal of Applied Psychology*, vol. 57, pp. 61–7.

Moray, N. (1969) *Attention: selective processes in vision and hearing* (London, Hutchinson International).

Morgan, G. T., Cook, J. S., Chapanis, A. and Lund, M. W. (eds) (1963) *Human Engineering Guide to Equipment Design* (New York, McGraw-Hill).

Morrell, F. (1961) 'Electrophysiological Contributions to the Neural Basis of Learning', *Physiological Review*, vol. 41, pp. 443–94.

Morse, N. and Reimer, E. (1956) 'The Experimental Change of a Major Organization Variable', *Journal of Abnormal and Social Psychology*, vol. 52, pp. 120–9.

Mosel, J. N. and Goheen, H. W. (1958) 'The Validity of the Employment Recommendation in Personnel Selection: I. Skilled Trades', *Personnel Psychology*, vol. 11, pp. 481–90.

Motowidlo, S. J., Loehr, V. and Dunnette, M. D. (1972) 'The Effect of Goal Specificity on the Relationship between Expectancy and Task Performance', Minneapolis, University of Minnesota, Technical Report, no. 4008.

Mowrer, O. H. (1960) *Learning Theory and Behaviour* (New York, Wiley).

Munro-Fraser, J. (1966) *Employment Interviewing*, 4th edn (London, MacDonald & Evans).

Munsterberg, H. (1913) *Psychology and Industrial Efficiency* (Boston, Houghton Mifflin).

Murdock, B. B., jr (1962) 'The Serial Effect of Free Recall', *Journal of Experimental Psychology*, vol. 64, pp. 482–8.

Murray, E. J. (1964) *Motivation and Emotion* (Englewood Cliffs, N.J., Prentice-Hall.)

Murray, H. A. (1938) *Explorations in Personality* (New York, Oxford University Press).

Munstein, B. I. (1963) *Theory and Research in Projective Techniques (Emphasizing the TAT)*, (New York, Wiley).

Mussen, P. and Distler, L. (1959) 'Masculinity, Identification and Father–Son Relationship', *Journal of Abnormal and Social Psychology*, vol. 59, pp. 350–6.

Nash, A. (1965) 'Vocational Interests of Effective Managers: a review of the literature', *Personnel Psychology*, vol. 18, pp. 21–38.

Nash, A. N., Muczyk, J. P. and Vettori, F. L. (1971) 'The Relative Practical Effectiveness of Programmed Instruction', *Personnel Psychology*, vol. 24, pp. 397–418.

Naylor, J. C. (1962) 'Parameters Affecting the Relative Efficiency of Part and Whole Methods: a review of the literature', U.S. Navy Training Devices Center Technical Report 950–1.

Naylor, J. C. and Briggs, G. E. (1963) 'Effects of Task Complexity and Task Organization on the Relative Efficiency of Part and Whole Training Methods', *Journal of Experimental Psychology*, vol. 65, pp. 217–21.

Necker, L. A. (1832) 'Observations on Some Remarkable Phenomena seen in Switzerland; and an optical phenomenon which occurs on viewing of a crystal or geometrical solid' *Philosophical Magazine* (3rd series), vol. 1, pp. 329–37.

Neel, R. G. and Dunn, R. (1960) 'Predicting Success in Supervisory Training

Programmes by the Use of Psychological Tests', *Journal of Applied Psychology*, vol. 44, pp. 358–60.

Neisser, U. (1967) *Cognitive Psychology* (New York, Appleton-Century-Crofts).

Nelson, T. M. and Bartley, S. H. (1968) 'The Pattern of Personnel Response Arising During the Office Work Day', *Occupational Psychology*, vol. 42 (1), pp. 77–83.

Newcombe, T. M. (1954) *Social Psychology* (New York, Dryden).

Newcombe, T. M. (1961) *The Acquaintance Process* (New York, Holt, Rinehart & Winston).

Newman, R. I., jr, Hunt, D. L. and Rhodes, F. (1966) 'Effect of Music in Employee Attitude and Productivity in a Skateboard Factory', *Journal of Applied Psychology*, vol. 50 (6), pp. 493–6.

Nisbet, J. D. (1957) 'Intelligence and Age: retesting with twenty-four years' interval', *British Journal of Educational Psychology*, vol. 27, pp. 190–8.

Noble, C. E. (1969) 'Outline of Human Selective Learning', in *Principles of Skill Acquisition*, ed. Bilodeau, E. A. and Bilodeau, I. M. (New York, Academic Press).

Norman, D. A. (1976) *Memory and Attention* (New York, Wiley).

Norman, W. T. (1963) 'Relative Importance of Test Item Content', *Journal of Consulting Psychology*, vol. 27, pp. 166–74.

Oatman, C. L. (1964) 'Check-Reading Accuracy, Using an Extended-pointer Dial Display', *Journal of Engineering Psychology*, vol. 3, pp. 123–31.

Opsahl, R. L. and Dunnette, M. D. (1966) 'The Role of Financial Compensation in Industrial Motivation', *Psychological Bulletin*, vol. 66, pp. 94–118.

Orne, M. (1962) 'On the Social Psychology of the Psychology Experiment with Particular Reference to Demand Characteristics and their Implications', *American Psychologist*, vol. 17, pp. 776–82.

Osgood, C. E. (1949) 'The Similarity Paradox in Human Learning: a resolution', *Psychological Review*, vol. 56, pp. 132–34.

Osgood, C. E. and Sebeok, T. A. (eds.) (1965) *Psycholinguistics: a Survey of Theory and Research Problems*, Indiana University Press).

Osgood, C. E., Suci, G. J. and Tannenbaum, P. H. (1957) *The Measurement of Meaning* (University of Illinois Press).

Osgood, C. E. and Tannenbaum, P. H. (1955) 'The Principle of Congruity in the Prediction of Attitude Change', *Psychological Review*, vol. 62, pp. 42–55.

Owens, W. A. (1966) 'Age and Mental Abilities: a second adult follow-up', *Journal of Educational Psychology*, vol. 57, pp. 311–25.

Owens, W. A. and Henry, E. R. (1966) *Biographical Data in Industrial Psychology: a Review and Evaluation* (Greensboro, N. C., The Creativity Research Institute).

Paivio, A. (1971) *Imagery and Verbal Processes* (New York, Holt, Rinehart & Winston).

Parson, F. (1908) *Choosing a Vocation*, (New York, Houghton Mifflin).

Pavlov, I. (1927) *Conditioned Reflexes* (Oxford University Press).

Payne, D. E. (1956) 'Role Constructs *versus* Part Constructs and Interpersonal Understanding', unpublished Ph.D. thesis, Ohio State University.

Payne, R. and Pugh, D. S. (1971) 'Organisations as Psychological Environments', in *Psychology at Work*, ed. Warr, P. B. (Harmondsworth, Penguin).

Payne, R. and Pugh, D. S. (1976) 'Organizational Structure and Climate', in *Handbook of Industrial and Organizational Psychology*, ed. Dunnette, M. D. (Chicago, Rand McNally).

Pelz, D. C. and Andrew, F. M. (1966) *Scientists in Organizations*, (New York, Wiley).

Penfield, W. (1958) *The Excitable Cortex in Conscious Man*, (New York, Thomas).

Penfield, W. (1969) 'Consciousness, Memory and Man's Conditioned Reflexes' in *On the Biology of Learning*, ed. Pribram, K. (New York, Harcourt Brace & World).

Perl, R. E. (1934) 'An Application of Thurstone's Method of Factor Analysis to Practice Series', *Journal of General Psychology*, vol. 11, pp. 209–12.

Pew, R. W. (1966) 'Acquisition of Hierarchical Control over the Temporal Organization of a Skill', *Journal of Experimental Psychology*, vol. 71, pp. 764–71.

Piaget, J. (1950) *The Psychology of Intelligence* (London, Routledge).

Pont, H. B. (1963) 'A Review of the Use of Information Theory in Psychology and a Study of the Effect of Age on Channel Capacity', B.Ed. thesis, University of Aberdeen.

Popper, K. R. (1968) *Conjecture and Refutations* (New York, Harper).

Poppleton, S. E. (1970) Unpublished studies of group selection procedures, (London, N11P).

Poppleton, S. E. (1971) 'Eye-gaze Behaviour, Personality and Sociometric Data', M.Sc. thesis, University of Exeter.

Poppleton, S. E. (1975) 'Biographical and Personality Characteristics Associated with Success in Life Assurance Salesmen', M.Phil. thesis, Birkbeck College, University of London.

Poppleton, S. E. and Lubbock, J. (1977) 'Marketing Life Assurance – Causes of Success and Failure in Life Assurance Salesmen', *European Journal of Marketing*, vol. 11 (6), pp. 418–31.

Poppleton, S. E. and Salaman, G. (1978) Unpublished research.

Porter, L. W. (1961) 'A Study of Perceived Need Satisfactions in Bottom and Middle Management Jobs', *Journal of Applied Psychology*, vol. 45, pp. 1–10.

Porter, L. W. (1964) *Organizational Patterns of Managerial Job Attitudes* (New York, American Foundation for Management Research).

Porter, L. W. and Lawler, E. E. (1968) *Managerial Attitudes and Performance* (Homewood, Ill., Dorsey).

Porter, L. W., Lawler, E. E. and Hackman, J. R. (1975) *Behaviour in Organizations* (New York, McGraw-Hill).

Porter, L. W. and Mitchell, V. F. (1967) 'Comparative Study of Need Satisfactions in Military and Business Hierarchies', *Journal of Applied Psychology*, vol. 51, pp. 139–44.

Postman, L. P., Bruner, J. S. and McGinnies, E. (1948) 'Personal Values as Selective Factors in Perception,' *Journal of Abnormal and Social Psychology*, vol. 43, pp. 142–54.

Poulton, E. C. (1974) 'The Effect of Fatigue upon Inspection Work', *Applied Ergonomics*, vol. 4, pp. 73–83.

Premack, D. (1959) 'Toward Empirical Behavior Laws: 1. positive reinforcement', *Psychological Review*, vol. 66, pp. 219–33.

Price, K. O., Harburg, E. and Newcombe, T. M. (1966) 'Psychological Balance in Situations of Negative Interpersonal Attitudes', *Journal of Personality and Social Psychology*, vol. 3, pp. 265–70.

Pritchard, R. D. and De Leo, P. J. (1973) 'Experimental Test of the Valence–Instrumentability Relationship in Job Performance', *Journal of Applied Psychology*, vol. 57, pp. 264–70.

Pritchard, R. D., Dunnette, M. D. and Jorgenson, D. O. (1972) 'Effects of Perception of Equity and Inequity on Worker Performance and Satisfaction', *Journal of Applied Psychology*, monograph, vol. 56, pp. 75–94.

Pritchard, R. D. and Sanders, M. S. (1973) 'The Influence of Valence, Instrumentality and Expectancy on Effort and Performance', *Journal of Applied Psychology*, vol. 57, pp. 55–60.

Proctor, J. H. and Thornton, W. M. *Training: a handbook for line managers*, (New York, American Management Association).

Pugh, D. S., Hickson, D. J. and Hinings, C. R. (1971) *Writers on Organisations*, 2nd edn (Harmondsworth, Penguin).

Raimy, V. C. (1948) 'Self-Reference in Counselling Interviews', *Journal of Consulting Psychology*, vol. 12, pp. 153–63.

Rawls, D. J. and Rawls, J. R. (1968) 'Personality Characteristics and Personal History Data of Successful and Less Successful Executives', *Psychological Reports*, vol. 23, pp. 1032–4.

Reeves, J. W., Wilson, V. W. and Stringfellow, C. D. (1951) *Studying Work* (London, N.I.I.P.).

Reich, W. (1950) *Character Analysis* (London, Vision Press).

Rodger, A. (1950) 'Industrial Psychology', *Universities Quarterly*, vol. 4, pp. 149–56.

Rodger, A. (1953) *The Seven Point Plan* (London, N.I.I.P.).

Rodger, A. and Cavanagh, P. W. W. (1962) 'Personnel Selection and Vocational Guidance' in *Society: Problems and Methods of Study*', ed. Welford, A. W., Argyle, M., Glass, D. V. and Morris, J. N. (London, Routledge & Kegan Paul).

Rodrigues, A. (1967) 'Effects of Balance, Positivity and Agreement in Triadic Social Relations', *Journal of Personality and Social Psychology*, vol. 5, pp. 472–576.

Roe, A. (1953) 'A Psychological Study of Eminent Psychologists and Athropologists and a Comparison with Biological and Physical Scientists', *Psychological Monographs*, vol. 67, (2, whole no. 352).

Roethlisberger, F. J. and Dixon, W. J. (1939) *Management and the Worker – an account of a research program conducted by the Western Electric Company, Hawthorne Works* (Harvard University Press).

Rogers, C. R. (1951) *Client Centered Therapy: its current practice, implication and theory* (Boston, Houghton Mifflin).

Rogers, C. R. (ed.) (1967) *The Therapeutic Relationship and its Impact: a study of psychotherapy with schizophrenics* (University of Wisconsin Press).

Rosenberg, M. J. (1960) 'An Analysis of Affective–Cognitive–Consistency' in *Attitude Organization and Change*, ed. Hovland, C. I. and Rosenberg, M. J. (Yale University Press).

Rosner, S. (1957) 'Consistency of Response to Group Pressures', *Journal of Abnormal and Social Psychology*, vol. 55, pp. 145–6.

Rothe, H. F. and Nye, C. T. (1961) 'Output Rates among Machine Operators. III. a non-incentive situation in 2 levels of business activity', *Journal of Applied Psychology*, vol. 45, pp. 50–4.

Rowe, P. M. (1963) 'Individual Differences in Selection Decisions', *Journal of Applied Psychology*, vol. 47, pp. 304–7.

Rowe, P. M. (1967) 'Order Effects in Assessment Decisions', *Journal of Applied Psychology*, vol. 51, pp. 170–3.

Rubin, G. and Smith, K. U. (1952) 'Learning and Integration of Component Movements in a Pattern of Motion', *Journal of Experimental Psychology*, vol. 44, pp. 301–5.

Rundquist, E. A. (1970) *Job Training Course Design and Improvement*, 2nd edn, San Diego Naval Personnel and Training Research Laboratory, Research Report SRR 71–4.

Rundquist, E. A., West, C. M. and Zifse, R. L. (1971) *Development of a Job Task Inventory for Commanding Officers of Amphibious Ships*, San Diego, Naval Personnel and Training Research Laboratory, Research Report SRR 72–2.

Runkel, P. J. and Damrin, D. E. (1961) 'Assessment *versus* Experimental Acquisition of Verbal Habits, in *Verbal Learning and Verbal Behavior*, ed. Cofer, C. N. (New York, McGraw-Hill).

Sachs, J. S. (1967) 'Recognition Memory for Syntactic and Semantic Aspects of Discourse', *Perceptual Psychophysics*, vol. 2, pp. 437–42.

Sahlins, M. D. (1965) 'On the Sociology of Primitive Exchange', in *The Relevance of Models for Social Anthropology*, A.S.A. Monographs, vol. 1 (London, Tavistock).

Sainsbury, P. (1955) 'Gestural Movements during the Psychiatric Interview', *Psychosomatic Medicine*, vol. 17, pp. 458–69.

Salmon, P. (1963) 'A Clinical Investigation of Sexual Identity', in *The Evaluation of Personal Constructs*, ed. Bannister, D. and Mair, J. M. M. (New York, Academic Press).

Sampson, E. E. (1965) 'The Study of Ordinal Position: antecedents and outcomes', *Progress in Experimental Personality Research*, vol. 2, pp. 175–228.

Sampson, E. E. (1976) *Social Psychology and Contemporary Society*, 2nd edn (New York, Wiley).

Sampson, E. E. and Insko, C. A. (1964) 'Cognitive Consistency and Performance in the Autokinetic Situation', *Journal of Abnormal and Social Psychology*, vol. 68, pp. 184–92.

Sarnoff, I. and Zimbardo, P. G. (1961) 'Anxiety, Fear and Social Affiliation', *Journal of Abnormal and Social Psychology*, vol. 62, pp. 355–63.

Schachter, S. (1951) 'Deviation, Rejection and Communication', *Journal of Abnormal and Social Psychology*, vol. 46, pp. 190–207.

Schachter, S. (1959) *Psychology of Affiliation* (Stanford University Press).

Schachter, S. and Singer, J. E. (1962) 'Cognitive, Social and Physiological Determinants of Emotional State', *Psychology Review*, vol. 69, pp. 379–99.

Schaeffer, H. R. and Emerson, P. E. (1964) 'The Development of Social Attachments in Infancy', *Monographs of Social Research and Child Development*, vol. 29, no. 3.

Scheflen, A. E. (1964) 'The Significance of Posture in Communication Systems', *Psychiatry*, vol. 27, pp. 316–31.

Scheflen, A. E. (1964) *Stream and Structure of Communicational Behavior*, (Commonwealth of Pennsylvania, Eastern Pennsylvania Psychiatric Institute).

Schein, E. E. (1965) *Organizational Psychology* (Englewood Cliffs, N.J., Prentice-Hall).

Schlosberg, R. (1954) 'Three Dimensions of Emotion', *Psychological Review*, vol. 61, pp. 81–8.

Schramm, W. (1962) 'Mass Communication', *Annual Review of Psychology*, vol. 13, pp. 251–84.

Schutz, W. C. (1953) 'Construction of High Productivity Groups', Department of Systems Analysis, Tufts College.

Schwab, D. P., De Vitt, H. W. and Cummings, L. L. (1971) 'A Test of the Adequacy of the 2-Factor Theory as a Predictor of Self-report Performance Effects', *Personnel Psychology*, vol. 24, pp. 293–303.

Schwab, D. P. and Heneman, H. G. (1969) 'Relationship between Interview Structure and Interviewer Reliability in an Employment Situation', *Journal of Applied Psychology*, vol. 53 (3), pp. 214–17.

Schwartz, H. A. and Haskell, R. J. (1966) 'A Study of Computer-Assisted Instruction in Industrial Training', *Journal of Applied Psychology*, vol. 50, pp. 360–3.

Schwartz, H. A. and Long, H. S. (1967) 'A Study of Remote Industrial Training via Computer-Assisted Instruction', *Journal of Applied Psychology*, vol. 51, pp. 11–16.

Scott, W. D. (1911) *Increasing Human Efficiency in Business* (New York, Macmillan).

Sears, D. O. and Freedman, J. L. (1965) 'Effects of Expected Familiarity of Arguments upon Opinion Change and Selective Exposure', *Journal of Personality and Social Psychology*, vol. 2, pp. 420–5.

Sears, R. R. (1963) 'Dependency Motivation' in *Nebraska Symposium on Motivation*, ed. Jones, M. R. (University of Nebraska Press).

Sears, R. R., Maccoby, E. E. and Levin, H. (1957) *Patterns of Child Rearing* (New York, Harper & Row).

Seashore, R. H. (1951) 'Work and Motor Performance' in *Handbook of Experimental Psychology*, ed. Stevens, S. S. (New York, Wiley).

Seashore, S. E., Indik, B. P. and Georgopoulos, B. S. (1960) 'Relationships among Criteria of Job performance', *Journal of Applied Psychology*, vol. 44, pp. 195–202.

Secord, P. F. (1958) 'The Role of Facial Features in Inter-personal Perception', in *Person Perception and Interpersonal Behavior*, ed. Tagiuri, R. and Petrullo, L. (Stanford University Press).

Secord, P. F. and Backman, C. W. (1964) *Social Psychology* (New York, McGraw-Hill).

Secord, P. F., Bevan, W. and Katz, P. (1956) 'The Negro Stereotype and Perceptual Accentuation', *Journal of Abnormal and Social Psychology*, vol. 53, p. 78.

Seidel, R. (1959) 'A Review of Sensory Preconditioning', *Psychological Bulletin*, vol. 56, p. 58.

Seymour, W. D. (1966) *Industrial Skills* (London, Pitman).

Sharp, S. E. (1899) 'Individual Psychology, a study in psychological method', *American Journal of Psychology*, vol. 10, 329–91.

Shaw, M. C. (1968) 'Underachievement: useful construct or misleading illusion', *Psychology in the Schools*, vol. 5, pp. 41–6.

Shaw, M. E. (1954) 'Some Effects of Problem Complexity upon Problem Solution Efficiency in Different Communication Nets', *Journal of Experimental Psychology*, vol. 48, pp. 211–17.

Shaw, M. E. (1964) 'Communication Networks' in *Advances in Experimental Social Psychology*, ed. Berkowitz, L., vol. I, (New York, Academic Press).

Sheffield, F. D. and Roby, T. B. (1950) 'Reward Value of a Non-nutritive Sweet Taste', *Journal of Comparative Physiology and Psychology*, vol. 43, pp. 471–81.

Sheffield, F. D., Wulff, J. J. and Backer, R. (1951) 'Reward Value of Copulation Without Sex Drive Reduction', *Journal of Comparative Physiology and Psychology*, vol. 44, pp. 3–8.

Sherif, M. (1959) 'Group Influences upon the Formation of Norms and Attitudes', in *Readings in Social Psychology*, ed. Maccoby, E. E., Newcombe, T. M. and Hartley, E. L., (New York, Holt).

Sherif, M. (1966) *Group Conflict and Cooperation* (Boston, Houghton Mifflin).

Sherif, M., White, B. J. and Harvey, O. J. (1955) 'Status in Experimentally Produced Groups', *American Journal of Psychology*, vol. 60, pp. 370–9.

Sidney, E. and Brown, M. (1961) *The Skills of Interviewing* (London, Tavistock).

Siegel, A. E. and Siegel, S. (1957) 'Reference Groups, Membership Groups and Attitude Change', *Journal of Abnormal and Social Psychology*, vol. 55, pp. 360–4.

Silver, C. A., Jones, J. M. and Landis, D. (1966) 'Decision Quality as a Measure and Visual Display Effectiveness', *Journal of Applied Psychology*, vol. 50 (2), pp. 104–13.

Silverman, D. (1971). *The Theory of Organisation* (London, Heinemann).

Silverman, R. E. (1970) 'Learning Theory Applied to Training', in *The Management of Training*, ed. Otto, C. P. and Fland, O. (Reading, Mass., Addison-Wesley).

Simon, H. A. (1960) *Administrative Behaviour*, 2nd edn (London, Macmillan).

Singer, D. L. and Whiton, M. B. (1971) 'Ideational Creativity of Expressive Aspects of Human Figure Drawing in Kindergarten Age Children', *Developmental Psychology*, vol. 4, pp. 366–9.

Singleton, W. T. (1959) 'The Training of Shoe Machinists', *Ergonomics*, vol. 2, (2), pp. 148–52.

Singleton, W. T. (1969) 'Display Design: principles and procedures', *Ergonomics*, vol. 12, pp. 519–41.

Sissons, M. Unpublished research reported in Cook, M. (1971) *Interpersonal Perception*, (Harmondsworth, Penguin).

Skinner, B. L. (1938) *The Behavior of Organisms: an experimental analysis* (New York, Appleton-Century-Crofts).

Slater, P. E. (1955) 'Role Differentiation in Small Groups', *American Sociological Review*, vol. 20, pp. 300–10.

Smith, K. U. (1962) *Delayed Sensory Feedback and Behavior* (Philadelphia, Sanders).

Smith, O. W. and Smith, P. C. (1962) 'An Illusion of Parallelism', *Perceptual and Motor Skills*, vol. 15, pp. 445–61.

Smith, P. C., Kendall, L. M. and Hulin, C. L. (1969) *The Measurement of Satisfaction in Work and Retirement* (Chicago, Rand McNally).

Smode, A. F. (1958) 'Learning and Performance in a Tracking Task under Two Levels of Achievement Information Feedback', *Journal of Experimental Psychology*, vol. 56, pp. 297–304.

Spearman, C. E. (1904) '"General Intelligence" Objectively Determined and Measured', *American Journal of Psychology*, vol. 15, pp. 72–101.

Spence, K. W. (1956) *Behavior Theory and Conditioning* (Yale University Press).

Sperling, G. A. (1960) 'The Information Available in Brief Visual Presentation', *Psychological Monographs*, vol. 74, no. 498.

Spooner, A. and Kellogg, W. N. (1947) 'The Backward Conditioning Curve', *American Journal of Psychology*, vol. 60, pp. 321–34.

Springbett, B. M. (1958) 'Factors Affecting the Final Decision in the Employment Interview', *Canadian Journal of Psychology*, vol. 12, pp. 13–22.

Stephenson, W. (1931) 'Tetrad Differences for Non-verbal Subtests; Tetrad Differences for Verbal Subtests; Tetrad Differences for Verbal Subtests Relative to Non-Verbal Subtests', *Journal of Educational Psychology*, vol. 22, pp. 167–85, 255–67, 334–50.

Stephenson, W. (1953) '*The Study of Behavior: a technique and its methodology* (University of Chicago Press).

Stogdill, R. M. (1948) 'Personal Factors Associated with Leadership: a survey of the literature', *Journal of Psychology*, vol. 25, pp. 35–71.

Strong, E. K., jr (1943) *Vocational Interests of Men and Women* (Stanford University Press).

Strongman, K. T. and Hart, C. T. (1968) 'Stereotyped Reactions to Body Build', *Psychological Reports*, vol. 23, pp. 1175–8.

Suinn, R. M. (1961) 'The Relationship Between Self-acceptance and Acceptance of Others: a learning theory analysis', *Journal of Abnormal and Social Psychology*, vol. 63, pp. 37–42.

Sultan, E. E. (1962) 'A Factorial Study in the Domain of Creative Thinking', *British Journal of Educational Psychology*, vol. 32, 78–82.

Super, D. (1957) *The Psychology of Careers* (Boston, Houghton Mifflin).

Suppes P. and Morningstar, M. (1969) 'Computer-Assisted Instruction', *Science*, vol. 166, pp. 343–50.

Sykes, A. J. M. (1962) 'The Effect of a Supervisory Training Course in Changing Supervisors' Perceptions and Expectations of the Role of Management', *Human Relations*, vol. 15, pp. 227–43.

Tagiuri, R. (1958) 'Social Preference and its Perception' in *Person Perception and Interpersonal Behavior*, ed. Tagiuri, R. and Petrullo, L. (Stanford University Press).

Tagiuri, R. (1969) 'Person Perception' in *Handbook of Social Psychology*, ed. Lindzey, G. and Aronson, E. (Reading, Mass., Addison-Wesley).

Tannenbaum, A. S. (1966) *Social Psychology of the Work Organisation* (London, Tavistock).

Tannenbaum, R., Wechsler, I. and Masserick, F. (1961) *Leadership and Organisation*, (New York, McGraw-Hill).

Taylor, C. W. and Holland, J. (1964) 'Predictors of Creative Performance', in *Creativity: progress and potential*, ed. Taylor, C. W. (New York, McGraw-Hill).

Taylor, F. W. (1911) *Scientific Management* (New York, Harper & Row).

Taylor, J. A. (1956) 'Drive Theory and Manifest Anxiety', *Psychological Bulletin*, vol. 53, pp. 303–20.

Terman, L. M. (1925) *Mental and Physical Traits of a Thousand Gifted Children. Genetic Studies of Genius, I* (Stanford University Press).

Terman, L. M. and Oden, M. H. (1947) *The Gifted Child Grows Up. Genetic Studies of Genius IV* (Stanford University Press).

Terman, L. M. and Oden, M. H. (1959) *The Gifted Group at Mid-Life. Genetic Studies of Genius* (Stanford University Press).

Theologus, G. C. and Fleishman, E. A. (1971) 'Development of a Taxonomy of Human Performance: Validation Study of Ability Scales for Classifying Human Tasks', *Technical Report No. 10*, (Washington, D.C., Department of the Army).

Theologus, G. C., Romashko, T. and Fleishman, E. A. (1970) 'Development of a Taxonomy of Human Performance: a feasibility study of ability dimensions for classifying tasks, American Institute for Research, Silver Spring, Maryland, Technical Report 5 (R70-1).

Thorndike, E. L. (1898) 'Animal Intelligence: an experimental study of the associative processes in animals', *Psychological Review*, Monograph supplement, vol. 2, no. 8.

Thorndike, E. L. (1913) *Educational Psychology, Vol. 2: The psychology of learning* (New York, Teachers' College).

Thorndike, E. L. (1924) 'Mental Discipline in High School Studies', *Journal of Educational Psychology*, vol. 15, pp. 1–22, 83–98.

Thorndike, E. L. (1932) *The Fundamentals of Learning* (New York, Teachers' College).

Thorndike, R. L. (1949). *Personnel Selection* (New York, Wiley).

Thouless, R. H. (1931) 'Phenomenal Regression to the Real Object', *British Journal of Psychology*, vol. 21, 339–59.

Thurstone, L. L. (1938) 'Primary Mental Abilities', *Psychometry*, monograph no. 1.

Thurstone, L. L. (1955) 'The Differential Growth of Mental Abilities', Report of University of North Carolina Psychometric Laboratory, no. 14.

Thurstone, L. L. and Chave, E. J. (1929) *The Measurement of Attitudes* (University of Chicago Press).

Tilley, K. (1968) 'A Technology of Training', in *Industrial Society*, ed. Pym, D. (Harmondsworth, Penguin).

Tinbergen, N. (1942) 'An Objectivistic Study of the Innate Behavior of Animals', *Biblioteca Biotheoretica*, vol. 1, pt. 2, pp. 39–98.

Toch, H. H., Rabin, A. I. and Wilkins, D. M. (1962) 'Factors Entering into Ethnic Identifications: an experimental study', *Sociometry*, vol. 25, pp. 297–312.

Tolman, E. C. (1932) *Purposive Behavior in Animals and Men* University of California Press).

Tolman, E. C. and Honzik, C. H. (1930) ' "Insight" in Rats', *Publications in Psychology*, vol. 4, p. 215 (University of California).

Torrance, E. P. (1965) *Rewarding Creative Behavior* (Englewood Cliffs, N.J., Prentice-Hall).

Touhey, J. C. (1974) 'Situated Identities, Attitude Similarity and Interpersonal Attraction', *Sociometry*, vol. 37, pp. 363–74.

Trattner, M. H., Fine, S. A. and Kubis, J. F. (1955) 'A Comparison of Worker Requirement Ratings made by Reading Job Descriptions and by Direct Job Observation', *Personnel Psychology*, vol. 8, pp. 183–94.

Treisman, A. M. (1964) 'Verbal Cues, Language and Meaning in Selective Attention', *American Journal of Psychology*, vol. 77, pp. 206–13.

Trist, E. L. and Bamforth, K. W. (1951) 'Some Social and Psychological Consequences of the Longwall Method of Goal-getting', *Human Relations*, vol. 4, pp. 1–38.

Trist, E. L., Higgin, G., Murray, H. and Pollock, A. (1963) *Organisational Choice* (London, Tavistock).

Truax, C. B. (1963) 'Effective Ingredients in Psychotherapy: an approach to un-ravelling the patient–therapist interaction', *Journal of Counseling Psychology*, vol. 10, pp. 250–63.

Truax, C. B. and Mitchell, K. M. (1971) 'Research on Certain Therapist Inter-personal Skills in Relation to Process and Outcome', in *Handbook of Psychotherapy and Behavior Change: an empirical analysis*, ed. Bergin, A. E. and Garfield, S. C. (New York, Wiley).

Tuckman, B. W. (1965) 'Developmental Sequence in Small Groups', *Psychological Bulletin*, vol. 63, pp. 384–99.

Tulving, E. and Madigan, S. A. (1970) 'Memory and Verbal Learning', *Annual Review of Psychology*, vol. 21, pp. 437–84.

Tyler, L. E. (1965) *The Psychology of Individual Differences* (New York, Meredith).

Uhrbrock, R. S. (1961) 'Music on the Job: its influence on worker morale and pro-ductivity', *Personnel Psychology*, vol. 14, pp. 9–38.

Ulrich, L. and Trumbo, D. (1965) 'The Selection Interview since 1949', *Psychological Bulletin*, vol. 63, pp. 100–16.

Underwood, B. J. (1957) 'Interference and Forgetting', *Psychological Review*, vol. 64, pp. 49–60.

Underwood, B. J. (1963) 'Stimulus Selection in Verbal Learning', in *Verbal Behavior and Learning*, ed. Cofer, C. N. and Musgrave, B. J. (New York, McGraw-Hill).

Urwick, E. (1947) *The Elements of Administration* (London, Pitman).

Valins, S. (1966) 'Cognitive Effects of False Heart-rate Feedback', *Journal of Personality and Social Psychology*, vol. 4, pp. 400–8.

Valverde, H. H. and Youngs, E. J. (1969) *Annotated Bibliography of the Training Research Division Reports, 1950–1969*, Wright Patterson Air Force Base, Ohio: Air Force Human Resources Laboratory, Air Force Systems Command.

Vernon, M. D. (1962) *The Psychology of Perception* (Harmondsworth, Penguin).

Vernon, P. E. (1950a) 'The Validation of Civil Service Selection Board Procedures', *Occupational Psychology*, vol. 24, pp. 75–95.

Vernon, P. E. (1950b) *The Structure of Human Abilities* (London, Methuen).

Vernon, P. E. (1953) *Personality Tests and Assessments* (London, Methuen).

Vernon, P. E. (1960) *Intelligence and Attainment Tests* (University of London Press).

Vernon, P. E. (1964) *Personality Assessment: a critical survey* (London, Methuen).

Vernon, P. E. (1967) 'A Cross-cultural Study of "Creativity Tests" with 11-year-old Boys', *New Research in Education*, vol. 1, pp. 135–246.

Vernon, P. E. (1969) *Intelligence and Cultural Environment* (London, Methuen).

Vernon, P. E. and Parry, J. B. (1949) *Personal Selection in the British Forces* (University of London Press).

Vroom, V. H. (1960) *Some Personality Determinants of the Effects of Participation*, (Englewood Cliffs, N.J., Prentice-Hall).

Vroom, V. H. (1964) *Work and Motivation* (New York, Wiley).

Vroom, V. H. (1970) 'Industrial Social Psychology', in *Handbook of Social Psychology*, ed. Lindzey, G. and Aronson, E. (Reading, Mass., Addison-Wesley).

Vroom, V. H. (1976) 'Leadership', in *Handbook of Industrial and Organizational Psychology*, ed. Dunnette, M. D. (Chicago, Rand McNally).

Vroom, V. H. and Yetton, P. W. (1973) *Leadership and Decision Making* (University of Pittsburgh Press).

Wagner, R. (1949) 'The Employment Interview: a critical summary', *Personnel Psychology*, vol. 2, pp. 17–46.

Walker, C. and Guest, R. (1952) *Man on the Assembly Line* (Harvard University Press).

Wallach, M. A. (1971) *The Intelligence/Creativity Distinction* (New York, General Learning Press).

Wallach, M. A. and Kogan, N. (1965) 'A New Look at the Creativity–Intelligence Distribution, *Journal of Personality*, vol. 33, pp. 348–69.

Wallach, M. A. and Wing, C. S. (1969) *The Talented Student: a validation of the creativity/intelligence distinction* (New York, Holt, Rinehart & Winston).

Walster, E., Aronson, E. and Abrahams, D. (1966) 'On Increasing the Persuasiveness of a Low Prestige Communicator', *Journal of Experimental Social Psychology*, vol. 2, pp. 325–42.

Walster, E. and Festinger, L. (1962) 'The Effectiveness of "Overheard" Persuasive Communications', *Journal of Abnormal and Social Psychology*, vol. 65, pp. 395–402.

Walters, R. H. and Parke, R. D. (1964) 'Social Motivation, Dependency and Susceptibility to Social Influence', in *Advances in Experimental Social Psychology*, vol. 1, pp. 232–76.

Walters, R. H. and Parke, R. D. (1965) 'The Role of the Distance Receptors in the Development of Social Responsiveness' in *Advances in Child Development and Behavior*, vol. 2, pp. 59–96.

Warr, P. B., Bird, M. and Rackham, N. (1970) *Evaluation of Management Training* (London, Gower Press).

Warr, P. B. and Knapper, C. (1968) *The Perception of People and Events* (New York, Wiley).

Warr, P. B. and Wall, T. (1975) *Work and Well-Being*, (Harmondsworth, Penguin).

Warrick, M. J. (1947) 'Direction of Movement in the Use of Control Knobs to Position Visual Indicators', in *Psychological Research on Equipment Design*, ed. Fitts, P. M., U.S. Army, Air Force, Aviation Psychology Programme Research Report No. 19.

Watson, J. B. (1919 *Psychology from the Standpoint of a Behaviorist*, 2nd edn (Philadelphia, Lippincott).

Watson, J. B. and Rayner, R. (1930) 'Conditioned Emotional Reactions', *Journal of Experimental Psychology*, vol. 3, pp. 1–14.

Weber, M. (1947) *The Theory of Social and Economic Organisation* (New York, Free Press).

Webster, E. C. (1964) 'Decision Making in the Employment Interview', Industrial Relations Center, McGill University, Montreal.

Wechsler, D. (1958) *The Measurement and Appraisal of Adult Intelligence*, 4th edn (London, Bailliere, Tindall & Cox).

Weick, K. E. (1966) 'The Concept of Equity in the Perception of Pay', *Administrative Science Quarterly*, vol. 11, pp. 414–39.

Weil, E. *see* Witkin, M. A., Lewis, W. B. and Weil, E. (1968).

Weiner, B., Heckhausen, H., Meyer, W. V. and Cook, R. M. (1972) 'Causal Ascriptions and Achievement Motivation: a conceptual analysis of effort and reanalysis of locus of control', *Journal of Personality and Social Psychology*, vol. 21, pp. 239–48.

Weiner, B., Frieze, I., Kukla, A., Reed, L., Rest, S. and Rosenbaum, R. M. (1971) *Perceiving the Causes of Success and Failure* (New York, General Learning Press).

Weiss, D. J. and Dawis, R. V. (1960) 'An Objective Validation of Factual Interview Data', *Journal of Applied Psychology*, vol. 40, pp. 381–5.

Weiss, D. J., Dawis, R. V., England, G. W. and Lofquist, L. H. (1961) 'Validity of Work Histories Obtained by Interview', *Minnesota Studies in Vocational Rehabilitation*, no. 12, University of Minnesota, Minneapolis.

Weiss, W. A. and Fine, B. J. (1956) 'The Effect of Induced Aggressiveness on Opinion Change', *Journal of Abnormal and Social Psychology*, vol. 52, pp. 109–14.

Welford, A. T. (1958) *Ageing and Human Skill* (Oxford University Press).

Wernimont, P. F. and Campbell, J. P. (1968) 'Signs, Samples and Criteria', *Journal of Applied Psychology*, vol. 52, (5), pp. 372–6.

Whiting, J. W. M. (1960) 'Resource Mediation and Learning by Identification', in *Personality Development in Children*, ed. Iscoe, I. and Stevenson, H. (University of Texas Press).

Whitla, D. K. and Tirrell, J. E. (1954) 'The Validity of Ratings of Several Levels of Supervisors', *Personnel Psychology*, vol. 6, pp. 461–6.

Whitsett, D. A. and Winslow, E. K. (1967) 'An Analysis of Studies Critical of the Motivator–Hygiene Theory', *Personnel Psychology*, vol. 20, pp. 391–415.

Whyte, W. F. (1955) *Money and Motivation: an analysis of incentives in industry* (New York, Harper & Row).

Wicker, A. W. (1969) 'Attitudes versus Actions: the relationship of verbal and overt behavioral responses to attitude objects', *Journal of Social Issues*, vol. 25, pp. 41–78.

Wilkins, L. T. (1959) 'Incentives and the Young Worker', *Occupational Psychology*, vol. 23, pp. 235–47.

Wilkins, L. T. (1950) 'Incentives and the Young Male Worker in England', *International Journal of Opinion and Attitude Research*, vol. 4, pp. 541–62.

Wilkinson, R. (1971) 'Hours of Work and Twenty-four Hour Cycle of Rest and Activity', in *Psychology at Work*, ed. Warr, P. B. (Harmondsworth, Penguin).

Wilkstrom, W. S. (1968) 'Managing by and with Objectives', *National Industrial Personnel Policy Study*, no. 212.

Williams, A. C. and Flexman, R. E. (1949) 'Evaluation of the School Link as an Aid in Primary Flight Instruction', *University of Illinois Bulletin*, vol. 46, no. 71.

Williams, H. L., Lubin, A. and Goodnow, J. J. (1959) 'Impaired Performance with Acute Sleep Loss', *Psychological Monograph*, vol. 73, no. 484.

Willis, X. (1962) reported in Chapanis, A. (1976).

Wing, J. F. (1965) 'A Review of the Effects of High Ambient Temperature on Mental Performance', Technical Report AMRL-TR-65-102, U.S.A.F./Aerospace Medical Research Laboratories, Wright-Patterson Air Force Base.

Wing, J. K. (1961) 'A Simple and Reliable Subclassification of Chronic Schizophrenia', *Journal of Mental Science*, vol. 107, pp. 862–75.

Wissler, C. (1901) 'The Correlation of Mental and Physical Tests', *Psychological Review*, monograph vol. 3, pp. 1–63.

Witkin, H. A. (1959) 'The Perception of the Upright', *Scientific American*, vol. 200, pp. 50–6.

Witkin, H. A. (1965) 'Psychological Differentiation and Forms of Pathology', *Journal of Abnormal Psychology*, vol. 70, pp. 317–36.

Witkin, H. A. (1967) 'A Cognitive-style Approach to Cross-cultural Research', *International Journal of Psychology*, vol. 2, pp. 233–50.

Witkin, H. A., Dyk, R. B., Faterson, H. F., Goodenough, D. R. and Karp, S. A. (1962) *Psychological Differentiation: studies of development* (New York, Wiley).

Witkin, H. A., Faterson, H. F., Goodenough, D. R. and Birnbaum, J. (1966) 'Cognitive Patterning in Mildly Retarded Boys', *Child Development*, vol. 57, pp. 301–16.

Witkin, H. A., Goodenough, D. R. and Karp, S. A. (1967) 'Stability of Cognitive Style from Childhood to Young Adulthood', *Journal of Personality and Social Psychology*, vol. 7, pp. 291–300.

Witkin, H. A., Lewis, H. B., Hertzman, M., Machover, K., Meissner, P. B. and Wapner, S. (1954) *Personality Through Perception: an experiment and clinical study* (New York, Harper).

Witkin, H. A., Lewis, H. B. and Weil, E. (1968) 'Affective Reactions and Patient–

Therapist Interactions Among More Differentiated and Less Differentiated Patients Early in Therapy', *Journal of Nervous and Mental Disease*, vol. 146, pp. 193–208.

Wober, J. M. (1961) 'An Experimental Study of Different Styles in the Administration of a Written Group Test', unpublished M.Sc. thesis, Birkbeck College, London.

Wofford, J. C. (1971) 'The Motivational Bases of Job Satisfaction and Job Performance, *Personnel Psychology*, vol. 24, pp. 501–18.

Wolf, M. G. (1970) 'Need Gratification Theory: a theoretical reformulation of job satisfaction/dissatisfaction and job motivation', *Journal of Applied Psychology*, vol. 54 (1), pp. 87–94.

Wolfe, J. B. (1934) 'The Effect of Delayed Reward upon Learning in a White Rat', *Journal of Comparative Psychology*, vol. 17, pp. 1–21.

Wolins, L. and MacKinney, A. C. (1961) 'Validity Information Exchange No. 15-06', *Personnel Psychology*, vol. 15, pp. 227–9.

Woodworth, R. S. (1938) *Experimental Psychology* (New York, Holt).

Wright, O. R., jr (1969) 'Summary of Research on the Selection Interview since 1964', *Personnel Psychology*, vol. 22 (4), pp. 391–413.

Wyatt, S. and Marriott, R. (1956) *A Study of Attitudes to Factory Work* (London, H.M.S.O.).

Wylie, R. C. (1961) *The Self-Concept: a critical survey of pertinent research literature* (University of Nebraska Press).

Yarrow, L. J. (1964) 'Separation from Parents during Early Childhood', *Review of Child Development Research*, vol. 1, pp. 89–136.

Yonge, K. A. (1956) 'The Value of the Interview: on orientation and a pilot study', *Journal of Applied Psychology*, vol. 40, pp. 25–31.

Young, P. T. (1959) 'Food Seeking Drive, Affective Process and Learning', *Psychological Review*, vol. 56, pp. 98–121.

Zajonc, R. B. (1960) 'Balance, Congruity and Dissonance', *Public Opinion Quarterly*, vol. 24 (2), pp. 280–96.

Zalesnik, A., Christenson, C. R. and Roethlisberger, F. J. (1958) *The Motivation, Productivity and Satisfaction of Workers*, Graduate School of Business Administration, Harvard University.

Ziegler, P. N. and Chernikoff, R. (1966) 'A Comparison of 3 Types of Manual Controls on a 'Third-order' Tracking Task', *Ergonomics*, vol. 11 (4), pp. 369–74.

Author Index

Subject Index